BLOOD FEUD

BLOOD FEUD

The Man Who Blew the Whistle on One of the Deadliest Prescription Drugs Ever

Kathleen Sharp

DUTTON

DUTTON
Published by Penguin Group (USA) Inc.
375 Hudson Street, New York, New York 10014, U.S.A.
Penguin Group (Canada), 90 Eglinton Avenue East, Suite 700, Toronto, Ontario M4P 2Y3, Canada (a
division of Pearson Penguin Canada Inc.); Penguin Books Ltd, 80 Strand, London WC2R 0RL, England;
Penguin Ireland, 25 St Stephen's Green, Dublin 2, Ireland (a division of Penguin Books Ltd); Penguin
Group (Australia), 250 Camberwell Road, Camberwell, Victoria 3124, Australia (a division of Pearson
Australia Group Pty Ltd); Penguin Books India Pvt Ltd, 11 Community Centre, Panchsheel Park, New
Delhi—110 017, India; Penguin Group (NZ), 67 Apollo Drive, Rosedale, Auckland 0632, New Zealand
(a division of Pearson New Zealand Ltd); Penguin Books (South Africa) (Pty) Ltd, 24 Sturdee Avenue,
Rosebank, Johannesburg 2196, South Africa

Penguin Books Ltd, Registered Offices, 80 Strand, London WC2R 0RL, England

Published by Dutton, a member of Penguin Group (USA) Inc.

First printing, September 2011
1   3   5   7   9   10   8   6   4   2

 REGISTERED TRADEMARK—MARCA REGISTRADA

LIBRARY OF CONGRESS CATALOGING-IN-PUBLICATION DATA
has been applied for.

ISBN 978-0-525-95240-4

Printed in the United States of America
Set in Sabon Lt Std
Designed by Leonard Telesca

To my first boon companions, my siblings: Danny, Kevin, Peggy, Patty, and Maureen

Contents

Prologue

In the moments before she became a widow, veiled in blood, Sharon Lenox was happier than she'd been in ages. Her fifty-four-year-old husband, Jim, had just returned home from the hospital where he'd spent the night receiving infusions of magnesium, potassium, and trace minerals. After enduring months of toxic cancer treatments, the six-foot-tall, 120-pound man had become so dehydrated, he'd required immediate medical attention. Now, on this mild winter evening in January 2008, a week after Jim's birthday, Sharon was standing at the kitchen sink, washing dessert plates in soapy water, listening to her high school sweetheart patter on about their future together.

Earlier in the evening, their five adult children, fourteen grandchildren, and assorted relatives had gathered at their modest home to celebrate Jim's homecoming. About fifty of them had squeezed inside the family room to eat cake, drink soda, and talk politics. George W. Bush was still president of the United States, but Senator Barack Obama was campaigning to become the next leader. Around eight P.M., the last of the kids had left. Jim was now resting on the couch while his wife cleaned up. Frail but effusive, Jim was elated at the prospect of living long enough to watch his grandchildren grow up.

"Remember when we beat cancer the first time?" he asked his wife. In 1998, they had learned that the disease was ravaging Jim's left lung.

In a bid for life, he'd undergone surgery to remove part of his tumor-riddled organ. The operation had scared Jim so much he had quit smoking and, for nearly a decade, had lived cancer free. Then, in April 2007, the doctors had found two new lung nodules inside his body. Sharon had taken a leave from her job delivering mail to shuttle her husband to doctors' appointments, chemotherapy sessions, and blood transfusions. By August 2007, Jim was showing "significant improvement," according to one report. Still, the oncologist had told Sharon that her husband would probably live only six months. She had accepted that fact, but not Jim.

"We're going to beat this cancer again, honey," he said, his voice deep and steady. Sharon just smiled. She stood at the sink, her hands trawling the soapy basin for stray utensils. She retrieved a dish, sponged it off, and admired how her solitaire wedding ring still sparkled amid the iridescent bubbles.

Suddenly, Jim fell silent. Sharon turned back to look at him and saw thick, dark blood oozing from his mouth. At first she didn't understand. Jim coughed and struggled to breathe while Sharon waited for him to speak. But no words came out. Then, Jim scooted to the edge of the couch, his eyes pleading for help. Sharon dropped the dish, reached for the telephone, and dialed 911. The emergency dispatch operator asked Sharon some questions. By then, blood was spurting out of Jim's mouth and nose, thick rivulets dripping down his chin. Sharon gave the operator her name, address, and telephone number, then cried, "My husband is bleeding and he can't talk." Jim was now coughing up "pieces of tumor and lung," according to a report filed later by the Anne Arundel County Police Department. Apparently, some of his tumor was lodged in his throat, choking him.

Jim's eyes were bulging, and he tried desperately to breathe as blood poured down his chest. He grew so agitated that Sharon prayed for him to pass out, and mercifully, he did. Sharon fell to the floor, too, and began administering CPR while the operator instructed her calmly from the speaker phone. Every time Sharon breathed into her husband's mouth, his warm blood gushed into her mouth. When she pushed on Jim's chest, more blood spurted from his nose. In no time,

Sharon's face and white T-shirt were soaked in crimson, and her long, ash-brown hair was matted with clumps of red matter. She continued rhythmically breathing into Jim's lungs and pushing on his chest, while the operator guided her resuscitation efforts, the soothing telephone voice violently at odds with the gory scene.

When the paramedics finally burst through the door, they found blood dripping from the walls and pooling on the floor. Sharon looked up from her husband's body and the rescuers took over, measuring his vital signs. Sharon telephoned a family member for help, but after twenty minutes, the paramedics gave up. When Jim's son-in-law finally rushed into the room, ready to assist, he froze in horror. There lay his children's grandfather, a tube protruding from his gaping mouth, his death-dulled eyes wide open, his head encircled by a halo of blood, sputum, and malignant growths.

"It looks like a murder scene," he thought.

Was it? Earlier that day, a nurse had walked up to Jim Lenox and without consent had injected him with an overdose of a drug that stimulated his red blood cells. At the time, that shot had angered Sharon. Now, in light of her husband's slow, torturous death, that injection loomed large in her mind. Had that drug killed her husband? And were others dying in the same grotesque way?

PART I

1

Meet and Greet

DRESSED in a suit and a psychedelic-colored tie, a nervous Mark Duxbury wandered through the first floor of a conference center, searching for his company's hospitality suite. It was cocktail hour along New Jersey's pharmaceutical corridor off U.S. Route 1, the highway that linked Washington, D.C., to New York City, and on this particular evening, March 1, 1992, several companies were hosting events at the private compound here in Plainsboro. Duxbury's new employer, Johnson & Johnson, had flown him and twenty-six other new hires to this wooded corporate retreat to induct them into the company with an intense three-month-long sales training program. Duxbury was eager to learn about the storied health-care giant, its new start-up, and the wonder drug he'd be charged with selling—just as soon as he could find the Lakeview Room.

He heard the party before he saw it: ice cubes clinking gaily against crystal, voices buzzing sotto voce amid the occasional burst of polite laughter. Duxbury stepped inside the room with its plastic ferns and water vista and quickly scanned the crowd. A hive of attractive women in dark skirts recited their personal histories as a group of clean-shaven men wandered over, trailed by a musky scent. Younger sales reps huddled in a corner, their voices loud and boisterous, while a more relaxed pride of veterans took turns offering an assessment of the industry's challenges. All seemed engaged in the preprandial ritual of the business class, sizing up one another before forming alliances and oppositions.

At the edge of the room, Duxbury tried to read the crowd. He was a lean five feet eleven inches tall and wore wire-rimmed glasses. His wheat-colored hair was clipped short on the side but topped by a pompadour. He seemed shy, but once he stepped into the circle, he moved easily in his tailored, Italian-made trousers.

Duxbury introduced himself to an affable group and immediately stood out. For one thing, he wore a hand-painted silk tie in wild shades of purple, pink, and magenta. For another, this wasn't just any tie but a playful Nicole Miller design that depicted an aorta, a scalpel, the acupuncture points of.the body, and a bold pack of Trojan condoms. His peers clustered around to touch the silky, anatomically correct neckwear; some cracked sly jokes. Duxbury basked in the attention. "My ties separated me from the robo-reps and were real icebreakers," he said later. In fact, without his sartorial statement, Duxbury would have faded into the eggshell-hued walls. People peeled away from other klatches to join the commotion in Duxbury's crowd. One sales veteran noted the fuss and studied Duxbury's pasty complexion, fair hair, and green eyes. "Mark was so pale, I thought he was an albino," said Dean McClellan.

McClellan was a tanned, dark-haired man dressed in snakeskin boots and a black-and-yellow, Hopi Indian–patterned sweater. With his well-groomed mustache, jug ears, and easy smile, he, too, cut an amiable, if not quite dashing, figure. The forty-six-year-old McClellan waited for the ruckus to die down, then moseyed over to introduce himself to Duxbury, who was fourteen years his junior.

McClellan spoke with a Minnesota inflection but lived in Tucson, Arizona, where he spent weekends building sheds in his yard and killing the occasional rattlesnake. He'd been working in pharmaceuticals since 1984, he told Duxbury, even though he himself eschewed taking drugs. "I prefer soaking up the sun as a tonic for my aches and pains," he explained. McClellan had just left a job at Boehringer Ingelheim, selling psychiatric and pediatric drugs to doctors in the Southwest. He didn't mention he'd been the company's top cardiac drug sales rep for three years running, but he did describe the dangers of driving along the weed-choked Mexican border every month with a trunkful of prescription drugs. "I keep a loaded revolver in my glovebox in case *los banditos* try to steal my drug samples," he finished, leaning in on his boots.

Duxbury smiled. As a native of Olympia, Washington, one of the wettest spots in the contiguous United States, he lived near the *other,* more benign, border. The only time he carried a gun was during deer- and bear-hunting season, when he and a friend would camp in the woods above Wenatchee and, inevitably, come home empty-handed. Duxbury was a weekend musician and had won several top Washington State awards for his skills on the clarinet and other woodwinds. At nineteen, he'd been selected to join the thirteen-member Walt Disney World All-American Players in Anaheim, California, where he entertained two million Disneyland guests one summer. Duxbury's band had played as the theme park's evening orchestra, backing up Vic Damone, Tony Bennett, and Chita Rivera. But at twenty-one, Duxbury had dropped his promising musical career to pursue a more lucrative job in sales.

"So, how'd you land at J and J?" McClellan asked.

"I sold drugs for hogs and dogs," Duxbury joked.

He'd started his career with Beecham Laboratories' Animal Health Division, retailing antibiotics for sheep, cattle, and pets. From 1984 on, he drove the back roads of Oregon, calling on ranchers and cattle buyers. Later, he traversed the freeways of California, selling to feedlot owners and veterinarians. His sales had boomed an outstanding 140 percent compared to an industry growth of 2 percent, and for that he'd won a shiny gold pin. In 1989, he had moved to Bristol-Myers Squibb, where he dealt in heart medicine for human beings. He was so good that he nabbed his company's Go-Getter National Achievement Award, which placed him in the top 10 percent of the BMS sales force nationwide. Since McClellan knew all about cardiac medicine, the pair began gossiping about the doctors on the cardiology scene.

As different as cactus and conifer, the two hit it off that night and began a long and sometimes tumultuous friendship. Duxbury believed that McClellan was the "most interesting guy" he'd ever met, while McClellan considered his new friend "a smart and funny chap."

A dinner bell ushered the new hires into a banquet room, where they found their place cards at white-linen-clothed tables. A tall, impeccably dressed man strode to the head of the room, a smile playing on his lips. He had an aquiline nose, wire-brush eyebrows, and an air of Episcopalian authority. Dennis Longstreet introduced himself as the president of Ortho Biotech and welcomed his guests to their new company, "Johnson and Johnson's first foray into the biomedical field." J&J had played a major role in every health-care trend since the late nineteenth century, and now, on the cusp of the new millennium, it was forging a path into the cutting-edge world of biotech drugs.

"You're part of a grand adventure," Longstreet announced, looking at the expectant faces. As waiters appeared to fill wineglasses, Longstreet raised a toast. "To the success of Procrit and to every one of you."

The room echoed his words in a cloud of huzzahs.

McClellan dined at a table with W. Thomas "Tom" Amick, Ortho's field sales manager. Amick was from Raleigh, North Carolina, and tried to project himself as someone to the manor born although he'd been working for J&J since 1974. He had mottled pink skin, limestone-gray eyes, and the bluster of a man who'd drink water from a fire hose. His energy was piercing, contagious, and capricious. Amick listened as McClellan and the other diners at the table introduced themselves. When a pretty young female rep started to detail her short résumé, Amick pounced. "The only reason you're here is because I told your district manager to hire you." She blushed, as her dinner companions silently inspected their plates.

McClellan was shocked. "Amick is totally out of line," he thought. But that was his new leader, curt and imperious.

From then on, whenever Amick walked into the room, the more ambitious hirelings would flock around him, eager to impress him. But McClellan and Duxbury kept away. "Amick manages by fear and intimidation," another rep explained, and the three agreed.

That night, the two new hires talked about the company's mixed message. Elegant Longstreet seemed to epitomize J&J's blue-chip, old-line, Waspish reputation. Yet Amick's three-bell-alarm, barking-orders mien typified the crass side of Yankee capitalism. One thing was clear. If Duxbury and McClellan wanted to rise to the top of this rarified institution, they'd need to know every molecule in J&J's new drug package and every term in its recombinant-DNA technology box. They'd have to influence physicians' prescribing habits, learn insurance codes, and find the quickest way to capitalize on the biopharma-sales rush that was electrifying medicine. In other words, they'd need to become Procrit "detailers."

—◆—

THE next morning, a brigade of worsted wool and polyester filed into a sterile classroom at the Merrill Lynch Conference and Training Center. Duxbury squeezed into a plastic chair-desk next to McClellan's, ready to learn about the drug that J&J expected to be its first biotech hit. At eight A.M., a doctor from the New Jersey Medical School lectured on the benefits of Procrit, followed by a hematologist from St. Luke's Roosevelt Hospital, who explained the revolutionary science behind it. Duxbury sat riveted by the radical story.

The synthetic protein *epoetin alpha* had been spawned at the dawn of biotechnology start-ups in the early 1980s in Thousand Oaks, California. There, in a skateboard suburb thirty miles north of Hollywood, a venture capitalist, a chemist, and a scientist who'd spent twenty years experimenting with blood molecules founded Applied Molecular Genetics. The firm had little more than a stack of stationery and a wish list of inventions, such as a genetically engineered organism to extract oil from shale that could recover billions of barrels; a protein that would make chickens grow faster and fatter; and an indigo that could replace the natural and chemical dyes used to color blue jeans.

The firm's founders, however, were keen on making a big splash with their product. It just so happened that the research scientist, Eugene Goldwasser, had spent most of his career experimenting with erythropoietin, or "epo," a hormone naturally produced by the kidney. Pronounced *ee-rith-row-poy-i-tin*, this human protein stimulated the bone marrow to make more red blood cells, which increased hemoglobin, the crucial, oxygen-carrying component of blood that gives people stamina and energy. Without sufficient red blood cells, we become exhausted, depressed, and anemic and suffer serious health ailments. As it was, patients with malfunctioning kidneys or unnaturally low levels of erythropoietin required constant blood transfusions. For them, transfusions spelled the difference between barely existing and fully alive. In the early 1980s, however, the nation's blood supply became suddenly tainted with a mysterious bug. The HIV virus that caused AIDS had yet to be identified, but suddenly people were dying after receiving HIV-infected blood transfusions. Fear and hysteria swept through hospitals. Researchers at pharmaceutical companies slowly realized that if someone could clone epo, he'd eliminate dangerous transfusions, save lives, and make a bloody fortune too.

Goldwasser had performed so many experiments on sheep and rats, he had already produced eight milligrams of pure human epo—the world's only supply. This tiny amount was enough to launch an effort to find a cure for anemia, and his colleagues at Applied Molecular Genetics—or Amgen, as it was called—quickly pegged synthetic epo as a priority. Patenting such a breakthrough could benefit not just AIDS patients but also people enduring kidney dialysis, chemotherapy treatments, major surgery, and who knows what else. The problem, however, was that blood contains two hundred or so proteins, while epo makes but a brief appearance. "It wasn't rocket science," Goldwasser once said. "It was a lot more complex." To find epo, a scientist needed to spot the tiny molecule swimming in the bloodstream, then "catch" it from a vast sea of more visible proteins.

In 1981, after raising $19 million in venture capital, Amgen started hiring scientists. One of them, Fu-Kuen Lin, was charged with finding a way to clone the epo gene. The son of a Chinese herbalist, he had a broad, patient face and poker-game eyes. Dressed in a white lab coat, the forty-two-year-old spent days and nights in Amgen's laboratory, examining X-ray film on a backlit screen and searching tirelessly for the gene coding for human epo. He and his female assistant Chi Kwei Lin (no relation) shared a staggering task—to find a gene on a single strand of DNA among some 1.5 million fragments of human genome.

It was the equivalent of finding a short string of consecutive words—one particular sentence—buried in the massive twenty-volume *Oxford English Dictionary*.

As the AIDS epidemic mushroomed, Lin raced against other well-funded researchers at Parke-Davis, Abbott Laboratories, and other firms based in Chile and Japan. Even the goliath Johnson & Johnson was hunting epo, but from a totally different angle. Its scientists tried to extract human epo from certain anemia patients whose kidneys go into overdrive to produce the protein. They spent two years on that effort, far longer than expected.

Lin kept at it, too, despite many failed attempts to solve epo's riddle. During the mid-1980s, Amgen's staff voted several times to kill the program, but Goldwasser was unwavering, and finally, after two years, Lin came up with an ingenious method to catch the elusive molecule. He created multiple short strands of DNA fragments that could "fish" for the epo gene; in late 1983, he actually "hooked" it. That Yuletide miracle allowed Amgen to raise $40 million in an initial public offering, and buy itself some time.

After spending another painstaking year trying to sequence the gene, Lin moved on to the next grueling task—cloning it. As Amgen's scientists watched, he inserted the human form of epo into the fast-growing cells of a Chinese hamster's ovary, and voilà! Out came a genetically engineered version of the hormone, which they called epoetin alpha. In late 1984, Lin filed for the key patent on the process of producing recombinant epo, and Amgen headed for the finish line.

News of its biotech breakthrough spread up the Pacific Coast, across the continent to Route 128 in Boston, down to New Jersey, and through the I-270 tech corridor outside Washington, D.C. Overnight, Amgen became legendary. But that wasn't enough. It needed to turn its discovery into a commercial product, and that couldn't happen without the imprimatur of the U.S. Food and Drug Administration.

Pharmaceuticals are bound by an arduous drug-approval process set by the FDA. Before a drug can be sold, it must be tested extensively in laboratories and in animals, followed by three phases of well-controlled drug trials on humans. It's a nail-biting, expensive process that can take years. At any point along the way, scientists may discover fatal effects, dubious benefits, or other red flags that can kill the project. But a happy ending to a Phase III study is the sine qua non of a drug application. In 1985, the gene-splicing shop was hoping that epo could replace the four-hundred-year-old practice of transfusing blood, which would give the patent owner a veritable gold mine.

Maverick Amgen soon found itself in the middle of biotech's own Wild West. Holding the world's first *big* genetically engineered drug patent in one hand, it fended off threats and offers with the other hand. Dow Chemical, Abbott Labs, and Parke-Davis called. Kirin Brewery purchased the Japanese rights to epo for $24 million, and J&J offered to buy Amgen outright. But the start-up refused. Instead, Amgen sequestered fifteen employees in a block of rooms at a cheap Quality Inn in Simi Valley to work on its FDA drug application. The job should have taken 280 days, but the group resolved to get it done in 90. When the J&J people heard of that ambitious goal, they scoffed, claiming it was impossible. But that just spurred on the Amgen crew, who worked around the clock in shifts, fortified by caffeine and sugar. Weeks crawled by until one day, an Amgen worker hung a bedsheet over the entrance to the building with a scrawled message: THE SIMI VALLEY HOSTAGES ARE FREE!

It had taken ninety-three days—an incredible record.

Amgen's staff had compiled all of the results from its studies and trials that, along with other data, filled 140 volumes that stacked nine feet high. Yet even *that* feat wasn't enough. The shop now had to push its application through the FDA maze, which could take another eighteen months. After spending $85 million and nearly six years on its dream, Amgen *still* had no sales product. Worse, it had run out of money. Desperate to continue, Amgen quickly cut a deal. It sold J&J all rights to the epo market in Europe, and rights to most of the U.S. market except dialysis, the one Amgen figured it could easily develop.

In return, the New Jersey firm promised to help steer epo's application through the regulatory channels. "That deal saved Amgen," Robert Erwin, director of the Marti Nelson Cancer Foundation, said years later. In June 1989, Amgen won FDA approval for its product, Epogen. In December 1990, J&J's version of the drug, Procrit, was approved but only for the HIV market. And in 1991, Ortho reps began selling their one and only product.

But no one could have foreseen the treachery that this union would produce. Nor could anyone imagine the horrific consequences of epo itself.

—⁂—

For Duxbury, the days of classroom instruction bled into dinners of chicken fricassee and too many late nights of hanging at the bar. By the second week, the group of affable, smart, and good-looking salespeople began to take on certain distinct traits. "There are a lot of egos in this room, and everyone wants to outshine everyone else," Duxbury told McClellan one night. But according to several accounts, the freshman class fell into three distinct cliques. There were the "thinkers" who hung out at the coffee shops and read all of the course work, such as McClellan; and those who had gotten their jobs because of political connections, such as a former babysitter for an Ortho manager. And there were people like the handsome African-American Henry Lovett, who had always worked for a living.

Individual traits emerged too. Duxbury was known as the witty, sarcastic one, rather like the rebel from the teen movie *The Breakfast Club*. McClellan was the serious one, even though he was unintentionally funny. He wore hats, sweaters, and boots to class, despite the room's thermostat reading of a comfortable sixty-nine degrees. He remained indoors most days but complained frequently about the "cold" eastern weather. One night, McClellan cranked his room temperature to eighty-five degrees so he could sleep, but his roommate, Raj Mehta, couldn't stand it and wound up sleeping in the cool porcelain bathtub. The next day, Mehta found another roommate, while

McClellan was given his own private room, where he nailed the thermostat to a steamy eighty-nine degrees.

Duxbury bunked with an Egyptian man who smelled of patchouli. He didn't speak much but was so keen on expanding his language skills, he watched late-night Spanish TV. Duxbury and McClellan referred to a group of good-looking ladies' men as the "cabana boys." They included a short Turkish weight lifter named Marc Ehab Elsayed and a dashing gentleman from Atlanta, Georgia, Holt Robinson. The women were less flashy. Joan Newman was a black marathon runner who wore track suits to breakfast. Christy Stark was a freckled-faced redhead with a megawatt smile. The tall brunette from Philadelphia, Elizabeth Shimshock, "had such a bland personality, I couldn't figure out why she went into sales," McClellan said. To the amazement of the men in her class, Shimshock would go on to win six top sales awards, more than most of them. Then there were the instructors, including a woman who flirted openly with the cabana boys.

As the second week dragged on, the group grew restless. "We are in the middle of nowhere, stuck in the woods, and don't have a lot of free time," said McClellan. "Yeah," Duxbury agreed. "This is the class from hell." When the students weren't studying epo in the classrooms, they were sharing meals in a bland room, after which they'd attend a lecture by a sales manager. Some days, the sales reps would organize a volleyball game, or jog round the twenty-seven-acre campus. But sooner or later, they'd all meet in the bar to tally up the day. Then they'd trundle up to the same floor of the cloistered hotel, where they'd sleep in rooms that overlooked the man-made lake.

One night, toward the end of the session, Duxbury accompanied four people to a rowdy bar in Princeton. He wasn't drinking. But the others ordered so many cocktails, the barmaid brought them complimentary beer bongs and Jell-O shooters laced with alcohol. "It's a stunt to loosen you up," Duxbury warned his friends. But the office party quickly degenerated into a sodden disaster, especially since the two females in the group were Ortho trainers and therefore supervisors. One woman was already dating a trainee, in violation of company policy, and was so drunk she had to be carried to the car. There, she lay in the backseat across the laps of two male trainees, writhing seductively to the music on the radio. "This is disgusting," Duxbury thought. As soon as the group reached the conference center, Duxbury helped carry the woman to the hotel lobby. But he refused to join the group in her room. As he described it afterward: "This was bad news coming at me like a semi."

To Duxbury, the manager's behavior was reckless and unprofessional. "If a male trainer had acted like that with female students, he would have been fired," he later told McClellan. Duxbury's sense of fairness required that the woman be held to the same standards as a man. So, the next day, he wrote a formal complaint. On the last day of class, a male manager appeared and apologized to the students. He said that the female trainer had been demoted for making "a Career Limiting Move—a CLiM." Neither Duxbury nor McClellan had ever heard that expression. But as the rep with the unbending principles, Duxbury would come to know that term very well.

—⁓—

It was a glorious spring morning, and Mark Duxbury drove a shiny new company car along the rim of Puget Sound. He passed fleets of purse seiners, gill-netters, and weekend cruisers, which rocked gently on the blue rippled water. The sound of trombones and trumpets blasted from a tape in his automobile cassette player. Every salesperson needs inspiration, and Duxbury was psyching himself up for a day of cold calls by playing big-band music. He was a full-fledged product specialist for Ortho Biotech, and today he'd meet a handful of potential clients in hopes of eventually signing some contracts. As he drove along the waterfront, he slapped his car's steering wheel in rhythm to the music while the boats bobbled and rolled.

Today was going to be a challenge. Ortho presented itself as a young, innovative company whose salespeople were more like technical advisors to physicians. But convincing medical professionals to treat Duxbury as an advisor was an entirely different thing. There were thirty thousand other drug reps working the country, most of them selling established brands, and Duxbury was introducing a new pharmaceutical from a new company to new accounts—the most difficult job a rep could get. He needed to gain the ear, if not the trust, of busy administrators who spent their days dodging guys like him. He believed he had the edge. After all, he represented Johnson & Johnson, the maker of No More Tears Baby Shampoo and Listerine mouthwash, the inventor of the first-aid kit and the ubiquitous cloth stretcher. Who in the medical field hadn't come across a J&J product? The company's reputation was such that it was the only corporation to share a logo with one of the world's most respected humanitarian groups, the American Red Cross. Duxbury figured it'd be relatively easy to sell Procrit, especially since the amazing drug could conceivably save lives. That's why he was calling on people today without the benefit of an appointment—well, that, and the fact that no one had answered his telephone calls.

Duxbury believed there were two types of people in the world: those motivated by fear and those inspired by fun. There were Eeyores, named after the dour donkey from the Winnie-the-Pooh children's books, and there were Tiggers, labeled for the bouncy, self-confident tiger that the salesman took as his personal mascot.

Eager to make a sale, Duxbury headed to Olympia. In the backseat of his Chevy Impala was his black bag, which measured two and a half feet high, two feet long, and a foot wide. His "detail" bag was a portable medicine cabinet that held everything a salesman might need, and inside were adjustable shelves to hold drug samples. Procrit, however, required careful handling, It had to be refrigerated at four degrees Celsius to retain its potency and, unlike a martini, could not be shaken, stirred, frozen, or exposed to the sun. As a result, Ortho reps couldn't carry samples of the sensitive medicine. So Duxbury filled the shelves with alcohol wipes, cotton balls, adhesive tape, and disposable syringes, all made by J&J. In other compartments he had packed coffee mugs, clipboards, ballpoint pens, and writing pads emblazoned with Procrit's name in blue sans serif type. Later, he'd hand out some of these tchotchkes to doctors and nurses. In the bag's pockets and flaps, he kept street maps of various cities in his territory, glossy brochures that described the drug, and some forms. Despite the load, his black bag still had enough to room to fit a dozen torpedo sandwiches in case he wanted to throw an impromptu "education" lunch for nurses.

The rep also had a binder that included a Procrit price list and a master directory of his potential accounts, his "call on the universe" list. Before Duxbury had joined the firm, his boss, Bob Nelson, had traversed the states of Washington, Idaho, Montana, and Alaska, gathering contact information for nephrologists, HIV specialists, and other physicians who were candidates for Procrit. But today, Duxbury had his eye on bigger game. As Tom Amick had said, "Hospitals are our most important customer class," since they place big orders. If Duxbury wanted to achieve his first-year sales quota, he'd have to land a hospital contract soon. The trick was finding the buyer. Every institution has its own purchasing system; sometimes the pharmacist places drug orders, other times the chief physician does. He was about to scout St. Peter Hospital to locate its procurement officer.

Duxbury drove past downtown Olympia and toward its eastern suburbs. Soon he saw the patient tower of Providence St. Peter. The building was a state-of-the-art facility on Lilly Road, made of tempered glass and concrete, and it had been gracefully expanded over the years to accommodate the growing legions of the sick. He pulled up to the building, parked his car, and grabbed his binder. Thinking it best to perform his reconnaissance mission incognito, he left behind his telltale black bag.

His mother, a registered nurse, had once worked at St. Peter, and Duxbury had visited her as a kid. He recalled the sight of the nuns who ran the place, their starched white alien headgear, their heavy skirts rough as burlap. When they walked, their belts of rosary beads clacked like strings of bone. He had been frightened by them, but now, standing in the busy lobby, he searched them out. Who better to guide him through the hospital's maze than a compassionate member of the Sisters of Providence?

Instead of religious habits, he saw only nurses in pastel uniforms, and men in lab coats and street clothes. Duxbury peeled off his suit jacket, hooked his finger in the designer label, and threw his coat over his shoulder. He strolled down the hall as if he were a physician coming on shift.

He spied a plain-looking woman in a dark pantsuit wearing a three-inch-long cross hanging from a silver chain. "Excuse me, sister," he said. "I'm lost."

The woman looked up, and Duxbury rewarded her with a smile. "I'm a sales rep for a division of Johnson and Johnson," he said. He reached inside his breast pocket and produced his business card.

"Hematopoietic Product Specialist," she read.

"Can you tell me where I'd find the pharmacist?"

"Which one?" she asked.

Bingo, Duxbury thought. There's more than one pharmacist here, which could be a sales bonanza.

The Catholic nun and secular rep chatted in the hall as people steered a path around them. St. Peter employed about nine hundred people and treated hundreds more. Many of its patients were poor, indigent, and elderly and therefore had no private health insurance plans. But part of their medical and prescription drug costs was covered by Medicaid or some other government program. The hospital's acute renal dialysis unit could treat fourteen people at a time, and more in its outlying satellite units. Although dialysis patients belonged to the Amgen reps, the hospital's AIDS patients who received the blood-booster Epogen fell into Duxbury's bailiwick, and soon the pre-dialysis group would too. The rep needed to find out how many such patients were treated here, and how he could transfer them to Procrit.

He met a social worker, a nurse, and a technician. With every encounter, he launched into the story of how California scientists had cloned the gene of the hormone erythropoietin, using cells from the ovaries of a Chinese hamster, and injected it into anemic people. The results were amazing. Pale skin turned pink, dull eyes regained their sparkle, and bodies began to make their own red blood cells. Duxbury was the kind of guy who could sell rings to Saturn if he thought it would help save the planet, and he truly believed in epo. "This drug really benefits some patients," he'd say. "Your transfusion candidates won't get infections or viruses that come from blood banks." Duxbury's enthusiasm for the product was contagious. If someone asked about side effects, he'd reply, "Procrit is like mother's milk." He'd pull out two medical studies he'd tucked inside his binder that demonstrated the drug's effectiveness. Anyone who read the articles could see that epo did indeed reduce the number of transfusions. But there wasn't any conclusive data about safety.

Duxbury made no sale that day, but his foray into St. Peter marked the beginning of a slow-building, low-pressure sales campaign that he hoped would bear fruit. And so it went, week after week, site after site. In time, the rep made a few sales to doctors who used Procrit for non-dialysis patients and AIDS sufferers. But the physicians prescribed the drug in small doses and only for six to eight weeks. He kept stopping by St. Peter, hoping to learn the name of its epo purchaser without appearing to be desperate.

Not much flustered Duxbury. He'd grown up in a pastoral setting in northeast Olympia, the second of three kids in a middle-class family. His parents, Duane and Faye, were high school sweethearts who, after graduating from college, bought a simple single-story, two-bedroom house in 1955 for about eight thousand dollars. The red-roofed house sat just at the city's limits, in a clearing in the forest, down a lane where only three other families lived in similarly practical wooden houses. Duxbury's dad had taught music in the North Thurston School District, traveling from school to school leading choirs, bands, and orchestras. Most summers, he put away his horns and trombones for hammers and nails, expanding the family homestead. Their first child was Duane junior, and four years later, in early spring, Duxbury arrived. When the baby turned one year old, his father parked him in a playpen on the lawn while he and the workers built an addition to the home. Each time a worker passed by, the diapered boy would raise his little hand and give a toothless grin. "His first word was *hi*," said Faye. "Mark was happy to talk to anybody, and once he got started, he never stopped jabbering."

A year later, the family welcomed Ruth Anne, and the three siblings spent their free days outdoors, running along a dirt road they called "the cows and bulls trail," horsing around the blackberry patch, or splashing in the pool their father later built with money earned from private music lessons. "It was a pretty idyllic time," Faye recalled.

Duxbury was especially close to his mother, a nurse with a bachelor's degree in science from the University of Washington. Faye always worked, either in a doctor's office, or a hospital ward, or a school infirmary. She'd arrive home laden with trinkets from pharmaceutical reps, and Duxbury would run out to greet her by shouting, "Mommy, what did the salesman give you today?" A miniature globe, an address book, a pen set—the boy collected these items as if they were treasures from a shipwreck.

Now he himself was a drug salesman, a "detailer," passing out calendars and pens and wearing totemic ties. On one of his visits to St. Pete, a nurse spied his ascot and squealed, "Oooo! I just love Tigger!" Soon he was a welcome presence inside the linoleum-floored fort.

But there was so much to learn. It would take months before he discovered the names of the pharmacists who ordered drugs for his types of patients, and longer still before those druggists would actually see him. On his rounds, Duxbury accumulated whatever information he could. Then he'd find the cafeteria, buy some coffee, and sit at a small table with his binder.

He'd record his impressions for his weekly activity reports—WAR dispatches, he called them—which were sent electronically to his boss in Seattle and to his boss's boss in New Jersey. In that initial WAR, he recorded the number of hospital patients, the protective nature of St. Pete's staff, and the fact that there was at least one pharmacist on the dialysis floor. He didn't think there was more than 10 percent of non-dialysis business at the hospital, and the nurses didn't seem to like epo. Maybe there was bad blood between St. Peter and Amgen. Or maybe the hospital had "once had a J and J rep with really bad breath," he theorized.

Forging new territory was hard work with an uncertain payoff. As he roamed the Northwest trying to sell his company's product, he did the numbers in his head. He'd heard that it took Ortho about $300,000 a year to support a drug rep; Duxbury's 1992 quota was only

$250,000. Even if he made his forecast, he wouldn't be paying his own way. Other numbers didn't add up, either, such as the amount of non-dialysis business in his market. At most, he figured he could sell $10,000 to $15,000 of Procrit a month. At that, he'd be 30 percent short of what headquarters expected from him. "This is no way to make money," it dawned on him. "And it's no way to keep this job." As Duxbury sped through the forested country, his natural effervescence struggled with his roiling gut.

2

The Deal

Dᴇɴɴɪꜱ Longstreet leaned back in his chair in his office in Raritan, which was control central for Ortho. A glance outside his window might have cheered another man. Clover pushed through the dirt, dogwood bloomed around the hundred-acre corporate park, and the shiny, late-model cars in the parking lot no longer wore ice and snow. Beyond Longstreet's door lay the precincts of other J&J divisions: Ortho-McNeil, with its top-selling acid reflux pills, Ortho Clinical Diagnostics, with its respected chemical tests, and Ortho Biologics, which ran an offshore manufacturing facility. The 1992 recession was probably squeezing other leaders inside these four-story cement buildings, but Longstreet and his lieutenants were getting absolutely crushed.

Nearly every problem could be traced back to Ortho's historic deal with its so-called partner, Amgen. Their relatively simple, five-page product license agreement (PLA) had been a source of conflict for as long as Longstreet could remember. Now Amgen was aggressively selling truckloads of Epogen to pharmacies, hospitals, and other groups that included Ortho's reserved *nondialysis* business. Amgen reps had been in the field for three years, sewing up most of Ortho's market with long-term contracts. Although Longstreet had repeatedly asked his corporate partner to stop, his cordial requests had gone nowhere.

The memorandum war had escalated to the point where Longstreet could almost see his opponent in front of him, spitting out his accusations in strings of yellow bile.

"Where's your data to support [your] assertions?" Amgen's vice president Paul Dawson demanded in one note.

"We [are] willing to provide you with this information if you will reciprocate with similar [data]," Longstreet replied.

"You [are] not telling the truth," Dawson sneered.

And so it went, page after acrimonious page. Was there ever a time when the two had gotten along?

Like a lot of couplings, the one between Amgen and J&J had seemed like a good idea at the time. In September 1985, the PLA joined the cutting-edge bioscience of a West Coast boutique to the marketing brawn of a venerable East Coast pharmaceutical. Similar deals between biotech firms and drug companies would follow, but none quite like this one, occurring at the dawn of the biotech era when everything was untainted by cautionary precedents. Many a petri dish had been wasted searching for low-hanging fruit, and epo was one of the few proteins that had a clear therapeutic use. The PLA had been so exceptional that analysts had called it "the deal of the century." But its most extraordinary element was that J&J had paid some $6 million for the rights to sell the drug everywhere in the world—except Japan and China—for all indications other than dialysis. That was *a steal,* and for a ridiculously low price plus royalties, J&J received access to all of the nondialysis markets in the United States that it could develop. This would prove to be an important distinction. As for Amgen, it got a quick cash infusion, allowing it to report $548,000 in fiscal 1985, its first annual profit.

At the time, Amgen thought it was getting the better end of the deal, with access to two hundred thousand U.S. dialysis patients and roughly $350 million in annual sales—four times the size of the predialysis sector. The partners had planned to file for regulatory approval of their drugs at the same time so they could enter the market together. As the holder of epo's patent, Amgen was responsible for submitting all papers to the FDA in hopes of obtaining approval for both drugs. To help its partner reach that goal, J&J spent millions of dollars providing Amgen with technical writers, environmental impact statements, and toxicity studies, and helping to navigate the byzantine regulatory process.

But at some point, Amgen's leaders realized they'd given away the store. The PLA asserted that J&J could go after "all indications for human use, other than dialysis," and that encompassed sickle-cell anemia, AIDS, hemophilia, cancer, maybe even depression. Angered at their oversight, Amgen's leaders began to undercut their New Jersey partner at every turn. Amgen declined to name Ortho as a distributor on its FDA application; it refused to supply Ortho's clinical trials and predialysis data to the FDA for its approval; its executives walked out of negotiations and even withheld crucial information from its so-called partner. The biotech firm refused to give J&J enough epo cell line so it could manufacture its drug in Europe and, when that failed, tried to charge Ortho twelve times its cost—as much as $300,000 per gram. It eventually agreed to charge only double its rate, and then threatened to completely disrupt Ortho's European supply.

Four years into the deal, Amgen had "forced Ortho, step-by-step, to relinquish its independence," according to a judge. In the end, it dropped Ortho's name entirely from epo's drug application and raced to get to market first. Hours after regulators approved Epogen's application in June 1989, the California firm shipped hundreds of thousands of vials worth $20 million, *in just one day*, cutting Longstreet off at the knees. Whatever income Ortho's chief had promised J&J's board for 1989 flew out the window, along with a year's worth of overhead.

Longstreet tried to apply for a drug license based on nondialysis use only, but the FDA said that was too similar to Amgen's dialysis license. He searched for a separate indication, but 1990 came and went. Whatever sales Longstreet had projected for that year also vanished. It took him nineteen months to obtain regulatory approval for Procrit, and then only for a narrow market—HIV patients who suffered anemia due to a toxic drug called AZT. By the time Procrit shipped in January of 1991 and Ortho reps were finally unleashed, Longstreet expected sales of $100 million that year.

Now, sitting in his office off Country Club Drive, the frantic leader needed a break, and quickly. Amgen was gobbling up epo's entire market, selling about $340 million of Epogen a year and laughing in his face. Longstreet had spent his whole career at the image-conscious J&J, trying to exemplify what legendary chairman Robert Johnson had called the "J&J type," a man of solid character and sound judgment. He had started at the bottom, selling controversial and, in some states, illegal birth control pills for a unit of the G-rated, family friendly J&J, clambering over Ivy League types to seize the reins at J&J's first biotech division. His courtly cunning would have shocked the organization man of the 1950s, yet he could not outflank Dawson.

Now, Amgen's vice president fired another missile in Longstreet's direction: "I have yet to receive any response . . . that Ortho intends to abide by the contractual restriction against [marketing] Procrit for dialysis."

Such topics, Longstreet sniffed, "may be best discussed at top levels." But while he had Dawson's attention, Longstreet went on to accuse him of selling long-term contracts at hospitals that served both dialysis *and nondialysis* patients. *You're poaching on our territory, old boy.*

Dawson would have none of it. "I'm still waiting for . . . Ortho's assurance that its agreements with customers are restricted to non-dialysis purchases."

"That has always been our intent," Longstreet assured him. Yet, what a shame, he added, that Dawson had refused to meet and discuss these very issues.

How dare you? Dawson responded. "I have not refused to meet with Ortho. . . . Your repeated efforts to blame Amgen for Ortho's difficulties make me think that your purpose is to divert attention from Ortho's own improper market activities."

Longstreet threw out some emotionally charged phrases, such as "posturing," "bad faith," and Amgen's "overall strategy to denigrate Ortho."

"I do not intend to dignify your accusations," Dawson bellowed.

As Amgen's first vice president of sales and marketing, Dawson was hard-nosed. The former G. D. Searle rep had spent the past four years building a sales organization to launch two of biotech's most lucrative products, a red-blood-cell maker and a white-blood-cell maker—Amgen's only crops. The dogged commander may have ranked beneath Longstreet in the pecking order, but he acted as his equal. In a way, Dawson's behavior was a barometer for the state of the PLA, which had been reduced to a whorl of lawsuits and counterclaims.

J&J had accused its partner of breaking their agreement by refusing to file a joint drug application; in June 1991, a judge concurred. Amgen had not only locked Ortho out of the market; it had aggressively sold to its partner's reserved sector prior to Procrit's debut. For that, the judge ordered Amgen to pay Ortho $164 million in damages.

Amgen was gobsmacked, as that was more cash than the firm had on hand. That summer day, Dawson and Amgen's CEO, Gordon Binder, called employees to the auditorium to discuss the shocking $164 million fine. Layoffs were possible, Binder admitted. "Bankruptcy is not out of the question." Many employees were so upset, they went home that night to scour their shelves for Johnson's Baby Powder, Rolaids, and other J&J products, and tossed them into trash heaps and bonfires just so they could be "a 100 percent J&J-free" household.

As it turned out, the $164 million fine did not destroy Amgen—nor did it deter it. Eight months later, Longstreet was still fielding reports that Amgen was burgling Ortho's lot. So, in February 1992, he lowered his musket at Dawson and fired. "I am very disturbed by information . . . that [you're promoting] Epogen for the treatment [of] exclusive Ortho indications."

Dawson had a different interpretation of the loosely written PLA. "Ortho has no rights to [nondialysis], nor are Amgen's rights limited to end-stage dialysis," he declared.

"Quite frankly," Longstreet responded, "I find it truly bizarre that you continue to insist that we had agreed to assign [predialysis] sales to you. We had simply agreed to consider such a proposal."

That's not true! Dawson cried, then called the CEO a liar.

Longstreet was exasperated. "I do not understand why you insist on misstating our position."

Apoplectic, Dawson accused Ortho of even *more* breaches. But before Longstreet could reply, his nemesis suffered a heart attack while touring Amgen's manufacturing plant. A few days later, on February 21, 1992, Paul R. Dawson died.

As spring now rolled through the bucolic fields behind Longstreet's office, even the graveyard at St. Bernard Roman Catholic Cemetery looked pleasant. Longstreet had once envisioned leading Ortho out of the corporate nursery and into the hall of fame, but that dream must have looked brash in the spring light of reality. Amgen had already forced Longstreet to slash Ortho's 1991 sales forecast from $100 million to $45 million. His estimates for 1992 looked optimistic too. He'd give no quarter to the enemy, and vowed to stem the red tide that was staining his office.

—❀—

Dawson wasn't the only casualty in the battle of the blood drug. While leaders at both companies continued to brawl over their pact, European racers pushed the boundaries of epo too. Initially, the results were thrilling.

Insert needle into ampoule; draw liquid; inject it into upper buttocks; and *ride*. Push the legs faster, lean into the wind, wipe the sweat from your brow. Because you're driving yourself hard, your cardiovascular system strains to keep up. It pumps blood that carries oxygen to your flexors and adductors, hopefully before the lactic acid burns the muscles and signals exhaustion. You ride harder, but the burn doesn't come. Instead, an explosive power propels you up the alpine peak. The blood pounds in your veins, eyes well with tears, and you fly to the finish line.

For cyclists, recombinant epo seemed better than amphetamines, caffeine suppositories, testosterone, cortisone, steroids, and all the other banned "vitamins" so common on the professional circuit. While other substances could be detected in doping tests, epo couldn't be. Plus, it seemed natural. One measure of health is the level of hemoglobin, the protein in your red blood cells that delivers oxygen to tissues. A healthy level for a male is between 13 grams of hemoglobin per deciliter (g/dl) and 17 g/dl. For a woman, it's 12 to 16 g/dl. To an athlete, the ability to raise one's hemoglobin by just 10 percent could spell the difference between placing in a race and winning, and that's what recombinant epo did.

In the late 1980s, one could easily obtain the black-market drug from clinical trials in Sweden, England, and the United States. Word on the street was that safety tests were under way to assure the world that epo was absolutely safe, and that was sort of true. But epo had issues. Scientists knew that boosting red blood cells also thickened the blood, which increased the risk of clotting. Blood clots lead to serious health problems such as strokes, heart attacks, and brain aneurisms. But at what dose? And under what circumstances?

Amgen and J&J were supposed to answer those questions in large, post-approval safety trials, according to Dr. Patricia Keegan, M.D., then a member at the FDA's biologic division. Manufacturers with products that purport to cure a disease usually submit safety trials *before* a drug is approved. But epo was a palliative drug that didn't actually cure a disease; it simply treated the *symptoms* of a disease. Since FDA approval standards for palliative drugs were more relaxed than they were for curative drugs, regulators weren't as strict about epo's trials. "They [the firms] didn't come in with safety studies at the time of their [drugs'] approval," said Keegan. "But they were asked to conduct those studies," first in 1989, when Epogen was approved, and again in 1991, when Procrit arrived. By late 1992, those studies were still under way.

Yet it was the cyclists zooming through the medieval towns of Italy and Holland who became epo's most visible guinea pigs. They easily bought vials of Eprex in Geneva without a prescription. Following the "more is better" maxim, they'd inject a high dose, followed perhaps by another one. Then came the adverse side effects. First, five Dutch racers died suddenly, followed by a Belgian. Then, seven more Dutchmen died, including Johannes Draaijer, a twenty-seven-year-old who had once raced in the famous, month-long Tour de France. He had started getting sick after using epo, his wife said. In February 1990, a few days after a race, Draaijer had died of a heart blockage. Although a doctor had pronounced him fit to ride that race and an autopsy revealed nothing, his widow tearfully confirmed his drug use. She told reporters that she hoped her husband's death would serve as a warning about epo's hazards.

Researchers blamed the athletes for abusing the drug at high doses in an unsupervised manner. By 1992, after standard dosage levels were known, even more cyclists who had allegedly used the drug died, many from cardiac failure. By then the Committee of Medicinal Products in the EU and the FDA in the United States had already given Epogen, Eprex, and Procrit their seals of approval. Despite the lack of solid scientific evidence, cyclists and patients alike assumed that the regulator's stamp meant the drug was safe.

—⚏—

PANDEMONIUM erupted in the lobby of the St. Francis Hotel as a group of Ortho sales reps burst though the doors. Duxbury quickly scanned the throng of boisterous people to see if McClellan was among them. The two hadn't seen each other for nearly six months and were looking forward to reconnecting. But when Duxbury didn't see the Arizona rep, he returned to the conversation unspooling near the wall. It was September 1992, Indian summer in San Francisco, and all of the hail-fellows-well-met reps from the Western region were converging here for a four-day sales meeting. Come nightfall, some thirty-six reps and their managers from four sales divisions would commandeer the lounge of this hotel, including people from as far away as San Diego, California; Bellingham, Washington; and Minneapolis, Minnesota.

The fourth quarter was always crunch time, when reps were expected to move more product and close the year on a high financial note. And this was an especially crucial moment. There was plenty of confusion as to which accounts reps could call on, and what they could say. Most of the salespeople had no clue about the ongoing war between Ortho and Amgen, but a handful of executives did, and they worried that the tug-of-war over markets was going to pinch Ortho's financial statements that year—again. Ortho could not afford another rout. The truth was, Ortho's revenues at that moment "were barely enough to keep the lights on," as one manager told Duxbury. Plus, Ortho's legal bills were proliferating like bacteria in a culture dish.

But none of this was spoken that afternoon in the hotel lobby, where excitement rumbled through the crowd like tremors before an earthquake. And no wonder. The freshman class of Procrit had spent months working alone, straining to make friends with virtual strangers, waiting for people who never showed, and enduring brush-offs. "Little Willy Lomans," some doctors called them, referring to the character in the classic American play *Death of a Salesman*. Or "drug droppers," as if these trained medical specialists were beasts of burden. After smiling through the insults, a rep would return to a motel room where the walls were thin, the mattresses were lumpy, and the blankets too thin (or too thick), only to discover that the couple next door who had made noise last night had used up the hot water. Ortho reps were paid well to tolerate these petty nuisances; a decent base salary, bonuses and commissions, a health-care package, pension, and company car went far in soothing the loneliness and stinging rebukes of being a traveling salesperson. The only time the reps saw their peers was at sales meetings like this one in San Francisco, and now they were free.

Ortho planners made sure to set these reunions inside luxury spots that oozed of privilege and status. Here, the reps were cosseted from the distrust, suspicion, and hostility they confronted every week on outside sales calls. Here, the middle-class workers could feel pampered and rich. On top of that, there was plenty of playtime. In fact, this particular meeting resembled a field trip for 180-pound schoolkids rather than the serious work session it purported to be. As soon as Duxbury spied McClellan, they made plans to meet later.

Located on Union Square, the iconic St. Francis Hotel had been built in 1904 by Charles Crocker, one of California's Big Four railroad magnates. It had survived fires, earthquakes, sex scandals, and military wars, while managing to host emperors, queens, and statesmen throughout it all, without interruption. Even now, at the tail end of the twentieth century, the Grand Dame was so genteel, her staff still offered to polish guests' silver coins, a service both reps took advantage of. For Duxbury, whose childhood vacations had been spent RV camping in an Airstream trailer, and McClellan, whose boyhood summers had been spent trimming trees in a string of dull towns, this hotel stimulated the imagination. The first morning, on their way down to breakfast, they paused at a landing to admire the marble pillars and crystal chandeliers.

"I'll race you down," said Duxbury.

And so they galloped down the steps, *thumpeta, thumpeta, thumpeta.*

Catching their breath in the lobby, the two men read an announcement board—WELCOME ORTHO BIOTECH! It listed the events for the next few days: the regional meetings, the evening dinners, and leisure activities such as golf excursions and ferry tours. Daytime hours were dominated by large group presentations, or small breakout sessions for each of the four divisions. McClellan and his co-workers in the Southwestern District, and Duxbury and his Northwest crew, got an earful of company news from official sources.

More than once, they heard others complain how hard it was to sell Procrit, even after nearly two years on the market. "I have a few mail-order pharmacies that aren't even carrying Procrit," one complained. Many criticized the complicated terms of the PLA. Employees knew that Procrit could help everyone with kidney problems, but they were arbitrarily limited to selling it for nondialysis patients only. Others groused about the incessant, urgent demands from their leaders. "Every ten minutes, it seems, I get a voice mail from my manager, or from his manager, asking me to resend a report or redo the profiles of the doctors in my territory," said one rep. The constant requests for more reports stole time from making a sale. McClellan, among others, felt as if he wasn't getting enough support from headquarters. Even something as simple as obtaining a Procrit brochure took weeks or even months.

But perhaps the biggest problem was the overly optimistic sales forecasts. In their enthusiasm at finally obtaining the FDA's blessing, Ortho executives had ordered too much factory product, and now tens of thousands of Procrit packs sat unsold in dozens of warehouses. Since the shelf life of Procrit was about eighteen months, much of the medicine was about to expire. That meant millions of dollars' worth of Procrit could be returned soon. In fact wholesalers had already threatened to ship back unsold dated goods, and as the year drew to a close, the pressure to move inventory intensified.

The poor communications, glut of expiring product, and high sales forecasts triggered several outbursts during that conference. At one meeting, Duxbury watched a new friend stand up and ask, "What is management doing?"

It was the Panic of '92.

—∞—

At night, after the meetings, many of the reps wound up in the Oak Room bar, an old smoking room from the Roaring Twenties. In the dim light, they discussed the events of the day, their company, and, inevitably, industry scandals. Most of the ruses, such as husk parties and lick-and-stick scams, involved getting free or discounted prescription drugs and selling them at full price. Such schemes were unique to America's pharmaceutical pipeline. This multibillion-dollar shadow world of drug distributors runs the gamut from seemingly respectable corporate suppliers to convicted felons. In between lie so many layers of merchants it's a wonder that the pipeline can accommodate them all.

Manufacturers like Ortho promote their drugs through their sales force. But reps don't actually deliver the drug the way that traditional salesmen do. Instead, the drug is moved through a variety of middlemen who process orders in seemingly nonsensical ways. Wholesalers like McKesson or Cardinal Health, for example, purchase drugs at a slight discount from the sticker price, then sell them at steeper discount to Ortho clients—such as drugstore chains like Walgreens and groups like the Hospital Corporation of America (HCA). This makes no sense until you realize that the wholesalers recoup their losses by billing J&J for the difference via "charge backs" and fees. Next come the pharmacy benefit managers, who work for an HMO or a group of employers. They buy huge volumes of drugs at discounts and distribute them to their members at a markup, pocketing the change. Insurance companies, employee plans, and even doctors do pretty much the same thing—buy wholesale, mark up prices, and sell retail.

These middlemen are the links between drug manufacturers and consumers, who include Medicare and other government and municipal funds. The charge backs, discounts, postsale rebates, free goods, and off-invoice payoffs are designed to deceive these payers by hiding the real cost of drugs. In fact, the entire serpentine system is so deliberately convoluted that the chain of transactions isn't clear to the regulators and policy makers who have a shot at streamlining it. So we're left with an ingenious twist on Soviet-style economics, in which every link in the drug distribution chain conspires to bilk the state— and taxpayers—into propping up their business.

It's not uncommon for drugs to change hands several times, going from one operator to another, even from one state to another. There are secondary wholesalers who sell to regional customers and closed-door pharmacies that serve nursing homes, AIDS clinics, and other closed systems. Secondary wholesalers have been known to buy discounted drugs and divert them to retailers at a markup—a practice that even the Big Three wholesalers have been caught doing. At the bottom of the chain are rogue operators who set up Internet pharmacies to sell Valium, Ritalin, and narcotics. Unscrupulous types at any of these levels can illegally obtain discounted medicines and sell them back to another link in the chain. Sometimes, they sell them back to the wholesaler from which they came, so that it's hard to tell who is scamming whom. A drug diverter could be a vice president at a "gold-standard" corporate distributor, or a tattooed felon pushing fake steroids on the Web. The most vulnerable people in the system, the self-employed, underinsured, and uninsured, tend to pay the most for medicine. Odder still is that the two groups that together purchase the largest volume of drugs, the federal and state governments, often get stuck with the highest bill, another bloat to the cost of American health care.

In the 1990s, mail-order pharmacies joined this conga line. And one name that popped up repeatedly at Ortho meetings was an outfit called Charise Charles.

—⁂—

A WEEK after leaving San Francisco, Duxbury and the entire Western Region flew east to Massachusetts to attend another meeting. This event, however, was a national sales meeting, and all four regions—with sixteen divisions and approximately 140 sales reps and managers—assembled, including Longstreet, Amick, and other executives. As soon as McClellan read the week's itinerary, with its scheduled cruise of Boston Harbor, he exclaimed, "We're going to sail on two oceans in opposite ends of the country in one week!" But that wouldn't be the highlight of this particular expedition.

It was here that Duxbury learned that the Southeast divisions were dramatically outperforming the Northwest. Apparently, Atlanta and Orlando were on track to win the company's highest district award, the President's Cup, given every year to the top performing district. Duxbury glanced at the seven other hardworking reps in his territory and thought, "It's not because the Southeast has better salespeople. Maybe they have more *nondialysis* business." The idea that any unit could so thoroughly trounce his own hardworking group bothered him.

Later, the Seattle rep met a smart, funny thirty-four-year-old black man from Kansas City, Missouri. Duxbury thought his territory was big, but Oliver Medlock had him beat by miles. He was responsible for accounts in Nebraska, South Dakota, Missouri, Iowa, and Kansas. Duxbury whistled, but Medlock was proud of his expanse. "I take it as a great compliment that management thinks I can do this. It's an opportunity for me to be Ortho's number one salesperson."

Duxbury said he felt the same way, and Medlock chuckled. He told the West Coast man that he, too, had started out in 1991 as a "wide-eyed" rep eager to sell what he'd been told was a $100-million-sales drug. But after a few months, he and several other Midwestern reps had felt misled. "Procrit is not the hot-knife-in-butter product that it's been made out to be," he confided to Duxbury. Nondialysis accounts in many territories equaled only 16 percent of the total epo market, and the AIDS segment was even smaller. "But management thinks we can get 70 percent of the market," he said. Some reps had tried to reason with their managers, but discussions had devolved into shouting matches. In one region, in fact, Ortho had hired a consultant to mediate between the two sides with little success.

The Kansas City salesman went on to say that he hoped his manager might readjust his expectations. "He's a pretty good guy. But we'll see what Amick says," Medlock added. "Nothing happens in the sales field without his say-so."

While Duxbury tried to sort through this new information, the next meeting convened. He quickly found a seat next to McClellan just as the roomful of reps began airing their complaints. One man said that Amgen seemed to have a lock on his AIDS market, something McClellan had sensed. "A lot of people hate us," chimed in a saleswoman, which rang true for Duxbury. Several reps had been chewed out by potential clients who were loyal Amgen customers. "This drug belongs to Amgen," a few had been told. One nurse had actually hissed at a salesperson, "You have *no right* to be here." Medlock said that he himself had visited several nondialysis offices in the Midwest only to be physically escorted to the door.

Duxbury and McClellan exchanged shocked glances: Amgen was clearly encroaching on Ortho's market. But how would Ortho retaliate? This wasn't addressed in the gripe session, and after forty minutes or so the assembly broke up.

Before the national meeting was called to order, Duxbury bumped into the Florida Division manager, Bennie Thompson. He was a jovial African-American with close-cropped hair and a ready smile who, at that moment, was handing out Charise Charles flyers. He was so close to the Boca Raton mail-order firm that Thompson reviewed its sales material, corrected misspelled words, and edited policy statements before the supplier placed its advertisements and distributed material. Duxbury introduced himself to Thompson and took a leaflet. It listed the most up-to-date discounts for Procrit packages, including overstock. Duxbury noted the bonus of free syringes. "This is a good deal," he said, and Thompson encouraged him to call with any questions. It was clear that Ortho enjoyed a cozy relationship with Charise Charles, but why? Duxbury knew this was not the time to ask. As other reps filed into the room, Thompson greeted them each with a flyer, his friendly voice booming, "Good selling, everyone!"

When the big sales meeting began, Amick exhorted the troops, "The goal is for Ortho Biotech to have a fifty-one percent share of the epo market," he said. Duxbury knew that was impossible, if Ortho reps were to stick to nondialysis and AIDS patients. But Amick had a strategy. He instructed his team that as long as even one vial of Procrit was used for a nondialysis patient at a dialysis center, reps could approach that clinic with a contract. Avaricious Amgen had made too many inroads into Ortho's terrain, and it was only fair that Ortho should sell into Amgen's dialysis sector too. "Convert, convert, convert" became Ortho's new mantra.

Later, in a smoky bar around the corner, Duxbury met a convoy of Ortho vets and learned more about Charise Charles. It turned out that Tom Amick, who had once been an Ortho division sales manager in the Southeast, had a friend. Marty Nassif owned an obscure mail-order pharmacy in Florida, where it was laughably easy to become a wholesaler. Mail-order druggists tend to spend their mornings sitting at desks inside their gated estates, taking telephone and fax orders, and shipping product by courier. Nassif had found a niche mailing epo to Amgen's clients at hospitals and centers around the country. But after a few years, he'd grown frustrated with the biotech firm. The Boca Raton resident wanted to find an alternate source of lucrative epoetin alpha.

And Ortho was the only other one.

Amick met with Nassif and offered what would later be called a sweetheart deal. Ortho would sell Procrit to Nassif's pharmacy, Charise Charles, at a 25 percent discount. Charise Charles could pass on some of that discount to Procrit customers and still turn a tidy profit. Furthermore, Ortho would pay a portion of Nassif's advertising costs and, as a perk, provide syringes so Charise Charles could give them to its customers. The gifts and discounts would help Ortho move product that was about to expire.

But then the two Floridians went further. They conspired to sell directly to freestanding dialysis centers, a judge later found. This was not against the letter of the PLA, but it strained its spirit. Later, Amick explained his logic. "Our salespeople [have] every right to go into a dialysis center, because there's nondialysis business [there]." Besides, he added, "We were not told we were *not* permitted to call on dialysis centers." And that was true, as far as it went. Nassif, for his part, gave Amick a list of all the freestanding dialysis centers to which he'd been shipping Epogen; Amick sent the list to Ortho reps around the country, encouraging them to use the back-channel supplier to "convert" Epogen business to Procrit. Once Duxbury heard this story, he had a eureka moment. "So that's how the Southeast does so well!" he said. The district used Charise Charles to convert Amgen's dialysis business.

On the last night of the conference, the bedraggled reps retired to the hospitality suite, which was packed. The cocktail chatter was about how everyone's sales forecast was about to grow even higher. Duxbury didn't believe it; McClellan, who spent his days educating doctors about Procrit, rather than selling it, didn't *want* to believe it. "They can't increase next year's targets when so many of us can't even meet this year's goal," he said. At one point, Medlock sidled up to Duxbury and said, in a low voice, "Every district is having a difficult time with sales." Ortho might have to revise its 1992 target downward, again, Medlock said.

"Wish I could shrink my sales target," Duxbury said, wistfully.

Medlock laughed a sharp bark. "Yeah, if I had the ability to make my forecast more realistic, I'd be in pretty good shape too."

By midnight, busboys had cleared the glasses, ashtrays, and bottles from the hospitality suite, and the party moved upstairs to someone's hotel room. Duxbury and McClellan participated in the pranks until the wee hours, losing themselves in the collective disassociation from the grown-up world at large.

A week or so after that meeting, crates of nearly expired Procrit began to move out the door, thanks to clever Charise Charles. That middleman helped headquarters inch closer to its target, but sales weren't strong enough to help Longstreet reach his 1992 goal. Tension in Raritan spread like scurvy on a galleon.

Around the same time, after the dogwood blossoms had died, Longstreet and Ortho took yet another hit. Amgen had formally accused Ortho of breaching the PLA, *again,* this time for failing to develop two other drugs. An arbitrator, retired U.S. District Court Judge Frank McGarr, heard the argument that the New Jersey company had pledged to create a hepatitis B vaccine and an interleukin-2 drug, and split the proceeds evenly with its California partner. But the process had taken more time and money than Longstreet had anticipated and the drugs never materialized. Amgen claimed that, as a result, it had lost income from the drugs' anticipated revenues, and this time the arbiter agreed. He ordered Ortho to pay Amgen $90 million.

The fine was another setback for Longstreet. The $132 million that he'd been banking on for 1992 sales fell short, and for the fourth year in a row, Ortho missed its financial mark. Around that time, Duxbury heard another disturbing rumor: Ortho might shut down as result of its abysmal failure. His J&J career might not last the year.

3

Medicine Road

THE idea that a leader can publicly deny a crime when, in fact, he ordered it is as old as court intrigue. In the twelfth century, there was England's King Henry II and the convenient murder of Thomas à Becket, the archbishop of Canterbury. During the Cold War, there was the U.S. government's nineteen-page "how-to guide" that detailed the art of political killings: "No assassination instructions should ever be written or recorded." That way, a CIA official could plausibly deny he had any knowledge of such a crime.

In Ortho's case, plausible deniability offered a solution to a nagging problem. It couldn't afford to pay another multimillion-dollar fine to its rival and its balance sheet was anemic. The company needed a foolproof way to make money, and fast. If Ortho's managers never issued *written* orders to take over Amgen's dialysis clients, then it could argue that no such order had been given. Its leaders could blame a creeping climb in dialysis sales to a fluke of the market. They could impugn a middleman like, say, Charise Charles. After all, Ortho couldn't be held accountable if a rogue supplier in Florida started shipping Procrit to Amgen's former clients. As Longstreet later explained, "What they do with the product when we ship it to them is out of our control."

In late 1992, Duxbury sat across the table from his boss, Bob Nelson, sipping coffee inside a brightly lit diner. Nelson was one of the first employees of Ortho Biotech, having joined in 1990. While waiting for the FDA to approve Procrit, he had crisscrossed the Northwest, meeting infectious disease specialists, nephrologists, and oncologists—his and his company's future clients. He'd collected their names and numbers on a master list and knew that plenty of business lay beyond the Cascade Mountains. Eastern Washington boasted agricultural sheds, processing plants, and industrial operations. Although the Hanford nuclear reactors had been decommissioned years before, they remained part of the most contaminated nuclear site in the country, constituting a large environmental cleanup effort. Nelson detailed other unhealthy characteristics of the area, including a commercial nuclear power plant, the Yakima Indian Reservation, and a U.S. military base.

"The area has an unusually large population of Hispanics and Native Americans—"

"—who tend to be predisposed to diabetes and end-stage renal disease," Duxbury completed the sentence.

The two understood each other perfectly.

Nelson said it was time for Duxbury to call on some of the dialysis accounts he knew in that area. One was an acute-care hospital with a dialysis center in Richland. Also, there were two nephrologists who bought a lot of epo for patients.

"You really need to hunt down those guys," said Nelson. "There's money to be made out there."

"I thought we weren't supposed to approach dialysis centers," Duxbury said. "Isn't that a violation of the Amgen licensing agreement?"

"No," Nelson replied. "We can call on nephrologists for *nondialysis* business only." As Amick had made clear at the national sales meeting, the company needed to get more aggressive about grabbing its share of business back from Amgen reps.

But Duxbury felt uncomfortable, partly because he'd never pitched to a nephrologist. Don't worry, Nelson said, and he coached him on a script that went something like this:

"I represent Ortho Biotech and would like you to stock Procrit for your nondialysis use." If the doctor said he didn't want to stock two identical products for two separate uses in his facility, Duxbury should say, "Since you won't dual-stock, my job is to do whatever is necessary to get Procrit used in your *nondialysis* patients."

A lot of physicians had good relations with their Amgen reps, Nelson said, so the rep should address that fact in his pitch: "If you chose to stock only Procrit in your institution, don't worry, Doctor. Amgen will still receive compensation through a clause in our marketing agreement." Duxbury didn't need to get technical, Nelson explained, but Ortho had agreed to pay Amgen for sales that "spilled over" into its turf—as Amgen had pledged to do for Ortho. What Duxbury didn't know was that the two companies were fighting over how exactly to measure those spillover sales.

Since every successful sales pitch has a closing line, Nelson lent Duxbury the following clincher: "Doctor, what do we need to do to get Procrit stocked in your pharmacy?" The two rehearsed the possible scenarios until Nelson was satisfied.

The next day, as Duxbury prepared for his sales trip to eastern Washington, he still felt uneasy. What was the correct therapy for dialysis patients? He had begun reading up on that when he received a $500 check from Ortho headquarters. The bonus was an unexpected delight, even though the rep wasn't sure what he'd done to deserve it. A few days later, he opened another envelope with an even larger check, this one for $1,400. It came with a note indicating that his "bonus" was for "sales effectiveness," whatever that meant. "I'm getting checks in my mailbox and I have no idea why," he thought. Nor could he explain the reason behind four other payments he'd spent so far that year, which totaled some $3,000. One check came with a congratulatory letter signed by Amick, who encouraged him to keep growing business. "Convert all nondialysis business to Procrit," the national sales director had written.

All that cash. Duxbury headed east of the Cascades to try a little plausible deniability.

—m—

A STEADY rain swelled the southeastern end of this basin, near the confluence of the Columbia, Yakima, and Snake Rivers. Duxbury drove into the Tri-Cities area, which consisted of several small towns and three cities. Once resplendent with sagebrush, the plains had been given over to a multinational agricultural and chemical processing plant, and a strange atomic experiment. In 1943, the government had evicted residents of a small farm town so it could turn it into a bedroom community for the top secret Manhattan Project facility nearby. Richland became "a closed city," restricted to those who worked at the world's first full-scale plutonium production reactor. Its mail addresses were purposely misleading—and still were, as Duxbury was about to discover.

During his previous visits to this area, he'd heard that Dr. John Boykin treated both dialyzed renal-failure patients and those with near end-stage renal disease—in other words, patients who were not yet hooked up to dialysis machines. Duxbury had several addresses for Boykin, including two in Richland and two in Yakima. Rather than stop at Boykin's office in Richland, the rep drove another eighty miles or so to Yakima, a sprawling town of seventy-two thousand that boasted one of the largest Rotary clubs in the world. Passing warehouses and packing sheds, Duxbury drove through town until he found what he thought was the right office. But it took him several months of fruitless visits to learn that Boykin was rarely in that office. Later that year, he discovered that most of the doctor's time was spent at the nearby hospital.

Duxbury drove to the facility, found its renal dialysis unit, and checked in with the woman at the desk. Then, he took a chair. He flipped through some magazines, got up, and paced the floor. Somewhere down the hall in a sterile room a group of sallow-faced people sat in vinyl recliners, their arms laced with bandages and tubes that hooked them to a noisy machine. Their kidneys no longer functioned properly and therefore couldn't remove the waste and toxins that were poisoning their systems, making them susceptible to infections and diseases. Ordinarily, malfunctioning kidneys would be a death sentence. But thanks to this expensive backup system of pumps and catheters, these patients could live a normal life span. The pumps sucked the dirty blood out of the body, filtered it through the machine, and pushed purified blood back in. Patients, and their insurers, paid about $40,000 a year to sit in this room for half a day, three days a week, so the wheezing machines could act as their kidneys. Despite the time and expense of their treatment, these people gladly endured the exhausting routine for a chance at living somewhat normal lives.

Kidney disease can damage the cells that make natural epo, so most dialysis patients tend to be anemic. That meant that, until recently, wheelchair-bound people also had to endure regular blood transfusions in which even more needles and tubes were poked into their skin and veins. But now they could roll into their doctor's office, get a shot of Procrit, and be home thirty minutes later. "They were thrilled with the change," said Dr. Charles Bennett, the renowned founder of Southern Network on Adverse Reactions (SONAR). Epo was administered at the low dose of 3,500 units, three times a week, for a weekly regime of 10,500 units. Yet over the course of their twelve-week therapy, most dialysis patients felt immeasurably better. "Epo really improved their lives."

The low dose was crucial. In early clinical trials, Amgen had injected a much higher, 10,500-unit dose into patients *in one shot,* which had triggered serious side effects such as high blood pressure, known as the "silent killer." Amgen had not fully addressed the question of whether lower doses would be effective while erasing the hypertensive episodes triggered by the high dose, according to court documents. At one point, a regulator had questioned whether moderately anemic, nontransfused renal failure patients even *needed* epo.

Ortho, on the other hand, had conducted trials using varying doses. It had found that the higher the dose, the bigger the risk of adverse reactions. So, initially, the FDA recommended a starting epo dose of 3,500 to 7,000 units. Dialysis patients received the low end of that. If the patient didn't respond after two weeks, the doctor could gamble on a higher dose.

To Duxbury, this proved that Procrit really did help people, which dovetailed with his own personal motto, "Do well by doing good."

He paced the floor of the hospital unit. Finally, someone returned and introduced Duxbury to Dr. Boykin. The physician was a short man with a round face and a fringe of dark bangs that hung over his aviator-style glasses.

Duxbury got to the point. "I've heard that you're treating nondialysis patients with erythropoietin. Is that true?"

It is, the doctor confirmed.

"Are you treating them with Epogen?

"Yes," Boykin said, growing testy.

"Did you know there are *two* brands of erythropoietin?" Duxbury explained that Procrit was the indication for nondialysis patients. Ortho Biotech had special purchasing programs for the doctor and his patients. "There are various ways to get Procrit."

"What sorts of ways?"

There were retail pharmacies, mail-order houses, and other avenues, he said. "But let me ask you: Why have you chosen to use Epogen for nondialysis patients?"

"Both drugs are the same price," Boykin answered, incorrectly. "I have a contract with Amgen, and I just want to stock one drug."

"Well, they are not the same price," said the salesman. "And I'm here to talk to you about Procrit for your *nondialysis* practice, which I think could be to your benefit."

Boykin read between the lines. He told the rep to meet him the next afternoon at his Richland office.

The next afternoon, Duxbury pulled up to Boykin's office. The doctor greeted him right away and took him to his private office. Duxbury then launched into the pitch he'd practiced with his boss. "I'm not here to promote Procrit for your dialysis patients," he started. "I want to be clear about that." Instead, he wanted to move Boykin's sixty or so nondialysis patients onto the drug Procrit.

Nephrologists routinely buy their own drugs at wholesale prices and bill the patient or his insurer at retail value. Because Procrit was often administered in a health-care facility, it was covered by Medicare. And since Boykin had been buying Epogen for his patients, his staff had been billing Medicare for it and getting reimbursed. He wanted to make sure that he could do the same with Procrit.

Duxbury assured him that Part B of the Medicare End Stage Renal Disease Program reimbursed doctors at the same rate for both drugs. He showed Boykin the drug's label and said: "See. The government recognizes both brands as epoetin alpha."

Soon, Boykin's administrator and nurse, Carleen Brown, walked in and joined the conversation. Duxbury explained that Ortho had a special Physician Rebate Program that was available to doctors who bought Procrit for nondialysis renal failure patients.

How much is that?

Duxbury opened his binder and pulled out his list of Procrit distributors, which included the nation's top suppliers: McKesson, Cardinal Health, and Bergen Brunswick. He then showed Boykin flyers from a few mail-order pharmacies. The two men reviewed all of the prices offered, but Boykin lingered on the promotion from Charise Charles. It offered Procrit at 8 percent less than the top retail price— lower than anyone else.

"This is *a lot* less than I've been paying Amgen," he exclaimed. "I had no idea I could even *get* these prices."

"And that's before our eight percent rebates," Duxbury piped up.

Boykin's face turned red. He counted himself as one of Amgen's best customers, with patients in two hospitals located in two cities. Yet here he was, paying top dollar for the same product that a mail-order outfit was discounting by 8 percent. The doctor was clearly unhappy with Amgen and asked for more information on Charise Charles.

"I'm not in the business of recommending one supplier over another," Duxbury hedged. But the middleman's prices were so low that Duxbury knew the doctor would probably place an order.

Boykin's nurse noted the supplier's Florida address and asked if this was a fly-by-night operation. In his best radio-announcer voice, the rep reassured her. "I know that Charise Charles is dependable; it packs its product properly and ships it overnight in a timely manner." The tight-lipped nurse just stood there, frowning. So Duxbury tried a little humor. "Don't worry. They won't leave your order on a doorstep in Des Moines, Iowa, in the middle of the summer, en route to the wrong address in Yakima, until you finally get it, with its ice pack melted and the medicine ruined."

Boykin chuckled, but Brown was not amused.

Then Boykin asked, "Do these prices apply to dialysis patients?"

"They apply to any purchase."

Then the doctor tried his own little joke: "I'd be pretty stupid to pay more for my Epogen dialysis patients than I'd pay for my Procrit nondialysis patients, wouldn't I?"

Duxbury's boss had warned him to avoid even *appearing* to promote Procrit for dialysis patients. Otherwise, Amgen could accuse Ortho of violating the PLA and the rep could lose his job. So Duxbury dodged the question and said, "What you do with the drug is your own business." *Plausible deniability.*

Boykin still didn't bite, so Duxbury moved in for the close. "Look," he said. "It's in my selfish interest to help you here. I'm just trying to make a nondialysis sale."

His candor disarmed both doctor and nurse. They then peppered Duxbury with a barrage of questions about the supplier's purchase terms, shipping, and delivery. But the rep couldn't answer all of their questions himself, so he called the mail-order druggist. It was after four o'clock in the afternoon in Yakima and seven P.M. in Florida, where the supplier was based, and Duxbury got a recorded message. He then called his boss in Seattle for help. Nelson told him he needed to set up this account in a "special" way, and gave the rep the private home telephone number for Marty Nassif. "He'll help you."

So Duxbury called Nassif. "I apologize for disturbing you at home," he began, "but I'm here in the office of Dr. John Boykin, owner of the Mid-Columbia Kidney Center. He and his nurse have some questions about buying Procrit from you." Duxbury handed the phone to Boykin.

The doctor grilled the distributor and, after several minutes, placed an order for a hundred vials of Procrit of 10,000 units each. The average wholesale price (AWP) was $11,400. But with the vendor's 8 per-cent discount, the bill came to $9,200, a huge savings. On top of that, Ortho would give the doctor a 7.6 percent rebate if he sent his Charise Charles invoice to Raritan as proof of purchase. It was like mailing in a cereal box-top for a prize. The rebate was supposed to be for doctors who used Procrit on nondialysis patients only. But Boykin clearly planned to use Procrit on all of his patients.

Next came the tricky part.

Boykin usually had his supplies shipped to his Mid-Columbia Kid-ney Center office. But the center's name would flag the account as a freestanding dialysis clinic, and such a large Procrit order shipped to a kidney center—and an Amgen client, at that—would be uncovered in an audit. So Nassif helped set up the account in a way that could camouflage the buyer's identity. Instead of naming the kidney center as the shipping destination, the invoice recorded the doctor's name and some innocuous street address in Richland. When all was done, it looked as if Procrit had been mailed to a physician's office.

In reality, it had been shipped to the fourth floor of the Kadlec Medical Center in Richland, where Boykin operated one of the larg-est kidney dialysis centers in the area. The Mid-Columbia Kidney Center was not supposed to appear on any of the paperwork. This was Ortho's plausible deniability in action: Secretly target Amgen clients; approach those customers under the guise of selling Procrit for the few nondialysis patients there; and unveil Procrit's much cheaper price offered by Ortho's surrogate, Charise Charles. Finally, but most importantly, cover your tracks by cloaking the identity of the new client. This would keep Amgen clueless about why it lost its account, place Ortho executives above reproach, and allow them to deny that they had ever ordered a systemwide covert operation.

For Boykin, the ruse would work, and he'd receive his rebate. But for Duxbury, plausible deniability would sputter, thanks to a mix-up on the invoice. The "ship to" window on the statement named the doctor all right; but the "bill to" window listed the kidney center. Duxbury would receive no credit for the arduous sale he had just made. If this dialysis sale were to be discovered by Amgen, Ortho could claim it had never encouraged its rep to convert the account; in fact, it hadn't even paid him for his sale. Ortho could simply reimburse Amgen for the portion of the sale that "accidentally" spilled over into its rightful dialysis market and keep its nondialysis portion. No harm, no foul.

As Duxbury drove home that night, he passed the orchards and fields and turned west toward the last stands of old-growth forest. Forging new terrain was hard work, and he thought of the men who had traveled here before him. In the nineteenth century, doctors had been scarce, and immigrants had brought their own cures for illnesses and disease: Irish dynamite crews believed that swallowing live frogs would cure their stomachaches; Italian workers wore garlic pouches to ward off cholera; Chinese miners used snake oil to ease their aching joints. In time, country "doctors" were bottling these exotic concoctions and loading up their wagons with tins and jars, hitting trails like the one Duxbury was traveling. These early pharmaceutical representatives sold miracle remedies from buckboard wagons that they'd pull off to the side of the road. Using big words and rapid-fire patter, they'd conduct demonstrations that were part folklore, part science, and mostly quackery. Some of the flimflam men mounted traveling theatrical productions like *The Kickapoo Indian Medicine Company* and *Dr. Balthasar and His Marvelous Miracle Medicine Show*. People lined up for miles to buy elixirs from these men, believing that the bottles would cure them and their loved ones of everything from allergies to death of two weeks' standing. It grew so blatant that the Indians called the Oregon Trail "the Medicine Road."

The commerce triggered a boom of products, and by the late nineteenth century, a raft of "medicines" had become patented. The law allowed medicine makers to protect their products' clever names without requiring them to list their ingredients. Many products contained caffeine, rubber, horehound, tar, morphine, laudanum, and 40-proof alcohol; no surprise that folks felt better after ingesting such cures. Some Westerners grew addicted to the Kickapoo cures, but in time the colorful snake-oil entrepreneurs were pushed aside by company men.

After the turn of the century, traveling salesmen dispensed their firms' patented mystery medicines by rail, horse, and car.

One such "traveler" was a strong-willed young man dressed in a beaver coat, gray spats, and pince-nez glasses. Clenching a black bag in one hand and a cigar in the other, Philip B. Hofmann wore a derby hat that made him seem taller than his six feet five inches. The greenhorn had been sent out West during the Great Depression to overcome the prejudice against medicinal "travelers" like him. His was a modern company with the latest in equipment and technology, and he intended to promote his patented health-care products—sterile bandages, antiseptic creams, and some hard-to-sell items. His company had a backlog of a product called Lister's Dog Soap, and to move it, the traveler devised an unusual sales pitch. He trained his dog, Sandy, to sit up at strategic points in his spiel and bark. Then he took his mutt on the road.

At one whistle-stop, the flamboyant salesman walked into a shop and commanded his dog, "Tell the pharmacist how much you like Lister's Soap." Sandy barked and wagged his tail. "Show the nice man how good you smell." The dog offered his paw to the druggist. "Now, tell him how much we need this order." Woof, woof, wag, wag. After this entertaining show, a druggist would usually buy Hofmann's line. By the end of the salesman's run, druggists west of the Mississippi had enough Lister's Dog Soap to last through World War II.

Duxbury didn't have a dog. And he wasn't about to perform any tricks. Yet he was just as clever and ambitious as that salesman. Thirty years after that mutt-and-rep show, the flamboyant Hofmann became chairman of Johnson & Johnson. He often boasted that he had never failed at anything, and the thirty-two-year-old Duxbury intended to make the same claim.

For him, Boykin's kidney center sale could be a real coup, his own Lister Soap sales fable. As he drove into the night toward Seattle, the traveler weighed the risk of getting caught against his chances of success. "It's a shot in the dark," he told himself.

But Duxbury really needed this sale to make his target for the J&J division.

—☁—

LATER Ortho's sales department mailed Duxbury a copy of the Boykin invoice and, boy, was it screwed up. "There goes my bonus," Duxbury told himself. Since the account clearly listed a freestanding dialysis center, he wouldn't get paid *any* commission on even a portion of his $10,000 sale. Duxbury could fight headquarters to get paid for what was rightfully his, but he considered the price. As it was now, Ortho could not plausibly deny this tainted sale, not with *Kidney Center* emblazoned across the bill. "Besides, Boykin is some two hundred miles away, and this account is more hassle than it's worth."

Dr. Boykin, however, was so pleased, he placed an even bigger Procrit order in February 1993. It came to $22,800, before rebate and discounts. Duxbury received a copy of that invoice, too, along with Boykin's first rebate check from Ortho headquarters, which the salesman was expected to hand-deliver. "It's positive reinforcement," his boss had explained. Whenever a salesperson gives a doctor a few hundred dollars *just for doing his job,* the physician is so appreciative, he treats the rep with newfound respect. Sometimes, he even reciprocates by placing another order. But since Duxbury wasn't getting paid for this deal, he didn't want to spend a day driving to Boykin's office to deliver his check. Plus, the payment reminded him that, no matter what Ortho managers said, Duxbury had stolen an Amgen client and had violated the spirit, if not the letter, of the PLA. "I don't want anything to do with this account," he thought.

"Never wanted it in the first place."

So Duxbury dialed headquarters and asked if he could express-mail the check to the customer. "And," he added, "I'd appreciate it if you guys would just mail any future checks to Dr. Boykin himself." The clerk agreed to both unusual requests.

Although Duxbury didn't receive any credit for the sale, his boss did. Duxbury's district also received credit for the nondialysis part of his sale, and that helped push the Seattle District up a few notches on Ortho's national chart. Later, in a districtwide message, Nelson publicly praised Duxbury's efforts and urged the other reps to follow his lead by converting mixed-use institutions.

At year's end, Duxbury made his forecast, barely. For that, he received a 3 percent "merit" raise, which brought his 1993 base salary to $45,500, the equivalent of about $70,000 in 2010 dollars. The medicine road rose up to lead another young ambitious man to prosperity.

4

Raise the Stakes

Duxbury grew into the challenge of selling Procrit. He didn't believe in the hard-sell approach, never had, and thought that salespeople in general got bad reputations because of a few dishonest ones. He wasn't indifferent to the monetary rewards and trophies that came with the job—far from it. He craved the attention and prestige that followed a top-tier rep. Yet, like most successful salespeople, he was driven by something bigger than personal gain. To him, making a Procrit sale meant that he had helped a patient by introducing her to an efficacious, vivifying medicine. A sale also signified that he had forged an authentic connection with another person, a buyer, which was no small thing when you're an itinerant worker. His philosophy was that if he could help patients and make a client look good, he'd eventually land the account. His clients became his friends, and what kind of a guy screws his friends for a living? "When done right, sales can be a wonderful experience."

His sanguine view was noticed by those he met on his daily rounds. One such person was an attractive, light-skinned black woman named Renee Matson, and for the past year or so, they'd grown especially friendly. The two had met a few years earlier when they were selling cardiovascular drugs, he for Bristol-Myers Squibb and she for Merck. The rivals would bump into each other on sales calls and quickly took to teasing one another with their rapier wits. Matson found Duxbury so lighthearted she was sure he was a happily married man. Around her, Duxbury felt like kindling in the presence of a spark. One day, he finally screwed up the courage to ask her out, and she quickly agreed. Beneath his easygoing demeanor, she saw a driving ambition, and the two began dating. They made a striking mixed-race couple, he with his heart-shaped face and flaxen mustache; she with her café-au-lait complexion and short raven hair. In early 1993, he proposed marriage, but she wasn't ready. Undeterred, Duxbury kept sparking her with his cheery, earnest courtship.

He loved the thrill of the chase, whether pursuing love or money. To him, the pharmaceutical profession was like a coliseum filled with charioteers and gladiators. Sales reps worked under harsh conditions, tolerated jeers and rejection, and strove to not simply survive the obstacles but surmount them with flair. A few wound up inspiring admiration and even acclaim, and Duxbury studied them. Every week, he received from Raritan a colorful play-by-play description of the latest joust or deal. He kept abreast of the national sales statistics, individual rankings, and weekly competitions. Sometimes the cheese was spread a little thick, as in the latest contest, for example. It was named after a popular television series called *Murder, She Wrote,* only instead of spinning tales about murder cases, Ortho reps had to sway doctors to write more prescriptions. In J&J's version of the game, "Procrit They Wrote," Duxbury already commanded a lead. He'd sold enough medicine to earn a coffee mug, was about to collect a videocassette movie (starring Angela Lansbury), and just might win a box of gourmet meats, called the Steak-Out. The grand prize: a London Fog trench coat.

Duxbury periodically flew back to New Jersey for more training. Traveling from his Seattle home to J&J's headquarters amounted to an eleven-hour day, including the three-hour time difference. At one point, he was called to a diversity-training seminar that reviewed company policy on racial discrimination and sexual harassment. Duxbury believed he was among the least racist, least chauvinistic men on earth; he'd been raised by a working mom and was dating a black woman. Even so, in February 1993, Ortho insisted that all employees attend the class. So Duxbury boarded a plane to New York City on the same weekend in which a bomb exploded beneath the World Trade Center in Manhattan. The incident had triggered a massive manhunt, clogged Eastern transportation routes, and delayed his flights.

While stranded in an airport, he called Renee. "I miss you," he said.

"Me too," she replied. Then she paused, uncertain how to deliver the news. So she blurted it out. "I'm pregnant."

Duxbury was elated, and Renee seemed happy too. He proposed to her again, and this time, she accepted. They cooed and jabbered until his flight was about to board. As he walked toward his departure gate, he yearned to be heading west rather than east. By the time he arrived in class early Monday morning, he was sleep-deprived and resentful. He listened to the teacher point out historical events in an effort to underscore how white men were responsible for things that the students themselves had not done. Yet any criticism of affirmative action programs was barred; Duxbury felt a subtle form of reverse discrimination. "We could be a rat species, the way the instructor is talking about white males," he thought.

He wanted to object but instead bit his tongue. After the session, he bluntly told the teacher, "You'll never convince me that this class was worthwhile."

Duxbury's disdain of the politically correct environment in which he operated would boomerang against him one day.

—❦—

In early 1993, it was time for managers to hand out new sales forecasts. Duxbury opened his mail and braced himself. He figured his new target was about to skip 20 percent from $250,000 a year to $300,000—which would be a hefty jump. Yet, when he saw his new figure, he nearly choked. His goal had *quadrupled* to $1.1 million. He immediately called his boss. "I have virtually all of the nondialysis business in my territory," said Duxbury. "What more do you want?"

"Mark," Nelson responded, "I hired you because you were supposed to be a hotshot. But I'm not getting my money's worth."

Duxbury's mouth snapped shut, while the rest of him objected strenuously. As his leg jackhammered and his nostrils flared, he made some mental calculations. One of his best clients was a doctor's office that bought $4,000 worth of nondialysis drugs every month. Duxbury could make five such sales a month for $20,000. That's how he had made his 1992 sales goal of $250,000. Only, now, he had to sell $100,000 a month, a mind-boggling amount. "It can't be done," he told his boss. "There isn't that much business in my territory."

Nelson didn't want to hear that. But over the next few days, Duxbury talked to a few reps scattered in other cities. McClellan's forecast had doubled to about $600,000, and others had gotten fat increases too. But he couldn't find any other person who'd been saddled with a *400 percent* increase. "My forecast is one of the largest increases in the nation," he realized.

In a way, it was flattering. "They must think a lot of you to give you such a big goal," McClellan told him. But Duxbury didn't see it like that. More likely was that someone in headquarters had made a mistake. The rep could help correct the error by breaking out the actual amount of nondialysis patients in his turf. He slowly began to collect those figures from his clients, certain his target would be readjusted.

In the meantime, he continued making his calls. A Wenatchee-based clinic bought $30,000 worth of Procrit a year for prerenal failure and AIDS, a measly $2,500 a month. St. Joseph Hospital purchased Procrit for its HIV patients, but the amounts were minuscule. In fact, few hospitals in his territory had much of a nondialysis sector at all.

In the meantime, his bosses asked him to estimate the total *dialysis* sales in his district. Since his compensation would be affected by these numbers, he decided to compile not just the dialysis figures but his rightful nondialysis ones too. It took several weeks, but in spring, Duxbury wrote a friendly memo to his boss and his boss's boss, William Ball. *Here's the total estimated dialysis business in my territory—$3.45 million.* He compared that to the total epo sales in his territory, $4 million. "That leaves me with roughly $500,000 in nondialysis business," he said.

So why, he asked, was he being saddled with a forecast of $1.1 million—double the amount of business that legally belonged to him?

His bosses said they'd take these figures to Amick.

—⚬⚬⚬—

In Raritan, meanwhile, a manager came across a shocking request. Two veterinarians had submitted Procrit invoices proving they'd purchased large amounts of the drug. Now the vets, one in California and the other in Georgia, wanted their 8 percent rebates from Ortho's popular Physicians Rebate Program.

Epo was becoming so established that dog and horse owners not only knew about the drug; they were doping up their animals to gain the racer's edge. Yet animals injected with even low doses of human epo showed signs of distress: a greyhound's natural ability to produce his own red blood cells crashed, leaving him severely anemic; a horse's blood turned to sludge, setting him up for pulmonary embolisms; some Thoroughbreds received such an epo "rush," they ran themselves to death, collapsing in heaps of sweaty flesh.

By 1993, researchers at Cornell and Rutgers Universities had begun to devise animal doping tests to stop such blatant abuse. Others mounted clinical trials to find safer versions of epo to help chronically ill pets. Yet still no word about the safety trials from the makers of Procrit, Eprex, or Epogen. Could it be that veterinarians had better information about the drug than doctors who treated humans?

—⚬⚬⚬—

Procrit vials began to move nationwide. Salespeople in not just Bennie Thompson's division in Florida, but Louisville, Kentucky; Topeka, Kansas; Asheville, North Carolina; Visalia, California; Burlington, Vermont; and Boston began converting Amgen customers to Procrit. Thanks to Ortho's supplier, Charise Charles, some offices started making their high forecasts.

As for Duxbury, he kept hammering away at St. Joseph, a "mixed-use" institution with both dialysis and nondialysis beds. Designed by the daring Chicago architect Bertrand Goldberg, the building incorporated geometric whimsy and space-planning concepts that helped make it an efficient institution. Duxbury could spot its circular tower from miles away, rising above Tacoma like a giant honeycomb.

He had cultivated a nice relationship there with a renal pharmacist named Robert Dimino, and one day, Dimino told Duxbury that St. Joe was in the process of developing a centralized pharmacy research unit. Among other things, the druggist hoped that his pharmacy would have the capability someday to run statistics on the hospital's patients, their medicines, and the pharmacy's expenses. "We don't have the type of equipment to do those things right now," Dimino confided.

"What do you need?" Duxbury asked.

"For starters, we could use a computer."

"Let me buy you one."

Dimino balked. No drug rep had ever made him such an offer.

But gift giving was commonplace at Ortho. Every district had several pools of cash that were earmarked for meals, events, and other offerings to clients. A regional director could dole out several $10,000 "educational" grants a year, dozens of luncheons for nurses, or a few lavish dinner "programs" for influential Procrit customers. The directors had a lot of discretion, but all of the grant checks were issued from Raritan, so Duxbury assumed they were legitimate.

Even so, Dimino reacted as if Duxbury had offered him a bribe.

"C'mon, Bob," Duxbury responded. "I'm not asking you to marry me. I just want to do a little business with you." The pharmacist said he'd check with his superiors.

Later, Duxbury told Nelson that they should "facilitate" St. Joe's purchase of a computer system. "It'll help us establish a good business relationship." Nelson, however, needed to justify the expense. He suggested that if Dimino would conduct some loosely defined "trial research" on Procrit, Ortho could buy him a computer. So, one January day, Duxbury took Dimino to lunch at a fine restaurant. After the two had placed their orders, Duxbury slid a check across the white-clothed table. "This'll help you establish a database at the pharmacy," he told his guest. "It's enough to buy a computer, some software, and whatever else you need."

The pharmacist looked at the $10,000 check and stammered. Duxbury assured him the check implied no obligation. "It's a symbol of our commitment to building a long-term, mutually beneficial relationship with St. Joe's." By federal law, large gifts tied to drugs that are paid for by Medicare are verboten, but a loophole allowed hospitals to accept money for research and "continuing education." But before Dimino could accept this substantial sum, he'd need to check with his boss, Al Linggi. After a few weeks, the hospital's managers decided to keep the "charitable gift," and from then on, Duxbury found himself warmly welcomed inside the efficient hive of St. Joseph.

As spring rolled on, Duxbury felt the pressure to sell. He and Renee had married and were living in her house a few blocks from the railroad tracks and the Tacoma Narrows Bridge. Since the couple was expecting a child, they had talked about Renee's quitting her job to stay at home with the baby. But in order to support his family in style, Duxbury would have to double his income and make at least six figures. It wasn't like he craved to be a master of the universe; he just wanted to be lord of his own two-car-garage manor, with a backyard barbecue.

He still hadn't received any word about his ridiculously inflated target, but he wasn't the only one complaining about the hefty numbers. Of Ortho's four national divisions, the Western Region seemed to be disproportionately affected by expectations, and another one of Ball's managers had just written him. "It's very frustrating," the manager complained. "When you look at [our forecast] figures, it is quite evident that they don't truly reflect the nondialysis market for epo." Ball shared his troops' frustrations. He collected these field dispatches, including Duxbury's memo, and sent them to Raritan, again requesting a more reasonable target for his district.

But Amick was unimpressed by the reports. To him, the moaning and groaning was the sound of salespeople trying to wiggle out of some hard work. He told Ball that if he wanted his target to shrink, he'd have to find "irrefutable evidence" from a third-party source that

Amick's goals were unrealistic. Otherwise, he told Ball to work with what was in front of him.

Every industry has its form of intelligence, a way to gain an advantage by obtaining private or secret information without the permission of those involved. For pharmaceuticals, one especially sharp tool was the Drug Distribution Data, which held a gold mine of personal information. Doctors and patients like to think that the details about their personal prescriptions are private, but the truth is that nearly every pill and injection purchased by the nation's hospitals, pharmacies, and doctors shows up in reports. These accounts mine data from insurers, wholesalers, drugstore chains, HMOs, the government, and the American Medical Association. In the early 1990s, these institutions began peddling their information to commercial clearinghouses like the giant IMS Health, and they in turn sold the intimate facts to Merck, Pfizer, and other pharmaceuticals, charging hundreds of millions of dollars a year. DDD reports, for example, allowed Ortho to pinpoint exactly where epo was being used, and which clinics were living up to their purchase commitments. Although sometimes you couldn't see the names of either patient or doctor in these reports, it was easy to identity a prescriber based on his ID number issued by the Drug Enforcement Administration.

Yet most doctors in 1993 had no clue that traveling reps knew more about their drug-prescribing habits than they did, and that fact alone gave a salesperson a huge psychological advantage. A doctor might think he was writing a hundred scripts a month for a certain medicine simply because of its merits, but maybe that $7,000 rebate check or the $10,000 "grant" had helped. Savvy pharmaceutical managers could actually link the timing of a gift with the subsequent placing of an order, and that told reps like Duxbury what sort of "marketing plan" worked best with certain clients. "If doctors knew that every drug they'd prescribed had been tracked, they'd go ballistic," McClellan once told Duxbury, and he agreed. That's why these drug reports were marked confidential. In fact, secrecy was such an integral part of them that IMS contracts specified that firms had to keep the physicians' data hidden from the doctors themselves. At the bottom of each DDD page was a warning: "This information . . . is confidential and is not to be disclosed. . . ."

Ball used this espionage tool to bolster his case for lowering his region's forecast. The DDD reports recorded the *actual* epo sales in his region—and in Duxbury's territory. The problem was that there was too much information: one had to chunk the drug sales by state, territory, and zip code; or by week, month, or quarter; or by any number of different ways. Ball had ordered the epo sales data, and when he received the six-hundred-plus pages of material, he had to analyze it. For that mind-numbing job, he and Ortho hired yet another middleman in the health-care pipeline—a high-priced consulting firm, which agreed to define Procrit's market in the Pacific Northwest.

Two months later, the consultants delivered their report, and in June 1993, Nelson summarized the results for Ball. Duxbury received a copy of that letter, too, and now, sitting in his office chair, he readjusted his spectacles to read it. There was "absolutely no doubt that greater than 90 percent of the dialysis market had been treated as nondialysis," Nelson wrote; Duxbury felt like rejoicing. But then Nelson hedged. He had identified specific retail customers, which, "if converted, would dramatically impact [Duxbury's] retail market share." This seemed contradictory, so Duxbury turned to the DDD report itself and found some serious problems. For one, it included in his territory a warehouse that housed $300,000 worth of epo—and nothing else. "That facility shouldn't even be part of my forecast!" But according to the high-priced consultants, it should be and added $300,000 to his forecast.

Duxbury called Ball and relayed this and other mistakes he had found. Ball listened sympathetically. But they had to wait for Amick's verdict.

Meanwhile, Nelson grew anxious with so much clandestine data floating around. All copies of the epo market reports had to be destroyed, but discreetly. "Whatever you do, Mark, don't throw those DDD books away," Nelson warned. "Amgen might pick those books out from our garbage." Corporate gumshoes rummaging through a rival's trash seemed like the stuff of spy movies. But the pharmaceutical industry, with its lucrative proprietary products, had grown skilled in the ways of skulduggery. Amgen itself had been the target of biotech's first "sting" operation in 1988 after an ex-employee had tried to sell the confidential formula for epo. Since then, Amgen, J&J, and other drug companies had installed ever more sophisticated surveillance systems, employing former FBI executives, foreign agents, and black-ops experts to guard their treasures from competitors and counterfeiters. That's why Nelson was nervous about being caught with reports that listed Epogen's sales. Fortunately, he had recently purchased a shredder for his office, which in 1993 was a rare sight. He collected the DDD reports from Duxbury and fed them through his machine. As Nelson ripped the lists of epo sales into strings of confetti, Ball sent Amick "irrefutable evidence" from the third-party consultant that the Western Region's numbers were off. Then, he waited.

Around the same time, yet another Western Regional meeting took place, this time in sunny San Diego. One afternoon, Duxbury and McClellan joined an expedition to Torrey Pines Golf Course, which bordered a natural reserve that was home to skunks, raccoons, and the dramatic-looking Torrey pine trees. The reps were joined by a few Ortho executives, including Tom Amick, and the party set out to play atop windswept cliffs. They were followed by a cart carrying a few young, pretty women who dispensed cold beers to the sweaty players. The game turned rowdy, and after an hour or so, Duxbury felt so relaxed, he turned to Amick and broached the subject that was on everyone's mind.

"Boy! This year's sales forecasts sure are brutal!" A few of the reps nearly choked on their beer; the managers leaned in to hear the vice president's reply.

"Get used to it," Amick snapped. "The forecasts aren't changing."

Duxbury stood back and let Amick take his shot. Then the group walked along the cliffs to the next hole, where wind-whipped trees looked as if they were about to fly. Duxbury and McClellan fell behind the group.

"Well, at least I know where the big guy stands," Duxbury said.

Duxbury had just started to adjust to the idea that his forecast would remain when, a few weeks later, he was thrown off course. Amick had not only refused Ball's plea to lower his region's numbers; he had actually increased them. That, in turn, had pushed Duxbury's forecast up 50 percent higher to $1.6 million.

One million six hundred thousand! That was five-and-a-half times more than what he had sold last year. Duxbury was so angry, he couldn't see straight. His wife grew agitated too. With their firstborn due in ten weeks, the rep now had six months to make what seemed like an impossible quota. He met with Ball and Nelson and pleaded in person. But Ball threw up his hands. "In order to correct this, Mark, I'd have to take money out of your goal and put it onto someone else's. I don't want to do that."

Duxbury knew that any further argument would amount to little more than a shoe-gazing exercise. Still, he warned his bosses, "The only way I can meet this quota is to steal dialysis business." Then it dawned on him: Robbery had been the point all along.

—⚍—

THAT summer, St. Joseph's epo contract with Amgen came up for renewal, and Duxbury moved in. He sensed that Amgen over the years hadn't given its top client much of a discount, especially considering the large amount of epo St. Joe purchased. He doubted if Amgen had ever given its client a rebate or a grant. But Duxbury had been wooing St. Joe's administrative director of pharmacy services, Al Linggi, for months, holding out those perks as an incentive to buy. One day, the rep again suggested that St. Joe could actually make money buying Procrit. *Perhaps that should be factored into the hospital's decision.*

Linggi considered that. "If the safety and therapeutic value of the two products are identical, I guess the determining factor *would* be economic," he admitted.

"So, if Ortho's product is identical to Amgen's, your decision comes down to finances, is that what you're saying?" Duxbury asked.

The druggist nodded and let the implications spill like pills across his desk.

Duxbury took the hint. "What if I gave you a significant discount on the product?"

"Then we could talk."

Duxbury couldn't slash prices without his boss's approval. But he had just secured the business of his future client. "I won't take up any more of your time," he said. "But I'll call you in a few days with a proposal."

Indeed, Duxbury and Nelson called on Linggi and presented Ortho's best deal. If the hospital placed a $250,000 order, it would receive an 8 percent discount. If it bought $500,000, it'd get a 9 percent discount. And if St. Joseph placed its entire $1.4 million order with Ortho, it would get the best package of all: a 14 percent discount off the AWP.

Amgen's rep had already submitted a bid, but the pharmacist looked Ortho's over and said he'd present Duxbury's proposal to his committee. A few days later, Amgen's rep returned to Linggi and learned of Duxbury's presentation. He offered to meet whatever price Ortho had offered. By then, however, it was too late; Linggi had seen in black and white the many advantages Ortho gave clients. When Duxbury called on Linggi later, the pharmacist warmly invited him in. "We're going along with the group," he said. Duxbury didn't understand and waited, perspiring under his designer jacket. Linggi added, "We're accepting your bid, Mark."

A wave of relief flooded the rep.

That summer, six months after Duxbury had given St. Joe a $10,000 check, the hospital switched its epo account from Amgen to Ortho. The initial order was only for $250,000, but Duxbury sensed this account would grow. In his Northwest territory, Procrit began to catch up to Epogen, and Duxbury's reputation grew.

5

The Cancer Indication

Iɴ April 1993, Longstreet and his troops received a huge commercial boost. Randomized, placebo-controlled trials of 131 anemic cancer patients demonstrated that epo resulted in a reduction of blood transfusions for them too. Epo helped bodies produce red blood cells so cancer victims could recuperate from their toxic treatments and prepare for another debilitating round. As a result, the FDA approved Procrit as a cancer therapy. Duxbury and the other reps were thrilled. Now, they could sell to a vast new market of approximately five hundred thousand people, far more than the fields of AIDS and nondialysis patients they'd been tilling. Duxbury in particular was relieved at the news.

"Business ought to pick up enough so I can actually make my forecast," he told McClellan.

The FDA had approved the new therapy based primarily on trials that proved Procrit reduced the need for transfusions. Neither Ortho nor Amgen had submitted any significant clinical, postmarketing trials to demonstrate the *safety* of epo, which they had promised to do. No one could be sure that Procrit was safe at even *recommended* doses according to several sources. But regulators weren't overly concerned. They figured that epo had established a track record in large renal patient populations over the past four years. "There was already a fair amount of clinic experience," Patricia Keegan of the FDA explained. Epo *seemed* safe. So the agency approved Procrit for chemotherapy-related anemia.

But as a condition for that approval, the FDA again told the two firms to practice some basic science: Conduct a randomized, double-blind, placebo-controlled pilot study to determine epo's safety in clinical settings. J&J began a postmarketing study of people to try to rule out detrimental side effects. "It was supposed to be a four-hundred-patient randomized study of those with lung cancer," said Keegan. Yet the trial did not fare well. About 17 percent of the patients had missing data, the rate of measurable responses to epo wasn't reviewed, and results were inconclusive. The companies were given more time to complete safety studies, said Keegan. "It would take a very, very long time," she added.

Longstreet didn't announce any of this to his sales force, and Duxbury assumed the FDA's seal of approval meant the drug was safe for most patients. But if someone's wife were to read the fine print on the package insert, she could build a small altar of caveats. "The safety and efficacy of Procrit therapy have not been established in patients with a known history of a seizure disorder." And this: "Carcinogen potential of Procrit has not been evaluated." And, most alarming of all, this: "The possibility that Procrit can act as a growth factor for any tumor type . . . cannot be excluded."

Epo as a tumor-growing agent? That was too perverse to be true. Yet, what were the survival rates of the miracle drug, as tested in a large patient population?

On the cobblestoned streets of Europe, where epo was still being abused, competitive cyclists had some clues. By the mid-1990s, a racer could pay about $6,000 on the black market for an epo regime, but forfeit a good deal more. Side effects included fever, chills, chest pains, and a creepy blue-gray darkening around the mouth. Former World Champion cyclist Joachim Halupczok experienced some of these symptoms at this time, including heart arrhythmia that many suspected was caused by his epo abuse. At twenty-two, the athlete had to retire from racing. A few months after Procrit was approved for U.S.

cancer patients, Halupczok collapsed while warming up for a soccer game. Minutes later, the twenty-six-year-old died. Epo was the prime suspect.

These red flags were ignored in Raritan, overshadowed by the huge potential of epo's long-anticipated approval for cancer. It wasn't just that Ortho had a new market; it could now sell higher doses. The standard Procrit regime for renal patients had been a low 3,500 units three times a week; for HIV victims, it was 7,000 units three times a week. But cancer patients would get 10,500 units three times a week—30,000 units every week! That was 50 percent higher than the original 1989 recommended starting dose of 7,000 units, enough to cause concern.

But for reps, the new high dosage translated into hundreds of millions of potential sales dollars. Duxbury added oncologists to his list.

—⚹—

THE wetlands that rim south Puget Sound came into view, and Duxbury steered his car onto the asphalt of Highway 101, keeping his eye peeled for the ten-story patient tower of St. Peter in Olympia. He parked in the lot, walked beneath the pungent awning of juniper boughs, and breathed in the smell. On his way, he glanced at Memorial Clinic located across the street. Duxbury had been calling on the nephrology group for months without success. He made a mental note to try them again.

Inside the hospital, Duxbury stepped into the elevator and struck up a conversation with a woman. She just happened to be St. Pete's financial counselor, and as soon as she learned that he was a Procrit representative, she groaned. "What's the matter?" he asked. She explained that some of the hospital's dialysis outpatients were not getting reimbursed for the epo drugs they were given.

"That's created a black hole in the pharmacy's budget," she confided.

"That shouldn't happen," he said.

"I agree. But it's been like that for years," she insisted.

So that explained the nurses' stony stares, thought Duxbury.

When the financial advisor stepped out of the elevator and walked briskly down the hall, Duxbury accompanied her, keeping up the conversation. She explained that early on it had been difficult getting reimbursed for epo. Even now, it was such a dicey issue that the nephrologists at the clinic across the street routinely sent about thirty of their patients to St. Peter's dialysis floor for injections. "That's odd," Duxbury said. He imagined the nurses wheeling dozens of renal-failure patients out of the clinic on gurneys, dodging oncoming traffic, their white sheets flapping, as they crossed the busy thoroughfare. It was an absurd tableau but no less preposterous than the situation itself.

Why hadn't the hospital filed insurance claims to get repaid for the drug? And if it had filed, why hadn't it gotten reimbursed? Without insurance money, Epogen and Procrit were too expensive for a nonprofit hospital. The financial counselor explained that local physicians had started Epogen as early as 1989. But when Procrit came on the market in 1991, there was a lag between the time when the FDA approved it for nondialysis and when Medicare began paying for it; the nephrologists at Memorial Clinic got caught in that window. As a result, they had lost tens of thousand of dollars using Procrit. Yet their patients needed the blood-strengthening medicine, so the physicians regularly sent their patients to St. Peter, whose staff charitably administered injections.

This was information that Duxbury could use! He verified the story, called Memorial Clinic, and visited the site a few days later. Four nephrologists and a clinic manager listened as Duxbury explained how they could benefit by treating their own patients. The doctors agreed to try Procrit on one condition. They didn't want to find themselves in a money-losing position again, if insurers refused to pay for the medicine. So Ortho had to give them the cash to purchase a month's worth of their drug.

Duxbury was taken aback; no client had ever made such a blatant request: *Give me thousands of dollars' worth of your commercial product, and I'll use it.* But he kept a straight face and promised to present their case to his boss.

Later, Duxbury met with Nelson at a local diner that prided itself on its fresh-baked pie. Over coffee and a slice of rhubarb, Duxbury relayed the situation. "We have an opportunity to sell $150,000 here, but there's a red flag." He told his boss about Memorial Clinic's demand. If Nelson was flabbergasted by the doctors' chutzpah, he didn't show it. Rather, Nelson told Duxbury to give the doctors a month's worth of free Procrit through something called patient trial cards. Each certificate was slightly larger than a three-by-five-inch index card but worth a thousand times more. Sequentially numbered, the cards could be converted into a month's worth of free commercial product for one patient, as much as four 30,000-unit injections, valued at approximately $1,200 retail. All the doctor had to do was fill out the trial card with his name, address, and signature, along with the initials of the patient he intended to treat. The rep then mailed the cards to Raritan, which in turn shipped a package of twelve chilled vials.

Though the cards were exchangeable for free product, they had no monetary value unless a doctor submitted claims to insurers, especially the U.S. Department of Health and Human Services. HHS underwrites, administers, and supervises Part B of the Medicare program, which covers hundreds of drugs like Procrit that are injected in a doctor's office. To cash in the free epo samples, one had to fill out a Medicare HCFA 1500 claim form with the patient's name, diagnosis, treating physician, the dates of Procrit injections, and units injected. About the only thing Medicare didn't require was a receipt proving that the claimant had actually *bought* the drug.

Sitting across the table from his boss, Duxbury said he didn't like giving the clinic "trial" cards. "We're giving them free Procrit, knowing they're going to file for government reimbursement," he said. "Isn't that Medicare fraud?"

No, his boss replied. "All you're doing is giving them Procrit. If they want to bill for the drug, that's their business." Nelson then gave Duxbury a dozen or so patient trial cards worth about $15,000 total. Later, the rep visited the clinic, proffered his cards, and asked the nephrologists to sign them. Then he returned to his office and faxed the signed trial cards to Ortho headquarters. A few weeks later, he followed up by telephoning the clinic's administrator. Not only had the doctors received their shipment of free commercial product; they'd injected a dozen or so patients with it. Even better, the administrator had filed a Medicare claim based on its retail price, and presto! The federal government had actually paid for the free drugs at 95 percent of the inflated AWP price. That was pure profit, the administrator exclaimed. Duxbury reported back to Nelson, "They're very happy to be making such good money on Procrit."

The rep followed up with another visit, and this time Memorial Clinic placed a legitimate order. Using discounts and rebates, the doctors made money on that deal, too, just not as much as before. They benefited from the gap between the inflated AWP rate set by Ortho and paid by Medicare, and the actual, lower price paid by Memorial. This "profit spread" was the key selling point in Duxbury's presentation, and now Memorial's physicians understood it. The clinic eventually signed a contract, and Duxbury grew closer to achieving his sky-high forecast.

But even sales like these did little to relieve the pressure at home. During her pregnancy, Renee became prone to depression. The couple argued incessantly and "intensely" about the ethics of Duxbury's deals to dialysis accounts. Renee had seen Ortho's memos to the sales force, stating that Procrit was for nondialysis only. "But that's different than your boss's orders," she'd claim, and rightfully so. "Can't you see that you're violating the marketing agreement?"

"It's okay," he'd respond, gently at first. "I'm covered. Management knows exactly what I'm doing. In fact, they've ordered me to do this!"

He had shown her every memo; she knew he'd been directed to gain a 50 percent market share in a territory whose nondialysis sales were 10 percent at most. "It doesn't compute," she'd cry.

Renee had helped Duxbury collect his facts for his memos, and she, too, had believed that Ortho would cut his unreasonable target. "They *have* to correct your forecast so they don't place you in the impossible position of violating the agreement." But after Amick had actually quadrupled his sales target, she grew angry. "There's no way Amgen is going to ignore your invasion! You have to quit this job immediately."

Duxbury had worked at Ortho for little more than a year. "I'm afraid if I leave this job now, it'll look erratic," he explained.

"That's better than becoming a scapegoat for Ortho," she yelled.

Then he'd wave the sheaf of memos in the air, remind her of the long paper trail, and that Amick himself had ordered him to convert these accounts. "I have total support," he'd shout.

Their arguments grew so explosive that, after three months, the couple no longer lived together. But each held out hope of reconciliation, especially when their child was born on September 30, 1993. Duxbury was present for the delivery. The couple named their baby after the African-American abolitionist and women's rights activist Sojourner Truth, a slave who had become the first black woman to sue a white man. They had wanted their daughter to be proud of her heritage and inspired by the heroic life of her namesake.

Holding his baby in his arms for the first time, Duxbury was overcome with emotion. Her tiny, tapering fingers, her perfect, pouting lips, her scent of morning and forgiveness. He vowed to do whatever he could to give his child a home with two loving parents. And he'd spend the rest of his life trying to keep that vow.

THAT autumn, Duxbury blazed through the state on a sales jag. He visited a large facility in central Washington and tried to persuade a wishy-washy decision maker to buy from him. He continued to trek out to the Tri-Cities area, meeting his contacts in Yakima, Kennewick, and Pasco. He fired up a buyer in Billings, Montana; helped convert a hospital in Boise, Idaho; and made nice with the cold shoulders at St. Peter. "I feel like a conversion there is a distinct possibility," he told his boss.

Driving, flying, and walking to every corner of his territory, he pushed himself. It helped that Ortho had developed other money-saving programs for its customers that no ordinary consumer could ever get. One plan functioned more like a savings account than a purchase agreement. During the first six months of a contract, a client could take as long as six weeks to pay its bill and *still* get a sizable discount. "The bigger the purchase, the bigger the markdown," Duxbury told his clients. If you ordered just $10,000 of the drug during a forty-five-day period, you'd get an 11 percent discount. But if you spent $100,000 or more, you could get as much as a 15 percent discount and take even longer to pay your bill. These deals allowed a client to hold on to its cash so it could compound interest. Duxbury found himself helping clients profit on both ends of the deal.

St. Joseph was one of his biggest clients and Al Linggi now a friend. In the four months since Duxbury had landed that account, the hospital had bought $500,000 worth of the drug. Now the rep wanted to nab a contract with the owner of St. Joseph, the Franciscan Health System. He convinced his bosses to cut another check and, this time, gave St. Joe a $20,000 "unrestricted educational grant" to "demonstrate our desire to truly be a long-term partner." That money was twice as large as Ortho's last gift, and the hospital managers were duly awed. "We are pleased with the professionalism that your company conducts business [with] and want to commend you for your efforts," Linggi wrote. The gift supposedly came with no strings attached, but it was used to train other pharmacists in the Franciscan Health System how to dose patients on Procrit. "Ortho Biotech's contribution to this training is greatly appreciated," wrote James A. Plourde, director of corporate, foundation, and group support.

Even so, by Thanksgiving, Duxbury was nowhere near making his forecast. Truth was, he wasn't sure if he'd keep his job. Then, in the waning days of 1993, he hit pay dirt. First, he landed a contract with Tacoma General Hospital, worth a cool $1 million. Then he heard from Linggi, whose group purchasing organization wanted to buy Procrit in bulk, giving him a $1.3 million deal. Those two megacontracts, along with a few conversions, meant that Duxbury had made his seemingly impossible quota—*and then some*. His last-minute Christmas miracle exhilarated Nelson and Ball and stunned the entire Western District.

Even Amick was impressed. Duxbury had achieved a fivefold increase in overall market share in barely six months. He'd increased his sales by an amazing 570 percent, becoming the top dog in the Western District. Furthermore, his territory had zoomed to first place on a section of the national charts, which meant he *and* his peers in the Seattle District would earn a trip. For that, his friends showered him with praise, and word of Duxbury's achievement rocketed throughout the three-hundred-person firm.

But not everyone was delighted. On his way up, Duxbury had climbed over several other ambitious players.

—✖—

As soon as McClellan heard of his friend's victory, he called Duxbury. "You blew us out of the water, Mark. Congratulations!"

"Thanks," said Duxbury. "How are you guys doing?"

McClellan's eight-person district had been in the running to win a trip too. A few weeks ago, his boss, Dwayne Marlowe, had been so confident his district had already won that he had told his staff to "start packing."

"But you took care of that," McClellan admitted.

Duxbury laughed.

"Marlowe thinks you won because you stole dialysis accounts," while the rest of Ortho had been trying to sell legitimately.

"Please," Duxbury snorted. "I was *ordered* to convert those accounts. Besides," he added, "if I hadn't sold dialysis, I'd be gone."

Duxbury paid no mind to the tittle-tattle. He had won and nothing could prevent him from basking in the glow.

McClellan, however, felt a prick of envy. He had worked hard that year, too, but couldn't seem to get any traction. He had made a fraction of Duxbury's 1993 sales, or $690,000. Yet he steadily drove across his tumbleweed territory, zigzagging through the scorching corridors of Arizona in the summer and the snowy passes of New Mexico in the winter. His territory started in Yuma, ran along the Mexican border through southern Arizona, and encompassed all of New

Mexico—nine hundred miles of mostly rural doctors working in spots like Mescalero, Cimarron, and Humble City. Some stops had trading posts of crafts; others had little more than a traffic light strung between two creosote-soaked posts.

After two years, McClellan had gotten to know his territory so well he dressed according to local custom. For the Indian Health Service clinics on the reservations, he wore his cowboy boots and bolo tie with the turquoise clasp. For the sole practitioners in rural outposts, he wore his black leather vest, pointy-toed boots, and Western hat. "That way, people will realize I'm just like them and not some city slicker from back East." But in the cities such as Santa Fe and Albuquerque, he dressed in a starched white shirt, navy blue suit, and conservative red tie, looking like a New Brunswick factory boss on winter holiday.

Up until recently, McClellan had sold Procrit only for AIDS and nondialysis. But now he promoted the drug for cancer victims too. The problem was a lot of doctors resisted his pitch. They didn't believe their patients with mild-to-moderate anemia actually needed another expensive drug, and a palliative one at that. So the rep had to convince them to buy, using Ortho rebates, grants, and patient trial cards that translated into free goods and cash. Slowly he, too, began adding oncologists as his clients, and his epo sales started to rise. McClellan wanted to be as successful as Duxbury was. At the very least, he wanted a spot on the next awards list and to be inducted into the club.

—⁓—

ONE Monday in early 1994, Duxbury stood in the airport of Great Falls, Montana. Stuck on the northern tip of the Great Plains, a hundred miles south of the Canadian border, he was so cold he felt as if he were standing on a glacier left over from the last ice age. Great Falls did in fact lie beneath what was once the Laurentide ice sheet and was now part of Duxbury's expanded territory.

His prize for being a top Ortho rep, he thought wryly.

Earlier that year, 1994, Duxbury had received another small 3 percent merit raise, which brought his base salary to $47,000. More than a third of his total compensation in 1993 had been bonuses, and he'd have to earn at least that much if he wanted to make a six-figure salary this year. Along with his minuscule raise had come this big territory, and now Duxbury was responsible for virtually all of the state of Washington, parts of Idaho, and the entire state of Montana. Thus, his trip to Great Falls. To get here, he had boarded a sixteen-seat, turbo-propeller-powered airplane with a skinny cylindrical fuselage. The Flying Pencil, he called it. Inside its small, cramped interior, Duxbury and a handful of other passengers had been buffeted by a chinook wind and somewhere over Coeur d'Alene, his stomach had twisted into a backward flip. An hour later, Duxbury had managed to disembark from the plane without incident and walk across the tarmac, his fingers frozen, his ears ringing, and his stomach still churning somewhere over Idaho.

This week, he'd meet a few more clients and prospects. One was a troublesome but chipper pharmacist. That young man inadvertently used the trademarked word Epogen as a synonym for the generic term erythropoietin, or epo, and his bad habit destroyed all of the groundwork that Ortho had already laid. Even if a doctor in a nearby hospital had specifically prescribed Procrit for a cancer patient, the pharmacist would carelessly fill that order with Epogen. In fact, that had just happened, and as a result, Duxbury wasn't receiving credit for the sale he'd so assiduously developed. As soon as he discovered the reason for his lost account, Duxbury called on the goofy druggist, imploring him to at least use the less-specific, medically correct term epo. "Better yet," Duxbury begged, "just say Procrit." So on this particular visit, the pharmacist greeted the rep with a big grin and hollered, "Hey, here's the Epocrit guy!" Even the exasperated rep had to chuckle. But he didn't let up: "C'mon, man, help me out. I'm trying to spread the brand name Prooo-criit," he said, drawing out the vowels theatrically. By the end of the day, the druggist conceded and the rep made headway in Big Sky Country.

Duxbury's schedule grew erratic, crisscrossing three states every month. He became expert at lugging his roll-on bag and sales material through hallways and lobbies, juggling a newspaper and a Styrofoam cup of coffee. He'd rent a car, then head out to a former-mill-town-turned-service-hub like Lewiston, Idaho, or stay in an ex–mining town with high cancer counts such as Libby, Montana. Inevitably, he'd develop a hospital prospect over lunch and take a doctor to an expensive dinner, after which he'd visualize the day when he could bag another big deal and feel that surge of oxygenated joy. "This is what a shot of Procrit must feel like," he'd imagine. In this particular daydream, he'd return to the hotel and call the wife with good news. But the wife wasn't there anymore, and the child he ached to hold was growing up without him to tuck her in at night.

At thirty-four, Duxbury was tasting the lonesome side of the dirt road, where even go-getters get depressed by the monotony of hotel check-ins, house specials, and the smell of the previous occupant's perfume clinging to the polyester bedspread. Once, he woke up in a strange motel, burning with a 103-degree temperature. He had to cancel his meetings and spend the day and night in a tub filled with ice. But most other nights on the road, he'd fall asleep with the names of his whistle-stops blurring together into one interminable place: Billings-Blackfoot-Butte-Missoula-Bozeman . . .

Was this life worth the toll? While he was pondering this question, he arrived home for a weeklong stay. Sorting through his mail, he found a note from Carol Webb, the vice president of sales and marketing. Duxbury, she said, was now a "key member of Biotech Sales," entitled to receive stock in Johnson & Johnson. Webb had enclosed his new stock agreement, along with a certificate for J&J shares. From then on, she wrote, he'd receive at least fifty shares of stock every year for as long as he remained at Ortho.

Duxbury stared at the yellow paper, bordered by filigree, and saw it was worth $1,900. He was now vested in the future of J&J.

A few weeks later, he opened yet another letter from headquarters. This one was from Amick, personally inviting Duxbury and his wife to an all-expenses-paid trip to the Ritz-Carlton near Laguna Beach, California. Duxbury's sales had blasted way beyond those of the fifty other reps in the sprawling Western Region, and he was its undisputed 1993 Biosphere Award Winner. That meant he had had the greatest overall growth in sales and would join a handful of other top-selling reps from around the country on vacation. Amick closed his note by giving Duxbury a rare compliment: "You are to be applauded."

Duxbury had just been inducted into the club and he wanted to share his news with Renee. Even though his wife had already filed divorce papers, the couple still felt affection for one another and even passion on occasion. Duxbury knew he wasn't easy to live with: He traveled most of the time, said provocative things, and could be contrary and even ornery. Sometimes he'd get so angry at her, he could see the fear in her eyes. But he'd control himself. He loved her and their child and still believed they could be together.

He dialed her number and told her about his achievement. "I not only made forecast, I exceeded it."

"So what? I swear you're going to get sued by Amgen one day," she said.

"No, I'm not. Amgen is breaking its agreement, too, you know. Besides, management is totally behind me."

"Your managers are going to hang you out to dry," she retorted.

"Look, I didn't call to argue." He read her Amick's invitation to join him and others in sunny California. "Will you come with me?" he asked. "It'll be good for us to get away together."

Renee hesitated, and Duxbury knew she was considering his offer. Maybe she'd see that the biotech drug business was more brutal than her industry. Maybe she'd realize that she'd been too suspicious and had misjudged Ortho. Seconds passed as he waited. Then, she answered in a voice as cold as a scalpel. "I don't want to participate in an event that celebrates improper, unethical, and possibly illegal sales." Then she hung up.

—⚏—

The rituals of a sales corporation are crucial to its success. This is especially true in start-ups, where the traditions that bind a group together have yet to take root. The Ortho tribe was nomadic and its members practiced daily rites in isolation: They stocked their medicine bags every morning; logged their miles in spiral notebooks; and filed their WAR pages every week. By performing such tasks scrupulously, one demonstrated the level of commitment expected by the corporation. The employees also shared similar ideals, such as selling Procrit far and wide and working long to play hard. But the core values of the organization were quantitative, revolving around numbers, rankings, and statistics. A few people endured the unrelenting pressure to make their quotidian benchmarks, but after a while, even the most driven grows dissatisfied with generating cash. Generally, people need something bigger than themselves, some grand, collective goal worth striving for. The President's Cup trip, with its Biosphere trophies, fulfilled that psychic need.

Duxbury prepared to celebrate himself and his peers in grand style, even if he couldn't bring his significant other. Instead, he invited a male friend who'd experienced a rough patch, and the two guys left drizzly Seattle for the persistently sunny clime of Orange County. They were whisked to the coast, where the region's crown jewel, Laguna Beach, rested in Mediterranean-style splendor. After checking into the Ritz-Carlton, they retired to a patio where they sipped syrupy cocktails and listened to the waves slapping the shore.

All weekend long, Duxbury found little messages on his bed or dresser. Once, someone left a plush robe arranged on his bed. Another time, he found a hundred dollars in scrip that he could use at the hotel gift shop. He and his friend found pleasure nearly everywhere: at the pool, where they were given an endless stream of free drinks, at the bar, where women sipped gin until their eyes sparkled (although not necessarily at them); and at the dinners, where they were treated like kings. One evening, Carol Webb went around to the tables and greeted every guest.

On the night of the ceremony, Duxbury walked into the dining room to the sound of music. Happy, major-key notes bathed the group in harmony as waiters served champagne from silver-plated trays. And the tables! They were exuberantly decorated with centerpieces of lit candles, hyacinths, lilies, and acrylic jewels. It was over-the-top, but then so was the entire conceit.

Duxbury shook hands with Bennie Thompson, whose Orlando Division had just won the President's Cup, making his the top performing division based on forecast and market share. "Bennie earned his award because he and his reps converted dialysis business," Duxbury told a friend. There were a few other reps who in 1993 had sold millions of dollars' worth of Procrit for dialysis use. Now, all of their careers were like roman candles, ready for blastoff. Duxbury had to pinch himself: A year ago, he'd been a piker, with sales in the bottom 10 percent, barely squeaking by on $250,000. Now, he was hitting $1.6 million.

After a four-course meal and several bottles of wine, the lights dimmed. Every culture has its totems, something that elucidates the underpinnings of the culture. So it was with Ortho Biotech. Longstreet, Amick, and Webb walked to the front of the room while Bill Ball addressed the group. Speaking with the slow dignity of one practiced in gravitas, the regional boss detailed how Duxbury had doubled his share of the epo market from 24 percent to 44 percent; how he'd leveraged one of J&J's multimillion-dollar contracts with a hospital chain, and converted four of its members to Procrit, and so on. "Mark is an extremely valuable member of Ortho," said Ball, and called the rep to the front. As the congregation watched, Longstreet gave Duxbury a signet ring, Ortho's totemic symbol of power. The ring was a real knuckle breaker; carved in the center of its square face was a diamond. Around its edges, scribed in bold black letters, was the name ORTHO BIOTECH. Longstreet handed the ring to Duxbury and said, "Your achievements on behalf of the company are greatly appreciated." The room applauded and the rep returned to his table. After the other gladiators were honored, the music, eating, and drinking resumed. Throughout the weekend, Duxbury frequently admired his gold band. It signified that he had arrived, and he vowed never to take it off.

Later, back in his office, Duxbury received another tribute. He had waited for weeks to learn the magic number of his 1994 forecast and, once again, had figured it would rise about 20 percent to, say, $1.9 million. But damn if it didn't double again—this time to $3.1 million—a staggering amount. Why was this happening to him?

6

Chosen One

Hair tousled from sleep, Duxbury poured a fresh cup of coffee and padded outside to the balcony of his condominium. He felt rested and energized from his luxury vacation and had decided to greet the dawn. Cradling a cup of black coffee, he stood quietly outside and watched the sun's first rays fall on downtown Seattle. They grazed the treetops that ringed Lake Union and poured molten light into the glassy water. As the sky changed colors, the birds burst into a cacophony, as if they'd been programmed from somewhere inside the Citiscape Condominium.

He had recently purchased an upstairs unit in this modern, Art Deco–style building, a lair for young professionals. His neighbors included the pretty news anchor for a local TV station, an attorney, and the dashing state congressman who occasionally slipped out of his girlfriend's unit before dawn. This secured building, with its underground parking and rooftop hot tub, was ideal for singles. Duxbury's own two-bedroom unit doubled as his Ortho office.

He turned back from the sunrise and poured himself a second cup of coffee. His eye fell on a nearby sippy cup with whimsical drawings. It was Sojie's favorite. Duxbury had turned his new home into a nest for his daughter. It was tough being a single divorced father raising a child with a hostile ex and a grueling travel schedule. He had sought the help of a family counselor and discussed how to juggle it all. "He was extremely worried about his little girl," said Vicki Boyd, the psychiatrist who advised him. "Mark's primary question was, If we're going to have to parent this child separately, what can we do to make her life as normal as possible?" Boyd referred him to the usual self-help books for divorced parents. Duxbury had stocked his condo with duplicates of the familiar toys and blankets that Sojie kept in her other house. "I don't want her to be a backpack kid, lugging clothes on her back," he had announced. He rather liked tripping over mermaid dolls and nesting blocks as he moved about his cozy bachelor pad.

That morning, after he had showered and dressed, he sat at his desk. The scent of lemon disinfectant emanated from the plug-in-a-socket air freshener that he used to mask the odor from the kitty litter box. He spent a few hours fielding telephone calls and electronic messages; apparently, everyone's 1994 sales forecast had jumped, primarily because of epo's new cancer indication. But the level of anxiety was rising along with expectations. Certainly, the potential for Procrit was huge, but revenues weren't automatic. "I doubt that a million dollars' worth of cancer business just suddenly appeared in my district overnight," Duxbury thought. He appealed the unfair figure and again his entreaties were swatted away. He and his fellow reps would have to spend months organizing events and luncheons in order to educate oncologists about the new therapy. But there was no sense arguing for a lower forecast; by late morning, he had printed out a few memos, assembled his price lists, and grabbed his satchel to begin his rounds.

Over the next few weeks, he called every oncologist in his territory, from the river basins of Washington to the grassy plains of Montana. By the time he'd actually meet a physician, Duxbury's antenna was already up, scanning for any telltale signs about his quarry. While delivering his pitch, the rep remained attuned to the twitch of a muscle, a glaze in the eye, that thing that no ordinary person would have caught. When all was clear, he'd move in for the close. If the doctor objected to switching drugs, Duxbury would use that objection to reveal Ortho's daily specials—the Early Purchase Incentive Program, the Physician's Rebate Program, the Physician's Supply House Program, or whatever innocuous-sounding plan Raritan had devised to undercut its rival.

Perhaps no other target received more of Duxbury's attention than St. Peter Hospital in Olympia. That facility purchased $1 million a year of epo from Amgen, and Duxbury dearly needed that account to close the gap in his $3.1 million target. One spring day, as the sun fell through the trees and dappled his balcony, he prepared for the hunt. He donned a Robert Daskal tie, its fuchsia, red, and taupe colors swirling like platelets on a lab slide, something a phlebotomist might appreciate. Then, he drove south and, forty-five minutes later, spotted the pearly patient tower of St. Pete.

Duxbury had spent two years wooing this client. He'd gotten to the point where the hospital's druggist, Tom Rowe, no longer shunned him, and for good reason too. Duxbury had rid the druggist of the stream of expensive Memorial Clinic patients who had crossed the street every month to get their injections at his facility. Memorial's nephrologists were now Duxbury's clients, treating their own patients with Procrit, and St. Pete was no longer hemorrhaging $150,000 a year. Rowe had thanked Duxbury profusely for that, and as Duxbury walked through the sliding doors of the modern hospital, Rowe actually waved at him.

But the druggist was worried—most of the epo used in this facility was earmarked for dialysis patients, and 10 percent of those people had no insurance. Duxbury had a solution: "I guarantee that if your hospital ever treats an uninsured nondialysis patient, Ortho will pay for that patient's drug." Ortho's Reimbursement Assurance Program had been created so even indigent patients could receive Procrit. The rep then steered his client through Ortho's other benefits, demonstrating how the rebates and discounts made Procrit less expensive than "Brand X." By the time he'd finished, Rowe's eyes had lit up; he could see the tens of thousands of dollars he'd save with Procrit.

St. Peter's contract with Amgen was about to expire in a few months, and Rowe admitted he was looking for a better deal. Duxbury smiled. "I'll come back in a few days with a customized proposal."

And he did.

Rowe submitted Ortho's offer to his purchasing committee, but it wasn't until June 1994 that the rep learned its decision. Alleluia! St. Peter was switching; Rowe placed an initial order of $250,000. After taking its 14 percent discount, the hospital enjoyed a lower net epo cost than it had been paying all these years. Duxbury had to ensure that this initial order would grow in the next few months. So, that summer, he gave Rowe a pharmaceutical thank-you card in the form of a $5,000 check, an unrestricted grant that implied more cash was on its way. If Duxbury could keep his customer happy, he'd wind up with the hospital's entire $1 million annual contract. He was inching toward his colossal forecast.

—⁂—

Dennis Longstreet sat in the witness chair inside a black skyscraper at One Liberty Plaza in Manhattan. Each of the law firm's ten floors encompassed nearly an acre of space, much of it framed by grand windows. Up here, a man could watch the cruise ships entering and leaving New York's harbor, sending up the occasional burst of celebratory fireworks. But Longstreet wasn't watching the show below; he was alert for any hand grenades that Amgen's lawyers might lob his way.

Ortho and Amgen had always known that each would inadvertently make sales that would slip into the other's turf. The tricky part was how to repay one partner for those "spillover" sales. After four years, the two were still arguing over terms of a formula designed to cure that problem. Amgen had proposed a complicated formula that gave it the highest possible remuneration and Ortho, naturally, had objected. It had suggested taking all epo sales, subtracting those Medicare called dialysis treatments, and treating the rest as Ortho's nondialysis market. But Amgen had balked. It owned the bulk of the entire renal market, and no matter how you figured, it would wind up paying Ortho for lost sales. Therefore, it was in no hurry to strike a deal. Why give up the hoard of cash that had "accidentally" slopped over from Ortho's pail into Amgen's bucket? Ortho was losing patience.

A judge had ordered audits that had revealed an intriguing pattern: Amgen's former vendor, Charise Charles, had been shipping Procrit to large dialysis chains that had once been Epogen customers. That morning, Longstreet was asked several questions about this anomaly. "Were Ortho's sales representatives instructed to place orders for dialysis centers through Charise Charles?"

"Not that I'm aware," the CEO replied.

Amgen clearly suspected that Charise Charles was an emissary for Ortho, and Longstreet had to tread carefully. More discoveries about Charise Charles could lead to a new battery of claims against J&J. As one of the biotech's attorneys had said, "The damage to Amgen in this spillover arbitration is not just the dialysis sales that Ortho grabs and camouflages as nondialysis. *It's the competition.*" Amgen shouldn't have to fight for market share against its own partner.

That morning, Longstreet answered questions patiently, yet when accused of any transgression, he was swift to deny it. He pointed out that Ortho had repeatedly tried to assure Amgen that it wasn't grabbing its market. Ortho's vice president Carol Webb had devised an honor system for just that purpose. She required customers to sign a Certificate of Use pledge in which they promised to buy Procrit *only* for nondialysis patients. Only then would Ortho pay the 8 percent rebates. If Amgen complained that Ortho's mysteriously growing dialysis sales demonstrated a breach, Webb could pull out the certificates to demonstrate that Ortho was still upholding its end of the deal. But Webb's system backfired. Some nephrologists felt insulted by the oath and, rather than sign a sworn statement, stopped buying Procrit altogether. Others blithely signed the certificates, promising to buy the drug for nondialysis only, while using Procrit for *all* of their renal patients. After cashing the $20,000 rebate checks, they'd repeat the ruse all over again. "Everyone was cheating," one manager admitted. By 1994, Webb's plan had provoked at least one lawsuit from an irate customer and a string of ill will from others.

While tugboat captains maneuvered in the harbor below, Longstreet picked his way through the minefield above. He managed to dodge most of the incendiary charges and, later that day, walked out of the door at One Liberty Plaza relatively unscathed. But the same could not be said for Ortho. After conducting more depositions, Amgen attorneys went after Charise Charles for helping Ortho break its PLA. There was talk of forcing J&J to give up its epo license entirely, so that Amgen could keep the booming market to itself. J&J didn't think that could happen, but just in case, Amick issued a clarion call to the troops that summer: Do not call on freestanding dialysis centers. *Plausible deniability is dead.* The sales force retreated but continued selling to mixed-use institutions.

As the rival companies continued to scratch for profits and share, they mounted new studies. These were not the long-overdue Phase IV science-based trials that the FDA had requested in 1989, 1991, and 1993. Rather, they were marketing-driven studies designed to expand sales of the multimillion-dollar drugs. Ortho began pushing Procrit for entirely new therapies, such as elective surgery and fatigue, while Amgen toyed with higher epo doses and hematocrit levels.

Hematocrit measured the thickness of blood; it was the ratio of red blood cells to the volume of whole blood. A sick dialysis patient, for example, usually has a level of 33 or so. A healthy woman has a hematocrit value of 42 percent; a man has 45 or so. But European cyclists using recombinant erythropoietin began to clock some amazing hematocrit levels of 50 and more, and researchers noticed.

In 1994, three moderately talented racers from the Italian team Gewiss-Ballan so thoroughly trounced the competition, experts suspected them of doping. That impression was reinforced when the team's doctor, Michele Ferrari, insisted that taking epo was no more dangerous than drinking lots of orange juice. The Italian couldn't possibly know if that was true, yet his public nonchalance about cheating marked a sea change in the world of professional cycling. From then on, it was understood that every serious contender had to inject himself with epo during the weeks before a race. Athletes began blowing up their hematocrits from 45 to a dangerous 56 or more. At those levels, a man's blood turned to sludge, forcing his heart to pump harder to push it through his thin-walled veins. "Pretty soon, you have mud instead of blood," one doctor explained. During a race, a cyclist might feel as if his legs had sprouted wings. But after the finish line, he'd slump on the side of the road, wheezing from shortness of breath, clutching his chest in pain, holding his stomach as diarrhea and vomiting set in. Such adverse side effects came from *moderate* doses, but *extreme* epo?

Amgen set out to find out how high it could push the hematocrit levels of seriously ill patients with chronic renal failure. It mounted a new study.

—⁂—

JIM and Sharon Lenox walked into one of their favorite diners, a rambling two-story place tucked off a leafy residential street in Odenton, Maryland. The couple had invited their five adult children to join them for dinner and had arrived early to grab a large table. They found their spot and Jim sat close to his wife, where they talked softly about nothing in particular.

At forty-one, Jim was tall and lanky, with startling green eyes and thick sandy hair. He had a face like garden statuary: four square planes relieved by elfin features. His wife of twenty-four years had a softer, worry-lined face, with a snub nose and long tawny hair tied in a ponytail. A trim five six, she fit snugly under the wing of her husband's long arm.

The two Catholic kids had met in a bowling alley in 1968 when Jim was fourteen and Sharon a few months older. Up to that point, they'd been good students. But the lively baseball player fell for the shy math whiz and they began skipping classes to meet on the sly. Jim recalled the first time they kissed, and she remembered how one exciting discovery led to another. By early 1971, she was six months pregnant, and they'd gotten their parents' permission to be married by the justice of the peace. Jim worked full-time at a diner, selling Pappy Parker's Fried Chicken. When their son Scott was born, the young parents could have tapped state aid for their hospital bill, but instead Jim paid $288 out of his own pocket.

A second baby, Jenny, arrived, then Joanne, and the couple made room inside their tiny two-bedroom apartment. They had no car, no telephone, and sometimes no heat or electricity. "But we love each other and have vowed to stay together," they agreed. Yet love wasn't enough. Sometimes they missed the rent. Once while Jim was at work, the landlord evicted his family and tossed their belongings in the street while Sharon calmly breastfed her baby. They borrowed money from her father to find a new place, but, by the time Sharon was twenty-two, she had five children underfoot. Finally, Jim landed a decent-paying job repairing underground gas mains for the Washington Gas Light Company. He rose every morning at five-thirty and took three buses to get to work on time.

After their eldest left home, Sharon was working at the U.S. Postal Service during the day and waitressing a few nights a week. Slowly, the couple repaid the relatives. After years of crawling into manholes, Jim was diagnosed with back problems and endured two surgeries. He found a new job as a medical biller, without benefits, but Sharon's job provided health insurance. All in all, life was good.

Now, with their kids either married or in college, the couple felt a freedom they'd never experienced in all their married years. They had leisure time. They had a few extra dollars, but all Jim and Sharon wanted to do was spend it on their family. So, here they were, waiting to treat their adult children, spouses, and four grandbabies to dinner and listening to a James Taylor song on the jukebox. Jim belted out the lyrics of "You've Got a Friend" to his wife, who giggled. Cancer was the furthest thing from their minds.

—〰—

At year-end 1994, Procrit sales were roughly $300 million—double the amount from the prior year. J&J's board seemed pleased, although revenues were half as much as Epogen's stunning sales of $720 million or so. Still, Longstreet had finally delivered. By 1994, the health-care sector was swelling into an industry, and investors and payers wanted to wring as much money from the system as they could. National for-profit chains snapped up community hospitals in Seattle, and monolithic middlemen bought mail-order houses like Charise Charles. As a supplier, J&J needed to centralize its services too. In 1994, it formed Johnson & Johnson Health Care Services (JJHCS) to help sell its myriad products to institutions by giving them rebates, fees, and other deals that lowered their sticker prices. Heading up the new company would be Longstreet, and among his hires were Bennie Thompson and Duxbury's boss, Bob Nelson, both of whom were skilled in these sales tactics.

As for Ortho, its new CEO was Carol Webb. This dynamic woman had come from Madison Avenue, where she had overseen retail accounts for two New York advertising agencies. A graduate of Bowling Green State University, Webb could disarm with her faint Southern drawl. Having taught science at an elementary school in Ohio, she also knew how to prod underachievers with gold stars. Tall, vivacious, single, and childless, the woman had devoted herself entirely to her career, and this was her moment. As one of the few females selected to run a J&J division, Webb vowed to push each member of her team "to fulfill your potential this year."

If anyone on J&J's board was concerned about a former ad woman leading a biotech division with a still-not-completely-vetted drug, no one raised an eyebrow. After all, this was the age of rapture for bio-drugs, and genetically modified hormones like epo promised to endow us all with more strength, more power, and überendurance. By tapping J&J's marketing prowess, Webb had a shot at fulfilling that promise and riding Procrit's rapturous wave.

—‌𝔪—

"I GOT all the Indian clinics in my territory," said McClellan.

"Well, aren't you the cowboy?" said Duxbury. "I've got most of the physicians in my territory."

"Yeah? I got all the nurses, so eat your heart out," said McClellan.

The two men were mentally calculating their sales to determine if they'd qualify for a Biosphere Award. McClellan had spent a year pounding the pavement, selling to doctors in the HIV, nondialysis, and oncology units. Some of his stock had slipped into dialysis patients, too, which couldn't be helped. All told, he figured he had sold $1 million in 1994. Duxbury had sold primarily to nephrologists and mixed-use hospitals; his sales were at least triple McClellan's. But had he made his 1994 forecast?

"I don't see how you can't win," said McClellan.

It was hard to argue with that. Duxbury had strong relationships at most of the institutions in his territory and owned 55 percent of the hospital business in three western states. He had also achieved the highest market-growth figure for physicians. But on that January morning, he was speculating. The final tally for 1994 wouldn't be announced until sometime in February. So Duxbury and McClellan turned their attention to other contenders. They wondered if the Pennsylvania woman with the personality of ragg wool would win again, or maybe some new yahoo from Florida would appear. It'd be great to see Oliver Medlock earn a Biosphere, and down the list they went, enumerating their odds-on favorites. About the only thing they didn't say that morning was how badly each wanted the other to join him in an all-expenses-paid vacation. Wouldn't that be outstanding? They continued talking in the clear, masculine cadence of those who had already won.

Early that year, Duxbury had received a new company car, a 1995 Buick sedan, whose interior smelled faintly of cowhide and wood chips. One morning, he found himself driving to the Seattle Tacoma International Airport to pick up his new boss, rain lashing down on his windshield. The steady slap of the wind-driven storm danced nicely with the bebop suite playing on his car stereo. Others might feel depressed during the long stretch of dark days, but Duxbury felt invigorated. Maybe he couldn't see five feet beyond his car hood, but damn if he didn't sense that 1995 was going to be a great year.

Meeting Michael Barton confirmed that. His new district manager was an affable dark-haired man with a waxed mustache and a firm handshake. As a graduate of the University of Utah Hospital Pharmacy Program, Barton was more knowledgeable about medicine than was your typical sales manager. He was the father of two young kids, and his wife owned a business in Salt Lake City, where he lived. Despite his geographic distance from Seattle, Barton assured Duxbury that they'd work closely together.

"I hear you have some of the biggest accounts in the region," said Barton.

"I do," said the rep without exaggeration.

Duxbury took his new boss on a whirlwind sales tour of his territory, introducing him to the buyers at four of his hospitals. At St. Pete, they found one of Duxbury's clients miffed after Ortho had failed to mail his rebate check in a timely fashion. Duxbury acknowledged the delay, apologized, and promised to take steps to eliminate any future delays. By the end of the meeting, the buyer had calmed down long enough to place another order of Procrit vials.

At St. Joseph, Duxbury introduced Barton to Al Linggi, who bought $1.6 million of Procrit a year. The three men went to eat, and somewhere between appetizers and dessert, Duxbury learned about a huge Procrit deal that was about to die. An Ortho manager was negotiating a $20 million Procrit contract with a purchasing group for a nationwide string of hospitals. But several hospital members were opposed to the deal. The next morning, Duxbury telephoned an Ortho manager in Raritan and gave him the lowdown. With barely a few days to close the deal, the manager contacted the reps closest to the holdouts, mailed them a few large "grant" checks, and told them to deliver the money to the recalcitrant voters. Days later, Ortho won the contract, most of which was dialysis business. The deal did nothing for Duxbury, but it impressed his bosses and hoisted the rep's star higher in Ortho's firmament.

After following Duxbury for a week or so, Barton shook his head in admiration. "It's impressive to watch the rapport you have with the staff pharmacists," he told him. *How do you do it?* From then on, the two developed a mutual respect, working together seamlessly. When St. Joseph missed the date to qualify for a big discount, Duxbury asked Barton to extend the deadline, and he did. When a different J&J division eliminated that hospital's "corporate dividend," Barton allowed Duxbury to give St. Joe a $5,000 grant, a little something "to help ease the financial pain."

Barton's trust allowed Duxbury to grow in new professional areas. The rep converted a hospital in Boise, Idaho, that wasn't even in his territory and which gave another rep a fat bonus. At a conference in Portland, Oregon, Duxbury met an impressive young woman and passed her résumé to headquarters; on his recommendation, she was interviewed and hired. Whenever a fellow rep's computer screen froze, Duxbury was there to help fix it. In the spring of 1995, he became the technology specialist in the Northwest District, and a committeeman who advised Raritan in purchasing new technology.

Raising Sojie, however, remained a challenge. Yet even Renee would say that Duxbury was a devoted father. Most weekends found him holding his eighteen-month-old on his lap, feeding her Cheerios, discussing the merits of Elmo, the bright orange cartoon character who knew his numbers by heart. He and Renee were still entwined in a relationship, but they often got their wires crossed. Sometimes he'd appear on her doorstep to pick up his daughter for their weekly visits, and Renee would be delighted to see him. She'd invite him in for dinner and, occasionally, ask him to spend the night. Other times, he'd show up bearing flowers and wine to find her steaming mad. "Don't you dare come past the front step," she'd say. He never knew what to expect. But in early 1995, the now-divorced couple was getting along well, sharing child-rearing duties, workaday struggles, and sometimes a nice meal. Duxbury still dreamed of raising their child in a stable, two-parent home, and Renee didn't discourage him. As a result, his characteristic patience and playfulness flourished.

But so did his flaws. During one performance evaluation, Barton chastised his star salesman for filing "sporadic" weekly activities reports. "You need to file them at the end of the reporting week." Also, your expense reports are usually late. "This is puzzling because it appears that you complete them on time, you just fail to turn them in," Barton said. Duxbury admitted that "my administrative skills are definitely an embarrassment." Duxbury honestly didn't think that anyone would care about sporadic reports as long as his sales continued to zoom. But he pledged to do better and signed the evaluation that became part of his official file, ready to be used against him someday.

The idea that bad times would ever appear seemed as remote as a country doctor. On the morning that the national sales rankings were finally announced, Duxbury saw that he had not only made, he had *exceeded* his 1994 target by some $100,000. He had sold $3.2 million, double the amount from the year before. It was another stunning achievement that put him and his Western Region in second place. In addition, he had forged a new Ortho record by becoming the first in his division to win two Biosphere Awards in a row.

Even Renee was impressed. When she learned that her ex-husband's career was on fire, she forgot that she had ever doubted him. Ortho was thriving, epo was exploding, and stealing clients apparently was de rigueur for biotech partners. Maybe she'd been too harsh on Duxbury. So when he asked her to accompany him on the awards trip, she accepted. That made the unconventional couple very happy.

As soon as McClellan and his wife, Beth, stepped onto the promenade of the Palm Springs Airport, McClellan spied a chauffeur holding a sign with his name. Beth followed her husband as he greeted the driver, helped retrieve their bags, and walked outside to the waiting limousine. Husband and wife slid across the cool leather seats and exhaled, as the limousine slowly pulled onto the Gene Autry Trail.

The McClellans were accustomed to deserts, but somehow this arid land felt richer, less hurried, and cleaner than their Tucson home. Waves of heat shimmered off the roadway, giving the boulevards a shine. Each stately, well-trimmed palm tree seemed to be a duplicate of the one before, too perfect even for phantasmagoria. When the limo rounded a corner into a wealthy enclave, Beth spotted the sign for Rancho Mirage. She turned and told her husband, "I guess we've arrived."

The stocky girl from Moorhead, Minnesota, was not accustomed to such royal treatment. She had married McClellan at nineteen, had finished college at night school, and had raised two kids in the course of a life spent in Minnesota and Arizona. While her husband spent weeks on the road, she kept life humming at home. Ortho realized how hard a detailer's job was on family life, which is why managers included the reps' spouses on these annual fandangos.

After the driver pulled into the Westin Mission Hills Resort, the couple checked in and found a message to meet for dinner at six o'clock. They left their villa and wandered a landscape dense with man-made boulders, illuminated waterfalls, and dark fans of palm fronds. At last, they came upon a mariachi band playing a ballad for a coterie of Ortho employees. Margaritas were flowing, and people were already sitting at brightly colored tables, lost in conversation.

The Duxbury party had missed their flight, but once they arrived, they, too, were enchanted by this oasis. At the President's Breakfast the next morning, they met the McClellans and, later, signed up for events. Beth had a complimentary facial. McClellan rode a hot-air balloon in the sky, gazing at the resort some hundred feet below: "Looks like an ant farm from up here," he yelled to his companions. Down on the ground, Renee and the others raced Jeeps over dunes, rode horses on quiet trails, shopped at tony boutiques, or congregated by the pool, close to the free booze.

As for Duxbury, he hit a few balls with his friends on the world-class Pete Dye Resort Course. Known for its elevated tees and pothole bunkers, the eighteen-hole golf course hid other, less obvious, hazards. Duxbury didn't know it, but Carol Webb, Tom Amick, Bill Pearson, and a few others on the greens had already given signed declarations, been deposed, or were about to testify in one of the suits. After its last round of subpoenas, Amgen had unearthed even more evidence of Ortho's conversions. As Duxbury putted the ball, the enemy was inching closer.

But here at the intersection of Dinah Shore and Bob Hope Drives, not far from Frank Sinatra's spread, the rep believed he was a star among luminaries. One night, the reps and their ladies and gentlemen were chauffeured to Liberace's estate with its rococo chairs and baroque candelabras. While the guests dined on Cornish game hens and wild rice, a Liberace impersonator appeared to serenade them on a Steinway. Beth was agog. She pointed to the man's Brylcreemed pompadour and whispered to her husband, "He looks just like him." Even the dessert that night was over-the-top— a white chocolate piano with cocoa keys sitting on a "rug" of raspberry sauce. Later, when McClellan and Duxbury retired to the bar for an after-dinner drink, Duxbury turned to his friend and said, "Since when was the last time we felt so free and easy?"

"Since never, that's when!"

The trip climaxed on Monday, April 3, at twilight, when Duxbury, dressed in a tailored suit, and McClellan, wearing a tuxedo and bow tie, waited nervously outdoors on a red carpet with their women, who were dressed to the nines. A slight breeze moved the palm fronds into ever-shifting runes; the sky burned a deeper shade of orange; a lizard scurried over a boulder. Then they heard the escorts before they saw them: kilted men playing an ancient warrior tune on drums and bagpipes. Some Biosphere honorees were already trailing the musicians, and as soon as the ensemble passed by, the two couples fell in line too. An outsider might snicker at the sight of adults dressed in dark suits and long gowns, following pied pipers in the desert sunset, marching to the "Celebrity D" room. But they'd be missing the point. This was a carefully orchestrated ritual designed to strike an emotional chord in this corps of big-game hunters, and whether it was the Highland drone, the tartan plaid, or the pomp and pageantry, the effect on at least two of the reps was profound.

McClellan's surname originated with a Scottish clan whose heirs had been sheriffs of Galloway since the thirteenth century, just as McClellan's dad and cousin had once been police chiefs in clannish Wheaton, Minnesota. McClellan wasn't keen on genealogy, but he'd mailed away for a brass plaque inscribed with the McClellan coat of arms and had hung it prominently in his guest bedroom. Duxbury, however, was riveted by the tales of his heritage. Years ago, an uncle had painstakingly traced the name (if not their bloodline exactly) to Duxbury Hall in Lancashire, England, the birthplace of Captain Myles Standish. The captain had arrived in America aboard the *Mayflower* and had cofounded Duxbury, Massachusetts, in 1632. A cursory search had shown the rep that his surname stretched back to the First Crusade and the Norman Conquest of England in 1066. "You're full of crap," McClellan had told him. "There's no way to back that up." But Duxbury insisted that he was descended from lords and knights.

Now, stepping to the pipes, the blood of their ancestors coursing through them, the two arrived inside the grand room. There Webb, Amick, and the others applauded as Duxbury, McClellan, and their fellows marched in. Holding a microphone in one hand and a drink in the other, Amick welcomed the champions to their banquet. An orchestra struck up an anthem, and the winners were led to tables crowned by astonishing five-foot-high glass vases spilling over with white gardenias, white roses, and silver lace.

The two couples sat next to each other and began a five-course dinner of wild mushrooms, swordfish, and beef filet. Renee and Beth swapped stories about their daughters, while the men ribbed each other about their ties. After dessert, someone tapped a silver spoon against a glass and the room fell silent. Winner after winner was called to the stage so Pearson could recite his or her deeds. When it was McClellan's turn, the Tucson rep stood between Webb and Amick as the highlights of his year were declaimed. Tanned and beaming, McClellan was then given his own gold ring. He was now a member of the club. After he sat down, Duxbury was called. He was praised in front of his peers not only for exceeding his forecast, but also for helping several people in his district reach their forecasts and for assisting others within the J&J family. "Mark had another phenomenal year," Pearson told the assembled, then turned to the rep: "We want you know that management at all levels appreciates what you've accomplished." Webb, dressed in a sleek black suit, kissed his cheek, while a sunburned Amick handed back to Duxbury his Ortho Biotech ring, which now held a new, sparkling diamond.

Applause followed Duxbury to his seat, where Renee admired his new jewel and slipped her arm around his shoulders. "I feel like a chosen one," he whispered in her ear. After the ceremony, the music and drinking continued, and a tipsy woman climbed on a chair to snip roses from the towering centerpieces. "Christy," yelled Amick, rushing toward her, "what the hell do you think you're doing?" She continued filching flowers as if she were in her garden at home. By eleven, the event shut down, but the champions were just getting started. Duxbury stood up and announced with raised fist, "Let's liberate the golf carts!" Several men cheered and rushed outdoors; McClellan grabbed a bottle of gin, while his buddies lifted some glasses and a bottle of Scotch. Flooding out to the warm night, the men found the golf carts sequestered behind a chain rope and commandeered a few. Under a waxing moon, they zipped recklessly over velvet fairways, yelling military orders to one another, and stopping at every other hole to clink their glasses in a Celtic and Anglo-Saxon toast. Occasionally, a rep would howl at the pack of coyotes that yelped in the craggy hills in the distance. After a while, Duxbury, McClellan, and the others returned the carts, giddy and exhausted. McClellan trundled off to bed, while Duxbury and two others changed into their swim trunks and met in the Jacuzzi. Soaking in the hot water, they watched the dazzle of stars overhead and sighed.

For Duxbury, this was as good as his life would get. Unbeknownst to him, Amgen attorneys had just written his name near the top on their "wanted" list.

PART II

7

The Deposition

1995

THAT spring, Duxbury was promoted to regional key account special-ist. He was no longer a mere rep toting a black bag, but an RKAS charged with spearheading companywide efforts to land long-term ac-counts that could propel Ortho's growth, through either money or influ-ence. Sometimes, he quarterbacked with another RKAS from one of the two hundred or so J&J divisions. For example, Duxbury and a special-ist from Janssen began making joint sales calls in the Northwest to promote Procrit and a pain reliever called Duragesic, a potent opioid skin patch. He and a rep from Longstreet's new division, JJHCS, bid on a contract for a large HMO in the Northwest—and landed it. In his new post, the salesman gained a broader perspective. The fortunes of publicly traded health-care companies were rising, subsidized in part by govern-ment payouts, under-the-table gifts from firms like J&J, and the misery of a growing, aging population. Doctors' offices, religious institutions, and nonprofits struggled to hold their own in the rush to privatization, and small players merged to help each other "fight the savage war be-tween us and for-profit health corporations," as one doctor put it.

Duxbury jumped into that pool, too, soliciting group purchasing organizations (GPOs) that represented dozens of small health-care providers. They leveraged their collective buying power to obtain the same discounted volume deals that corporate chains received. HMOs,

POSs, PPOs, and other acronymic bodies fell into Duxbury's basket too. One was Group Health Cooperative of Puget Sound, which had grown to encompass customers in several states. The HMO purchased millions of dollars' worth of pills, stents, and gauze every year, many from J&J units, and Duxbury began cultivating that account. Working with a rep from Longstreet's unit, he offered it a $20,000 "dividend" during its first year of a long-term Procrit contract. He liked knowing he could extend discounts, rebates, and grants not just from Ortho, but from JJHCS too.

To help him land the big fish, Duxbury's managers shrank the size of his territory to thirty golden miles from Tacoma up to downtown Seattle. Here lay premier medical facilities. Best of all, his forecast rose by a mere 20 percent, instead of the 100 percent pole vault from the two prior years. His target was $3.6 million and to get there, he'd need to land a few jumbo accounts.

Duxbury met regularly with Barton, usually at a twenty-four-hour diner that prided itself on fresh baked pies and sausage gravy. One day, he pulled into the lot of the green-and-yellow restaurant twenty minutes before their appointment. He asked for a booth and was led to one near a speaker that piped in the narcotic sounds of Muzak. He ordered a pot of coffee and reviewed his notes. By the time Barton came through the door, Duxbury had lined up his strategic points.

First, he reported on the progress of his bigger accounts, including Group Health. Next, he brought Barton up to speed on his physicians. Then he voiced his desires.

"I'd like to focus more on oncology," he started. He'd heard stories of how anemic chemotherapy patients, after a month of Procrit injections, felt revived. Some would rise from their beds and walk outside or drive to the market. He wanted to help those patients, and after he put down his coffee cup, he looked Barton in the eye.

"I'd rather spend ninety percent of my day trying to grow our oncology business than trying to convert large hospitals."

"But you're bringing in sales for Ortho, which is a big part of your job," Barton replied. After all, he, too, had a forecast; he needed his top rep to help pull in the dollars.

"I understand," Duxbury argued, "but part of our function is to make sure we're advocates for patients too. I thought the whole idea was to educate oncologists about how their chemotherapy patients could benefit from epo. And I'm not doing that."

Instead he felt bogged down by converting accounts. His figures showed that the hospitals in his territory purchased $3 million worth of epo a year, "but most of that is for dialysis patients." He pulled out a memo he'd written that broke out those numbers by account. This memo was similar to all the other ones he'd prepared for his managers over the past two years. He handed it to Barton and said, "It's in our best interest to get this stuff removed from our forecast for ethical reasons." Clearing dialysis sales from their forecasts would also free them to grow oncology sales. "That's where the future is," he urged, and Barton nodded. Plus, Duxbury added, more growth means increased market share. "And that translates into bigger bonuses for everybody."

Okay, okay, said Barton in surrender. He'd take Duxbury's case to Raritan.

But Amick had seen these figures before, and Duxbury's annual exhortations to lower his forecast were growing tiresome. As the new executive director of sales, Amick didn't need a squeaky wheel hounding him about dialysis sales when he already had Amgen riding him about the same damn subject. As it was, Amgen's attorneys were trying to turn the spillover arbitration into a more serious claim, and had just presented their latest pet peeve to the judge: *Has Ortho deliberately and systematically stolen our dialysis patients?* If so, it was time for a corporate-style divorce. After deliberating in the spring of 1995, the judge ordered Ortho to turn over all documents related to the topic. Amick complied by commanding Ortho's staff to collect all of their memos, e-mails, weekly activity reports, and papers related to Charise Charles, its successor IV One, their owner Marty Nassif, and others.

As for Duxbury and his persistently obnoxious memos, they were ignored. Headquarters felt no need to wash renal sales from an individual forecast. That left Barton and Duxbury no choice but to continue converting accounts and selling to mixed-use customers. Barton delivered the message to Duxbury in a matter-of-fact fashion, but the rep could practically feel the lash of Amick's reprimands. He agreed to drop the matter but couldn't resist a parting shot: "It's a constant source of frustration that I can't do more with oncology.

"I think it's a huge mistake."

In May, Duxbury responded to Amick's all-points bulletin for dialysis-related papers. He spent most of the day pawing through his files as the cat rubbed against his legs, meowing. He gathered whatever he could find, including his infamous memos, and express-mailed them to J&J's attorneys in New York.

Then, in June, the inconceivable happened: Duxbury was subpoenaed. He was so distressed that he assumed he was being dragged into the Ortho-Amgen litigation. But had he read his summons carefully, he would have learned that a circuit court in Seminole County, Florida, was ordering him to testify in a case filed by Charise Charles against Amgen. Recalling the memos he had sent, he feared the worst. "This is too much," he thought, and J&J attorneys agreed. They tried to quash the subpoena, claiming that the demand was "unduly burdensome and oppressive," accusing Amgen of mounting "an impermissible fishing expedition into the affairs of a nonparty to this action" and of squeezing Duxbury for information to use against his employer in its long-running arbitration. The tug-of-war slopped into summer. Duxbury held out hope that maybe, just maybe, he'd escape testifying. Yet his summons had been clear—*Fail not, at your peril*—and Duxbury discussed the worst-case scenario with Barton.

He had sent the attorneys his messages to management that proved they had scouted the Northwest for Amgen's dialysis sales. The anxious rep confessed that those papers might jeopardize Ortho and its product license.

"What happens if they depose me about all that?" he asked Barton.

"Don't worry," his boss replied. "You're very valuable to the company and have the full support of management."

—m—

A<small>T</small> lunch hour on a stifling August day, Duxbury stood on the sidewalk of a busy thoroughfare in Manhattan, facing a polished granite tower. The nearsighted salesman searched for the name of the law firm on the sharp-edged wall but missed it in the glare of the noonday sun. He figured he was at the right place, and the pale northwestern man walked into the lobby of Patterson Belknap Webb & Tyler. Known for its litigation muscle, this midsize firm had once been the stomping grounds for Rudy Giuliani, mayor of New York City; Edward Cox, son-in-law of President Richard M. Nixon; and Robert Morgenthau, longtime district attorney for New York County and the inspiration for Adam Schiff, the fictitious DA on TV's *Law & Order* and, therefore, the image of the quintessential American DA. Patterson Belknap represented some of the world's biggest blue-chip firms, including Coca-Cola, General Electric, and Johnson & Johnson. Although Duxbury had a right to enlist his own attorney, separate from Ortho's counsel at Patterson Belknap, his employer had neglected to tell him that, he'd later claim. The rep waited anxiously in the lobby, until a young man in a conservative suit holding a walkie-talkie led him to the inner chambers, which turned out to be no short walk away. In his ten years of selling pharmaceuticals, Duxbury had toured factories that manufactured opiatelike narcotics and warehouses that stocked millions of dollars' worth of choice drugs. But he had never witnessed the level of security that he found inside this high-toned office. Duxbury was led through a maze of doors, up elevators, and down hallways, each of which required a pass card and a secret code to enter. He tried to make small talk with his escort, but the man was as friendly as Plexiglas.

If only Duxbury's career were as bulletproof as this place, he'd come out okay.

Finally, he was deposited in a large, elegant conference room. That's when Duxbury received another surprise: Charise Charles had sent its attorney, Jerry Linscott, from the Orlando office of Baker Hostetler, to examine him. The balding, white-bearded man seemed pleasant enough, but his presence puzzled the rep. "I thought this was a termination suit between Amgen and J and J," Duxbury said. No one present was inclined to tell the rep about the details of this case or its relation to Ortho, not even Duxbury's (and Ortho's) attorney, Thomas DeRosa. But the mail-order wholesaler Charise Charles was suing Amgen for halting its Epogen supply—which Amgen had done after it had caught Charise helping Ortho violate the PLA. To defend itself, Amgen had pulled in some Ortho reps who had sold Procrit to dialysis centers, such as Duxbury. But Ortho wasn't named in this suit.

The man who would conduct most of the deposing was Paul Pizzo, a litigator from one of Florida's oldest firms, Fowler, White, Gillen, Boggs, Villareal & Banker. With his ruddy face and bushy black eyebrows, the Tampa native looked as if he'd rather be anywhere but here on this sticky Friday afternoon. As Amgen's attorney, he was responsible for steering the Ortho rep into muddy waters, and he began by asking a few innocuous questions. Like a good soldier, Duxbury gave the man his name, title, and address along with the names of his hospital accounts. The two discussed DDD figures and various other methods for measuring sales. Then Pizzo pounced.

"Is it among your goals to convert hospitals to [use] Procrit?"

"It depends," Duxbury said warily.

Ortho's attorney objected. Pizzo struggled to rephrase the question when the witness rescued him. "Are you asking me, 'Are there times when I've converted accounts . . . that I know [had] dialysis business?'"

"Yes," said his prosecutor.

Having asked the question correctly, Duxbury then answered it: "Yes."

The interplay continued for the first hour. When asked if he'd ever converted an institution, the rep named two large hospitals as examples. He looked into the videotape camera and added that he hadn't set out to steal customers from Amgen but had little choice. "My concern is that I get business that belongs to me." If I absorb dialysis sales, so be it. "If I weren't doing this, Amgen would be taking my business."

The cardinal rule for any witness on the stand is to answer prosecutors with a simple yes or no. Never volunteer information. Yet, oddly enough, J&J's high-priced attorneys did not reveal these rules to their witness, nor had they bothered to prepare him. As a result, Duxbury behaved like a chameleon, changing at whim. When pressed about Ortho's policy on conversions, he grew restrained and self-deprecating: "I'm just a lonely grunt in the whole system. I couldn't speak for [Ortho] in any legitimate way." When treated kindly, he turned garrulous and found it hard to turn off his switch. In the presence of a professional clawing for incriminating evidence, Duxbury volunteered information he wasn't even asked for. At one point, he disarmed the room by confessing a venial sin: "I'm not known for being great with paperwork." When Pizzo started fishing for tidbits about Ortho's alleged breach, the salesman gallantly defended management. Then, a minute later, he pulled out a noose. "If you read the documents that I provided, there is at least one letter complaining explicitly about how much dialysis business was included in my forecast."

Pizzo quickly took a break to review the pernicious letter. When he returned, he lobbed his missile at Duxbury's sale to Dr. John Boykin. "In the course of your meeting, you discussed the fact that Mid-Columbia Kidney Center—"

Duxbury brusquely cut him off: "I didn't discuss that."

Pizzo stopped. "You did not discuss that?"

"Are you implying that I brought it up?"

Pizzo had to start over: Did Boykin ask if he'd get a rebate for buying Procrit?

Duxbury confirmed that was true.

"So, it came up?"

"Yes, it came up." *But the doctor brought it up, not me.*

Pizzo then asked the same question in a different way. But before Duxbury could answer, J&J's attorney objected. And so it went in herky-jerky fashion for the rest of the afternoon: lunge, protest, retreat. The more precise Duxbury tried to be, the more Pizzo rephrased his query, adding a word or nuance. Duxbury began to sweat. The questions grew so tricky that J&J's attorney, DeRosa, admonished Pizzo, saying, "It'd be better if you asked him a question instead of restating his testimony." When Amgen's lawyer asked the rep for the fifth time if he had told Boykin he'd get a rebate, Duxbury exploded.

"No, no, no, no, no," he shouted. "You're not listening to me!" He glared at the roomful of attorneys.

Pizzo stepped back.

Duxbury reined in his anger, but sarcasm dripped through. "Is there a part that's not clear?" he asked. Neither Pizzo, nor Linscott, nor DeRosa responded to his question.

"I don't like this game," Duxbury thought.

Pizzo recovered enough to continue poking around the Boykin sale, so much so that Duxbury tried to downplay the event. Yet Pizzo would not let it go, and Duxbury grew frightened. "Why is he making such a big deal out of a ten-thousand-dollar sale?" he thought. At one point, the rep objected, "This is all out of proportion." When the terrierlike lawyer bore down on the rep, Duxbury threw up his hands. "I don't know what you want!"

Finally, around seven P.M., the interrogators allowed their prey to walk out of the claustrophobic conference room. Standing outside on the Avenue of the Americas, Duxbury breathed in the muggy air; it smelled faintly of steaming garbage and grilled hot dogs. He lit a cigarette. Then he tried to reconcile the day's proceedings with his grumbling intuition.

Nearly half of the afternoon had been spent nitpicking the details of a penny-ante deal with a nephrologist in eastern Washington. No one had inquired about the much bigger conversions at Memorial Clinic, St. Joseph Hospital, or any of Duxbury's other accounts. "If I was sitting in the Amgen chair, I would have asked about the other deals." He couldn't shake the feeling that most of his documents had escaped notice and considered why that would be. Perhaps the documents he'd handed over weren't so incriminating after all; or maybe Amgen was looking for something bigger than what he could deliver. There was the remote possibility that Ortho's attorneys had withheld some of his papers, but such prestigious lawyers wouldn't dare risk a sanction.

Duxbury's reverie was broken by the sound of laughter pouring out of the cafés and bars up the street. He imagined Wall Street brokers, who pump stocks, had just hoodwinked their banker friends, who paper over losses. Maybe the corporate attorneys had been setting him up too. After all, this was Manhattan, the heart of American capitalism, where shades of gray proliferate on their very own color wheel. His unease continued to gnaw at him like an animal sensing a steel trap. Then, he hit upon a Tigger-like idea. Perhaps the *real* reason no one had asked about his documents was because his career really was bulletproof. He chewed on that theory for a minute and decided to go with it. Stubbing out his cigarette, the salesman bounded up the street.

—ɷ—

Back in Seattle, Duxbury summarized the uncomfortable proceedings to Michael Barton. "I don't think my testimony was damaging," he said. "I answered the questions honestly while using as few words as possible, and while putting Ortho in the best light possible." He didn't complain about being placed in the insufferable position of having to tell the truth, protect his firm, and save his job—all at the same time.

He also told McClellan about the experience. But his friend had already heard the highlights. "You told Amgen's attorneys exactly what's been going on in your neck of the woods." He warned Duxbury to be careful. "You're a company liability now, Mark."

Duxbury brushed away his friend's concerns. "It's okay, Dean." He reminded McClellan that Barton had assured him that Raritan backed him completely. Then the Seattle salesman went on to re-create for McClellan the focal points of his six-hour deposition. Somehow, with the passage of time and distance, Duxbury's nail-biting ordeal had become an entertaining tour de force. He had *sliced* the prosecutor's arguments, *pummeled* his assumptions, and lanced his case with a few well-executed verbal glissandos. "I told them Amgen was poaching our nondialysis business too." *You should have seen me.*

Duxbury convinced himself that his deposition had been harmless and that his career truly was unassailable. Such wishful thinking was one way to keep his sales and spirits aloft. But it blinded him to the forces that were marshaling against him.

The first hint of attack appeared in New Jersey. As a member of Ortho's Incentive Compensation Review Task Force, Duxbury flew to Raritan for a weeklong meeting that included Amick, Pearson, and others. The session quickly deteriorated into a strident discussion of bonuses. One faction wanted to keep the "pay-for-performance" structure while another argued that the pool be divided among more people. Duxbury didn't like that idea. "It's a twenty-eighty world," he said. Twenty percent of the people do eighty percent of the work. "Why would I break my back to achieve a tough forecast if I'm not going to earn *at least* the same money I did last year?

"That makes no sense."

One manager preferred rewarding more, albeit less successful, people.

Okay, said Duxbury. "But socialism doesn't work. If you do this there'll be an exodus of top sales performers."

But Pearson defended the new concept. "This plan will incentivize more performers, while still giving top people a sizable bonus." He urged Duxbury to adopt a "teamlike" approach. But the RKAS retorted that he feared for "the People's Republic of Ortho Biotech." At the end of the weeklong meeting, Amick announced a dilution of the bonus pool. It seemed to Duxbury as if the outcome of the task force had been preordained, and he returned to Seattle perturbed that he had wasted precious sales time.

Later, when Pearson was promoted to national field sales manager, the impolitic salesman called to congratulate his new supervisor. "No hard feelings, I hope," he said.

"No," Pearson replied. But the chill in his voice said otherwise.

Duxbury worried more about his list of two hundred doctors, fourteen institutions, and dozens of pharmacies. One day he called on a new client, the Western Washington Cancer Treatment Center, arriving with an oncology nurse educator named Patricia Buchsel. Her job was to help salespeople by speaking authoritatively about Procrit with other registered nurses. A new hire, she was obviously nervous, so Duxbury tried to put her at ease by giving her some background. The center was a privately held facility that had been built around a magnificent maple tree whose colors changed with the seasons. "Cancer patients can look at it while they're getting their chemo," he said. When they entered the space age–style lobby, he introduced himself to the receptionist. But once she heard the name Ortho, she ignored them. Duxbury asked to see a nurse, but one never arrived. He asked to speak with the administrator, and this time a burly man came out. Before Duxbury could offer his hand, the man rudely showed him the door.

Outside, Buchsel was flabbergasted. "They were openly hostile to us."

"That's never happened to me before," he said. "I'm sorry."

On their way to the next appointment, Duxbury played a bebop music tape, which she didn't like, and asked about her knowledge of military history, which was zilch. They pulled into another premier facility and Duxbury talked with a snobbish doctor who liked participating in clinical trials funded by drugmakers. Duxbury was polite, but Buchsel thought he was too casual. After a few more visits, she grew uncomfortable with his quirky personality and "different" interests. She went home that night worried that she'd made a mistake joining Ortho.

On their next outing, they called on Tacoma General Hospital's Cancer Center. There, Buchsel witnessed the warm connection Duxbury had with the staff. She marveled how quickly and successfully he enrolled some of its oncology patients in an Ortho-funded study about Procrit and cancer-related fatigue. From then on, she fell into a pleasant, productive work relationship with the rep and loosened up to the point where she considered Duxbury a "pal."

Yet someone would soon twist their relationship into something more.

8

On the Border

1996

STRADDLING a bar stool in Tombstone's famed Crystal Palace, Mc-Clellan bought Duxbury a beer and raised the frosty mug in a toast to the paleface.

"Here's looking at you, bud," McClellan said. He drank thirstily, white foam coating his dark mustache.

Wearing pressed denim and new Western boots, Duxbury scanned the dark interior of this tourist spot, lingering on the spicy costumed barmaids and the graying gunslingers. "This looks more like the Geritol Palace," he said dryly.

Tombstone was quite nice in February. Duxbury had left dreary Seattle the day before, flying to Tucson to spend a long weekend with his co-worker and friend. Ostensibly, the RKAS was in town to teach McClellan how to "pull through" an order of Procrit at Tucson Medical Center—the region's biggest private hospital. The two had headed out Friday morning to meet the pharmacist, and Duxbury had demonstrated how to cement the big new order.

Then they had hopped into McClellan's car and headed southeast to a corner of the desert that once ate men alive. Speeding past the Whetstone Mountains, they had admired some of the prettiest grasslands north of the border. They had entered rugged Cochise County, named for the legendary Apache leader, and McClellan had repeated some of the stories he'd read in his *Time-Life Old West Series*. But Duxbury had been uncharacteristically quiet.

As they sat on creaky bar stools, Duxbury related his woes over his cold beer.

By now, he was spending as much time as he could with his daughter, which amounted to every other weekend and whatever weekday he could scavenge. He was also paying a generous $1,000 a month in child support. He still hoped that he and Renee could work things out, but the events of the last few months had angered her and they were arguing again. She believed his testimony would cost him his job and scolded him for not having listened to her in the first place. In the meantime, she had started dating, and he'd taken to calling her ten times a day, first begging, then badgering, her to stop seeing her "boy toy." Their sniping affected Sojie, who grew increasingly upset at her parents' fighting. Dropping Sojie off at child care turned into a heart-wrenching routine, with both father and daughter crying good-bye.

Things got ugly. One evening, Duxbury had rushed from work at five P.M. to pick up his daughter at the Tacoma day-care center, as arranged. But Renee was already there, in a foul mood and demanding to talk to Duxbury immediately. She'd heard that he was about to go on a trip with another woman and demanded to know if this was true. Unwilling to expose the toddlers to a scene, Duxbury stepped outside and Renee took Sojie. Duxbury didn't protest and instead drove off. But that seemed to enrage Renee. She followed him in her car to the freeway entrance and tailed him for several miles as he headed north. At one point, her car was practically riding the back bumper of his automobile. He pulled off the road, stopped the engine, and walked to her window. "Please stop following me," he said. "This is dangerous." She started yelling, so he returned to his car and pulled onto the freeway. There she was again, revving the V8 engine of her Pontiac Trans Am, tailgating him at high speed. He slowed down, pulled off the freeway, and again pleaded with her to take their child home. Renee hurled obscenities at him. Then she turned to reach for something—a semiautomatic. Duxbury grabbed her arm, and she winced, saying what he already knew. "I'm carrying my gun." Duxbury needed help.

He jumped back into his car, drove to the parking lot of Lyon's Grocery Store in Seattle, and ran into the telephone booth.

Renee's black car screeched into the lot, too, turning a few heads. She got out of her car and made a beeline for her ex-husband, the hem of her dark dress flapping.

"I'm calling the police," Duxbury said loudly. "Get away from me."

Duxbury dialed 911 and said, "I'm being harassed and need help." Before the operator could ask a question, Renee grabbed the phone from Duxbury and disconnected the line. When the operator tried to call back, she got only a busy signal.

By then the two were struggling in the booth and attracting a small crowd. Duxbury pushed Renee against the glass and she punched and hollered. At one point, she kicked him in the groin with her sharp-toed high heel. He doubled over and groaned. But Renee kept socking him in the chest, face, and shoulders. Aghast at the violence, a grocery store employee ran inside to use the store's phone. *Hurry! There's some kind of fight between a white man and a black woman!* Minutes later, two members of the Seattle Police Department pulled up in time to witness Renee's fusillade of fists. While Sojie sat in the car, an officer managed to calm down her mom. Upon questioning, Renee freely admitted that she had a Walther handgun and handed it over, along with two magazines and twelve rounds. The police seized the cache, handcuffed the woman, and drove her to the precinct, where they booked Renee for assault.

Duxbury was left hunched on a curb with a bleeding lip, a ripped shirt, and several bruises. The officer asked if he wanted medical attention, but he declined. Instead, he carried Sojie to his car and, as the officer instructed, drove to the precinct. There he turned his daughter over to one of Renee's relatives.

When Duxbury finished his story, McClellan's eyes were as big as saucers. "A gun, a baby, and speeding on the freeway? That's nuts!" he said. He ordered another round.

Duxbury said he could have decked his ex-wife but had chosen not to. "There's something emasculating about being beaten by a woman, especially one you love," he said. It seemed like the more he tried to please Renee, the more foolish he looked. Renee had been ordered to attend anger management class, Duxbury added. "But I haven't seen much change in her behavior."

When their beers arrived, Duxbury took a swig, then continued. He told McClellan about the backroom machinations between Ortho and Amgen. Several other reps had testified in Amgen's suit against Charise Charles, including Susan Beutler of San Francisco, Dorie Good from Pennsylvania, and Oliver Medlock of Kansas City. The first two reps were infamous for making big dialysis sales, but good old Medlock had steadfastly refused to do so. In fact, he had complained so often about how Pearson and Amick had directed the sales force to "go out and sell dialysis," he had started secretly recording his conversations with supervisors, a form of protection. The summer that Duxbury was in Manhattan, being cross-examined, Medlock was also being quizzed. When the lawyers learned of his secret tapes, they subpoenaed them, too, and spent three full days questioning the Kansas City rep. By the time Medlock had returned to work, he felt vindicated. But his mood didn't last long. A few weeks after he divulged his managers' taped dictums, the African-American was fired for "poor sales performance." Now he was truly cynical, pounding the pavement for another job.

McClellan shook his head at the wreckage. "You could wind up on the street, too, my friend," he said.

This time, Duxbury didn't squabble. Staring down at the scratched surface of the bar, he confided to McClellan, "I requested my personnel file a few weeks ago. I thought it might give me a clue about my future with Ortho."

Then he looked up and saw the elaborate back bar, the ornate mirror, and his own glum expression staring back. "Well," he said suddenly, in a cheery voice, "enough about me and my problems." He turned to his friend and said, "Tell me about yours!" The two laughed, and Duxbury started feeling better.

They drained their drinks and wandered into other thirst parlors, comparing the false fronts and dance-hall girls. Tombstone looked much like it did in 1880, when Wyatt Earp owned part of a saloon, his brother Virgil was U.S. deputy marshal, and their self-destructive friend Doc Holliday was a fixture at the card tables. The history buffs passed through the courthouse museum, caught a reenactment of a murder trial, and toured Boothill, so named because many of the three hundred people were buried there, allegedly, still with their boots on. McClellan took pictures of Duxbury smiling next to the graves of those who had been shot during the infamous Gunfight at the O.K. Corral. Duxbury's favorite marker had been erected for a Wells Fargo agent who'd perished in a dispute over a package. His epitaph read:

HERE LIES LESTER MOORE
FOUR SLUGS FROM A .44
NO LES NO MORE.

Toward the end of the day, McClellan led his friend to an enclosure surrounded by a high brick wall. In the center of the courtyard stood a replica of the Tombstone gallows where men had been hanged for various crimes. It had a ladder with thirteen steps—one broken—that led to a platform. Above that hung a crossbar with two neatly tied nooses; a sign forbade anyone from climbing up to try on the neckwear, but Duxbury moved closer. "Law's gonna catch up to big, bad Mark," McClellan teased him. His friend said nothing. The late afternoon sun cast an eerie rose glow over the scaffold, and a sudden breeze swung the ropes as if ghosts still dangled. Abruptly, Duxbury turned and said, "We'd better head back."

In the car, they retraced the trails where desperadoes had once robbed stagecoaches and cowboy gangs had rustled cattle. They spent the rest of their weekend fishing in Patagonia Lake, drinking suds, and shooting the empties in a ravine where stray bullets wouldn't ricochet far. Duxbury's Colt .45 and McClellan's .357 Magnum did great damage to the Bud Light cans. After a few hours of target practice, the men loaded the bullet-riddled cans into the car trunk and drove back to McClellan's, where they took turns crushing the aluminum containers with a new woodsplitter. They played like eleven-year-olds until Sunday morning, when Duxbury boarded a plane for home.

Later, McClellan placed the photos from that weekend in one of his leather-bound albums. He lingered on a picture of Duxbury, standing in front of Tombstone's scaffold with his back to the camera. McClellan hoped his friend could turn himself and his career around and avoid the gruesome fate that McClellan foresaw in that picture. What McClellan missed, however, was that the gallows held twin nooses. There was rope enough to strangle two.

—⚭—

WHILE Duxbury tooled around Arizona, his boss grappled with work. Because of family responsibilities, Mike Barton found it difficult to leave Salt Lake City as often as he wanted. He oversaw dozens of reps in Idaho, Montana, Washington, and Oregon and, as district manager, was expected to spend at least a hundred days a year on the road. Yet he managed to do his job while traveling about sixty days a year. In fact, he was in his Salt Lake City office consulting with one of his managers out West when he took a frantic call from his boss, George Mooney.

Mooney claimed there was a "crisis" involving Mark Duxbury. Evidently, Pat Buchsel had registered her reluctance to work with Duxbury, due to his "inappropriate and sometimes sexist behavior." Mooney told Barton to contact Buchsel and another female employee to determine whether Duxbury was, in fact, sexually harassing women. "You have to take this matter seriously and investigate immediately," Mooney insisted. As soon as Barton hung up, he pushed aside his other pressing matters and focused on the investigation.

He called the female rep with whom Duxbury had worked, but she didn't have much to say. *Yes, Mark sometimes pulls juvenile pranks.* But as soon as she tells him to stop, he does. Next, Barton called a few of Duxbury's other co-workers, but none of them knew of any untoward conduct. Finally, he dialed Buchsel, explained why he was calling, and heard the surprise in her voice. "That's weird," she said. "I've never made a complaint of sexual misconduct against Mark to George Mooney." Sure, Duxbury could use some "grooming," but she had never seen him offend anyone and had certainly never seen him exhibit sexual misconduct. "In no way should he be removed from his position," she emphasized.

Barton couldn't find anything to corroborate a "crisis," and he wrote a two-page memo to Mooney detailing this. Duxbury was among his best sales reps and was too valuable to lose without good reason. Barton therefore suggested that the salesman undergo a training program to improve his professional behavior, especially with the teaching institutions. If the RKAS didn't improve in sixty days, "I recommend that this be a considered a human resource issue and be managed accordingly."

Mooney wasn't happy with Barton's solution, and neither was Bill Pearson. As the field executive responsible for Ortho's sales force, Pearson had good reason to dislike Duxbury. He wasn't a "team player." Who could forget Duxbury's sarcastic remark about management's new, watered-down bonus pool at "the People's Republic of Ortho Biotech"? In the spring of 1996, as Pearson worked in his home office in a master-planned community near Houston, he mulled over the Duxbury "problem." The rep had produced documents for the *Charise Charles v. Amgen* lawsuit that proved his bosses had told him to convert Amgen business. Duxbury's testimony had been so damaging that on August 31, 1995, six days after he'd left the stand, Amgen had filed yet another suit to terminate Ortho's licensing rights. The biotech company had tried this three times before—in late 1988, when Ortho performed a dialysis trial; in February 1989, when Ortho failed to develop two other drugs it had promised; and in January 1992, when Amgen accused it of failing to develop the cancer market. In each case, divorce had been denied.

But now, Amgen claimed that its partner had purposely stomped on the PLA by selling epo to freestanding and hospital-based dialysis centers for several years. "Ortho's breach is substantial, continuous, and company-wide [and] has been carried out with the active participation, encouragement, and direction by all levels of Ortho's management," the new suit claimed. If the biotech company could break up this commercial union, it would sound the death knell for Ortho and

Procrit. J&J would have to fire hundreds of Ortho workers, including Duxbury and McClellan, and shut Ortho's doors forever. If Judge McGarr were to grant this divorce, rival Amgen could wind up with exclusive rights to the fastest-growing sector of the entire market—cancer—and reap the fruits from years of J&J's research, development, and promotion. J&J's attorneys at Patterson Belknap pleaded with the judge not to end this lucrative, albeit oppressive, relationship, for that "would be devastating to Ortho Biotech."

Not one to rush judgment, Judge McGarr delayed a decision until he could determine if Amgen had followed the rules for termination. Had it given its partner, Ortho, proper notice of a default, as outlined in the licensing agreement? The arbitrator was forced to put that question on hold to address another long-standing dispute over the spill-over formula.

Duxbury, of course, had no clue about the legal maneuverings and their impact on J&J. Nor could he know about the gathering storm headed his way.

Outside of Houston, behind a street canopied by pines and magnolias, Pearson strategized with Mooney on how to contain Duxbury. The trumped-up sexual harassment charge had been their solution, but Barton had snipped that bud, and now they had to "handle" him too. A few weeks after closing the Duxbury investigation, Barton flew to Spokane to meet with his boss, Mooney, and interview candidates for a sales position. In between appointments, Mooney casually suggested that Barton fire Duxbury. The Utah manager froze. "I know he's a bit unorthodox," Barton responded, "but he's bringing in more money than anyone else in my district."

"Why do you want him fired?"

Mooney didn't answer. But he suggested that Barton needed to improve his own leadership skills and "identify more with the management team." *Firing Duxbury would go a long way to proving your commitment to your role as district manager.*

"I work for you, George," Barton began. "If you want to me to fire someone, I'll do it, but not without first following some ethical and legal guidelines." J&J had a written policy on terminations that specified how to proceed: Provide warnings, place worker on probation; create a time by which the worker must improve. None of that had happened yet with Duxbury, Barton explained.

"How would you feel if someone fired you out of the blue, for no specific reason other than the fact that you're a little different?"

Mooney didn't reply. But Barton had just flunked his test.

A few days later, Mooney recounted this episode to Pearson. In a confidential letter, the two decided that Barton was failing in his duties. They had given him both "written and verbal directions" on how to improve his field activity and administrative chores, to no avail. About 90 percent of Barton's responsibilities lay beyond his home base in Utah, and now, after eighteen months, that was suddenly a handicap. Since Barton couldn't—or wouldn't—move to the district's hub in Seattle, Pearson decided to demote Barton as soon as possible.

Around Memorial Day 1996, Ortho held a biregional district meeting in Denver. Later, Mooney asked Barton to share a cab back to the airport. On the way, Mooney informed Barton that he was being demoted immediately and had three choices: take a sales position in Salt Lake City; move to another firm within the J&J family; or leave the company entirely. Barton accepted the demotion. But a few weeks later, after a very difficult spell, he resigned. Ortho gave him a generous severance package of nearly seven months' pay; in return, he agreed not to sue J&J. Before long, Raritan began searching for a new manager to live in Seattle.

When Duxbury learned of Barton's resignation, he called him to wish him well. His former boss was gracious, then paused. "Watch your back, Mark." Barton described the past few months of executive plotting, beginning with Mooney's bogus charges against Duxbury and his order to fire him. "My demotion," Barton explained, "was due largely to me refusing to fire you." For once Duxbury was speechless. Before he ended the call, Barton warned him again: "Be wary of George."

From that day on, Duxbury descended into a memorably horrid summer. Two weeks later, Renee called and invited him to lunch. Pleasantly surprised, the rep dressed up to meet her at a restaurant.

After placing his order, however, he was served with a restraining order preventing his visitations with Sojie. Renee worried that Duxbury's work troubles were impairing his fatherly duties. "You're putting so much pressure on Sojie, I'm concerned about her emotional well-being," she explained. Harsh words were flung across the table, until Duxbury abruptly left. He had to hire an attorney to defend himself against his ex-wife's allegations and wound up selling his favorite saxophone to pay his legal bills. But it was worth every penny. The following month, his visitation rights with his three-year-old daughter were restored, along with their Saturday morning ritual of watching *Blue's Clues* over bowls of milk and cereal rings.

—◆—

In August 1996, Duxbury's career took a puzzling turn. A rep from northern California named Keith Wood was promoted to Northwest District manager. The first sign that something was amiss was the fact that Wood was promoted at all, Duxbury thought. A slight, pale figure with red hair, Wood had maintained an undistinguished Ortho career. Moreover, he worked some eight hundred miles away from Seattle, in the San Francisco area, which was a hundred miles farther than Salt Lake City was. Duxbury ignored the signals.

He started off by giving Wood a tour of Swedish Medical Center and Seattle's Pill Hill, with its old buildings and stunning views of Elliott Bay. Duxbury provided a historical commentary of the neighborhood too. In the 1890s, it had been a leafy retreat for Seattle's upper crust. King County's first official courthouse had been built here, forcing attorneys to hike from their downtown offices up this steep hill, cursing all the way. They called the summit Profanity Hill until the courthouse moved, and now the spot was full of churches, universities, and medical facilities. Wood chuckled at all the right places in Duxbury's spiel. After accompanying him on his rounds, Wood took the rep aside.

"I know about the difficulties you're having with your ex," he said solicitously. To try and relieve some of the pressures, he was going to realign the rep's territory. "How nice," Duxbury thought. But a few weeks later, he saw the realignment, and his heart sank. Wood had shrunk his territory to a small fifty-mile area between South Seattle and Olympia. Even worse, his new turf excluded most of the oncology clinics in Seattle, Tacoma, and Olympia—the places he'd been serving for the past few years. Staring at the map, he realized, "This is clearly designed to make my sales figures look bad."

There was no time to take up the matter with Wood, as a few days later, Duxbury joined half of Ortho's national sales staff at a biregional meeting in Tucson. In the lobby of El Conquistador Golf and Tennis Resort, he met McClellan. After lugging their bags to their rooms, the two friends arranged a reconnaissance of the five-hundred-acre resort. They grabbed some drinks and a canopied golf cart, and tooled around the eighteen-hole golf course, the lush gardens, and the hiking trails in the Sonora Desert. As the hours passed, Duxbury experienced déjà vu. The setting sun turned the swimming pools into pewtered plates and the mountain's red outcroppings into charcoaled flames. In the ebbing light, his mind turned to that night in Palm Springs eighteen months ago, when he and his friends had glided over fairways after being honored by their chiefs. How Duxbury longed to recapture the mood from that magical desert trip!

This particular meeting was devoted to seminars revolving around 1996 sales objectives such as "Meeting our profit commitment to Johnson & Johnson by achieving our forecast." The most important goal seemed to be growing the "Phase IV trials" that could expand a new Procrit market.

Ortho often used "minitrials" and so-called Phase IV studies— postapproval studies—to promote its drug. In 1996, the big campaign centered on a "quality of life" trial. QOL, however, was an ambiguous term at best. A poor quality of life wasn't a disease per se. Rather it referred to symptoms ranging from physical ones, like fatigue and insomnia, to psychological ones, such as unhappiness and ennui. *Quality of life* was medically defined as the degree to which a person enjoys the possibilities of life, and Ortho's marketers contended that Procrit could induce a better QOL.

Amgen had already managed to squeeze that term onto Epogen's label, under the heading "Clinical Response to Epogen, Chronic Renal Failure." The product insert stated that Epogen patients experienced "statistically significant improvements" in most QOL parameters, such as more happiness and better sex. Ortho wanted a similar sentence under the cancer heading, and understandably so. By now, about one million Americans a year were diagnosed with cancer and they suffered from fatigue, poor quality of life, and anemia due to lack of iron, among other factors. *Imagine how Procrit sales would soar if we could promote our drug for those patients.*

But the company had two problems. One was the law. While doctors are free to prescribe medicine for any use and dosage they see fit, drug companies are forbidden from promoting a drug for indications not listed on the label. If caught pushing an off-label use, a company could pay a steep fine, suffer criminal sanctions, and even lose its license to sell products. The second problem was regulators. The FDA had approved Procrit only for chemotherapy-related anemia. As Dr. Patricia Keegan of the FDA explained, "The drug was approved so patients could avoid blood transfusions. And fatigue is *not* an indication." If J&J marketeers wanted to add QOL to the drug label, they'd have to provide compelling scientific evidence. So that's what they tried to do.

As early as 1994, Ortho began sending reps into oncologists' offices to try to persuade them to enroll patients in "minitrials" and Phase IV marketing studies. Unlike independent Phase IV scientific trials, these studies had no protocol, no efficacy or safety endpoint, lawsuits would later allege. These sales trials had no FDA registration numbers. Duxbury and McClellan claimed these fatigue studies were just a way to get doctors to prescribe the drug in a risky off-label manner.

Ortho paid each oncologist about $550 for every patient up to five, or nearly $3,000. The cash was supposed to compensate doctors and nurses for filling out the study's paperwork. But reps like McClellan routinely did that, reviewing confidential patient files to select the subjects and recording their personal information. "I got a good start on

[Dr. X's paperwork] this week and should be able to get five [patients] enrolled," McClellan reported to his bosses. It wasn't until years later that reps realized they'd been violating patient confidentiality laws.

The expensive national sales campaign convinced oncologists to enroll 2,300 of their patients in Ortho's study. A few doctors took grants of $10,000 and more to write articles about the QOL trial. In May 1994, the journal of the American Society of Clinical Oncology published one such piece, and, anticipating another, Ortho announced a "promotional preparation [and] SALES TRAINING!" to teach reps how to parlay the article into QOL drug orders.

Around the same time, Ortho found a well-respected researcher willing to write yet another piece about the QOL study. Dr. John Glaspy, a professor at the School of Medicine of the University of California, Los Angeles (UCLA), had taken grants from both Amgen and Ortho to study epo and its effects. Ortho surmised that if Glaspy's piece about its study landed in a prestigious medical journal, regulators might be persuaded to add QOL to Procrit's label.

So McClellan, Duxbury, and the others promoted the off-label use for fatigue. Years later, both men would learn that off-label promotion is a federal crime—something that the lawyers and leaders in New Jersey certainly should have known.

Throughout the week, Duxbury couldn't help but notice the disturbing number of new faces. At night in the bar of El Conquistador, he searched for old friends. But he couldn't find the reps who had sold so much Procrit for dialysis, nor those who'd testified in an Amgen case. "Didn't you hear?" McClellan asked. "A lot of those guys have been fired or resigned." The two estimated that about 50 percent of the sales force had been replaced by newcomers, many of them fresh out of college.

Every Ortho sales meeting came with a keynote address, and this time national sales manager Tom Amick took the podium to deliver a rousing one. In what would soon be called the "come to Jesus" speech, Amick sternly lectured the troops on ethics. He emphasized the importance of Amgen's litigation and how seriously it needed to be taken.

He scrunched his face into a scowl, paced the floor like a drill sergeant, and enunciated his words clearly. From this day forward, he barked, *market share* would no longer be used to measure sales performance. "Contrary to any previous understanding there is no such thing as 'market share,' only 'market share growth,' and anyone who tries to convert dialysis business will be terminated immediately." Sitting in the audience, Duxbury witnessed the backs of the assembled stiffen; a few shellacked heads swiveled to check their neighbors' response. Could this be true? The entire room of salespeople had just been put on notice that overall *epo growth* in their zone would be the *only* standard of performance. Exactly how that would impact bonuses had yet to be revealed, but insecurity settled on the crowd like smoke on artillery. Amick repeated himself in raspy, staccato bursts. "I never want to hear the words *dialysis* or *market share* again." *By the way,* he added, "there's been no infraction of the marketing agreement. And no one has lost their job because of that."

Duxbury leaned into McClellan and whispered, "What a bunch of BS." Later, in the bar, they joined other reps, who chortled over Amick's message about "fair play."

"That was an unbelievable performance," said one man. "What a joke!"

One rep reminded the group that Amick hadn't acted alone. "Longstreet and a lot of other people had the opportunity to stop the conversions, but they didn't." Duxbury just listened, nursing his drink. In this murmuring cave of speculation, he realized that none of these guys had as much to lose as he did, and, for the first time, he saw both sides of his impossible position. Over the years, he'd received numerous *written* advisos indicating that Procrit should not be promoted or sold for dialysis use. At the same time, he (and others) had been given *verbal* orders to do the exact opposite. Duxbury had tried to leave a trail of his objections to those orders, only now it hit him: Amick, Pearson, and other leaders had been conspicuously silent on the issue, at least on paper. How clever of the professionals, he thought.

Another water-cooler item bubbled up. There was talk that Raritan wanted to erase dialysis sales from all forecasts. If true, it didn't console Duxbury. William Ball, Michael Barton, Bob Nelson, and a lot of other people who were no longer at Ortho had tried to eliminate those sales years ago. "That idea's been driven from the bottom up, not from the top down," he told McClellan. But coming from headquarters, it sounded like money laundering—washing past sales from official records. Duxbury grew worried.

—⚏—

A LINE of buses pulled to a stop on the back side of the Santa Catalina Mountains, behind El Conquistador, and disgorged about a hundred pharmaceutical salespeople amid the dust, exhaust, and diesel fumes. Once the air cleared, Duxbury, McClellan, and their friends smiled. They were all dressed casually and several people wore Western gear of Levi's, Tony Lama boots, Stetsons, and bandannas. The group was corralled toward an open bar and barbecue grill, where the grease of red meat splattered onto hot coals. An organizer welcomed them with trays of cold drinks and announced that, after the cookout, they'd move to the shooting range for the highlight of the evening, a quick-draw contest. The crowd buzzed over the prospect of a Wild West gun-slinging competition.

Contestants were given authentic holsters to wear. The leather sat low on the hip and angled down on one side where the gun hung. The bottom of the holster had a rawhide thong that tied around the thigh, so that when you drew your gun, your holster would remain in place. Organizers handed out real Colt Single Action Army revolvers, which had been the weapon of choice in the West since the 1870s, when the Colt SAA was introduced. Some called the guns Peacemakers, but Duxbury preferred the term *Equalizer* because "having a Colt on your hip made you equal to any man." They had cylinders that tilted out of the frame for loading, but these revolvers held not real bullets but blanks. "When I shoot, I like to make sure I hit something," Duxbury complained.

"Like a sales target?" someone ribbed, and his circle burst out laughing.

"I'm trained for accuracy, not speed," he replied good-naturedly. On occasion, he'd spend a Sunday afternoon at a firing range, shooting five hundred rounds of ammo. But he didn't perform well in quick-draw contests, which would be clear soon enough. He, McClellan, and the others grabbed some drinks while they eyed the juicy steaks on the grill. Here was a chuckwagon buffet as envisioned by corporate team builders: smooth wooden benches arranged around tables of checkered cloth; lanterns propped up on boulders and stumps; aluminum pots of steaming buffalo chili, cowboy beans, and Indian fry bread. After dinner, the crowd was divided according to region, then split further into districts. Each team faced off against another, and after a few rounds, the Seattle District was eliminated, much to Duxbury's relief. "Now I can sit back and enjoy the show." It was at times like these that Duxbury reveled in the emotionally satisfying bond of his fellow reps. Lone-star sales folks and deputized detailers could face off against one another in lighthearted diversions that didn't threaten one another's survival. As Duxbury looked around, he saw J&J's drug distributors thoroughly enjoying themselves on the edge of the Mexican border, drinking, singing, and shooting *pistolas* into the clear night.

McClellan, meanwhile, was on his fourth drink when he took another turn. Each shooter had to wait for a light to appear; that was the signal to pull the trigger. The pistols were single action, meaning that you had to pull the hammer back to cock the gun while you drew it from the holster, then fire when the muzzle was aligned with its target. Dueling against McClellan was his boss, Dwayne Marlowe, who at one point handed the rep yet another drink, hoping that more liquor would skewer his aim. McClellan cheerily accepted the cocktail, took a sip, drew his gun, and hit the cardboard bull's-eye. "Ah," the crowd exclaimed, not quite believing what it had just seen. Marlowe seemed to be getting mad: The more McClellan drank, the faster he drew. Pretty soon it was just the two of them standing in the dirt, McClellan and Marlowe, going mano a mano. The boss stopped, got himself a glass of water, and brought his opponent another gin and tonic, his sixth drink of the night. Each man gulped from his glass and waited. The green light flashed and Marlowe drew. But by that time, McClellan had already pulled his gun out of the holster, cocked the hammer, aimed, and fired. He hit the target dead center in 0.48 of a second, less than a half a second, beating his boss by a long shot and winning the evening contest. The crowd erupted in cheers, and Duxbury ran over to shake his buddy's hand. McClellan took home a bronze plaque—and Marlowe's enmity.

9

Blues

LONG, oyster-colored strings of rain fell from the sky, hitting the pavement like pieces of cracked shell. Duxbury was driving out of the remote westernmost corner of Washington, passing small fleets of stern trawlers and trap setters that rocked in synch with the Charlie Parker tune pouring out of his tape deck. As the storm hailed down, the typically optimistic salesman tried to concentrate on the up-tempo, twelve-bar rhythm. Any minute now, his favorite song would jump-start the circuits in his brain, activating the dopamine cells that would spread pleasure sensations throughout his body. Duxbury concentrated on the music, its beat echoed by the car's windshield wipers, the passing trucks' tire flaps, and the gushing drainpipes that hung from the wind-beaten buildings. Bebop ran circles around the basic eight-note approach to music, and the musician loved how Parker's blues changes defied the standard metronome. Duxbury himself had mastered the complicated notes of "Chi-Chi" on the saxophone, and those chords always filled him with a sense of possibility. He had spent this Sunday alone on the wild, sparsely populated western coast, walking the wave-wracked beaches and forest sanctuaries. As a kid, he had chased shorebirds along this stretch of sea, poked pieces of driftwood into the mudflats, and fearlessly swum the waters that crashed against the rocks. Most summers his parents had brought him, his brother, and his sister here for vacations, and every season Duxbury had performed some daredevil feat. Here is where he had always felt invincible and fully alive. But after spending the day on the treacherous coast, jazz riffs running through his brain, he felt only melancholy. It was late, and heading east from Grays Harbor, it seemed as if the wipers, the truck flaps, and everything else around him were getting juiced on "Chi-Chi." Not him. The one song and place that usually brought him joy had abandoned him.

His thoughts were tangled. For one thing, the new boss was riding him hard. Usually, managers followed reps on their rounds once a quarter or when there was a big presentation afoot. But Keith Wood scheduled regular visits with Duxbury and shadowed him so vigilantly, he felt as if headquarters were watching him through a one-way observational mirror. It was surreal, this caged feeling, especially since the Northwest District manager didn't seem to be working with anyone else. Indeed, other reps in the district actually *complained* about the lack of guidance they received from Wood. At times, Duxbury felt as if he had his own personal tormentor.

Still, he tried to give Wood the benefit of the doubt. Duxbury had started the year with lofty goals, along with a "hot list" of thirty retail accounts that frequently purchased epo without specifying Ortho's brand. The rep tracked these numbers through DDD reports, tracing each epo sale back to the buyer. If he found that a script had been written for Epogen, Duxbury visited the doctor to persuade him of Procrit's higher financial yields. So far, after a few months in this retail sector, he had managed to dominate 65 percent of that market. As for hospital conversions, he had made headway with the elite Swedish Medical Center, thanks in part to a $15,000 grant he had given its researcher Saul Rivkin. The center had already started twenty of its patients on Procrit, but then its purchasing group had left, and Duxbury had to start all over again with a new gatekeeper. A similar thing had happened with the Veterans Administration facility, and Duxbury's goal of growing his hospital sales 30 percent by year's end now looked impossible. Still, he was king of that group, owning 83 percent of that business.

All in all, he believed he was doing well. His weekly reports were on time, his office was more organized and open for inspection, and he continued receiving bonus checks and gifts for his "remarkable growth"—including one for obtaining the highest retails sales in his district. Duxbury was on track to make nearly $100,000 this year.

He didn't claim to be perfect; his expense reports were sometimes tardy. But Wood harped on this weakness constantly, noting the inadequacy of the rep's last four reports. Duxbury reviewed those papers and found that most of the "errors" stemmed from a lack of explanation, not a shortage of receipts. "But we live in a no-error environment, and I will take my lumps," he told Wood.

In the midst of all this, Renee sued him again, and Duxbury wound up with a more rigid custody schedule. He spent some weekends and every Wednesday evening with Sojie, and had to pick her up from day care between five and five-thirty, no exceptions. The designated place for transferring the child was the police station near Renee's house. If Duxbury needed to leave town at a time when he was scheduled to be with Sojie, he now had to notify his ex-wife *in writing* at least three days prior to departure. He also had to verify that his trip was business related. "Acceptable proof would be travel tickets issued by [Ortho]," she stipulated. He was prohibited from telephoning Renee except in an emergency; otherwise there was *no* flexibility in the new arrangement.

As if that weren't enough, Renee also wanted to see his pay stubs and income tax returns to "determine if child support should be readjusted." Sojie's mother wanted to get more money at a time when her child's father was straining to increase his income. If stress could be squared, Duxbury would embody the equation.

—⚹—

Duxbury stood on a balcony of his condo overlooking downtown Seattle and reminded himself that repeats matter. He slowly exhaled the last, treble-clef note from his saxophone, and a moan filled the air. (Or was that a horn from a houseboat below?) He waited out the pause. Then he blew again, pulling from deep inside himself, letting the note linger in the air, pushing the sound down to the shore, where it slipped into the water. After an hour of practice, he cradled his sax and rested in the moonless night.

Music was Duxbury's balm, and he had his father to thank for that. Duane Duxbury Sr. had loved music and had yearned to play professionally. But months of shooting M13s in the National Guard without protective ear guards had ruined his hearing. Plus, let's face it, the man didn't have "the touch." So he spent his life teaching music to public school children and private students. Yet he had never met a child with the natural gifts that his own son possessed. When Duxbury was three years old, he could handle a flute; when he was eight, his father gave him an E-clarinet because the tyke couldn't reach B-flat on a standard instrument. Mark's fingers had leapt along the spine of the "kinder-clari," producing clear, bright notes. His hands did the same thing on other wind instruments—the oboe, trombone, horn, flute, and tuba. He could play piano and guitar. But it was on the saxophone that Duxbury could really swing.

His dad had been determined to see his son make something out of his God-given talent. "I was funneled into music," Duxbury would say later. He was forbidden to play any sports because of the risks of injuring his face and hands, and most afternoons, after three-thirty, the former National Guardsman would run his sons, Duane junior and Mark, through the scales. The older boy spent hours painfully practicing. But the younger one easily advanced; he could read sheet music, play complicated numbers, and breathe in a circular manner to lengthen his notes. Music had made him a leader. During football season at Olympia High School, the smartly dressed drum major would march his band onto the field, whistle them into formation, and conduct rousing sets for the crowd. Later, when Duxbury formed a trio, his dad built a studio so the boys could record their idiosyncratic blend of jazz and bluegrass. Duane senior pushed his son to join the Washington All-State Band, among others, and to compete in Northwest music contests, where his boy earned top soloist performance honors—three times.

As Duxbury grew older, however, music became his bane. "My dad was a frustrated musician who tried to live vicariously through me," Duxbury later said. He'd always been a difficult man who fought with his own kin, said an uncle, Alyn. "He was a perfectionist who'd turn apoplectic over pretty minor things. And he didn't cut anybody any slack." When Duxbury turned fourteen, Duane senior turned his hypercritical glare on his son, calling him "lazy" for not practicing more. He sneered at the teenager's Spyro Gyra albums and ridiculed his taste. When Duxbury took home a report card that read "Not working to capacity," his father almost threw him against the wall. At sixteen, Duxbury ran away from home to live with a professional photographer and his wife in town.

Yet music endowed him with full-ride musical scholarship offers from four colleges. Duxbury accepted one from Washington State University but, after two years, left and took another one from the University of Washington. There he played lead tenor saxophone in the school's jazz ensemble, replacing a guy named Kenny Gorelich, who'd later be known as Grammy Award winner Kenny G. Bored, Duxbury then switched to yet another school, Evergreen College, and moved home. That's when the boy who had once examined dying dragonflies in a jar decided to study medicine. He signed up as a double major, adding premed. But when his father heard this, he sat his son down and said, "If you get your music major, I'll pay for everything, and you can continue to live here for free. But," he added, his dark eyes turning stormy, "if you follow through on this premed [nonsense], you'll have to get your butt out of this house by Monday morning." Duxbury left that weekend. On Monday, he began taking science and math classes. He supported himself by giving private music lessons—just as his father had once done. But after a particularly cold winter living in a damp basement, Duxbury gave up. With only three science classes to go, he dropped out of the premed program and graduated with a bachelor of arts in music performance/life science.

For years, Duxbury had resented his dad, but fatherhood had pulled the thorns from his boyhood memories. "My dad had worked like a dog for thirty years, providing for his family, until he retired at the age of fifty-one," Duxbury realized. A year into his retirement, in 1982, Duane senior fell while digging a septic tank at his vacation home in Ocean Shores, Washington. He'd had a stroke and lost some cognitive function. With the help of his wife, Faye, he slowly regained his ability to read, drive, and walk. He even took up painting. But a decade later, he was felled by another stroke. Afflicted now with Crohn's disease, he became a "medical nightmare," said Duxbury. Faye continued caring for her husband until the day she came home from work and found him on the bathroom floor. He'd lain there for five hours, wedged between the toilet and the sink, crying in vain. That's when Faye moved him into an assisted care facility, a place he called "hell."

Duxbury occasionally visited him on Sundays. The first time he took Sojie, he wasn't sure how his bigoted father would react to his biracial granddaughter. But he needn't have worried; the moment Duane senior saw the little girl, he was smitten. Duxbury watched the two play make-believe, astonished at his father's newfound tenderness. "I never thought I'd hear Dad sing 'The Big Bird Song,'" he told his mother.

I N late October, Wood surprised his salesman with an overnight package containing the last four months of his expenses and a memo outlining his alleged mistakes. His boss repeated the claims that Duxbury's receipts didn't match his listed expenses, some receipts were "missing," and his odometer readings were "incomplete." Some of Wood's criticisms were contradictory. Duxbury, for example, had used a Visa card instead of American Express because one vendor didn't accept the latter. Yet Wood scolded him. "Begin using vendors that accept this card, and use your Visa or personal check as necessary," which is exactly what Duxbury had done. Wood's memo also contained several grammatical and spelling mistakes—he addressed his letter to "Marc" rather than Mark—and Duxbury felt the entire exercise was so trivial, he didn't bother to respond.

Instead, he decided to show Wood the solid relationships he had developed with his clients. One day, the two were scheduled to call on Swedish Medical Center. For the occasion, Duxbury donned a new silk tie painted with flesh-colored pills, a blue-tipped thermometer, and a box of gauze stamped with Johnson & Johnson's red logo: STERILE, the box read. Duxbury was so tickled by his serendipitous find, he thought that Wood, a stickler for detail, would be amused too. But his boss didn't even comment. The rep drove him to Swedish Medical and parked on a knoll overlooking downtown. He waited for Wood to get out, but instead of accompanying Duxbury on the call, the manager begged off. "I need to do some work; I'll just stay here in the car," he said.

Duxbury shrugged, walked inside the building, and started to make his rounds. The $15,000 grant money Ortho had given Swedish had helped induce the center to buy about $100,000 worth of Procrit. Duxbury checked with the staff to make sure the patients were responding; he dropped by the back office to make sure insurers were reimbursing it at the retail price; he talked to a few doctors, trying in ways both subtle and direct to move them toward a bigger order. An hour or so later, Duxbury returned to his car and found Wood reading something on Duxbury's computer. He immediately saw that someone had rummaged through his briefcase; it was splayed open in the backseat, amid a scattering of his personal papers. Wood had also removed Duxbury's laptop from its case, unlocked his security code, and clicked through his documents. The rep knew that because, at that moment, his boss was reading the résumé that Duxbury stored on his laptop. Stunned, the rep blurted out, "Keith, are you spying on me? You have no right to look at my personal papers!"

Wood looked up and nonchalantly said, "You don't own this laptop, the company does. As your supervisor, I'm entitled to see what's on it."

Duxbury barely controlled his rage. He climbed into the driver's seat and savagely twisted his key in the ignition. As he drove Wood back to the airport, the miles passed in icy silence. Duxbury left Wood at the curb, but on the way home his anger turned to fear. There was no denying that Ortho was trying to get rid of him, and from that point on, Duxbury grew hypervigilant. Every time he headed into a client's office, he looked over his shoulder. Every time he returned from a sales call, he inspected the exterior, interior, and belly of his car, searching for any sign of tampering or surveillance . . . or worse.

—m—

ON November 1, Wood met Duxbury to formally review his performance; Duxbury was expected to rate himself, too, using Ortho's five-point scale that ranged from outstanding to unacceptable. Wood spoke for twenty minutes or so, referring often to his handwritten notes, and Duxbury realized with a sinking heart that Wood's assessment of his performance was worlds away from his own. The salesman had rated himself superior or competent in nearly every category, based on comparable figures in his district. But Wood castigated him for missing his original ambitious goal of growing sales in the hospital, retail, and alternate-care sectors. He was especially critical of Duxbury's weekly activity and expense reports, which were "well below standard." That was the only one of six categories that the boss and his charge agreed on. Wood's other ratings were "garbage," Duxbury thought.

Then, just when the rep thought that things couldn't get any worse, Wood gave him a blank review form. "Sign it," he ordered. Duxbury was shocked; Wood just sat across the table, a snarl clenched in his jaw. Duxbury's mind spun through the various moves he could make. If he didn't sign the form, Wood would get mad and devise another trap for Duxbury. After all, he could add whatever he wanted to the blank form, after the fact. If the rep *did* sign the sheet, he might mollify his boss long enough to inform headquarters about Wood's outrageous ploy. So, without a word, Duxbury signed it. A few weeks later, he received a copy of his review, only this time the blanks had been filled in with Wood's heinous scores. Duxbury had rated himself "superior" in his hospital category, not unreasonable given his 83 percent share, and "competent" in all areas except administration, where he admitted he "needs improvement." Overall, he considered himself competent. Wood, however, had marked him competent in only two skills and below standard in the others. He'd branded the rep as "needs improvement," one rung above "unacceptable," the point at which they push you off the train.

Duxbury reread his boss's summation, terror coating the roof of his mouth. He lit a cigarette, paced the floor, and resumed his seat. After a conference with his knees, he raised his face toward his own ego wall, where some of his awards and commendations hung in gilded frames. "Jesus," he said aloud. "How did this happen?" He never thought he'd end up like this, a has-been at thirty-six. For the next few mornings, he got up and dressed for work as usual, in starched shirts and wool slacks. But gone were the days when the self-assured man sat on the compensation committee in Raritan, contributing his advice. He no longer soaked up high-level computer training so he could edify his peers in new technology. That fall, Wood also stripped him of his district computer specialist title. As if to underscore the rep's new lowly status, he also demoted him from Seattle project leader to just another team player. Duxbury girded himself for what he thought was coming and started calling corporate headhunters.

—⚏—

"Wood's doing some funny things with my numbers."

"Like what?" McClellan asked.

"Turning big ones into little ones." Duxbury explained how he believed his boss was rigging his accounts to make him look bad. Some of his retail sales, for instance, were lower than the national average. Yet his overall market share was unusually high, and that's what counted, he told McClellan. "Figures are supposed to be hard and fast."

"Not in this business," McClellan replied. The veteran salesman had witnessed many ways in which companies shift facts to fit a desired outcome. Of late, he had begun to suspect that Ortho was doing the same to him, but he kept his notions to himself.

"Keith is playing games with me, and I don't like it," Duxbury groused.

"Now, hold on there, Mark. Don't confront him. Just hang on for a while."

"And then what?"

"Look." McClellan tried the reasonable approach. Thanksgiving's just around the corner, then Christmas will arrive with a long break. "After that, things will settle down." Any day now, the FDA was expected to approve Procrit for elective surgery patients, who tend to lose blood during their operations. Instead of transfusions, surgical patients would soon be able to get 40,000 units of Procrit to help boost their hemoglobin levels. "So," McClellan concluded, "we're going to be busy promoting the new surgical use. Keith won't have a lot of time to play any games."

"I don't know . . . ," said Duxbury, sounding unconvinced.

"Don't rock the boat," McClellan said sternly.

Duxbury made it to the last week of November. He had four days of rest ahead of him, until Monday, December 2, when he was scheduled to fly to San Francisco for a district meeting. But the night before Thanksgiving, Wood telephoned to tell the rep to stay late Monday night in San Francisco. "I want to spend some time alone with you after the district meeting," Wood explained.

Duxbury panicked. He had a few past-due expense reports and a messy storage locker, which, in an extreme case like this, could be grounds for dismissal. Sensing that he was to be fired, he called the only other person who had a vested interest in his job: Renee. "This is an emergency," he started off. "You've got to help me." He explained his abysmal job rating, the unfinished reports, and disorganized car trunk and locker. A hush filled the line; if her ex-husband lost his job, she'd lose financial support. Renee agreed to help stave off the crisis. A day or so after Thanksgiving, she spent nearly eight hours helping Duxbury re-create the last few weeks of travel, organizing his receipts, recording his mileage, and describing every jot and nickel. The next day, they drove to Duxbury's storage locker, where she helped stack Ortho brochures, systematize boxes of Procrit mugs and pens, and label other material, in case his superiors surprised him with a visit.

Duxbury went to bed Sunday evening but tossed all night. Hours before dawn, he got up, dressed, and drove to the airport, where he boarded the flight to San Francisco. Arriving early for Wood's district meeting, he handed his boss an envelope containing all of his overdue reports. The manager looked startled once he realized the package's contents, but he didn't smile or nod. Instead, Wood started the meeting, whose big topic, sure enough, was promoting the new 40,000-unit surgical dose of Procrit. At the end of the day, other reps headed back to their offices or to the airport; Duxbury stayed behind. Then, Wood handed him an envelope.

"I'm giving you a warning letter, which I want you to sign."

Duxbury read the rehash of the same old concerns about his lax paperwork, the way his car "reflected a state of disorganization," and how he'd been late to a meeting three months earlier, which was not "the first time he'd been late." His sins and failings sounded like a broken record, framed in the most serious way. A "verbal warning will become part of your personnel record," Wood explained—the same personnel record that Duxbury had been trying for months to obtain. The warning would remain on file for a year. If the employee showed "consistent improvement in both field and administrative activities," the black letter would be removed from his file. Otherwise, it could lead to "further disciplinary action." It had been copied to three other managers.

But all Duxbury saw was that his status had been downgraded to "Does not meet standards"—the second lowest grade on Ortho's totem pole. That made him ineligible for bonuses, which represented 40 percent of his income. The only bright note was that Wood repeated his pledge to Duxbury: If the rep solved his problems within ninety days, he'd be reinstated to competence and could jump back on track.

—⚭—

DUXBURY's rivals, the ones at Amgen, were flailing too. Reps at that firm could sell only to anemic dialysis patients, and by now, 90 percent of those people were getting Epogen. Amgen's market was saturated, its sales couldn't grow much bigger, and Wall Street analysts feared that the ballyhooed biotech firm had lost its edge. Ortho, however, was booming. Its reps were promoting Procrit not just for nondialysis and AIDS patients, but also off-label for fatigued cancer patients. Very soon, Ortho's epo sales would eclipse those of Amgen, the inventor and patent owner of the wonder drug.

Amgen hoped that results from its Normal Hematocrit Cardiac Trial (NHCT), a scientific randomized study, would rejuvenate its brand. Did a higher dose of Epogen equal a better quality of life for dialysis patients? As it was, Epogen's label limited dosage to achieve hemoglobin levels of 10 to 12 g/dl. But Amgen tested its thesis by giving elderly renal patients higher doses to push hemoglobin to 13 and even 14 g/dl, and hematocrit to 42 percent—the numbers of a healthy young woman. Tragically, the NHCT didn't deliver. Patients in the high-dose, high-target group suffered *more* deaths and heart attacks than those treated with the low goal of 10 g/dl. Indeed, the results were so fatal, a safety monitoring board stopped Amgen's trial.

For years, anecdotal evidence of epo-injected horses galloping to death, "hopped up" greyhounds falling down, and Dutch cyclists dying from epo overdoses had plagued Epogen, Procrit, and Eprex. Now, Amgen's own study showed an undeniable and fatal health risk associated with these drugs. But rather than issue a stern public warning, the FDA simply revised the product label: Doctors could increase risks and fatalities if they dosed up patients to hemoglobin levels of 12 g/dl and higher. That was it.

When Duxbury and McClellan heard about Amgen's study, they shook their heads. Shame on Amgen for giving old men with renal and symptomatic heart diseases high doses in the first place, said Duxbury. "You couldn't have picked a worse class of patient for that trial," McClellan said.

The aborted study impacted Ortho's plans. In 1996, it had submitted an FDA application for a new, high-dose indication for its drug. The J&J division had conducted a Phase IV trial, injecting high doses of 40,000 units into young, healthy subjects. Ortho wanted permission to sell its high-dose therapy as a way to reduce potential blood transfusions for anemic patients scheduled for one-time noncardiac, nonvascular elective surgery. But after the NHCT fiasco, Ortho's high-dose proposal looked dicey too. In fact, the FDA was so concerned, it extended the review period for Ortho's application, pending more safety data about the new indication. This was not a good sign.

But Webb, in a July 24, 1996, memo, assured her reps the delay meant nothing. Ortho's proposed hemoglobin target for the new therapy wouldn't exceed 13 g/dl and the high dose was supposed to be limited to a *onetime* injection. "We remain confident, based on our submission and the many conversations and productive relationships we've been able to maintain with some key FDA reviewers, that our application is sound and strong, and that sometime during the third or fourth quarter of this year, we will have approval to market Procrit for this [surgery] indication."

Surprisingly, Webb turned out to be right. In December 1996, the FDA approved a onetime 40,000-unit Procrit injection for anemic surgical patients only, giving Ortho the lead. Ortho would try to flip this regulatory approval into an even larger pool of unsuspecting patients, but that scheme was still to come. At the time, however, both Amgen and Ortho were told to complete studies about the connection between epo and potentially fatal blood clots. The dejected Amgen researchers had to return to the laboratory to find something, *anything*, that would hoist their brand higher than their rival's.

Lost in this pharma arms race was any word about the risks of epo at already approved low doses and hematocrit targets. Where was that science-based, randomized, controlled safety study? The FDA was still waiting. . . .

—⁓—

THAT winter, Duxbury minded his p's and q's. He rarely wore a flamboyant tie, didn't tell any jokes, and walked in lockstep with the other reps, as McClellan had advised. He smoked more cigarettes, which serrated his voice to a raspy lower octave, and ate poorly, if at all, which turned his already pale cast to paraffin. If he had once grown pudgy from all those pizza lunches and martini dinners, he now lost weight. His nights were sleepless, and morning left him with dark circles below bloodshot eyes. Yet, for ninety whole days, from December to February, he was a zero-defect robo-rep, the sort of guy he had once mocked. He didn't complain—and neither did his boss Wood. Duxbury had clearly improved in his field and administrative duties, and his sales were up too. In February 1997, he packed his suitcase for a national sales meeting in Charlotte, North Carolina, expecting to be reinstated to the Wolf Pack, with bonuses and full privileges.

On opening night of the four-day-long Ortho conference, four hundred good-looking conventioneers drifted genially through a softly lit room. Duxbury hesitated on the perimeter of the arena, probing for the mood and personalities in this ocean. He took in the scene: The tables were decorated with strange papier-mâché creatures and phantasmagoric arrangements of flowers that gave off a cloying smell. There was the distinct whiff of singles bar action too: Pretty young female reps, whom Ortho veterans called Pharma Barbies, promenaded near the center of the floor, while buff young men, "Ken dolls," cruised the outer ring. These were the recent college graduates who had replaced so many experienced salespeople in the past year, disheartening the remaining veterans. Duxbury circled the rim in search of a friendly face. *Swoosh*. There was the orca-size director of special assignments. *Swoosh*. There was a pod of managed-care executives, whose expense accounts paid for nightly trays of caviar and champagne. *Swoosh, swoosh*. There was Amick moving toward Pearson and a few others from headquarters, colorful drakes whom Duxbury would just as soon avoid. He jumped into the crowd and swam past the gold chains, signet rings, and clinking glasses of wine and ale. Here, within the well-lubricated pit, Duxbury heard the ping of serious money. They said that Procrit had just hit the $1 billion sales mark; if true, that meant this crowd of sharks and minnows had collectively gone from zero to ten figures in just six years—an astonishing feat no matter where you stood. Duxbury waded deeper into the waters to find a friend.

This national meeting was a pivotal one. Early in the session, the troops were treated to a presentation by the legendary Peter T. Tattle, the group chairman for J&J's pharmaceuticals in the Americas. Tattle had started as a sales representative for Ortho Pharmaceutical Canada in 1965, climbing the rungs of sales, marketing, and product management on both domestic and international ladders. Now, at the top, he was responsible for all pharmaceutical businesses in the Americas, including Ortho-McNeil Pharmaceutical, Janssen Pharmaceutical, Janssen-Ortho in Canada, Ortho Biotech in the United States, and pharmaceutical businesses in Mexico and the rest of Latin America. He lived in Princeton, New Jersey, contributed to conservative causes through a political action committee called J&J Employees' Good Government Fund, and sailed a yacht. After an effusive introduction, he stepped onstage to a burst of applause. Then he made a chilling statement. "Will all non–J&J employees please leave the room?" Duxbury and McClellan exchanged sharp looks; a few reporters and vendors walked out. Tattle issued another command: "Please turn off any recording devices." A few mechanical clicks ricocheted around the room. Finally, he signaled for the lights to be killed; then he launched into a brisk slide show about the global performance of J&J's enormous drug business. Duxbury was fascinated to learn some facts and made a few discreet notes with his gravity-defying Fisher Space Pen, the same model used during man's first moon landing in 1969. Hunched over his knees, McClellan scribbled away in the dark with his special-order, military-issue flashlight pen. No one else seemed to be taking notes of this momentous lecture, and at one point, the Tucson rep whispered to his Seattle friend, "I don't understand why everything J and J says is such a big secret."

When the last slide clicked off, Tattle signaled to someone behind the curtain. The room remained dark, but a spotlight flicked on to illuminate the chairman. In an informal yet somber manner, the pharmaceutical chief described the importance of J&J's image: the folksy, 110-year-old, blue-chip icon that every mother trusts. Lately, however, several events had sullied that image and embarrassed the board's directors.

First, Tattle said, Ortho Dermatologics had illegally promoted its acne product, Retin-A, for facial wrinkles. Under the law, a doctor can prescribe a drug for nearly anything, but a company can promote products only for FDA-approved uses; otherwise, this member of the Dow Jones Industrial Average Index was no different than a flimflam man pushing snake oil. When the FDA learned of Ortho Dermatologic's alleged crime, it subpoenaed its sales documents. But instead of handing over thousands of pages as required, company mandarins destroyed them. In 1995, the unit was sentenced by the U.S. District Court of New Jersey on charges of obstructing justice. It also settled Justice Department charges, paid $7.5 million in fines and restitution, and received an FDA reprimand. Destroying documents to thwart a federal investigation was pretty outrageous and had generated bad publicity. Tattle listed a few other scandals: J&J reps had been caught stealing documents about a rival's product launch; a J&J employee had stolen a copy of a confidential study protocol for another competitor's new product; J&J Consumer Products division had settled Federal Trade Commission charges that it had exaggerated the failure rate of condoms while advertising its own spermicidal jelly, K-Y Plus Nonoxynol-9. Tattle complained to the Ortho crew just how expensive it was to defend such shameful, high-profile cases.

Oddly enough, the chairman of J&J's pharmaceuticals didn't mention the elephant in the room. J&J was facing the prospect of a yet another headline-worthy scandal that was incubating right here in this crowd. Subpoenas, stealing sales, illegal promotions; Duxbury at the time was thinking of Amgen's claims against Ortho. But years later, he'd look back at this moment and realize he'd gotten it all wrong. It wasn't the dialysis conversion that would shock nursing mothers or even Peter Tattle. No. It was the Procrit scheme that Duxbury, McClellan, and the other reps were promoting: parlaying the FDA-approved, 40,000 unit, onetime dose for surgery patients into the nationwide sales launch of an unapproved, high-dose regimen for all cancer patients. Ortho's off-label cancer promotions were about to escalate and, if discovered, could crack J&J's venerable image beyond repair.

—◆—

ON the last night of this meeting, Duxbury and McClellan walked into a grand room that was crackling with live jazz music. Webb and Amick were personally welcoming members of the sales force to this blowout party, and the New York City band, with its horns, percussion, and cymbals, lent an air of cool sophistication to the Ortho congregation. Platters of hors d'oeuvres circulated, the open bar grew thick, and the posturing from the opening night had been amped up several notches, along with the pulsating bass of the live band. When it was clear that most of Ortho's reps had squeezed into this room, a radiant-looking Webb stood up to the microphone: Procrit sales had hit $1 billion in 1996! As a result, she said, everyone would soon get a $2,500 bonus and . . . The rest of her words were drowned out by war whoops and shrill screams. McClellan and Duxbury exchanged high-fives, and McClellan began describing a new boat he'd been eyeing. Duxbury didn't want to assume he'd get a bonus. So, drink in hand, he wandered around the room to get confirmation.

He found Wood standing in a circle of managers that included Pearson. "Hi, Keith," he began. The band launched into a funky dance number, and bodies crowded onto the floor, their hips gyrating to the music. Duxbury couldn't hear a word of what Pearson was saying, and shrugged his shoulders to indicate that while pointing to the animated dancers. Then he leaned into Wood's ear so his boss could him clearly. "I've complied with your requests." *My sales and administrative work are up to par, and I should be taken off probation.* Duxbury added, "I expect I'll be eligible for this bonus."

Wood looked at him. "I'll let you know," he shouted. Just then the band struck up a soul tune, and Pearson, George Mooney, and the other managers bobbed their heads to the beat. Then Wood swung around to face Duxbury.

"Say! Why don't you play the saxophone with the band?"

"I can't do that."

"C'mon, it'll greatly impress management. Besides," he added, looking genuinely friendly, "it'll help get you off probation."

Duxbury's stomach churned. He didn't like command performances; his dad had forced him into too many acts, and this was an especially tough crowd of critics. But if one turn on the saxophone would get him off probation, he'd try it. He waited for the band to take a break, then walked onstage. He sheepishly explained the situation to the saxophone player and motioned to the floor where his bosses stood, looking at him expectantly. The other band members drew near to listen. The rep's request was unusual, but the musicians came up with a tune they could play with a stranger. Duxbury offered to sanitize the instrument's mouthpiece by soaking it in a glass of Maker's Mark whiskey, and the drummer chortled. But Duxbury was serious, so someone brought a glass of whiskey to the bandstand. The saxophonist handed over his instrument to the drug rep, who bowed. After tasting the whiskey to ensure its bona fides, Duxbury plunked the mouthpiece into the glass, then jawed some more with the band. When it was time to strike up again, the band leader used the microphone to introduce Duxbury.

The band opened with a blues number, grooving in a fine interplay. Then the focus switched to solo improvisations. The keyboardist caressed his notes; the drummer nailed a polyrhythmic interlude; the bassist wrangled his upright instrument like it was an alligator struggling to slip into Delta mud. Then the musicians all stepped back and left Duxbury alone in the spotlight. With his feet slightly apart and his eyes closed, he played a four-chord blues riff. He began to sway, his body moving back and forth with the spontaneous notes. He hunched his shoulders and bent like a reed in the wind, the better to slide into the high scales. He nearly dropped to his knees and ripped out an intervallic scream. It sounded like he was pouring out his pent-up pain into a few haunting tones, all the while inching closer to the edge of the stage. McClellan felt goose bumps prickle his arms. He looked over and saw Wood's mouth fall open. Even the half-soused audience stood still, like parishioners in the presence of a snake-handling preacher. Duxbury seemed oblivious to them all. With his eyes closed, he belted out the last bewitching note, blowing for all he was worth, allowing the final note to fill the room before dying.

There was a hush . . . followed by a roar. Those who had been sitting now jumped up to give the salesman-musician a standing ovation.

Men wolf-whistled; women raised clapping hands above their dizzy heads. The applause lasted for what seemed like minutes and a lobster-faced Duxbury climbed down from the stage, uncharacteristically embarrassed. "I feel like a trained seal in a circus," he thought.

A group rushed up to him. Men pumped his hand, women stroked his arm, and everyone exclaimed, "Dux! That was wonderful!" Even his scrawny boss pushed close and blurted out, "Jesus, Mark. I had no idea you could do that."

Duxbury graciously accepted the accolades. But the room began to close in on him. He had never intended to reveal this side of himself, and a part of him resented it. "This had better be worth it," he thought. He scanned the room and realized that *everyone* was smiling at him, including Wood, Pearson, and other executives. Duxbury smiled back wanly. *Set me free*, he wanted to shout. *You can't keep me on probation indefinitely!* Duxbury set out to find McClellan and moved awkwardly through the crowd.

10

Quality of Life

SOMEONE once said that jazz music is an intensified feeling of non-chalance. No doubt Duxbury had a gift for music. But now, in the aftermath of his knockout debut at Ortho's last national meeting, he realized that he needed to transfer his intense feeling for the blues to saving his day job. He became ferociously disciplined on the surface, filing timely reports, calling on accounts, and practicing a form of professionalism that was devoid of his usual spunk and spirit. Every week or so, he'd compulsively stack files and boxes in his car trunk, focusing intensely on cultivating detachment. But no matter how he tried, he couldn't transcend his worries. The truth was, he couldn't feel nonchalant about a job that mattered a great deal to him. It was his livelihood, his career, and in a confusingly primal way, it represented his identity as a man. If he lost his salaried position, he'd be incapable of making child-support payments, and his ex-wife would emasculate him further by withholding visits with Sojie. Such a punishment would be redundant. If he were to fail his child, Duxbury would be the first to pull out the psychological whips and inflict his own thirty lashes. Indeed, if he should lose the one thing he loved, he wasn't sure what sort of destruction he'd be capable of—on himself or others.

He hoped he'd never find out.

By 1997, his take-home pay had dwindled to about $2,600 a

month. The $1,000 child support payments, mortgage, and living expenses chewed up most of that. A $2,500 bonus would mean so much, and he waited for word from management. Finally, on February 24, Keith Wood sent Duxbury a memo acknowledging their conversation in Charlotte. His boss noted some improvements, yet added strange new concerns about his performance. Duxbury scanned the letter, which had been copied to Bill Pearson and others, and cursed. "He's manipulating my damn DDD numbers again," the rep cried.

First, Wood complimented him for delivering his reports on time. However, the dates on which he said Duxbury had delivered them were all wrong. That was no minor thing, since the object of the game was accuracy and timeliness. Wood went on to criticize Duxbury for having one large hospital account that comprised 72 percent of his sales. If St. Joe disappeared, Wood said, Duxbury's sales would fall precipitously.

"That's an interesting observation," Duxbury thought. "But it has nothing to do with reality." Furthermore, Wood ignored the fact that Duxbury had recently sold $500,000 worth of Procrit to St. Joe, thrusting the Tacoma hospital onto the Northwest's list of prime customers—and Duxbury into one of its top reps. Yet Wood had found a way to criticize him for developing St. Joe from zero sales to a $2.2 million client within three years. It was stupefying!

Wood then compared Duxbury's 1996 sales growth, allegedly 12 percent, with that of another Seattle rep, who had supposedly scored 39 percent growth. But those numbers were wrong. About $250,000 worth of sales from Duxbury's account had been incorrectly allotted to the other guy. That error not only deprived him of his sales gains and bonus; it created a corresponding loss on his side of the ledger. Wood should have known this and, as a manager, helped rectify it. Yet here he was, spreading this canard in a do-or-die review of Duxbury's performance.

The more Duxbury scrutinized his sales numbers, the more chicanery he saw. The rep's list of accounts no longer contained dialysis centers, but his forecast still reflected *$3 million from past dialysis sales*. That huge number remained in the base against which Duxbury was measured and grossly distorted reality. Imagine selling an additional $150,000 of Procrit a year on a $1.5 million forecast, thus growing your sales a respectable 10 percent. Now, measure that same $150,000 bump against a $4.5 million base, and you wind up with a measly 3 percent annual growth. At Ortho, that was grounds for dismissal. Looking at the number of total sales, Duxbury's increases were bigger than nearly anyone else's in his territory. But those improvements were deliberately obscured by management. The huge amount of dialysis business Duxbury had once sold—business that never should have been there in the first place—was now being used against him. In horror, he realized Raritan was deliberately punishing him for following earlier orders.

"Bastards," he bellowed.

Duxbury sat down and performed his own careful analysis. Using the same DDD figures, he demonstrated that if Wood subtracted the illegal dialysis sales from his base, Duxbury had sold *41 percent* more Procrit in 1996 than in the prior year. That was a spectacular number compared to the sales growth of the Northwest District (29 percent), the Western Region (23 percent), and the national sales force (24 percent.) By all rights, Duxbury should be winning another diamond for his ring. At the very least he should be taken off probation.

After completing his analysis, he included these numbers in a two-page letter to his bosses. He closed with a firm, respectful appeal. "I'm requesting an immediate restoration of my performance rating to at least 'meets standard,' and full eligibility for bonus compensation."

But Wood refused and kept Duxbury on probation. In addition, the manager moved the target even higher. The rep now had to *exceed* the regional average for at least three months, Wood said. Even worse, Duxbury had to achieve that goal within the *next thirty days*, by the end of the first quarter. That was devious, and Duxbury's thoughts returned to that night in Charlotte when Wood had pestered him to perform onstage, holding out the promise of his bonus. He now believed that Wood had tricked him onstage in order to show Raritan's bosses that he could control the stubborn, resilient rep. The upshot was that Duxbury would remain caged for a while. But he wouldn't allow that to break him.

—ⅶ—

AFTER receiving Wood's memo, Duxbury resolved to show him just how effective he was in the field. Wood was skeptical about the oncology sales Duxbury had made to St. Joseph, so Duxbury's first order of business was to introduce his boss to the hospital's buyers. To do that, Duxbury needed the particulars of Wood's next Seattle trip. His boss had nailed down the dates but didn't provide his arrival and departure times until the day before his visit. That left Duxbury scrambling at the last minute to set up a schedule of appointments. He telephoned a few more customers, requested meetings, accepted regrets, and filled most slots for their two-day session. Wood had ordered him to keep most of Thursday, March 13, free because he wanted a "low-key" visit.

That didn't make sense to Duxbury. Why would his manager fly from San Francisco to Seattle, arrive at noon, and spend a "low-key" session in the field with his supposedly troubled rep? Duxbury called Wood and pressed: *Is there anything in particular you expect from this trip?* The boss said only that he planned to review DDD numbers and Duxbury's performance. Other than that, Wood insisted he had no expectations. Duxbury hung up but sensed that something was off.

On Thursday morning, he picked up Wood from the airport and drove him to the Sorrento Hotel. Built in 1909, in time for the Alaska-Yukon-Pacific Exposition, the landmark hotel had a redbrick face, wrought-iron gates, and moss-soft carpets and drapes. The family-owned hotel epitomized the unfussy graciousness of the woodsy Northwest. Plus, it sat in the center of Pill Hill, near most of Duxbury's biggest clients, such as Swedish Medical Center, Virginia Mason Hospital, and others. Over lunch in the Hunt Club, the two sat in a banquette as Duxbury diplomatically pressed his case for his bonus. Once again, Wood refuted Duxbury's claim about increasing business. Duxbury let his fork drop and clatter loudly against the china plate.

"Fine," he said angrily, dabbing his mouth with his napkin.

"I'd like to verify your assertion, that's all," said Wood, looking surprised.

"Aren't numbers good enough for you?" Duxbury struggled to maintain his composure, while Wood sat there, unblinking behind spectacles. "Let's ask someone at the hospital's cancer center for their opinion."

So off they went to the car. They said little on the forty-five-minute drive south, but once inside the Tacoma hospital, Duxbury grew sociable. As the two impeccably dressed men passed through the halls, several nurses and doctors greeted Duxbury by name. A few peered closely at his tie, which on this day was a bland beige number. Duxbury introduced Wood to two of the hospital's druggists. They both complimented Wood on Duxbury's excellent service, and the rep began to feel better. Next, Duxbury sought out an oncology nurse, Julie Peerboom, who greeted him cheerily. He had helped Peerboom schedule three in-service seminars so Ortho's nurse-educator Patricia Buchsel could instruct the staff about QOL and Procrit. "We've got some new information about treating cancer patients for fatigue," Duxbury said, glancing over at Wood. He seemed pleased.

Then, the district manager himself began to pepper Peerboom with questions about her use of Procrit. She summarized it for him.

"Before 1996, we hardly ever used Procrit in our oncology department. But Mark," she added, "has been very persuasive. We now have between ten and fifteen cancer patients on Procrit at any given time." Wood seemed excited.

In the lobby, Duxbury suggested they visit Tacoma General Hospital, which was less than a mile away. But Wood declined. Instead, he got on the telephone and spent the next half hour retrieving his voice mail and talking to his wife. Alarm bells rang in Duxbury's head; his boss was behaving in a grossly unprofessional manner, and if the rep had spent field time making personal calls, Wood would have written him up. As the boss continued chatting on the phone, the rep discreetly jotted down the times and duration of Wood's nonurgent calls. When the manager finally rang off, it was nearly five P.M.—too late to make any business rounds.

The next day, Friday, Duxbury and Wood arrived at the Madigan Army Medical Center at Fort Lewis in time for their appointment with

Dr. Ken Bertram and, Duxbury hoped, the chief of oncology. Duxbury quickly signed in at the front desk and asked the receptionist for two visitor's badges. She handed them over, and the rep scurried to the oncology unit. Wood, however, engaged the receptionist in a long, inane conversation about classic movies. It was an unusually busy morning at the center, and the woman attended to several other visitors as Wood chattered away. Duxbury went back to retrieve his boss for their meeting. But Wood ignored him. Duxbury interrupted him a few more times until, after twenty minutes, he gave up. They missed their chance to introduce themselves to a key decision maker at what could be a huge Procrit customer, and Duxbury was crestfallen. When he finally pried his boss away from her desk, the receptionist looked relieved. The rep dragged his boss down the hall in time to meet an oncology pharmacist, Lieutenant Colonel Beaudoin, who shook Duxbury's hand and told Wood, "Mark must be doing something right. We just got our first cancer patient on Procrit." Duxbury then buttonholed a purchasing agent, who reported increased demand for Ortho's drug, thanks to Duxbury.

Once they'd completed their rounds, Wood threw him another curve. "By the way, I've changed my departing flight out of Seattle today from two P.M. to five P.M.," he said. "That'll give us more time to spend in the field."

"You're not giving me much notice," Duxbury objected. Most doctors avoid meeting reps on Friday afternoons. "It's too late to set up any more appointments."

Even so, Duxbury gamely offered to drive his boss to two other oncology customers nearby. Incredibly, Wood declined to meet them. Instead, he asked Duxbury to drive him back to the hotel, located forty miles away. By the time they arrived in Seattle, it was nearly noon, and Duxbury had to wait while Wood checked out. Inexplicably, Wood started conducting business on the telephone. Suspicious, the rep noted the time in his spiral notebook. He considered taking a brisk walk outside to cool his rising temper, but raindrops were falling on the hotel's green awning, sounding like fingertips drumming impatiently on his head. Wood made another call and Duxbury ducked into the Fireside Room, where he ruffled the fronds of a giant fern, walked past the hearth and its steady fire, and sat in a Victorian-style chair that could have come straight out of *The Magnificent Ambersons*. Wasn't that one of the black-and-white movies that Wood had yakked about earlier at the army hospital? As Duxbury recalled, the film revolved around a bully who dominates everyone around him. The rep got up to check on his boss, glanced at his watch, and lit a cigarette. By the time Wood got off the phone, it was ten after one, and he had spent seventy-five minutes on noncritical issues. Duxbury was steaming mad.

His boss then announced he was hungry, so Duxbury drove him to one of his favorite restaurants, Ivar's, on Seattle's waterfront. The two sat uncomfortably at a wind-worn table, watching seagulls dive for bits of fish and chips. Duxbury broached the subject of why his high sales were not reflected in his DDD reports, but Wood excused himself to use the phone. "I need to check in with my wife and retrieve messages," he explained. "*You understand work and family balance, don't you?*" Wood added conspiratorially. Duxbury spent the next forty-five minutes staring at the metal-gray harbor.

By the time Wood reappeared, it was three-fifteen. There was no sense trying to catch an oncologist or client at that point. So Duxbury drove Wood to the airport in plenty of time for his flight. The two reviewed Duxbury's business plan as Wood acted bored.

Driving home, Duxbury wondered, "Why did Keith bother flying up here?"

Something was wrong. Or was Duxbury imagining things?

A week or so later, Duxbury received a surreal letter from his boss. Wood started by describing a completely different sales appointment, saying that they were able to "catch" Julie Peerboom and meet for a "few seconds" with the hospital pharmacists. He lamented that "nothing [had] transpired that would grow our epo market." Despite what he'd heard from the buyers at St. Joseph, Wood *still* didn't believe that Duxbury had sold more Procrit for cancer patients in the past year than the prior year. And though Wood had specifically told Duxbury *not* to make appointments for the afternoon, he used the free time against the rep. "I soon realized that you had no plan for the balance of the day," Wood wrote. As for Friday, what a "disappointment." Wood blamed Duxbury for being late to "our informal meeting with Dr. Bertram at Madigan," rather than own up to his bull session with Madigan's receptionist. He then chastised Duxbury for failing to close a single oncology sale in his presence. "There was plenty of time after lunch to walk into at least one local key account, but instead we ended up at the airport with time to spare. . . ."

Duxbury slumped. Here was an ambush of such naked malevolence that he could only sit dumbfounded before its power. He reviewed the facts. Wood had specifically told him he had no expectations for their "low-key" meeting. In fact, he'd *resisted* seeing more clients, preventing Duxbury from possibly making a sale. Instead of actually working with Duxbury and Ortho's clients as he was supposed to, Wood had spent more than three hours on the phone—or *25 percent of their field time together*— attending to mundane matters. Yet Wood was wagging his finger: "My minimal expectation for these days was that we would meet with a few of your top oncologists." Duxbury felt as if he'd been thrown into a carnival fun house. He read on. "I continue to have concerns around your ability to organize and plan for effective field days without direction," Wood wrote. "You will not be rated competent until you can demonstrate consistent field performance, especially [in regard to] gaining access to your key physicians." In other words, Duxbury was still on probation for some unknown stretch of time. Wood's twisted account had been copied to Bill Pearson, George Mooney, and a human resource manager in New Jersey.

Duxbury tried to howl but nothing came out. Was that passionate detachment? He called McClellan for advice but got no answer. Duxbury was alone on this one. He rose from his desk, poured himself a cup of coffee, and stood before a window. He caught his image reflecting in the pane. The light from a lamp pooled his features, showing lines of determination around his mouth and anger in his eyes. "Keith is lying, and I'm not going to sit around passively and watch him destroy my career," he thought.

"This is war."

He returned to his desk and wrote Wood a scathing four-page letter refuting every one of his points. Then, he leveled the boom. "[G]iven the extent of the errors, omissions, and misrepresentations in your memo, I am formally asking that you be replaced as my supervisor." He demanded that his job rating be restored at least to "meets standards" and copied his four-page treatise to Pearson, Mooney, and three others. He mailed it and, figuratively, reloaded. Ortho's executives simply couldn't allow this sick situation to fester any longer. Could they?

———

AFTER Seattle's merciless rain and Ortho's chilling office politics, Duxbury was happy to ramble around Atlanta for a few warm spring days. He lost himself in the Peachtree City, exploring its byways and plazas, most of them named after Georgia's fuzzy fruit. The view was nice too. Southern belles strolled during their lunch hour, wearing gauzy skirts, soft frilly blouses, and sherbet-colored gloss on their lips. The women here looked like ripe fruit waiting to be plucked but exuded a contradictory air of noli me tangere. Duxbury, for one, had no desire to touch the ladies.

He was here to mix with the sales staff of Ortho's sister company, Janssen, a division of Ortho-McNeil-Janssen Pharmaceuticals of New Jersey. The company focused exclusively on selling prescription medications for schizophrenia, bipolar 1 disorder, and symptoms of autism. Since employees from divisions within the J&J family could attend meetings hosted by sister divisions, Duxbury was here to learn about Janssen and its product, Risperdal. He'd always been fascinated by the brain. Plus, he was trolling for a new job.

He walked into the tan-walled hotel that hosted Janssen's national sales meeting. In the lobby, he read the poster board schedule of the multiday event, the week's arc looking all too familiar. There were the opening night's ritual of cocktails and banter; the subsequent days of stodgy workshops and PowerPoint slides; the leisure activities capped

by the free-form contrapuntal rumbas to the bar, where stalwarts speculated on the corporation's latest enigmatic shift. Years later, Janssen
would become embroiled in allegations that it illegally promoted Risperdal to overactive ten-year-olds. But that week, Duxbury moved
innocently between the scripted events and gossipy watering holes.

Midway through the convention, he filed into an auditorium to
hear a speech by Ronald Gelbman, J&J's worldwide chairman of
pharmaceuticals and diagnostics and a member of the Executive Committee. Here was a man who liked to "foster open communication,"
as he once wrote in a piece about leadership. Presently, Gelbman
walked onstage to applause, then launched into a speech about ethics.
Like Peter Tattle, he touched on the spate of recent scandals, including
the federal settlement over Retin-A. But Gelbman went further. He
talked about the fine line between answering a doctor's questions
about a drug's off-label use, and introducing such treatments in order
to make a sale. Gelbman stressed the importance of "doing the right
thing" and explained the proper way to promote J&J products. Duxbury saw an earnest man who seemed sincere about demonstrating
integrity, every day. "That's why I joined J&J in the first place," Duxbury thought. *Integrity.*

As he left the session, the rep couldn't help but contrast the director's refreshing speech about ethics with Ortho's "quality of life" campaign for Procrit. Four months earlier, Amgen's NHCT disaster had
prompted regulators to slap a warning on the label alerting doctors
that high doses could kill. Regulators had repeatedly said that the drug
should not be promoted to treat fatigue and other anemia symptoms.
So how could Ortho legally push Procrit to dying cancer patients for
an off-label use like fatigue?

Duxbury wanted to know.

The well-respected *Journal of Clinical Oncology* had just published
Ortho's uncontrolled, marketing-driven QOL study in its March 1997
issue. The peer-reviewed article was written by the "The Procrit Study
Group": Dr. John Glaspy of UCLA along with Ronald Bukowski of
Cleveland Clinic, David Steinberg and Charles Taylor of the Univer-
sity of Arizona, Simon Tchekmedyian of Pacific Shores Medical

Group, and Saroj Vadhan-Raj. The *JCO* article listed not just those men, but all 516 physicians who had assigned their patients to this trial. Each doctor had been given free drugs and been paid for testing his patients, and Duxbury figured the study had cost Ortho at least $2 million. A key element was dosage: If a patient's hemoglobin level did not climb to a "satisfactory" level (or reduce the need for transfusions), a doctor could inject him or her with 20,000 units of epo, three times a week. That was twice the standard dosage.

Ortho treated this as a "clinical trial." But there were few signed patient consent forms, no placebos, and no strict Institutional Review Board monitoring, as there'd be in an FDA-registered clinical trial involving humans, according to several sources. The QOL experiment didn't seem right to Duxbury, nor did the *JCO* study's numbers. For example, only 48 percent of the 2,342 enrolled patients had completed the four-month treatment. About 13 percent of the patients had incomplete or no data; 6 percent had dropped out due to "inadequate" response; 3 percent had an adverse event; and 18 percent had complications or died. Eight percent of the patients were unaccounted for, making the study incomplete. Duxbury worried most of all about those people who had died. "None of the deaths was reported to be drug related," Ortho's sales material assured him. But that statement was nowhere to be found in the medical journal's piece. Despite problems with 52 percent of the Procrit Study Group's experiment, Glaspy and his coauthors wrote that the higher the dose, the higher the hemoglobin, and the better patients rated themselves, based on unscientific measures such as activity, energy, and overall "feeling." Their conclusion? "[Q]uality of life in this group of patients can be improved by aggressively treating anemia."

Duxbury mulled this over on his long flight home, along with Gelbman's "do the right thing" speech. By the time he walked into his office, however, several disconcerting messages were flashing on his computer screen. Reps *had* to use the *JCO* study "to promote the efficacy and safety of Procrit . . . on a patient's Quality of Life," according to one sales document. Ortho's brass planned to submit the flawed study to the FDA—for the second time—"with hopes to get QOL onto our label!" The medical journal article was hailed as a corporate coup, and another victory for the Procrit state.

Buried on Duxbury's desk was a note from Keith Wood. He wanted Duxbury to set up an in-service QOL training for his clients and to reference "our recent *JCO* publication." Could this growing campaign become J&J's next scandal?

"I wonder what Gelbman would make of this," Duxbury thought.

He composed an e-mail to Gelbman, entitled, "Ethics regarding off-label promotion." Duxbury explained how impressed he had been with Gelbman's ethics talk in Atlanta; he described Ortho's *JCO* study, which "may eventually be an excellent marketing tool." But the study focused on how treating anemic cancer patients with Procrit improved their quality of life, "a claim which is distinctly beyond . . . the FDA-approved package insert claims." Duxbury's question was this: Is it proper for Ortho managers to order reps to conduct seminars on the *JCO* study?

Duxbury sent the message on April 8, 1997. A few days later, Gelbman responded. "This is a complex area where a quick answer is not as good as a discussion," J&J's drug chairman began. He said that Duxbury could legally set up a seminar and ask a doctor to speak about Procrit for "anemia in cancer patients." He could ask the doctor to touch on "all aspects of treatment." But he couldn't tell him what to discuss. "That would be wrong."

"Jesus," Duxbury snorted. "I already know that."

The chairman suggested that Duxbury fax him Wood's letter, which ordered him to promote "our recent *JCO* publication." But after re-reading Gelbman's response, he sensed that the chairman was waffling. "He didn't even answer my question." The salesman turned away from his computer. He threw open his window and drank in the fresh air. An old saying ran through his head: *Fool me once, shame on you. Fool me twice, shame on me.* Duxbury had tried to stop Ortho's plan of stealing Amgen's dialysis sales, with no success. He had tried to stop Ortho from its questionable QOL promotion, to no avail. He decided that Gelbman couldn't be trusted, and he wouldn't get fooled a third time, he told himself. Unfortuately, that promise he wouldn't keep.

—m—

Walking into a Western Region meeting in the San Francisco head-quarters, Duxbury needed answers to other questions too. Why had he been investigated for sexual harassment? Why had he been denied a bonus and slapped with probation? He wanted to get to the bottom of the witch hunt and had just consulted an attorney who specialized in personnel law. He had shown her Wood's memos that distorted facts, and his letters repudiating his boss's version of events. He had gone so far as to collect affidavits from witnesses, including the receptionist at the army base. The attorney had reviewed it all and theorized that Duxbury was cursed with a manager who was drunk on power. "Contact human resources and let them know about this," she said. "Ortho won't be able to allow this kind of stuff to continue." He had paid her hourly bill and taken her advice: "Keep writing everything down."

But Wood was *still* Duxbury's boss and growing more bellicose by the day. He scheduled Wednesday afternoon sessions with Duxbury that threatened to run past five P.M.—the time that Duxbury by court order needed to pick up Sojie and begin his weekly visit. When the single dad objected to the Wednesday sessions, Wood demanded that he send him proof of his visitation duties. Seething with resentment, Duxbury wrote down his parental rights, tallied up his visitation hours, and showed that he saw his daughter a mere thirty-six days out of the year. "I am *deeply* offended that you would try to encroach on *even one minute of this time,*" he told Wood. Duxbury demanded a written apology from his boss. It never arrived.

Now, striding into the regional sales meeting, he saw even fewer familiar faces amid the audience. Duxbury seemed to be the only one left who had been ordered to sell to dialysis centers.

During a break in the meeting, he walked up to regional manager George Mooney, who was standing in the lobby, and confronted him. "What's going on here, George?" *Why am I being squeezed like a ketchup bottle?* Mooney jerked his head toward a far corner and, without saying a word, walked over there. Duxbury followed. As the two men faced each other, Mooney took out his wallet. *Let me show you something.* He removed a business card for a J&J staff attorney in New Brunswick and explained, "There's history in this region that I don't even want to know about." Mooney had been ordered to call this attorney immediately if anybody ever brought up this "history." Mooney flipped over the card and pointed to another telephone number, scrawled in pencil. He said that if anyone approached him after hours, day or night, Mooney was supposed to contact the corporate lawyer at his unlisted home number.

Duxbury's blood froze. What was this "history" and why wouldn't George name it? Was this just another session of gloveless torture, inflicted by orders from on high? The rep felt his heart fluttering and his senses heightening to the point of paralysis. He realized that Mooney was watching closely to gauge his reaction. The rep tried to back away from the executive, who still held the white card. Duxbury smiled weakly, but it was no use; his undisguised terror showed, and Mooney saw it.

The salesman summoned enough power to return to the lobby. He moved past the circle of backslappers and impresarios, and thought, "What the hell is happening?" He spent the rest of the day in his room, staving off a panic attack. That night, he met McClellan, who asked, "Are you okay, buddy?" Duxbury shook his head, and his friend steered him to the bar and ordered their usual tonic-and-Tanqueray and Highland single malt Scotch. Maybe the 80 proof whiskey would burn away the questions brawling in Duxbury's head, and it did for the night. But, later, while waiting in the airport for his flight home, Duxbury could count the rail cars piling up in his train-wrecked life: Wood's increasingly sadistic demands; Ortho's ever-shifting performance targets; Duxbury's slowly shrinking income; Renee's constant demands; and, underneath it all, Sojie's heartbreaking needs. Some days Duxbury woke up, went to the washbasin, and recoiled at the sight of the stranger staring back at him in the mirror—the raccoon eyes, thinning hair, and hollowed cheeks. His clients and associates began asking him, sotto voce, "Are you all right?"

The salesman still hadn't received a copy of his personnel file. So, at the urging of his attorney, he arranged to meet Mooney in San Francisco, this time in the presence of a human resources manager. During the meeting, he brought up the unreasonable standards against which he was being judged. He confronted the regional manager about the bogus sexual misconduct investigation Mooney had ordered Mike Barton to undertake. "I want to see the written complaints about my behavior," Duxbury said.

There aren't any written complaints, Mooney said, his voice soothing. "I had simply heard things and wanted Mike to look into it." Mooney went on to say that Barton had taken the investigation "way too seriously." He glanced at the woman from human resources, who frowned. Apparently she hadn't received notification of the serious charges, as was required. Mooney leaned back in his chair and casually said, "I never expected Mike to write a *report*." But, he added, when he'd received Barton's summary of his investigations, Mooney had read it.

"Where's the copy?"

"I destroyed it."

"Shouldn't that be in my personnel file?"

"I don't see why," Mooney said.

Duxbury was about to fire another question when the human resources woman interrupted him. She agreed to investigate the reasons why Duxbury's managers would allegedly "harass" him. But the way she said those words didn't reassure him.

The meeting adjourned, Duxbury then descended into the basement of Ortho's San Francisco office, an old warren of rooms off a cold hallway. He had received permission to browse through his file but felt as if were walking into a crypt, disturbing the dead. He faced columns of army-green filing cabinets and found his dossier. He noticed it wasn't very thick, considering that he'd been at the company for five years now. Duxbury stood under the rude lightbulb that hung from a wire and flipped through his papers. Something wasn't right, but he couldn't put his finger on it. He found a chair and sat down. He reviewed the contents again, page by page, past the petty memos, the distorted "work-with" records, verbal warnings, and substandard performance evaluations. What was missing? He was shuffling through the papers a third time when it hit him. "There's no trace of my glory days!" He rifled furiously through the papers, searching for the congratulatory letters, notices of bonus money, achievement awards, and Biosphere announcements. But there were none. From the period of 1992, when he joined Ortho, until about 1995, there was no hint of a good deed or glowing word. He looked up, stared at the basement wall, and felt a knife in his back. "That's the period in which I was converting dialysis accounts." He started to gag.

Duxbury ran to the men's room, his footsteps echoing down the deserted hall as though someone were chasing him. He pushed open the bathroom door, slid across the floor, and fell into a stall. On his knees, he heaved into a porcelain bowl. Everything inside him revolted. In between his retching, he hugged the toilet as though it were his only line to reality.

When there was nothing left inside, he sat up. "I'm being set up," he realized.

11

Gaslighting

As soon as Duxbury walked into her office, Vicki Boyd knew that something was wrong.

"Are you okay?" the therapist asked.

"No, I'm not okay."

Boyd was shocked at the sight of the man standing before her. It had been a year since the therapist had last seen Duxbury, and she was alarmed at his physical appearance. His hands and head shook involuntarily, which didn't make sense. Outside was a sunny May day, perfect for the boaters and kayakers who paddled around Lake Union. Yet here, inside the office, Duxbury looked as if he'd just come in from a cold, trash-strewn alley. A shirt hung loosely from his bony shoulders, the corners of his mouth were cracked, and his bloodshot eyes darted around the room as if looking for an escape route.

"What's going on, Mark?" Boyd asked gently.

The distraught man launched into a litany of his symptoms. His former habit of waking in the middle of the night after a few hours of sleep had now progressed into full-blown insomnia. That, thought Boyd, explained the heavy bags under his eyes. He said he couldn't eat, and when he did, he turned nauseous and threw up. That, she noted, accounted for his dramatic weight loss. "I'm now a liability to my company, not an asset. Or that's what my managers think of me," he said timorously. Boyd could see why but needed him to articulate his feelings.

"Why do you say that?" she asked.

He told her that he was certain he was going to have to testify in a "case" known as *Amgen v. Ortho.*

"What is the issue?" she asked.

"It has to do with ethical problems."

"You really need to talk to some legal experts about this, or someone who knows that field better than I do."

The rep just snorted. "Yeah, maybe I should contact the chairman of J and J's worldwide pharmaceutical division," he said sarcastically. Boyd frowned, and Duxbury laid out the story of how he had heard Gelbman's speech about ethics, and how Duxbury had contacted the chairman with his concerns about Ortho's possibly unethical practices. But the chairman's waffling response had told Duxbury all he'd needed to know. Now the rep suspected that Gelbman had contacted Raritan officials about the salesman's concerns, leaving him vulnerable to attack.

"I know things that my managers don't want anyone else to know," he told his therapist. "And because of that, I represent a threat to nearly every executive at Ortho."

Boyd urged him to seek outside professional advice.

He had already sought legal counsel and had just hired a Seattle attorney to help him keep his job. But he didn't dare tell his lawyer about the larger issue preying on his mind. He couldn't explain it to just anybody—it sounded nuts. But he felt danger looming. He had a recurring dream of opening a door and falling into an abyss. It made no sense until he remembered struggling in the closed quarters of his New York deposition. At the time, he'd thought he had narrowly escaped that trap, but now he wasn't so sure. He looked at Boyd and spelled it out: "I think I'm going to be hauled into court."

"I believe you," Boyd assured him. That seemed to calm Duxbury.

He then described how Wood had bullied him into signing a blank performance review; how he'd discovered documents missing from his personnel file; how his bosses were inflating his sales goals and deflating his performance, and the whispering lies about him. He'd heard rumors of Ortho's escalating fight with Amgen, only this time, he didn't know how to decipher these signs. "If I let someone else know about the bigger issue, I could lose my job. I can't tell outsiders."

At that point, Duxbury began to gag. Boyd stood up to help her client, but he sprang out of the chair and ran to the bathroom. She heard the unmistakable sounds of violent retching. Then Duxbury reappeared, his face ghostly and his hands trembling.

"I've never seen you like this," Boyd told him. What would make a grown man vomit? "Do you want to continue?" she asked.

He nodded and started to cry. "My life is worse than ever, Vicki. I've never been under this much stress. They say I'm underperforming, and it's come true." He'd grown to hate that word *performance*.

The vomiting had been happening for several weeks now, and, initially, he'd visited his general practitioner for help. The doctor had prescribed one drug to ease the insomnia, another to cure the nausea, and a third to help him concentrate. "But nothing seems to be working. I mean, the drugs just aren't solving the problem.

"They're making things worse," he confessed.

Now he didn't know where to turn. He worried about missing a mortgage payment, a child support check, and failing to meet his sales target. It had gotten to the point where he couldn't even show up for a friendly sales visit without losing his breakfast. "I can usually handle this stuff. But this . . ." His voice trailed off. "I can't seem to get on top of it. I've tried to do it on my own, but it's not working." Boyd let Duxbury ramble for a while, until he circled back to his greatest fear— being forced to testify against his employer. "That'll just seal my fate of never being able to work in this industry again."

Their session was nearly over. Boyd urged him to talk to his personal attorney about his legal worries. "If you can do that, we'll figure out a way to get you feeling better soon," she assured him.

Duxbury looked at her. "I know I need to stand up to them, but can I?"

"If you need to stand up to something, whatever that might be, I'll help you." And with that, he left.

Boyd was so alarmed at her patient's condition that she contacted the human resources division at Ortho Biotech. "It's clear to me that this man is extremely distressed," she told the woman on the other line. "Due to medical reasons, I believe he's unable to perform his work adequately." *What is required for an employee to obtain leave of absence?*

Around the same time, Duxbury went home and dialed Ortho's Employee Assistance Plan. After talking with a nurse, he asked to be placed on short-term disability. "But in order to qualify for disability," the nurse said, "you have to continue seeing your family doctor to improve your general health. And you have to seek psychiatric counseling."

Without hesitating, Duxbury agreed to those conditions. Requests for documents were faxed to and from the therapist, Ortho's human resources specialist, the company's disability case worker, and the patient himself. Duxbury was told that the necessary paperwork to finalize his medical leave would soon follow.

Duxbury continued meeting Boyd weekly to explore the reasons behind his anxiety. Ortho's expectations of him kept growing, unfairly, he believed, and now he wasn't sure what his targets were. More terrifying were Wood's deceitful accounts of their "work sessions," and their effect on him. Duxbury explained how he'd had been told to do one thing, then been criticized for *not* doing something entirely different. Lawyers had urged him to document everything, so Duxbury found himself writing more formal complaints and sending them to more people, while making fewer sales calls. Just recently, he'd written a letter to six of his superiors, including Carol Webb, again complaining that Wood had forced him to sign a blank document. But the human resources manager had responded by writing, "Keith maintains that he did not ask you to sign a blank form." End of story. As for Duxbury's claim that managers were retaliating against him for testifying in the Amgen case, human resources assured him that his testimony hadn't even been provided to Ortho's management. Besides, she wrote, "Ortho Biotech was not even a party in the case in which your deposition was taken."

Was Duxbury the only one to see the connection between his testimony and his current nightmare? The only thing he'd been deposed about was his Ortho sales. Five days after his deposition, Amgen had filed its case against Ortho, accusing the company of cheating. Hell, maybe Duxbury *was* crazy, he told Boyd. Why, just a few weeks ago, Wood had told him to host a daylong education luncheon for nurses. Duxbury had set up a first-class event and reported back to his boss proudly. But Wood had exploded: "I *never* ordered you to do this," he had hissed, and berated the rep for being so extravagant with Ortho funds.

Listening to all this, Boyd felt a chill run up her spine. "They're gaslighting you," she said quietly.

"What?" Duxbury said.

"It's called gaslighting," she repeated, louder this time. The term comes from the classic 1944 movie *Gaslight,* in which a scheming husband (Charles Boyer) tries to drive his new bride (Ingrid Bergman) crazy. The husband will do anything to protect his murderous secret, and, to him, that means psychologically torturing his trusting young wife. Strange things begin to happen to her: Gaslamps dim and brighten for no apparent reason; pictures disappear from the walls; footsteps sound in the sealed attic. The husband insinuates that his wife is either responsible for these actions or imagines them. But she insists that's not true. Gradually, she grows unsure of herself and her own impressions. The husband tries to break her emotionally so that he can lock her in an asylum, inherit her house, and continue his sinister designs without hindrance. He nearly succeeds until a homicide detective visits the nearly hysterical woman to investigate an unsolved murder. "You're not going out of your mind," he tells her.

"You're slowly and systematically being driven out of your mind."

Boyd applied that film noir scenario to actual situations from her psychotherapy practice. "I see this often in domestic violence cases," she said. "The batterer tries to condition the person to believe that what they *think* is going on really isn't happening. It's a subtle but powerful type of reprogramming in which the dominant person tries to weaken the subservient one." She watched Duxbury closely for his reaction.

"My God," he said under his breath. His superiors *did* consistently deceive and trick him. They changed his goals constantly; told him what was wrong was actually right, and vice versa. They even denied that what he himself had seen or experienced had ever happened. "My God," he repeated, only louder this time. He wiped his brow as if clearing his brain.

Boyd continued. "It's a form of psychological abuse. Pretty soon, you grow suspicious of your own perceptions and scared of your own shadow."

"That's exactly how it feels," Duxbury said, his eyes lighting up.

For the rest of that session, he talked excitedly about his experiences while she confirmed the psychological pattern.

This time, he didn't vomit.

—⁂—

IN June, Duxbury was diagnosed with severe and recurrent depression. His medical team began treating him with a smorgasbord of drugs. He returned to his family doctor, who was flummoxed by his patient's physical condition. "It's one thing to lose your appetite, but it's another thing to eat and be unable to keep your food down." The doctor tried a few more drugs, but Duxbury's problem grew so persistent, he was in danger of becoming malnourished. He'd been given Zoloft but had read that it caused sexual dysfunction, a disorder that Duxbury didn't need on top of everything else. So he stopped taking it. He was given Xanax for anxiety but didn't like the wooziness it caused him. He wanted to stop taking that drug too.

When Boyd heard about his lack of pharmacological progress, she referred him to an advanced registered nurse practitioner. Donna Poole specialized in psychotropic drugs and, after a session, placed him on a few low-dose drugs, including Trazodone to help him sleep. Poole reported this to his health-care payer. Then, she and Duxbury waited to see if the new prescriptions provided him with any sort of relief.

In his sessions with Boyd, Duxbury delved deeper. He talked about how Wood had broken into his computer and briefcase and how he'd felt as if he were under surveillance. Boyd couldn't believe it. The more she heard about Ortho, the more worried she became. She didn't share her concerns with him, as he was anxious enough. He now smoked a pack of cigarettes a day, had cut back on his morning caffeine, and abstained from the evening cocktail. But rather than progressing, he felt himself slipping. One day he suffered a full-fledged panic attack that incapacitated him. "It's like someone is standing on my chest," he told Boyd later. "I can't hear anything, there's too much white noise in my head."

Even though Duxbury had been placed on medical leave, his health did not improve. He spent hours alone in his Seattle condominium, isolated from clients and friends, doped up on medications that seemed to worsen his symptoms. He'd hear the phone ring, only to pick it up and hear the buzz of a dial tone. He'd hear his boss yelling at him, only to turn around and realize he was alone. Was he imagining things? After a few weeks of mental anguish, Duxbury became convinced that he was losing his mind. He returned to Boyd's office and tearfully explained the phenomena.

"You're having flashbacks," she told him. He was like a soldier who, after being sent home, continues to hear the whistling bombs and rat-a-tat guns. She believed that with rest, Duxbury's symptoms would ease. But when the "white noise" didn't fade away, she realized that her patient, on top of everything else, was experiencing auditory hallucinations.

Then there was the issue of insurance. In June 23, 1997, a caseworker from Kemper National Insurance Services contacted Boyd, needing "written objective documentation" in order to approve Duxbury's disability. Boyd provided it. The insurer then told the psychotherapist that the caseworker would call every week after Duxbury's appointment to check on his progress and "substantiate" his disability. "When Mr. Duxbury has improved to a sufficient degree," the insurance woman said, Boyd would have to document his condition and name his "work release date." Don't worry, the Kemper rep added. The necessary paperwork would follow.

Duxbury's insurance covered only 40 percent of his $100 visits to Boyd, and even less for Poole. So the distraught, out-of-work patient had to pay the balance himself. One time, he bounced a check to one of his providers. On his next appointment, the mortified patient paid with a wad of cash.

Poole, meanwhile, seemed mystified by Duxbury's reactions to the drugs. She had prescribed Paxil for his tremors, but the medication didn't help. She had increased its dosage, but he developed "generalized body twitches." Duxbury was desperate to drop that drug, too, but rather than stop taking the medication, Poole advised him to "tough it out." If Duxbury's depression didn't improve or his twitches dissipate in the next few weeks, then she'd lower the dosage. But on his next appointment with her, he burst into her office and yelled, "I can't stand Paxil." Poole told him to cut his daily tablets in half until his prescription bottle was empty.

By July, however, nothing seemed to work. He still exhibited extreme anxiety, along with insomnia, depression, and anorexia. His caregivers continued the Trazodone for his insomnia but placed him on Prozac to combat his twitches. In one of her reports, Boyd wrote, "He's not a good medication candidate, as he has a lot of side effects." That was an understatement. The experts agreed that, pharmaceutically, it'd be a "very long haul" for Duxbury. No one could imagine just how costly Duxbury's drugs would be.

—m—

WHILE the rep fought daily to maintain his sanity, he tried to find another job. He contacted nearly half a dozen drug companies, including NeXstar, Purdue Frederick, and Genetics Institute, which had a patent for its own form of epo and had also battled Amgen. Word of Duxbury's job search got around, and he heard from reps he hadn't talked with in years. Most of them wished him well. But one fellow was blunt. "You might as well find yourself another line of business, Mark. From what I hear, there's no room for you in this line of work anymore." Headhunters had gotten the same impression, and Duxbury grew certain that his firing was imminent. He loved his work and still believed in the therapeutic value of Procrit. But he had to face facts. One day in Boyd's office, he finally owned up to it. "My days are numbered. I don't think I'll ever have a job again." He'd already missed one child support payment and was ashamed of himself and afraid for his future. "There's no way to get out of this maze," he said, sounding like a man whose life was about to end.

In August, Poole referred the patient to additional specialists, including a neurologist, but he still didn't improve. "I feel like I'm descending into hell," he said. He found himself walking the house at all hours of the night, talking to himself and other voices. He was seeing a neurologist, a psychologist, a physician, and a nurse practitioner, and now he wanted to bring in a soothsayer. "If I could just see what lies ahead for me, I'd be all right," he believed. "At least I could *do* something about it."

Then, in the midst of all this, Duxbury's father died on September 2. He thought he had made peace with his dad a long time ago, but death brought a flood of memories and conflicting emotions. The verbal abuse and derision were the things that Duxbury now recalled. After his father had passed, Duxbury spent much of a moonless night pacing around his small, nine-hundred-square-foot home, trailing out to the balcony, looking out at the lake, and returning to his kitchen, his flashbacks in dogged pursuit.

He suffered more panic attacks. During one episode, he was in the grocery store when he suddenly felt as if he were standing in the ocean, knee-deep in salt water. He faced the shore when, out of nowhere, he was knocked over by an immense wave. Falling underwater, he gasped for air, lost in a swirl of sand and kelp. He tried to scream but his voice abandoned him. When finally he surfaced, shivering and wild-eyed on the floor, he saw the faces of strangers hovering above him.

Then Kemper National Insurance Services introduced him to another form of agony. The paperwork that was supposed to have followed was stalled somewhere in insurance hell. Boyd had experienced "communication difficulties" with Kemper, while Ortho's human resource department had informed Duxbury his benefits were in jeopardy. "[W]e have not received the Employee Medical Certification Form." Duxbury had no clue what that meant. So he called the human resources woman the next day and explained his situation. That seemed to mollify her. Or so Duxbury thought. Later, despite Boyd's assessment that Duxbury's treatment would take six to twelve months, Kemper's case manager peremptorily decided that Duxbury's benefits would cease immediately. Boyd received this disturbing notice a few days before that deadline.

As if his money troubles, "gaslighting," physical illness, and depression weren't enough, he was now ensnared in the maddening bureaucracy of a "health" company. On September 4—two days after his father's death—Duxbury was notified that his benefits would cease the very next day.

Several of his supervisors, from Keith Wood on up to Tom Amick, had been kept informed of these developments. On September 8, 1997, George Mooney wrote Duxbury a formal letter. Since the rep hadn't reported to work yet, or even informed his managers when he would return, Mooney delivered an ultimatum: Show up in the next three days or be fired.

Duxbury tried to appeal, but to whom? It became apparent that a gross miscommunication had prompted Kemper to stop paying his medical bills. The necessary paperwork that was supposed to have followed never did. Without insurance to cover his sessions with Boyd, the patient was on his own. Duxbury wrote to his regional director at Ortho, explaining that he hoped that "Dr. Boyd's recommendations will be honored and that [my] disability will be reinstated." If only life were that simple. He contacted both Ortho's director of human resources and Kemper's mandarins, pleading for the proper documents for his appeal. "I must know . . . the criteria for qualifying for short-term disability!" he explained. Someone electronically sent him J&J's personnel manual, but Duxbury couldn't open it. "I've experienced major technical problems with it," he wrote back. *Can't you tell me in plain English what I need to do?*

He was now stuck in a perverse sociological experiment, with various middle managers trying to impress him with their own importance. Yes, they had power. But couldn't they please use it to help move him along this Kafkaesque game board? By necessity, he became obsessed with the microscopic points of corporate policy and procedure. Common sense grew scarce. When Ortho's personnel division informed him that, based on company rules, he must return to work on October 5, he blew up. "But that's a Sunday! Is everyone conspiring to drive me mad?" He studied J&J's rule book and cited "Reinstatement Procedure: Section 40.5.2" to argue his case, but details were never his forte and time was running out. On October 2, Boyd herself wrote to the J&J Appeals Committee at Kemper National Insurance Services in Plantation, Florida. She restated her professional opinion that Duxbury needed "drug therapy and supportive psychotherapy" for another six months, and repeated his symptoms: panic attacks, sense of foreboding, weight loss, tremors, involuntary vomiting, and insomnia. Her diagnosis, along with that of Poole, was that he suffered from "major depression, recurrent and severe," and was unable to work. She was sorry his papers had gotten lost in the bureaucratic maw, she added. But really! "The communication difficulties with Kemper regarding [his] benefits may very well have heightened Mark's condition."

In the end, Ortho acquiesced. It gave the rep until the first week of November, or six months after Duxbury had first asked for medical leave. He finally returned to work, a bloated punching bag of a man with haunted eyes, palsied hands, and nicotine-stained fingers. Exhausted, he sat down to his desk on November 5 and began plowing through the pile of mail and messages that teetered near his computer. One memo caught his eye. It indicated that Amgen and Ortho had indeed been slugging it out in a closed Chicago courtroom for the past few months, its lawyers trolling for witnesses. Duxbury felt relieved to learn that his instincts had been right all along. But the foreboding that he had felt had emanated not from Amgen's suit to terminate Ortho's contract, but from the *spillover* battle. On September 16, Judge McGarr had ordered Amgen to pay Ortho for the years of sales it had made to Ortho's customers. Duxbury had to read the message twice: It was Amgen, not Ortho, that had overstepped the boundaries of market share. For all of its dialysis conversions, Ortho hadn't come close to seizing as much of its rival's sales as the Amgen rival had "stolen" from it.

Duxbury looked out his window. The weak autumn sunlight fell through the trees, casting runes upon his balcony. The judge's decision changed everything. Granted, some of Duxbury's sales had been wrong. But they hadn't been as egregious as he'd once thought. In light of the latest ruling against Amgen, Duxbury didn't feel especially guilty of wrongdoing. He hadn't been crazy after all.

Then Duxbury got another surprise: Keith Wood was no longer his supervisor. Instead, a man named John Woodhouse stepped in and, that day, called to welcome Duxbury back. He suggested they meet, and on Friday, November 7, Duxbury walked into the familiar green-roofed diner where he had spent hours writing his WARs. The aroma of freshly baked berry pies greeted him. He slid into a leather booth and placed his satchel on the Formica-edged table. A pleasant middle-aged waitress in a green apron soon appeared.

"What are we having?"

"I don't know about you, but I'll have a cup of coffee."

A few minutes later, Woodhouse came through the door, Duxbury stood up to greet him and made a point of squaring his shoulders.

The Northwest District manager was nearly a decade older than the battle-scared Duxbury, but he appeared to be boyish in comparison. The fact that Woodhouse was an eager new hire accentuated that impression. A Michigan University graduate, he was tall and lean with sloping shoulders. Duxbury wondered if he could handle the weight he'd be asked to carry in the "messy" Northwest District. After a few niceties, the two reviewed Duxbury's goals.

"Your first order of business should be reestablishing yourself with your primary accounts," Woodhouse told him. Duxbury also had to focus on growing Procrit sales in oncology. The way to accomplish this, Woodhouse explained, was to target doctors whose patients had breast, lung, and ovarian cancer and give them trial cards for a new Phase IV promotion. Duxbury blanched; the company was *still* handing out free drugs that could be redeemed for federal cash. Wasn't that wrong? He wanted to ask the question but instead listened as Woodhouse spelled out his expectations. It was the same old mantra, and after forty minutes or so, Woodhouse gathered up his papers to leave.

"Remember, Mark," he said. "Epo growth comes by establishing Procrit therapy as the standard of care."

"Righto," said Duxbury.

As Woodhouse slouched out to the parking lot, Duxbury exhaled. "Gee, that wasn't so bad. He seems like a reasonable guy. . . ."

12

The Overdose Plan

Late 1997 to July 1998

ONE had been more bloodthirsty than the other. From 1991, Amgen had been hollering that Ortho had been acting in bad faith by "surreptitiously" selling the blood drug to freestanding dialysis clinics (FSDCs). To determine if that was true, Judge McGarr had ordered an audit of the partners' books. It had taken months to find a set of numbers on which the two could agree, and several years more to devise a formula that wouldn't trigger another feud. Based on his calculations, McGarr had come to a surprising conclusion: Spillover sales were "inevitable and could not be prevented by either party."

That wasn't what Amgen wanted to hear.

Each company in 1989 had agreed to compensate the other for sales made in the other's exclusive market, and over the years, each had jockeyed for dominance. The result was surprisingly catawampus; Amgen had to pay Ortho $78 million for the period 1991–1994, during which the biotech firm had locked in long-term contracts in Ortho's exclusive nondialysis and cancer markets. That figure, plus $18 million in interest, meant that Amgen had to pay its enemy again, this time a cool $96 million.

Now came the "cleaning operation." As part of the judge's order, Ortho had to "wash" all dialysis sales from its lists. In other words, it had to remove accounts that Amgen could claim were dialysis. To arrive at that figure, J&J's lawyers, along with Price Waterhouse accountants, crunched Medicare data to identify all renal sites in the country. Then they matched those sites against Ortho's targeted hospitals. If the two matched, Ortho multiplied the number of dialysis patients in each targeted hospital by the average amount of epo it figured each patient used per year; the sum was subtracted from the hospital rep's 1997 sales goal.

Duxbury could scarcely believe it. The formula flushed dialysis sales from the base of every Ortho rep—including his. This had been his crusade for four years. But to actually see it coming true was too incredible. He didn't quite believe it. He opened his new "cleaned" DDD book, which showed such a dramatic change in his year-to-date sales that he had to blink.

Without $2 million in dialysis numbers dragging down his base, the rep's midyear 1997 sales put him in twentieth place out of thirty-eight reps in the Seattle region. The clean numbers effectively took him off the bottom of Ortho's pile and placed him among the top 25 percent of all reps in the nation. Far from being substandard, Duxbury had actually outperformed the average salesperson in two big categories in his district, his region, and the nation.

The picture grew clear, and contradicted his manager's assessments. He'd need time to absorb this radical new information.

Duxbury had no illusions that his constant exhortations had had anything to do with Judge McGarr's ruling. Still, he felt vindicated by the court. No more conversions, no more dialysis sales, no more plausible deniability.

So why was he so angry? Those conversions had caused him unremitting pain over the years. They were a big reason why his marriage had broken up and why his four-year-old daughter now ping-ponged between two single parents. Because of dialysis, he'd been hauled into court against his will, which had contributed to his problems and mental breakdown. Other Procrit reps such as Oliver Medlock had paid dearly for these conversions and, now, poof! Those sales didn't even exist. *The volume of dialysis sales that Ortho had always denied existed was being removed.* On a more disturbing level, what Duxbury had done at Ortho's bidding was now considered *dirty*.

The rep got up from his desk, walked over to the window, and opened it. He tried to steady himself by filling his lungs with fresh air. Rain had fallen, leaving a slick tarp on the rooftops and sidewalks across the street. He stared at a large puddle, breathing in and out, until he had calmed himself down. No sense dwelling on the past, Boyd had told him. The new, improved sales figures looked good. "It'll be easier for me to make my goal, and honestly too," he believed.

The balance of the year rolled on peacefully. He and Sojie joined the rest of the family—his mother, his brother, his sister, and their respective families—in sharing holiday meals and exchanging gifts. He began to eat better, step more lightly, and tell jokes again. "What do you call Santa's helpers?" he asked his mom one day. She shrugged and he replied, "Subordinate clauses." Duxbury laughed the hardest, and by the time New Year's Day rolled around, he had recaptured much of his former self. He actually began looking forward to attending a national meeting, his first company gathering in nearly a year. He set his sights on the last week in January 1998.

—⚏—

DUXBURY had never told McClellan why he'd been absent from work. And McClellan hadn't called his friend during that horrendous period. Several Ortho managers already knew about the Seattle rep's "problems," but Duxbury felt it was no one's business. Truth was, he was ashamed of his weakness and depression. The less he talked about it, the better he felt. He still worried about being called to testify in Amgen's interminable arbitration with Ortho. But the ominous dread that had once clawed at his brain had vanished, leaving him to return to socializing with peers and strangers again. With a new boss and clean sales slate, Duxbury's future looked bright.

To attend the national meeting, Duxbury didn't even have to board a plane. He simply drove up to one of the toniest addresses in Seattle, the Olympic Hotel, located downtown. Built during the Roaring

Twenties, the hotel and its interior resembled nothing so much as a Gatsby mansion. The hotel's antique mirrors, late Renaissance-style carvings, and ornate staircase with wrought-iron railings were too rococo for his taste. But the choice of hotel signified that Ortho was riding high financially. Duxbury waited in the grand lobby until he spotted McClellan, his "doppelgänger," as he was now called.

The two made a point of staying close and, in one session, took adjacent seats at the back of the room. They fully expected to hear the speaker reveal some exciting new strategies with his "top sales plan" and came armed with Procrit notepads and pens. But the man gave a rudimentary talk and the two veterans grew bored. They began passing notes that mocked the earnest discussion. When the speaker intoned, "You must always meet the doctor," McClellan wrote, *"for a three-martini lunch."*

"Make sure you bring your black bag," the speaker continued.

"And place the three-martini lunch inside," Duxbury wrote back.

"Be good to the nurses."

"Especially if they're young and blond," McClellan scribbled.

"Make a point of meeting all the nurses too."

"Preferably after five at a bar."

And so it went, until the two were doubled over in hysterics, their shoulders convulsing noiselessly in straight-backed chairs. The speaker had no clue about the sophomoric shenanigans in the last row, but some members of the audience turned back to glare at them. The friends covered their writing pads; McClellan wiped away a tear, and Duxbury tried to catch his breath. As soon as the talk ended, the two jumped out of their seats and ran into the hallway, where they finally burst into pent-up laughter.

"That was only way I could stay awake."

"I haven't laughed that hard in a long time," Duxbury said, wiping his glasses.

The two crumpled their notes and threw them in the trash, but a few hours later, McClellan returned to pick through the garbage and retrieve the evidence.

"What are you doing?" Duxbury asked.

"I don't want any of our bosses to find these."

"And I thought *I* was paranoid," said Duxbury.

They attended other talks, including "Fatigue and Pain," about how to sell Procrit for off-label QOL use, and a discussion about using free "minitrial" drugs to enlist new prescribers. But the big presentation that everyone was expected to attend took place in the honey-colored Spanish Ballroom. Duxbury, McClellan, and nearly eight hundred other men and women took their seats under soaring twenty-foot-high ceilings and regal chandeliers. Ortho had been on a hiring jag for the past eighteen months, gearing up the oncology and surgical sales machines, and Duxbury watched dozens of new faces file into the room. Then Amick took the podium. This was a momentous occasion, the launch of Ortho's most ambitious Phase IV promotion yet.

The FDA had steadfastly refused to approve Procrit for fatigued cancer patients. Yet sales of Procrit were neck-and-neck with those of Epogen, hovering around $1 billion. Many cancer patients and their doctors *still* preferred treating their anemia with blood transfusions instead of the inconvenience of visiting the doctor three times a week for a shot. How much better if patients could get an injection just once a week, or QW, as a doctor would write it? That, as Amick explained it, lay at the heart of Ortho's new sales campaign.

Leveraging the onetime, 40,000-unit shot into a high-dose regime for cancer victims suddenly became a top sales priority. To persuade doctors to join the national promotion, Ortho reps would pay each one $500 per test patient; some doctors could collect an honorarium and many could earn about $5,000 for joining these trials. The crowd applauded.

Without the imprimatur of regulators, however, this high-dose promotion was illegal. Furthermore sale reps were not supposed to conduct clinical trials. Legally, the reps could answer doctors' questions about their drugs' off-label uses, but they were prohibited from initiating physician conservations about such practices. Yet documents from that day's national sales meeting show that reps were told to "(provide) mini-trials on once-a-week dosing on all offices who [sic] are currently using three-times-a-week dosing" and to "document the outcomes of these patients."

Duxbury knew that high doses triggered higher risks; the NHCT had proven that. So where was the medical justification for jacking up Procrit doses?

Duxbury turned to McClellan and whispered, "Patients could suffer strokes and heart attacks under this cockamamie plan." But the Tucson man stared straight ahead. Amick went on: The high-dose promotion was one of his "top five strategies" for the year. The new promotion was designed for speedy results, Amick added. "Our goal is to have thirty percent of our physicians converted to a once-a-week dosing regime by June," five months away.

But why risk a 33 percent higher dosage? Duxbury chewed on that. If enough doctors tanked up enough patients, 40,000 units would become the community standard in oncology. The FDA would be more likely to approve the high dose, and more importantly, Medicare would then have to pay for it. Here was a clever backdoor way to goose sales.

Duxbury was witnessing a massive overdose scheme.

But Amick stirred his troops, and the next hour sped by in a blur of goals tied to Phase IV QW promotions: Schedule speakers' programs; pay doctor "advisors" to talk up the high-dose plan; tap Ortho's Clinical Affairs to sway Medicare to pay for the injections; and use Ortho-funded abstracts to tout the "safety" of them. When the meeting finally broke up, Duxbury's head was reeling. He walked over to the bar, grabbed a soda, and joined a circle that included Woodhouse, George Mooney, and a few others. In the center was Amick, holding forth about QW.

"It's a brilliant strategy," someone told the national sales director.

Genially, Duxbury spoke up. "I'll bet the FDA would like to hear about this."

The circle froze, and everyone stared at Duxbury. "What I mean," he said, still smiling, "is that this off-label promotion is pretty audacious!" In other words, it's illegal.

Amick's face flushed, and Woodhouse glared at him. First one man and then another moved away until only Duxbury remained, sipping his soda alone.

Later, Duxbury and McClellan met a few other veterans in a former haberdashery that was now an oak-paneled bar. Duxbury told McClellan what he thought of the QW study. "This is nothing but a thinly veiled attempt to pump profits."

McClellan studied the pressed-tin ceiling. "Stop stirring up trouble, Mark."

"I mean it, Dean. This is massively illegal."

"I don't believe you. You said the same thing about the fatigue promotion."

"And I still say it," Duxbury said, growing upset. "You can't promote an off-label use of a drug until the FDA says it's okay."

The taciturn man didn't want to argue, but he thought his friend was needlessly roiling the waters. J&J wouldn't stand for the 40,000-unit-dose promotion if it were illegal. McClellan also believed that Duxbury sometimes liked to be the center of attention. Why else would the Seattle rep challenge Amick in front of other managers? McClellan lit into his friend.

"Even if you are right about this, you shouldn't badmouth the plan in front of the guy who designed it. That's asking for trouble."

"What about the patients?"

"Ortho wouldn't do anything to harm people," McClellan said.

"I'm not so sure," Duxbury said. But he let the matter rest.

Later that week, the reps broke into groups for dinner, and McClellan's party went to the Space Needle, a 605-foot-tall structure and one of Seattle's most visible landmarks. Up there was the SkyCity restaurant, a giant circular room where diners gawked at the dazzling views. A few reps went outside to the cold, wet observation deck, with its 360-degree panorama of the city and mountains. But McClellan stayed inside, admiring the restaurant's cantilevered windows that tipped so far out into the air, you felt like you could eat the clouds. In the dim room, lights from nearby skyscrapers sparkled gold against the black sky. The reps ate as the restaurant slowly rotated, and, at one point, McClellan spied a private party holding forth in a nearby glass room. "Isn't that Carol Webb?" he asked.

Sure enough, there were Webb, Amick, and a few other executives.

They were talking jovially with several white-haired gentlemen, whom McClellan recognized as J&J directors. "They're celebrating something," he said. The group had ordered what looked like the restaurant's signature dessert. The Lunar Orbit was a concoction of gourmet ice creams, syrups, and sliced fruit, set over dry ice and topped by ten-inch sparklers. It coughed smoke rings and sprouted steam plumes and was causing quite a stir. Someone at the J&J party turned to see the Ortho reps eating with the hoi polloi in the main room, and he sent over two bottles of Dom Perignon, along with his compliments.

Later, when McClellan told Duxbury about the incident, Duxbury laughed. "I guess Ortho had a pretty good year."

Indeed, Ortho had bested its own record from the prior year. It wasn't official yet, but revenues for 1997 were $1.170 billion—a 17 percent jump from the previous twelve months. Since Ortho was having its best year ever, that meant Webb was, too, and based on the SkyCity party McClellan had witnessed, J&J's directors were happy.

Now Ortho's CEO had to follow her attention-getting act with yet another high-wire performance in 1998. Her J&J division had barely beaten Epogen sales of $1.107 billion last year, and rival Amgen was about to challenge her with a new epo brand. Webb needed to make sure that her company and the J&J juggernaut would continue to soar, and the Procrit high-dose initiative just might be the ticket. How far would the pearl-roped president go? More importantly, how far would Duxbury go?

—⁂—

AFTER that eye-popping conference, Duxbury tried to cling to his newfound optimism about his career. When he learned that his territory was about to be realigned, he hoped he could pick up some of his old hospital accounts. But when Woodhouse revealed the plan, Duxbury's heart sank. His new territory included mostly physicians' accounts located in a thirty-mile radius between Tacoma and Olympia. "This is a much smaller region than what I had last year." Furthermore, his account list included no large Procrit accounts but plenty of oncologists he'd have to develop as clients. "This is like starting all over again," he said.

He scanned the list again and felt another blow. Duxbury's closest account was forty miles way from his Seattle home office. This would add at least two more driving hours to an eight-hour workday, leaving little room for the rest that Boyd and his doctors had prescribed. The rep felt himself inching closer to the level of stress he had suffered last year.

Unable to sleep that night, he took an extra tablet of Trazodone the following evening. He worked his accounts by trying to form new associations. He didn't want to call on the unfriendly Western Washington Cancer Treatment Center, whose manager had so rudely kicked him out two years ago. But Woodhouse expected him to maintain that account, so he called on its administrator, Melody Edgington. The serious woman would later become interim director of oncology at the center and didn't suffer fools.

This was a heady time for medicine and not just for Procrit. Federal regulators had just approved Viagra, a "little blue pill" for erectile dysfunction, and Pfizer was saturating the media with suggestive advertisements. Viagra jokes were common in Pill Hill lunchrooms and Seattle coffeehouses, and on that particular day, Duxbury thought he'd try to wring a smile from Edgington. He told her what he believed was a mild joke that he had just heard from another client.

"Why are men on Viagra not allowed to take iron supplements?"

"I don't know," Edgington answered, warily.

"Because they keep pointing north!"

Edgington looked disgusted; Duxbury quickly realized his mistake.

"I'm so sorry," he said. "I didn't mean to offend you."

"It's okay," she assured him. "You're forgiven." But Duxbury noticed that her lips remained pursed against his patient trial offer. He feared the administrator had tucked away his little penis joke so that she could bludgeon him with it later, when he least expected it. In the old days, a slip like this wouldn't have bothered him. But the rep began sweating in her presence. "It's just a minor fact of life," he told himself. "Get on with it." He finished his sales pitch and, as ordered by his boss, paid her center $500, so he could spend a day shadowing an oncologist on his patient rounds. As much as Edgington disliked Duxbury, she later accepted $5,000 worth of free Procrit as part of Ortho's Phase IV promotion. When Duxbury followed up later, he learned that Edgington's facility had been reimbursed by Medicare for the free drugs—or so he later claimed in a federal lawsuit.

Even though the administrator didn't like the rep, they still did business, and he felt certain she'd place an order soon.

Duxbury continued calling on the center's satellite units in the area. This time, however, it wasn't sour Edgington who flustered Duxbury but a middle-aged African-American man. One day, the two began talking about a controversial ballot measure headed for the state's election that fall. Known as Initiative 200 and sponsored by one of California's affirmative-action opponents, it sought to prohibit racial and gender preferences by state and local governments. Advocates on both sides of Initiative 200 voiced their views and the African-American argued against its passage; he believed that centuries of racial discrimination needed to be redressed with affirmative-action programs. Duxbury believed the entire definition of *race* had grown obsolete.

"My daughter is a mixed-race child," he said. "How would you categorize her?"

"She's partly black," the man said, "and therefore a victim of oppression."

"Yeah, but look at her." Duxbury pulled out a photograph of his five-year-old, dressed in a stylish outfit and smiling next to her plain-vanilla father. A few people gathered around to admire the picture. "She's a privileged child, and I mean that in a good way," said Duxbury. "That's why I question these race labels.

"I don't think they mean much anymore."

Some people disagreed, and Duxbury listened to the healthy debate. When it was over, everyone returned to their business. But the African-American glared at Duxbury, who realized that somehow, he had made another enemy.

And no amount of schmoozing with clients satisfied Duxbury's demanding bosses. One criticized the rep for being too passive with the Western Washington center. So, he organized an evening-long educational dinner for Edgington's staff, her patients, and their families, to promote Procrit as an off-label therapy for fatigue. He enlisted his "pal" Pat Buchsel to help "educate" the group. On the night of the dinner, he deposited at every seat a swag pile of educational materials, tote bags, water bottles, and T-shirts. When the guests arrived, the rep stood at the front of the room to welcome them. He publicly thanked Edgington and her staff and introduced Buchsel. Then the cash-strapped salesman made sure each guest enjoyed the four-course dinner while he slipped an extra meal into a brown bag so he could eat it later that night alone. After dinner, he buttonholed one of the center's top oncologists and asked, "Will you host a round-table dinner discussion with some other doctors later this year and 'talk up' the benefits of the new forty-thousand-unit dose?" The oncologist agreed, and Duxbury crept closer to closing a deal with the facility. Then, Edgington complained to Woodhouse that the sales rep was being *too* aggressive in his efforts. Duxbury could only curse. "I can't seem to do *anything* right at this place."

About the only thing Duxbury wasn't doing was aggressively promoting Phase IV QW trials. He'd given free drugs to some oncologists but hadn't signed up many patients. The sick and diseased couldn't possibly know the safety risks associated with high doses of epo because the reps themselves didn't know. "I wouldn't be surprised if none of the patients were informed of these experiments," he said years later. Instead of relying on busy doctors to select "optimal" study patients, many reps reviewed patient medical records. Records show that some Phase IV trial subjects started with hemoglobin levels of 9.3; a few had levels of 10 and above, which were considered "normal." Yet Ortho was gambling with their health. Duxbury didn't know if the high doses were harming people—and he certainly didn't think they were killing them. But Duxbury believed these Phase IV promotions breached medical ethics and later complained in court and to congressional leaders that they violated patient confidentiality laws and fraud statutes.

Woodhouse, however, interpreted his reticence as a flagrant disregard of orders, and jumped on the rep. In April, he set up a two-day work session with Duxbury and visited several institutions in hopes of signing oncologists to the new promotion. Woodhouse was shocked at how little Duxbury had done on the trials. When Duxbury tried to explain, Woodhouse chastised him for not "training" even one doctor to increase just one patient's hemoglobin levels. *Why aren't you paying clients to advocate QW dosing?* "You should bring your doctors up to speed as quickly as possible."

At Woodhouse's direction, Duxbury gave Western Washington $5,000 worth of free Procrit, which convinced them to join Ortho's high-dose study. Memorial Clinic got $32,000 worth of drug and Rainier Oncology $20,000 with the same results. But that wasn't enough to keep the rep out of trouble. In a now predictable, stomach-churning routine, Duxbury received a stern warning letter from Woodhouse in April. Based on the recent field sessions, Duxbury had failed to "select" patients for the QW trials. One doctor said he already dispensed a lot of Procrit, but "we know . . . that he is far from using Procrit as the standard of care." Woodhouse ordered Duxbury to sign two prescribers to become paid Procrit "advocates," and to press one of them "to treat to an optimal hemoglobin of 12," which could be a dangerously high level. *Use the Ortho-funded fatigue studies to cajole doctors to join Ortho's blood drive.*

Left unsaid was that Duxbury already had the second-highest sales in his district.

Woodhouse had copied Duxbury's "nasty-gram" to the new regional director, Bob Ashe, and to Amick in Raritan. The rep tried to calm his shaking hands by exhaling anger and inhaling calm, just as his therapist had taught him. He felt ridiculous, but after a minute, he could finally hear himself think. Then he knew with certainty that he was about to get fired. A year ago, he had doubted his abilities and had confessed to Boyd, "I don't think I have what it takes to stand up to them." But he himself had set things in motion, and there was no turning back. Now he needed to accept the consequences. He had to prove to himself, more than anyone else, that he was strong enough to take whatever punishment "they" could inflict.

—⟋⟍—

Every year, the American Cancer Society organized a huge patient event called Relay for Life. The fund-raiser gathered cancer survivors, their families, and caregivers at various events in Tacoma, Puyallup, Gig Harbor, and other cities around the nation. Duxbury had seen the local events as an opportunity for Ortho to raise Procrit's visibility with patient groups; he had managed to convince headquarters to pay $10,000 to be the sole corporate sponsor for the local events. Duxbury still believed that Procrit could help cancer patients fight fatigue. He'd heard stories about how moderate drug doses made survivors feel better and more energetic. The fact that there wasn't any conclusive evidence on that score didn't bother him as much as, say, the high-dose plan. But his belief in the benefits of *moderate* doses of Procrit for cancer patients made it easy for him to throw himself into the Relay for Life.

He recruited a well-regarded doctor to speak on epo's role in managing anemia-related fatigue for patients and asked Pat Buchsel to show up. He spent weeks arranging the design and production of custom-made T-shirts, water bottles, tote bags, and other goodies to be inscribed with Ortho's commercial tag, *Stand Up to Fatigue*. On race day, he'd distribute these gifts to members of his relay teams.

Duxbury and Ortho also gave the American Cancer Society a $3,000 grant to plaster Ortho's logo on the back of hundreds of medals to be given to the "racers." He and a few ACS volunteers attended to the minutiae tied to such corporate events: the stages, microphones, balloons, permissions, flyers, parking, advertisements, and porta-potties. A few days before the event, Buchsel called to say she couldn't attend, and Ortho's paid advisor, the doctor, backed out too. Duxbury notified Woodhouse of these changes, but the supervisor didn't seem to mind. Duxbury returned to work and, after putting in long hours for weeks, rose early on Friday, May 15, the day of the first race. He drove to a mall to pick up Woodhouse, who also begged off. "I'm going to be on a series of conference calls all morning, so I'll miss the event."

The two agreed to meet at the relay site later that day.

Duxbury drove to a Tacoma school stadium where the event was to take place. He supervised the hanging of a large red banner blazoned with STAND UP TO FATIGUE; he tied dozens of brightly colored balloons nearby, set up a display table, and arranged the memorabilia and fatigue "assessment" materials. When the victory lap began, he cheered on the sidelines for the race-walker hobbled by uterine cancer and the bald jogger with breast cancer. Throughout the morning, Duxbury got swept up by the gusto of the participants and the poignancy of their survival stories. They made his own imminent corporate demise seem less toxic.

At noon Woodhouse arrived. Cool and officious, he spent part of the lunch hour in a white tent, talking with volunteers and nibbling on refreshments. Woodhouse informed Duxbury that he needed to make several more "important" telephone calls that afternoon; the rep fought a wave of déjà vu. Hadn't another boss played the same telephone game with him just a few years ago? Hours later, at three-thirty, Woodhouse finally showed up again. Duxbury started to give him a tour of the costly, Ortho-sponsored event site, but his boss ordered him into his car. There, in the dark sedan, with the windows partially rolled up against the blue day, Woodhouse tore into him.

"I'm very disappointed in your performance here, Mark."

"What do you mean?"

"We talked about you getting a clown."

"We never discussed any such thing!"

"Well, I wanted a clown for the kids. And you didn't even bring a display table."

"I didn't have to," Duxbury said, his voice rising. "The American Cancer Society brought one for us. Didn't you see it?"

The boss ignored that comment and listed other ways in which the $10,000 race was a letdown. After lecturing for fifteen minutes, he asked Duxbury to exit the car. Then Woodhouse drove off, leaving him standing in the street.

"He's gaslighting me!"

Preternaturally calm, Duxbury returned to the relay. He spent the rest of the afternoon walking around, taking time-stamped photographs of the tables, gifts, and banners that bore Ortho Biotech's name. By late afternoon, the crowd had swelled to several hundred people, and dozens of relay "team" members came over to thank Duxbury for his help. Thom Murray, a director of the local division of the cancer society, shook his hand. "I'd call this a huge success," he said. Later, he'd report that Duxbury's work had helped the ACS raise $775,000 for advocacy, research, and patient services. Everyone, it seemed, considered the event a resounding success.

A week later, however, on May 22, Woodhouse sent Duxbury a memo. "When we met on the morning of May 15 . . . you explained that you had not followed through in securing any of the materials needed for this program." *I didn't say that!* The note listed other missing elements that were "unacceptable," and the rep felt himself losing it. Needing to check his perception of reality, he showed the letter to several people who had participated in the two-day event; to a person, they were stunned. "I'll help you respond to this memo," first one woman said, and then another. Within a week, Duxbury had collected a half-dozen photographs and statements from seven people who not only praised his event but refuted his boss's version of it.

Duxbury didn't know what to do next. He approached Woodhouse and explained that his boss's note contained several mistakes. "I'd like you to correct the record so it reflects actual events." But Woodhouse refused. So Duxbury continued calling on accounts and attending meetings during the day, while at night he compiled his own letter that rebutted Woodhouse's claims. The rep had no illusion that this would safeguard his job. But he needed to do this to protect his reputation. Plus, if someone at headquarters investigated Woodhouse's deceitful account, he might remove him from his position—as they'd done with Keith Wood. Duxbury closed his letter to Woodhouse by writing, "I am deeply concerned that you would make so many serious and untrue statements on a document that is intended for my permanent record." He asked that the personnel department investigate the matter and suspend any more "work sessions" between Duxbury and his boss until the investigation was completed.

On July 6, Duxbury took his dispatch to a prearranged meeting with Woodhouse at a mall. Instead of walking into a chain diner as they usually did, Duxbury detoured into Kinko's. As his boss stood by, the rep made a few copies of his formal complaint along with the attached photos and third-party statements. An old hand at this sort of thing, Duxbury had copied his correspondence to Amick, the human resources manager, and two other high-ranking supervisors. He allowed Woodhouse to read his epistle, including the part that expressed Duxbury's utter lack of confidence in his supervisor's ability to tell the truth. After Woodhouse read the letter, he slapped it down.

"That's not going to change anything."

"It'd better change. I don't trust you anymore," said Duxbury.

"Well, if I can't work with you, I'll get Bill Pearson to do it for me."

Duxbury hadn't expected that zinger.

He calmly faxed the memo to the other managers and spent the next hour working with Woodhouse as planned. The session went smoothly until Duxbury was placed in yet another untenable position. He simply had to complete a big Phase IV project, Woodhouse ordered. If he didn't, he'd get fired on the spot. That would leave Duxbury without any severance pay, benefits, or the possibility of unemployment checks. The rep wasn't ready for that. Later, he tried to complete a few Phase IV sign-ups, but it was like the left side of his body boxing against his right side.

He grew exhausted, had trouble sleeping, and lost weight. His nerves rattled like chains being pulled out of a metal box. One evening, as he drove home from another long and stressful day, he found himself yearning for resolution.

Finally, on Thursday, July 16, Duxbury received a message to take part in a telephone conference call at eleven o'clock the next morning. He called his attorney in Seattle, but she couldn't make the meeting. "Make sure you take detailed notes," she advised. "Ask that the conversation be monitored by someone from human resources. Make sure you have *some* legal representation."

The next day at the appointed hour, Duxbury dutifully called the mysterious telephone number. John Woodhouse was on the other end of the line.

"What's this about, John?"

"I have nothing to say. We need to wait for Bob Ashe," Woodhouse said, referring to his new regional director.

Ashe soon came on the line and immediately informed Duxbury that an "HR representative" was unable to attend the meeting.

"I want a delay so that I can have some legal representation," said Duxbury.

Ashe refused. Then he told the six-year sales veteran that he was being terminated for sexual misconduct and for making racial slurs.

"What?" Duxbury blurted out. Then he remembered his Viagra joke and Edgington's indignant reaction. But a racial slur, where did that come from?

"I don't understand," said Duxbury. Then, with a sinking feeling, he recalled the glare from the African-American affirmative action proponent.

"I've received a letter of complaint about you," he said. Officials at the Western Washington Cancer Treatment Center wanted Duxbury to stop calling on them—or it would cease buying Procrit.

"I'd like to see a copy of that letter," Duxbury said.

"Actually, I don't have a copy. But it exists."

Duxbury didn't believe that. Ashe explained the rep's options: He could either resign and receive two weeks' severance pay along with any unused vacation pay, or be fired and receive nothing, not even unemployment checks. The way Duxbury figured, Ortho had no cause to fire him. He could fight his termination and maybe obtain a settlement for the past few years of torment. But he was tired of fighting.

"I'm not sure what to do," Duxbury told Ashe candidly. "But if I accept a termination, can I change my mind next week?"

"Sure," Ashe told him. And with that, the call ended.

Duxbury consulted his attorney and, on Monday, July 20, submitted his resignation. He had to meet Woodhouse one last time at a neutral spot in a parking lot and submit to one final uncomfortable ritual. Duxbury handed over his company car, its keys, a fax machine, his computer, and other Ortho property. Woodhouse accepted the goods while avoiding Duxbury's eyes. An armed security guard stood to the side of the duo watching the exchange, his ropelike arms crossed over a barrel chest. After Duxbury had transferred the last bit of property, he handed Woodhouse a copy of his resignation letter that detailed the circumstances behind his forced departure.

Woodhouse accepted his resignation, asked him to sign some documents, and gave him copies of those papers, along with some other papers. Then, after stripping Duxbury of every Ortho thing, Woodhouse left. The burly guard offered to drive the jobless, wheelless man home. Once inside his kitchen, Duxbury poured himself a glass of Scotch and sat down with his satchel. He thumbed through the documents he'd been given, including something called the "Employee Secrecy Agreement." Duxbury noticed he had signed that paper in February 1992, when he had been an idealistic new hire. He read the fine print, which said that he had agreed never to discuss confidential information about Ortho, its product, promotions, or any of its written materials. But instead of intimidating him, the secrecy pledge gave Duxbury an idea.

PART III

13

The Millionaires' Club

SNAP. Twigs from the cottonwoods crackled underfoot. *Rustle.* Branches from the huckleberry bushes were pushed side. *Crunch.* Duxbury saw the aspens move as some wild animal made its way through the grove. He tried to quietly inch closer without frightening his prey. But the way his breath huffed from his gaping mouth and his heart pounded against his ribs, he was scaring himself. It'd been several seasons since he had stalked a white-tailed deer, and now, as big drops of rain plopped against his Gore-Tex jacket, he knew the deer were creeping deeper into the thicket. Duxbury stopped in his tracks to listen to the sounds of the woods.

Earlier that week, Duxbury and a friend had pushed into the recesses of the Cascade Mountains, licensed and loaded to hunt deer and bear. They had set up their tents and nestled into a leafy spot. It was October, and Duxbury had spent the past few weeks trying to adjust to that precarious spot on the seesaw where he was finally free of Woodhouse, Amick, and the Ortholites but was frozen in midair, unsure of where he'd land. He'd already run through the two weeks of severance pay Ortho had given him in late July—about $2,000, just enough to cover a few child support payments. He had wasted no time filing for benefits with the state of Washington's Employment Security Department. He knew that unemployment checks would not amount to much, but they'd tide him over until he could bag his next sales job, a campaign he'd already mounted.

Yet August had passed and September, too, without a job offer. Worse, he hadn't heard from the state about his unemployment claims; doubt had settled in. He had told the department about his menacing work environment, explaining that "any reasonable person would have resigned under the circumstances." Why hadn't he heard back? Maybe there'd been complications. Perhaps an Ortho minion was attempting to distort the facts of his mandatory resignation. Duxbury had anticipated that. One of his last official acts at Ortho had been to cover that possibility, and his exit letter had detailed the ugly affair: He'd been "one of the lucky recipients" of a subpoena, had testified for his employer's rival, had told the truth about Ortho's misdeeds, and wound up as "the last [deponent] to leave the company. There is virtually no one left who had any knowledge of these activities, other than upper management." He'd included his managers' devious letters and had closed by saying, "I've asked that Ortho Biotech refrain from disputing my claim for unemployment insurance, but haven't received any assurances to date." Naïvely, Duxbury thought that would protect him. But two months later, he still hadn't heard a word.

Yet, here, in these mountains four thousand feet above sea level, even in the bone-chilling rain, he could honestly say that life was good. Autumn had ignited the trees into golden plumes and shamed the once-verdant berry bushes into scarlet tramps. The riotous colors, decaying smells, even the way the rain fell softly through the canopy of branches, made Duxbury feel completely alive.

He took cover under a tree and reviewed his position. At home, Duxbury had followed up with headhunters and every week mailed six résumés and made a dozen calls. He'd contacted the North Seattle Job Service Center for help in fine-tuning his job search skills. And he waited for his unemployment check. Clawing at the edge of his mind was the ghost of the subpoenaed documents he'd handed over to Ortho. Apparently, they had vanished into the ether, and that worried him. Then, in late September, he'd received the letter he'd been waiting for. He ripped open the note from the employment department and read greedily. It said that Ortho had claimed that Duxbury had been "terminated" for making a "racial slur and a sexually suggestive remark," which was harassment. Therefore, he'd been fired with cause and couldn't collect benefits.

"Argghh!" Duxbury had roared, pushing his chair to the floor. Once again, he felt the blunt force of casual cruelty. Someone at Ortho had deliberately twisted the record in order to block his measly jobless check. "They're screwing me again!" Duxbury had bellowed. Would this New Jersey outfit play with his head until the day he died?

Then he stopped. "They picked the wrong guy to mess with," he decided.

Duxbury performed a simple act that would catapult him in an entirely new direction. He picked up the phone, dialed a California number, and heard a woman answer, "Amgen."

"I'd like to speak with Gordon Binder, please." Duxbury was transferred to the office of the chairman, and he introduced himself to Binder's secretary. The salesman explained why he was calling, and the secretary suggested that he e-mail her boss. Duxbury's note was short: *I'm a former sales rep for Ortho who testified in your company's lawsuit against Charise Charles about Ortho's dialysis sales. I'm concerned about certain aspects of my deposition and would like to talk to you.*

Two hours later, Duxbury's phone rang. It was Amgen's vice president and corporate counsel, Robert Brauer; surprised, Duxbury quickly recovered and explained. In 1995, under subpoena, he'd handed over documents related to the *Charise Charles v. Amgen* suit. But at his deposition, he'd been questioned about only 10 percent of those papers. "I believe that Ortho withheld certain documents I turned over," he said. He worried that he'd be held responsible for their omission and talked at length with the Amgen officer. Brauer proposed that they meet, and the rep agreed. In the meantime, Duxbury called an attorney, who warned him not to violate the secrecy agreement he'd signed with his ex-employer. "Don't give J&J any reason to sue you," she said.

After that, he and a friend had decided to lose themselves in the mountains, which was where Duxbury was now, trying not to think of his sketchy future. Just then, he saw the aspen leaves ripple. Crouching lower, he slowly approached the spot, lowered his rifle, and heard the sound of a something floundering in the bushes. Then he saw a flash of black fur. Holy shit! It was a bear, and the thought froze him in his tracks. He prayed the animal couldn't pick up his all-too-human scent of sweat and fear. But just in case, he climbed into the crook of a tree, pulled his hood up against the rain, and waited.

He kept his eye on that aspen, but his mind drifted to his meeting with Amgen's attorney. Duxbury had arrived at the Marriott Hotel near Sea-Tac Airport on a Friday morning. The high-ceilinged lobby had wood beams, a fire blazing in the hearth, and two Brooks Brothers types sitting on a brown leather couch. Clutching his satchel, Duxbury walked up to the man who was talking; Brauer rose and shook the rep's hand firmly. Then he introduced Howell Melton Jr., Amgen's outside counsel at Holland & Knight in Orlando, Florida.

The three moved to a table where Duxbury emptied his valise. Inside were the same papers that he had handed over to J&J attorneys in 1995. Now the Amgen lawyers went through them, one by one, as the rep explained their significance. Neither of the attorneys had seen these memos before. After a few hours, the trio moved to the dining room, where they ordered lunch and continued talking about Ortho's dialysis sales to Amgen clients. After five hours, Duxbury felt wrung out, but Brauer wasn't finished. "We'd like you to submit to an additional deposition."

"You'll need to subpoena me," the salesman replied. He wasn't about to testify voluntarily against Ortho. And he didn't want Amgen cherry-picking his papers. "I'll do it, but only if you use *all* of my documents this time." The lawyers agreed and set a date, which was a few weeks from then.

Duxbury heard the trees rustle again and scanned the ground below. That's when he saw a pile of fresh bear scat, still steaming slightly. He carefully climbed down, picked up a twig, and poked at the pile of ursine excrement: red skin, pale pulp, and amber seeds. This was the detritus not of berries but of apples. Duxbury remembered the orchard he had passed and realized, "This bear isn't lying in wait for me. He's drunk!"

Duxbury surmised that the creature had gorged on fruit that had fermented on the ground. The bear was "probably scared out of his wits," Duxbury thought. He could wait until the animal lumbered off, or . . . The hunter ran exuberantly toward the rustling bushes, waving his hands like a boy and hollering gibberish at the top of his lungs. The beast half-roared, half-moaned as it stumbled away.

A few days later, Duxbury and his friend drove down from the mountains, recounting the drunken bear story several times, polishing the nugget with each retelling. "I wish I could have seen him cockeyed and weaving," said Duxbury, laughing.

"Do you think he was hungover the next day?"

"I don't know, but I'll bet Mama Bear tore into his sorry hide!"

As the car bumped along the dirt road, pixels of civilization began to coalesce, initially as a mailbox on a post, then into an old filling station with rusted pumps. A suburban mosaic began to take shape, and Duxbury fell quiet. Soon, the city itself would emerge. The closer they got to the interstate, the more Duxbury felt the branches of the forest pulling him back, wrapping their arms around him. A ripe odor clung to him. It was either a trick of his mind or the tang of Ortho Biotech curling toward him. In a month, he'd have to testify against them. He tried to shake off this feeling of being a marked man.

—◆◆◆—

A BREEZE blew off the California coast, bending the snapdragons that danced along the cliffside garden and ruffling the table linens on the veranda. McClellan inhaled the perfume from the flowers mixed with the briny sea air. He scanned the magnificent shoreline of Laguna Niguel and sighed. It wasn't every day a desert rat like him got to see a blood-orange sun slip into the Pacific Ocean. The man turned his back on nature's canvas and returned to the private room he'd rented.

Everything needed to be perfect for tonight's meeting of what McClellan called the Millionaires' Club.

McClellan, Bill Pearson, and a few other executives had invited about twenty oncologist clients and their spouses to an all-expenses-paid weekend at the opulent Ritz-Carlton resort. An elite group, these doctors purchased about $1 million a year in Procrit, ranking among Ortho's top customers. This junket was not just a reward for the busy prescribers; it was an all-stops-out weekend to persuade them to prescribe Procrit in a risky, off-label manner. "Remember," McClellan had been told, "the idea is to get the docs to increase their dosage." Ortho had paid for their five-star-hotel lodging, their sumptuous meals, valet parking, golf fees, and even their caddie tips. The hosts had considerately allowed plenty of leisure time in the weekend schedule so the doctors and their wives could enjoy the romantic setting on their own. In return, Ortho hoped that these influential physicians would become disciples of the high-dose regimen.

That evening, as the guests trickled into the private room, McClellan greeted them with a warm handshake and chilled cocktails, the "grip and grin," as he called it. Some doctors wore formal bow ties; their women were swathed in satins and jewels. After a civilized half hour, they sat down to sup on lobster, steak, and baby arugula. No business was broached. But the following morning, after a rich breakfast, McClellan led the men to a roundtable discussion during which each doctor explained how he experimented with Procrit. One guest, Dr. Suresh Katakkar, injected 40,000 units a week into some patients. Another doctor, whom McClellan had just met, shot up his people with 10,000-unit doses *over ten days straight*. His 70,000 units-a-week regime was more than double the recommended dosage, and McClellan frowned. "That seems a little extreme."

"Oh, no," the doctor insisted. "I haven't seen any side effects so far."

"But how do you get insurance to pay for the high dose?"

"My patients work in Hollywood," the man sniffed. "They pay cash." The others nodded knowingly. If you cater to the cash-rich, you don't hassle with insurers.

Later, on the golf course, several of the doctors continued the discussion with McClellan. He reported to his bosses, "I'm sure that a few of these guys went home to try some of the experiments." Of course, if the doctors, of their own volition, wanted to experiment with the drug on their own patients, that was fine. But it was illegal for Ortho to promote such practices. Yet the marketing event did just that. McClellan never did follow up on what happened to the dosed-up patients discussed at the roundtable, but Pearson at headquarters considered the millionaires' event to be a smashing success.

Ortho had also formed advisory committees made up of academic physicians and clinical oncologists. These advisors weren't just doctors but department chiefs and influential people known as key opinion leaders (KOLs). They were paid an honorarium to establish Procrit as the standard of care and to attend Ortho "conferences" that might include dozens of less noteworthy doctors. Ortho footed the bill for any transportation and the KOLs' luxury accommodations, as well as for those of other, not so influential, physician attendees. McClellan helped organize several of these seminars; he even selected some of his customers to be speakers. "Some guys want to give three or four speeches a weekend so they can get three or four thousand dollars," in addition to their all-expenses-paid trips, he told his boss. A few actually wrangled such high fees. In little time, Ortho assembled Procrit Advisory Boards of KOLs who specialized in every imaginable type of cancer. The idea was "to build thought leader endorsement [sic] to establish Procrit as standard of care," not just for chemo and HIV, but also for fatigue and other unapproved treatments, according to one national memo.

Heading the list were several distinguished professors, division heads, and physician chiefs from Johns Hopkins University, Harvard Medical School, the University of Chicago, Memorial Sloan-Kettering Cancer Center, Emory University Hospital, Cornell University, Long Island Jewish Medical Center, the University of Texas MD Anderson Cancer Center, and other top-rated facilities. A memo listed the names of some eighty doctors. Dr. Nicholas J. Vogelzang of the University of Chicago, who had prepared a paper for Ortho on fatigue management, was a spokesman for the Fatigue Coalition, an innocuous-sounding group bankrolled by Ortho, and had recently been quoted in a *New York Times* story that suggested the off-label Procrit use for tired cancer patients.

Dr. John Glaspy of UCLA penned articles about Ortho-sponsored studies, while several other doctors agreed to "influence their colleagues to use Procrit" for cancer-related fatigue. Dr. Jerome Groopman of Harvard Medical School performed J&J-funded clinical trials on epo, sat on Ortho's fatigue advisory board, and was sometimes quoted in *The New York Times* extolling the "exciting" palliative drug for AIDS patients. Ortho's Speakers Bureau paid these and other doctors $1,000 or so for every speech they made about the blood drug. Often, attending doctors received hourly credits toward their annual continuing medical education (CME) required by most state licensing boards. Top cancer researcher and Ortho consultant Dr. David Cella of Northwestern University flew from Chicago to Tucson several times to address groups of doctors and fellows at the Arizona Cancer Center. He was given a suite at the stately Arizona Inn, a luxe boutique hostelry. For his "Anemia in the Oncology Patient" speech, Cella was paid $2,000 plus expenses, while members of his audience received 1.5 hours of CME credit.

Ortho didn't give money to doctors who cast aspersions on its drug; it also didn't reward advisors who moved between epo's two camps. Ortho had paid Glaspy to develop a fatigue scale that its reps used to educate other doctors, and he had authored the seminal fatigue study published by *JCO* in 1997. But when McClellan learned that the doctor consulted for Amgen, too, "it became a bit of an ethics problem." After the rep reported his findings to Raritan, Glaspy was dropped from Ortho's advisory council.

Still, by 1999, the company had at least one paid advisor or speaker inside nearly every top cancer facility in the nation. "I feel good about this," McClellan told Duxbury. But the former Ortho rep wasn't so sure. At what point did advisory support and speaking fees become kickbacks and bribes?

—⁂—

JIM Lenox woke up one morning with his knee aching again. The strapping forty-four-year-old had run his body hard over the past twenty-seven years, sliding into third base, kneeling on concrete slabs, and playing horsey with the kids. Now that his youngest had just graduated from college and since his wife's insurance covered his medical bills, he could attend to the many personal needs he had postponed over the years.

In July 1998, Jim underwent a routine physical exam in preparation for a knee operation. The doctor tapped his chest, put on his stethoscope, then heard a "strange rattle." The physician put down his instrument. "Forget the knee," he said. "Let's get a CT scan of your chest." A week later, the Lenoxes were sitting in the doctor's office looking confused as they heard that universally dreaded diagnosis:

"You have cancer."

Tests showed that Jim had lung tumors, which wasn't surprising. For decades, the father of five had been a moderate smoker. Still, he'd always been active, golfing, fishing, and playing on softball teams. As Jim tried to process the news, his usually stoic wife broke down in tears. She couldn't believe it, nor could she bear the idea of losing her husband, especially now as they were hitting their stride. These and other thoughts jangled through her mind as the doctor outlined a course of therapy. Jim squeezed her hand and whispered, "Don't worry, honey. We'll beat this, I promise."

A week or so later, she found herself driving him to Johns Hopkins Hospital, one of the top-ranked institutions in the country. Built in 1876 in the Queen Anne style, it loomed like a crimson-robed duchess over a gritty black neighborhood in East Baltimore. The building, with its polygonal tower topped by a gray dome, inspired awe. Even its flush red brickwork boasted surgical precision. Part church, part place of higher learning, and part charitable healer, Johns Hopkins was an American icon whose structures were listed on the National Register of Historic Places.

The Lenoxes swept up the stairs to a carved stone doorway and wended through the complex until they found the right room. That September, Jim underwent surgery and had most of his left lung removed through an eighteen-inch incision on his back. He then endured thirty-five radiation treatments, nearly one a day for seven weeks, with Sharon and their four-year-old grandson, Christopher, by his side. His red blood cell count took a beating, but the treatments worked.

By year-end, Jim was pronounced cancer free, and the entire family celebrated with a bountiful Christmas. Jim quit smoking, returned to work, and every six months underwent CT scans to make certain the disease did not return. Jim and Sharon believed they had beaten the devil. They began revisiting their old haunts, such as the bowling alley where he'd stolen her first kiss.

—ɷ—

MCCLELLAN, meanwhile, had turned into a pied piper of sorts. With his jug ears, perennial tan, and shirt-sleeved chivalry, some nurses thought the fifty-year-old resembled Clark Gable in *The Misfits*. McClellan, however, was a company man. On his long drives under the thunderheads and dazzling white clouds of Route 66, he memorized the Johnson & Johnson credo. "We believe our first responsibility is to doctors, nurses, and patients . . . ," he recited solemnly to the windshield. "In meeting their needs everything we do must be of high quality." . . . *We must provide competent management, and our actions must be just and ethical.* When he had committed all 309 words to heart, he felt like a J&J man, "who knows his job and has inherent good judgment . . . a man of civic consciousness and responsibility."

He didn't read any medical journals except those provided by Ortho. He didn't question his bosses. Even though his drug's product insert specifically warned that Procrit should *not* be used in patients with multiple myeloma tumors, McClellan pitched epo for precisely those patients. To assuage the skeptics, he and other Ortho reps were given a study of forty-one such patients that concluded, "EPO is a safe and effective treatment for the anemia associated with MM." McClellan had underlined the pertinent passages, even though the FDA prohibited that practice as promoting off-label use. But the rep followed orders. "DO NOT hand over the paper without mentioning why it is important . . . to the use of PROCRIT," his manager had written. Mc-Clellan also promoted epo for radiation patients, which was unapproved.

McClellan didn't like being shadowed by managers, so whenever one visited, the rep made life unpleasant. He'd turn off his car's air-conditioning unit, pick up the boss at the airport, and at noon drive the supervisor to a Mexican restaurant to eat the biggest, most *picante* enchilada. As the manager wolfed down his meal, McClellan would bombard him with numbers and names, until the man began sweating. Then McClellan would ferry his boss to appointments while blasting the car heater. After stopping to buy some Bromo-Seltzer, the poor man would finally holler, "Jesus, Dean! Can you at least turn off the heater?"

Headquarters tended to leave McClellan alone.

He roamed where few reps had gone, visiting federal clinics on Indian reservations in the Southwest and creeping into military bases. Twice a year the Davis-Monthan Air Force Base hosted pharmaceutical reps so military doctors could review their wares. McClellan memorized the names of several hospital staff members and began visiting them on base regularly. He'd stop at the gate, tell the guards that he was there to sell "blood products"—a magic phrase that acted like *open sesame*—and be waved into the inner sanctum. He became such a familiar face that McClellan hornswoggled his way into getting a rare military pass. From then on, he'd flash his badge and a smile to gain entry to nearly every military installation in his territory. Lieutenants at Davis-Monthan AFB liked him so much they allowed him to drive an F-16 simulator, used to train fighter pilots. It cost $2,000 an hour to test a pilot on this equipment, and McClellan was given sixty minutes to prove his mettle in the simulated cockpit. When he emerged, tense and perspiring, he was told that he'd performed better than the two trainees ahead of him. Photos were prohibited on base, but the salesman persuaded a uniform to snap a picture of him at the control panel of the federal toy.

Even better was that McClellan obtained stationery from the military base. He used it to type standing treatment orders for anemic chemotherapy patients: "Initiate Procrit [at] 40,000 units," he wrote. *If patients didn't respond after four weeks, gun the needle up to 60,000 units.* McClellan notified the doctors of his orders and added, "I have put a lot of work into this to make it easy." And it paid off. High-dose Procrit instruction sheets were posted in hallways, nurses' stations, and supply rooms throughout the base, making the unapproved high dosage part of the military's standard treatment.

McClellan pressed deep into his territory, past Navajo grazing lands and Apache mineral rights. He loved the silent beauty of the Chuska Mountains and the late-afternoon fuchsia sky of the Rio Grande Valley. One bright sunny day, he drove along the interstate in a snow-globe world of white sands and cumulonimbus clouds. Suddenly, traffic stopped in both directions. McClellan got out of his car and spied a cable strung across the road. It turned out to be a guide for a missile that eventually appeared, moving faster than a speeding bullet. "Well, I'll be darned," McClellan thought. He was close to White Sands Missile Range, an impenetrable, top secret facility near Holloman Air Force Base. From that day on, he began looking for an entrance into its medical facilities. One time, he saw three bat-shaped F-17 planes screaming overhead, accompanied by flares. The aircraft followed those flares just as surely as McClellan tracked his sales quarry, and one morning, McClellan swallowed hard and pulled up to the gate of Holloman AFB. He acted as if he'd done that a thousand times before.

"Hi, there!" he said, flashing his military pass. "I'm here to see the chief of pharmacy." Much to his surprise, the guard waved him through. Since Procrit was listed on federal formularies, McClellan simply had to educate the base's pharmacist about the wisdom of switching. And he did.

—⟪⟫—

McCLELLAN jackknifed his body into a folding chair, bent his head down, and flipped through confidential files. He desperately searched patient charts to find a few people he could stick into Ortho's Phase IV minitrial. Nurses in pastel smocks moved around him, occasionally upsetting his concentration. McClellan had signed up the facility's doctor for Ortho's promotional study, but the nurses had been too busy to select "trial" subjects and fill out the paperwork. Without this information, his client M.D. would not collect the $500 per patient he was expecting, and time was running out. So the work fell to McClellan, who hunched over files that he balanced unsteadily on his knees.

It may have been a violation of privacy law for the rep to review the personal details of a patient, but his boss had urged him to be proactive. Besides, he'd grown accustomed to it. He had spent the past few years filling out patient trial cards so the doctors could get free drugs and join Ortho's studies. The cards required patients' initials, but McClellan routinely made them up, starting at the front of the alphabet and writing "AB" for one patient, "CD" for another, and so on. He'd fabricate a patient's illness, writing "lung cancer" in the space. Sometimes, he'd leave the diagnosis line blank. His boss, Dwayne Marlowe, would help by writing in "CA" to indicate cancer, even though Procrit wasn't indicated for cancer victims—only for anemic chemo patients. In any case, it didn't seem to matter if you were sloppy on these forms. McClellan filled in the doctor's name, address, and amount of free drug the client wanted. The only thing he didn't do was forge the doctor's signature. Once the physician signed the cards, McClellan mailed them to New Jersey.

Each form requested a month's supply of Procrit and was worth at least $1,200. McClellan often carried eighty or so of these cards in his black bag, nearly $100,000 worth of scrip. He handed out minitrial cards to doctors like they were candy corn for trick-or-treaters. One doctor took $3,600 in free drug cards during a luncheon; another grabbed nearly $10,000. What the rep didn't stop to consider was that the free drug could dilute Procrit's true "net price" and "best price" figures that Ortho reported to the government. Those numbers helped calculate the AWP of the drug, which Medicare, Medicaid, and other insurers used to pay providers.

By the spring of 1999, Ortho's hyping of the high doses had turned so brazen that a few doctors complained to the FDA about it and sent materials they'd been given at luncheons and meetings. One was a "supplement" to *Oncology Issues,* an organ of the Association of Community Cancer Centers. The article had been subsidized by an Ortho grant and reported that the Georgetown University Medical Center (whose doctors belonged to Ortho's advisory groups) used the unapproved 40,000-unit shots as a starting dose. *So you should too!* Regulators immediately contacted J&J and said the article was being "used to validate that this is a recognized method of treatment at a large cancer center." *Please stop,* the FDA essentially responded. Citing instructions used by Allegheny University Hospital in Philadelphia and the University of Texas MD Anderson Cancer Center—both prestigious facilities whose doctors were paid Ortho speakers—the FDA told Ortho's parent that the handouts were "false, lacking in balance, and misleading," since they contained "a representation or suggestions not approved" by regulators. The FDA told the company to instruct its sales force on the federal rules prohibiting off-label promotions.

Two months later, the FDA fielded yet *more* complaints of Procrit promotions, this time from physicians *west* of the Mississippi. Once again, the regulators ordered Ortho to set up companywide training sessions about illegal promotions. McClellan, however, kept priming the off-label pump. The message he continually received from headquarters was, *Get your docs to escalate the doses!*

The rep put his back into his living. He lugged around copies of an Ortho form that nurses could use to assess patient fatigue. It recorded a person's name, hemoglobin count, hematocrit level, and chemo cycle. "Do you tire easily?" McClellan's one-pager asked. Most patients circled a 10, the highest level of exhaustion. When asked to name their most rigorous activity, a woman wrote, "Going out to eat." Yet when Procrit was offered, a few patients declined. "Too ill," wrote one poor soul. But most patients tried it, and McClellan never followed up to see how they fared.

He concocted a number of forms that gave Ortho's marketing trials a patina of official business. McClellan invented a patient graph that showed dates they were injected with high doses and how their hemoglobin numbers zoomed. He filled out QOL study sheets, tracking severely ill patients by recording the dates they received low doses of Procrit—10,000 units three times a week—as well as the fateful day they were doubled up with risky doses of 20,000 units three times a week. Then, he recorded his QOL findings. "Could care for family members once again," he wrote for one patient. "Longer periods between transfusions," he said of another. But had he looked closer, he would have seen that the majority of his cases fared poorly during his Phase IV project. "Cancer to the brain was worse, but anemia was better," he wrote for patient No. 3. Several people felt so sick, they refused treatment. Three out of five people were dying, based on one set of McClellan's homemade forms, some due to disease progression. Had this been part of a scientific trial, the 66 percent death rate would have set off alarms. But it was just one rep's field study, and McClellan didn't even notice the morbidity rate in his own handiwork.

Nurses needed attention too. To help them collect continuing education credits, McClellan hosted a luncheon for the forty or so members of the Oncology Nurse Education Society in Tucson one day. Using the nurses' education books as a guide, he devised his own official-looking presentation about fatigue for the room. The event lasted an hour: He spent forty-five minutes talking about Procrit and quality of life, and the nurses received 3.5 hours of CME credit.

He didn't realize that his off-label promotional efforts were illegal. Besides, he was driven by the same American Dream as the Great Gatsby or Willy Loman. "I want to be a millionaire," he once told Duxbury. He'd been toiling hard since he was a scrawny, eighty-pound ten-year-old, working after school at the grocery store in Wheaton, Minnesota (pop. 1,400). He had to scramble up a mountain of hundred-pound sacks of potatoes, stacked ten feet high, and lug one down. Then he'd open the bag, throw out the potatoes "filled with crawly maggots," and divide the rest into ten-pound sacks. Up and down the precarious stacks he scampered, hoping not to get crushed by an avalanche of spuds and earning a dime for every ten-pounder he tied. He was so productive that he made twenty dollars the first week.

"They decided that was too much for a kid, so they paid me sixty cents an hour after that."

In the summer of 1961, when McClellan turned thirteen, his dad hired him on his migrant tree-cutting crew. "I'll pay you only fifty cents an hour, but you'll get to put in long hours," his father told him. No kidding. McClellan spent sixteen hours a day climbing trees and chainsawing branches without a hard hat, safety net, ear mufflers, or even a rope. One hot day, the kid was hanging seventy-five feet above a sidewalk, trying to saw a huge branch near a utility line, when the branch snapped, pinned his leg to the tree, and landed on the power wire. As McClellan told Duxbury, ten thousand volts shot through his leg, and he writhed in agony. Down below, men hollered hysterically as arcs of electricity jumped from one power pole to the next on down the street. Each time the arc jumped, McClellan's body sizzled like a slice of bacon. As he struggled to maintain consciousness and avoid falling to his death, he himself was awed by the crackling coils of light. Finally, the electrical hula hoop ran into a transformer, blowing the wires and ending McClellan's aerial near-electrocution.

He continued cutting trees during summers, moving from town to vale with his dad's primitive chain-saw gang, sleeping in two-dollars-a-night flophouses and earning $48 for a six-day week. He couldn't wait to leave home, though, and moved on to the University of Minnesota. At nineteen, he married Beth, and they had a son. In 1970, within minutes of graduating with his bachelor's degree in education, McClellan, Beth, and their child climbed into a 1946 Ford pickup and drove two hundred miles south until they reached a town just shy of St. Cloud, Minnesota. There, McClellan worked as a teacher and principal for rural schools, existing on a four-figure salary, battling below-freezing winters, and helping neighbors dig their hogs out of mud bogs every spring. After work, McClellan would drive to St. Cloud to attend night school, where he earned two master's degrees.

His siblings, meanwhile, had grown into small-town burghers, wielding influence in their respective corners of the prairie. McClellan's brother was a superintendent of schools who parlayed his public perks into private advantage. One sister married the son of Wheaton's mayor and maintained a house in Fargo, North Dakota, and a stupendous manse in Lake of the Woods. Another sister invested in real estate with her husband and was worth $10 million. "I'm the only person in my family who isn't a millionaire, and because of that, I'm the black sheep of the family," McClellan lamented. He quit teaching and obtained a Realtor's license but didn't make much commission selling $10,000 houses, and *still* his siblings snubbed him. So one day, after an especially harsh winter, McClellan packed his family into the car and headed south to Arizona. "We expected to see covered wagons and dusty streets," he recalled. Instead, they found the bleak boulevards and smoggy skies of urban Phoenix. They kept on driving until they found a more picturesque spot in smaller Tucson. By 1985, McClellan had a son in high school, a three-year-old daughter, and a five-bedroom ranch house at the foot of the stunning Catalina Mountains. But he was gone most of the time, missing his kids' soccer games and school plays, selling a product that his wife didn't understand. And, now, in 1998, after forty years of work, he *still* wasn't a millionaire.

"I'm Mr. Average," he had to admit. "I've been mediocre my entire life." To remedy that, in 1998 he attended a "Success" business seminar, shelling out $225 and driving to Phoenix's America West Arena. He mingled with approximately fourteen thousand other success seekers who hoped to grab the golden keys to happiness. What they found was a spectacle of lights, music, and special effects in which business tips were leavened with patriotic slogans, Christian prayer, and celebrity flash. Sitting in the stands, McClellan applauded Notre Dame's football coach, Lou Holtz; Britain's former prime minister Margaret Thatcher; General Colin Powell; and TV host Larry King. He listened to an übersalesman, the seventy-two-year-old Zig Ziglar, reveal the "Gold in Goals: The Skills of Motivation," and jotted down aphorisms. "Success is dependent upon the glands—sweat glands." "If you learn from defeat, you haven't really lost." But the one that stuck in McClellan's mind was this: "Don't look back unless that's where you're heading." By the time the evangelical Peter Lowe came onstage and shouted, "Do you *really* want to achieve a level of success beyond what most people achieve?" McClellan and the crowd roared "Yes!" and rose to their feet like one giant centipede.

Reflection was useful to McClellan primarily as a way to map success. He began meticulously plotting his goals, blocking out each "action" step he needed to take to execute his dream. Client follow-up was key to his modus operandi, and his strategy began to work. By early 1999, he had finally beaten Duxbury's sales record. McClellan had sold $4.2 million worth of Procrit and was on his way to realizing his full sales potential.

—⁂—

Duxbury mopped the floor of his condo in a zenlike state. *Squee-chah, squee-chah, squee-chah.* His repetitious actions kept time to a wordless koan: Funny how a domestic chore can become a hallowed ritual when you realize it's the last time you'll perform the task. Duxbury loved his high-end condo, its lake-view location and cozy size. But he could no longer afford it. No job and no money had forced him to show his home to Realtors and potential buyers. It was not a great time to sell property, and Duxbury was about to hold a fire sale.

He had been searching for jobs in the pharmaceutical industry for nearly a year now, talking with recruiters and sending out résumés. Someone at Amgen had approached him with a job, but once the interviewer learned of his role in the company's continuing litigation, he balked. "Your knowledge of the case precludes you from working here," Duxbury was told. Crestfallen, he considered leaving the drug business. But he couldn't think of any other job he wanted more.

Then there was his unemployment case. The state had refused to pay his benefits because he had failed to show that a "substantial deterioration of working conditions or unreasonable hardship existed in the workplace." So Duxbury dove into his ocean of papers and plucked the most egregious examples of abusive treatment. If he couldn't persuade authorities that he had resigned under "extreme hardship," he'd have absolutely no income for quite a while.

On Monday, November 9, 1998, he prepared for a teleconference with administrative judge Jill Geary and an Ortho attorney. But minutes before the scheduled hearing, the judge called to postpone it briefly. Ortho had just informed her that a new lawyer would attend the meeting but needed time to prepare. Duxbury returned to packing boxes and, thirty minutes later, dialed the number for Geary. Also on the line was a Patterson Belknap lawyer, who had had no clue about the case. Since the burden of proving work-related misconduct fell on the employer, and since Ortho hadn't sent any evidence to back up its claim of Duxbury's misbehavior, Judge Geary ruled that Duxbury was entitled to his state benefits. Duxbury exhaled so loudly that both judge and lawyer heard his relief. "This decision makes a huge difference in my day-to-day existence," he explained. Duxbury was about to hang up when his instinct for self-preservation kicked in. What if Ortho contested the verdict? Duxbury asked the judge for a copy of the audiotaped hearing "that includes your final decision." The judge agreed.

Duxbury and McClellan kept in touch by e-mail and telephone. Periodically, the Tucson rep would ask the unavoidable: "Have you found a job yet?" Duxbury didn't mind. Besides, it was cathartic to talk to his friend, and McClellan always made him smile. But eventually, Duxbury grew concerned for his friend's welfare. "I don't want you to get in trouble from Ortho for talking with me."

"How's anyone going to know?" McClellan asked.

"Human resources, legal, the chief of security . . . They have their ways."

"Don't get paranoid, Mark."

Duxbury knew that Ortho reps like McClellan had to submit their telephone bills as part of their monthly expenses to be reimbursed. So he tried to program his phone in such a way that his number would be hidden from headquarters.

A week after Thanksgiving, Duxbury steered his car through the water-swollen streets of downtown Seattle. La Niña storms had topped the city's potholes with oily tiaras and clogged her gutters. Duxbury had twice circled the fifty-five-story skyscraper where he was scheduled to appear, but in this downpour, the structure looked like a gray-blue metallic curtain. When it had opened in 1988, critics named it one of the nation's three best new office buildings, but locals called the knobby-topped high-rise the "spark plug tower." He finally descended into a dry garage and parked.

He rode the elevator to the forty-fourth floor. Earlier in the week, he had reviewed his 1995 deposition and wondered whether he should testify for Amgen in its case against Charise Charles. Duxbury had even put the question to Robert Brauer in his charmingly blunt way. "If I get sued by J and J, will you defend me?" The vice president had demurred and didn't offer to pay for the rep's testimony. Now as the elevator doors slid open, as silent as a snake's jaw, Duxbury felt trapped. "I have no one here today," he realized. He almost turned back but remembered that he'd committed himself. So he wandered down the hall and found the wood-paneled conference room.

He greeted Brauer and Melton and nodded to a third man, Jerry Linscott of Baker Hostetler, representing Charise Charles. Linscott had been sympathetic toward Duxbury in the deposition three years earlier. But that was a lifetime ago, as he was about to learn. Duxbury took a seat by the glass-eyed video camera, and the show began.

First, Melton led him through the documents, detailing Procrit's prices, Charise's deals, and all the rest. Several hours later, it was Linscott's turn, and whatever empathy he'd shown the witness before had vanished. Linscott sparred with Duxbury over so many issues that the rep tried to defend himself. "I came into Ortho Biotech to be a technical expert. What I walked into was a street fight between two huge companies . . . a winner-take-all battle."

Linscott didn't seem to care. "Do you think Charise [did] anything wrong?"

The rep turned Jesuitical. "What do you mean by wrong, specifically?"

I mean, said Linscott, something "contrary to the law and morals of public standards." I mean Webster's definition, he added.

"I don't know if that's what [the dictionary] says," Duxbury said, uneasily.

The opponents went at it, hammer and tongs, each side getting in a few blows. "I'm not trying to be evasive," an exasperated Duxbury finally said.

"I'm just looking for the truth; that's all I'm looking for, Mr. Duxbury," the man said.

Amgen's Melton interrupted. "I think your questions are argumentative. You have asked this about ten times, Mr. Linscott." *You're now officially harassing the witness.*

But Charise's attorney ignored the objection. Instead, he demanded that Duxbury give him the criteria for Charise's "bad" actions. Since Duxbury had never defined the supplier's behavior in that way, he steadfastly refused to answer the questions. Finally, after seven hours, the prosecutor cut loose his weary deponent. Duxbury left the room feeling like a fly that had been chased around the kitchen with a rolled-up brief. He crawled into the elevator and descended to the pit of the building. How easily he spotted his dingy 1987 Nissan Pathfinder amid the rows of late-model European cars.

On his way home, he hunched over the wheel and listened to Coltrane. The deposition had been more adversarial than the last one—only, this time Duxbury didn't focus on his own performance. Instead, he replayed his opponent's parries and tried to discern a pattern. What had happened to move this chess game closer to an inquisition? One particular question rang in Duxbury's head: "Procrit is a life-saving drug, is it not?" Linscott had asked.

"No," Duxbury had answered.

"Procrit is a benefit to people who are suffering anemia, is it not?"

"Yes," he'd said, warily.

"Enhances their ability to live life . . . does it not?"

Duxbury had hesitated. Illegal promotions, phony experiments, off-label bribes, and overdose schemes—how could these crafty deals be life-enhancing? At the time Duxbury had answered affirmatively, but later he'd wish he could take it back. That snarling, badgering question began to circle back and fall on his head like a thousand reprimands. *"Procrit enhances a patient's ability to live, does it not, Mr. Duxbury?"*

—⚊—

On December 31, 1998, five months after Duxbury resigned from Ortho and four months after he should have started to receive his state benefits, he held his first unemployment check. After deducting money for child support, his weekly stipend came to $200. He had never fought so hard for so little. But it was too late. He had already sold his house at roughly 25 percent below appraised value and had netted just enough money to squeak by for another few months. He was shaken by the pummeling he had taken and, like a boxer, had heard the faint sound of the referee's count. He'd gotten up before the bell, but it was still early in the match.

14

"Strength for Living"

1999 to 2000

Heat waves rose from the asphalt, the steering wheel hot to the touch. It was early July, midday, the worst time to be delivering pepperoni-and-onion pizzas. Duxbury pulled up to a stoplight and glanced at the car next to his jalopy. Well, hullo! The blonde in the convertible smiled back, her hair grazing her bare shoulders, her halter top revealing. For a second, Duxbury forgot he wasn't a professional in a light tan suit but a minimum-wage slave in a red-and-blue paper hat. Their eyes locked—was that a "come hither" look?—and time seemed to stop. But when the traffic light turned green, the woman slowly mouthed the words *pizza boy,* then sped off, robbing the Domino's man of his smile.

Life had changed drastically for Duxbury. He tried to keep self-pity at bay, but, damn, it was hard. A few months earlier, in March, he had walked out of a fine interview with a decent man from Watson Laboratories, a verbal offer in hand. Duxbury had filled out the paperwork and supplied references; all that was left was verification of Duxbury's employment at Ortho Biotech. But the human resources people in Raritan had refused to answer their counterparts at Watson, despite numerous faxed requests and telephone calls. A month later, Watson withdrew its offer, and Duxbury resumed his hunt. With a sales track like his, Duxbury usually got to the interview room. But invariably, someone would ask, "Why'd you leave your last position?" He'd give the short version, explaining that he'd been forced to testify in litigation about Ortho's marketing policies in regard to its PLA with Amgen. That, in turn, had resulted in his departure, along with those of several other deposed reps. But invariably that would only prompt more questions like "You mean a lawsuit?" and "What marketing policies?" At that stage, Duxbury could see the curtains coming down on this scene. As he'd leave, he'd tell himself, "Maybe that company pushes the ethical envelope in their own promotions." More likely the manager didn't want to hire a guy who was involved in a suit between two titans. Would-be employers worried that the litigation would require him to offer more testimony or, at the very least, distract him from the new job. Others simply didn't want to hire someone with a gap in his career trajectory. "It's enormously frustrating," he told McClellan.

In June 1999 Duxbury's unemployment benefits expired, leaving him without any cash to buy gas to haul ass to his shrinking number of interviews. So, when he saw a HELP WANTED sign in the window of a pizza parlor, he applied. He landed a job that paid $5.15 an hour, roughly $150 for thirty hours a week, and he felt darn lucky about it too. Instead of scanning a doctor's ego wall to tailor his sales pitch, Duxbury now peeked into other people's messy apartments through a half-opened door. He tried not to stare at the customer's face as he exchanged his warm box of dough for a fistful of dollars, performing an awkward do-si-do that didn't always end with a tip. He slept on a couch in a friend's apartment, wore socks with holes, and paid his bills by delivering pies. Was he being punished for something? Every time he rethreaded the film through the sprockets in his mind, he arrived at the same conclusion. "All I did was respond to a subpoena. If I had refused to testify, or if I'd lied," he thought, "I'd be in an entirely different situation, either in jail or in management." Telling the truth was the right thing to do. Yet he had never imagined that he'd wind up like this, in the fast-food line, swathed in eau de garlic and crowned by a tissue beanie. No, he'd definitely had something else in mind, only now he couldn't quite remember what it was.

Then one night, while watching television, he saw a commercial that opened with a piano playing a few bars of hymnlike music. On the screen, a large black woman looked into the camera and declared, "I made an omelet." Cut to a vigorous old man, clad in lumberjack plaid, exclaiming, "I picked an apple!" Cue the youngsters carrying baskets of red fruit. Duxbury's heart warmed at the shots of old-fashioned kitchens, wicker bushels, and farm kids. The artful pastiche was complemented by just the right chords of Americana. Then came the burn: "This is about Procrit," said the narrator. As confirmation, the brand name filled the screen along with its scientific term, epoetin alfa. Duxbury sat dumbfounded. The theatrically trained voice continued, "If you are a chemotherapy patient and feel tired and weak, ask your doctor about Procrit." Yet these actors didn't look like chemotherapy patients. They were not bald, bruised, or blue, with skin stretched taut on their skulls. The omelet-maker was overweight and scab-free; the apple-picker rosy-cheeked and clear-eyed. But what really floored Duxbury was the gorgeous shot of a young, plump woman with luxuriant dark hair—the very picture of health. Again, he heard the Voice: "Procrit is the natural way to regain red blood cells lost during chemotherapy."

"It is not natural," Duxbury told the television.

The narrator ignored him. "In studies, only diarrhea and edema occurred more often with Procrit than with a placebo."

"Half true!" Duxbury yelled. There was no mention of hypertension, seizures, strokes, or the dreadful results from the Normal Hematocrit Cardiac Trials.

At first, Duxbury couldn't believe his ears. Here was a multimillion-dollar drug promotion for fatigue, an unapproved indication for Procrit. This was an illegal campaign and false advertising to boot, he believed. Why would regulators allow J&J to break the law, and more importantly, why would J&J be so brazen about it? A few days later, he asked McClellan about the ad. But his friend was effusive.

"Isn't it great? It'll help lift sales."

"But, Dean, it's deceptive," Duxbury said. "Look at the actors. They don't look like chemotherapy patients to me. They look like healthy people!"

"I don't see how J&J's lawyers would allow the ad to run if it was wrong, Mark."

That was exactly Duxbury's point, but he bit his tongue. He didn't want to lose the goodwill of his old friend.

Over the next few weeks, he had plenty of opportunities to catch the "Strength for Living" commercials. They played frequently, targeting the over-fifty, Geritol-for-lunch bunch. When he heard the tinkling ivory keys, Duxbury would lean forward on his couch-bed to better study the cunning arrangement of sounds, words, and cinematic images. As colors flooded the screen, the disembodied voice went on: "Call now, and learn how Procrit can help you get back the strength you need, your strength for living." Cut to the young woman tossing her curly dark mane in the face of millions of viewers. Cue to the bouncy mother throwing a ball to her son. Near the end of the sixty-second ad, a gold sunset spilled across the screen—along with the 800 telephone number. Each time Duxbury saw that, he grew outraged at the deceptive message. In his mind, there was no doubt that the sleight-of-hand campaign, filled with subliminal off-label messages, broke U.S. law. The commercial implied that Ortho's drug could reduce fatigue and weakness in anemic people, even though none of that had been proven in randomized science-based trials.

He thought back to his dark days at Ortho, when he tried to match J&J's high-toned talk about ethics to the low-down tricks of its subsidiary. Then it hit him. "So that's why Ronald Gelbman was so blasé when I reported the fatigue promotions," he thought, slapping his forehead. When Duxbury had contacted J&J's chairman of pharmaceuticals in spring 1997, the company was already preparing its Procrit for a fatigue media blitz. "This is a gray area," Gelbman had told the rep. But what he'd really meant, Duxbury realized, was, *This is the core of our $20 million ad campaign. Shoo fly!*

To the rep, "Strength for Living" was just another phrase for "quality of life." But what he didn't understand was how regulators could allow such quackery. Hadn't snake oil peddlers gone the way of the Victrola?

—m—

Dr. Patricia Keegan was among those who approved the nation's medicines, drug trial designs, insert labels, promotions, and advertisements. To visit her office in Rockville, Maryland, one had to run a gauntlet of gun-wearing guards, surrender an identification card, and submit to an escort. The rigmarole was meant for the safety of regulators. "People think we have a warehouse of drugs here, so we have to be careful," explained a gatekeeper. But no cache of narcotics lay inside the FDA fortress—only mounds of drug studies and promotions that needed to be reviewed on behalf of the American public.

Every day Keegan and her colleagues tried to balance the legitimate medical needs of U.S. consumers with the commercial desires of global pharmaceuticals like J&J. In a strange and peculiar way, the FDA site was like the Raritan compound in that both were within spitting distance of a country club *and* a cemetery. But there the resemblances ended. Keegan worked in a dyspeptic, low-ceilinged building off the droning Rockville Pike. Outside her window stretched several miles of black-topped strip malls packed with pet stores and noodle shops. And although she and her staff worked twelve miles northwest of the nation's capital, they weren't immune to political pressures. In 1999, in fact, the stress inside this particular building was mounting, partly because of the barrage of new advertising material from epo's promoters.

Although J&J and Amgen still fought in private courtrooms, they presented a united front when dealing with Washington. As epo's licenser, Amgen was responsible for upholding FDA rules; as a licensee, J&J had to cooperate with its partner to fulfill the agency's directives. So together, the pair had to answer to regulators. Keegan had been dealing with these two companies almost since she first arrived at the agency in 1990. A short, plump woman with cropped dark hair and spaniel-brown eyes, she was a board-certified M.D. in internal medicine and medical oncology. The regulator could be spotted in the halls of the Center for Biologic Evaluation and Research (CBER), dressed in an argyle sweater and sensible shoes, slogging to a meeting with members of the Drug Marketing, Advertising, and Communications Division (DDMAC) and other colleagues. Keegan was so well respected that by 1999, she'd been promoted to deputy director for the Division of Clinical Trials Design and Analysis.

Part of her job was to paw through volumes of drug applications and studies bound in red, orange, and blue covers, indicating different phases of trials. She also helped review advertising material for some of the nation's 4,500 drugs. Her office was packed with material, and memos were stacked precariously in towers on the floor or lined neatly in mail crates. Amgen and J&J had just added to the pile with a barrage of ad submissions.

Procrit's "Strength for Living" ads marked a sea change. For most of the twentieth century, pharmaceutical ads had been confined to print, where the seller had been required to summarize a drug's precautions, side effects, and contraindications. This was impossible in TV ads, since screen crawls of eye-squinting type do not make for snappy sixty-second spots. But as the drug industry grew, it began flexing its muscles and in 1997 pressured the FDA to ease its advertising rules. That altered the landscape in two significant ways: Pharma could reach beyond its customary print ads that targeted physicians and present its case directly to the unsophisticated consumer. And drugmakers no longer had to reveal all the risky reasons not to buy the product they were so earnestly pitching. All J&J and the other drug companies had to do was provide viewers with another means of acquiring the same cautionary information. Enter the 800 numbers and the officious shrug-off, "Consult your doctor."

Before the rules changed, in 1995, drug firms like J&J had spent about $313 million on these "direct-to-consumer" ads, most of it in magazines. But by the time Duxbury caught Procrit's spiel, that figure had more than quadrupled to $1.4 billion. By 1999 TV screens were flooded with sound bites about Allegra (for allergies), Prozac (for depression), Zocor (for cholesterol), and Valtrex (for herpes). And now, in between come-ons for Budweiser beer and McDonald's Happy Meals, was a plug for Procrit.

The J&J ads presented a thorny problem inside the FDA. It turned out that the same phrases that had irked Duxbury concerned Keegan and her colleagues. "Procrit is safe and effective," the ad brayed. But that wasn't entirely true. No adequate study had demonstrated that epo was safe at any dosage, and the drug firms' long-promised safety studies were still missing. Epo surely helped some anemic patients avoid blood transfusions, but now that doctors understood how the HIV virus infected blood banks, that benefit was hardly a lifesaver.

There were other untruthful elements to the campaign. J&J had run a large ad in the October 25, 1998, issue of *Parade* magazine. The headline asked chemotherapy patients, "Do you feel tired all the time? Please tell your doctor. There's a treatment for tiredness." But the roll failed to mention that Procrit was not intended for all chemo patients—only those with nonmyeloid tumors. Plus, it didn't include all the patient information it was required to, and instead printed a summary. Worse still was the statement that there was a cure for fatigue, wrote William Purvis, director of the advertising staff at CBER. "Procrit is intended . . . to treat anemia associated with certain chemotherapeutic regimens, not 'tiredness' in general," he wrote. He called the ad "false and misleading under the [law]" and told the drugmakers to stop running it.

A month later, Ortho Biotech pulled the advertisement. By then, however, it had been running for five months, reaching more than seventy-four million readers who had glanced at it not just in *Parade* but in six other national magazines too.

Then there were the beautifully evocative, subliminally suggestive TV ads. The commercial's thick-maned actress and twinkly-eyed grandfather inspired thousands of viewers to dial Procrit's 800 telephone number. Operators answered these calls seven days a week, twenty-four hours a day, repeating the same scripted advice to the tired and sick. This toll-free rep, "dedicated solely to Procrit," was equipped with a headset and keyboard to take down vital information. She'd then send out an "education" packet, perhaps with a free writing pen or pad. By month's end, the call center had mailed more than 10,000 packages—more than 360,000 since the campaign first launched in 1997. J&J paid its ad makers at Ogilvy & Mather about $20 million to devise these and other "awareness programs," and the return on investment was handsome. The promotion swept hundreds of thousands of patients into medical offices, where they harangued their doctors for epo prescriptions. A few caregivers refused to give the expensive drug to those who demanded some "strength for living." Other physicians didn't bother to argue. In the world of HMO medicine, where appointments were shorter than a flea's femur, some doctors would just as soon whip out an Rx pad than argue with a patient, just to keep the line moving.

Several FDA staff members wanted to rein in J&J's ad men. "They can't mislead, and they can't lie," said one. Others took the middle road: "But can they imply? Can they extrapolate?" Keegan listened to the back-and-forth as the mail carriers dumped crates and packages into her office. By 2000, J&J had grown even more aggressive. Keegan and staff reviewed a video for cancer patients and their families that said, "There may always be some fatigue with cancer . . . but it can be helped." J&J failed to balance that bold statement with a qualifying one. An Ortho banner made an "inappropriate analogy" between low red blood cell counts and weakness, suggesting that "Procrit can be used to treat tiredness." One of the company's many Web sites claimed that Ortho's drug raised "energy levels," while a tabletop display boasted that it "treat[s] all tumor types." And Procrit's glossy brochures still encouraged patients to ask "your doctor about fatigue." J&J submitted ads for FDA review as much as nine months *after* running them or delivered them without the complete broadcast or print date. J&J's "tardy submission of materials [was] not acceptable," said one official.

But patients had no idea of this deceit. To them, Procrit was safe, and the ads honest. One study found that 50 percent of consumers thought that direct-to-consumer ads had to be preapproved by regulators; 43 percent believed that only drugs that had been proven to be completely safe could be advertised, while 21 percent thought that only extremely effective drugs could be promoted. The makers of Lister's Dog Soap, however, proved them wrong on all counts.

Yet the federal agency, with its $1.1 billion annual budget, continued to try to hold its own against the $29-billion-a-year revenue-generating giant. On June 30, 2000, the FDA sent J&J a stern six-page letter listing several aspects of its dodgy Procrit ads. Keegan and the others said that the promotions needed "to more accurately bring in

Procrit's approved use rather than an open-ended general discussion on the symptoms of fatigue." They asked the company to "immediately stop distribution" of these materials.

A covey of legally vetted letters, dressed in obfuscating, sometimes obsequious, tones, arrived in Rockville, from New Brunswick. J&J managers were confused by regulators' "interpretation of the Federal Food, Drug and Cosmetic Act" and its "advertising provisions" for Procrit. They wanted to have a "dialogue" about the issues, and set that proposed meeting's agenda by including several attachments and a list of questions, including one no-brainer: "Is it FDA's position that language in a company Web site is to be written in language understandable to the consumer?" The company then closed its aggressive note in a passive way: "We wish to work cooperatively with FDA to address the allegations." One had to read the letter a few times to understand that J&J wasn't about to withdraw its ubiquitous ads no matter what the lawmen said. Its stance was unmistakable—rejection straight from an aerosol can.

It was all too much for Keegan and the staff. The volume of promo drug pieces to review tripled from roughly ten thousand items in 1997 to thirty-two thousand in 1999, while staffing inside Keegan's division remained stagnant. The staff began to issue dozens of warning letters to several drug companies, including several to repeat offenders. Before long, it was mailing fourteen warnings to GlaxoSmithKline, six to Schering, five to Merck & Co., and several to J&J, about its deceptive sales gimmicks. Although Congress had endowed the FDA with authority, regulators were no more able to ensure that Procrit ads were accurate than they could guarantee that epo was safe. J&J continued flouting the law on prime-time television, in lurid color, preying on seriously ill people.

—m—

Pump your legs faster, lean forward, push yourself to answer that ringing doorbell. Quick! But your feet move like bricks, your veins bulge like balloons, and your breath wheezes like a bellows. *Ring,*

ring, ring. Finally, you open the door only to blink at the empty porch. Then you glimpse the mail carrier hopping back into his truck and driving away with your package. Once again, you've missed the delivery of the prescription medicine that could help relieve the frustrating symptoms of anemia.

That was the message Ortho wanted to convey inside its virtual reality tour bus. The eighteen-wheeler weighed fifty-five thousand pounds, stretched seventy-eight feet long, and offered a thrilling e-ticket ride into a three-dimensional, surround-sound, sensory world—for free. As one tour guide said, "I used to work for Disney at Epcot Center, but now I've shifted from entertainment to medical education . . . and it's far more rewarding."

Visitors walked into the parked theme bus, where guides greeted them. They viewed a ten-minute introductory video about "cancer-related fatigue," not the FDA-approved indication of chemotherapy-induced anemia. Then visitors moved to one of five "pods." They were fitted with a helmet that had headphones, goggles with "eyes," arm straps with motion sensors, and foot pedals. Guides could control the pedals' resistance, so guests could feel just how difficult it was for an anemic person to move around. Your "eyes" saw their reality; your headphones piped in sounds and directions to steer you through the 3-D world. Then you ran the gauntlet: You had to pick up the telephone, turn off the whistling kettle, and answer the door quickly, among other tasks. In reality, you'd probably accomplish this in a matter of seconds. But not in Ortho's world, where guides adjusted your StairMaster pedals to turn light steps into leaden shuffles. Due to exertion, "a person [might] feel dizzy or a little nauseous," read instructions. If so, just lead the guest back to the greeting area and provide "some refreshments."

Ah, but if you had enough erythropoietin in your system, this wouldn't happen. If you received Procrit injections, you'd fly through the stations! To demonstrate, a guide might loosen the pedals' resistance and throttle you back down to reality. By the time a doctor stumbled out of Ortho's fun house, he'd feel enough empathy for the anemic to begin prescribing Procrit.

That was the whole point of the ICRA—Insight into Cancer Related Anemia—exhibit. Ortho had spent $1 million to build its motorized West Coast wagon so that oncologists might understand how important it was to address "quality of life issues" in their patients. It had a second unit puttering around the East Coast. "With the help of a vast team of engineers and thought leaders," Ortho had pioneered the effort to "reach a wider range of oncologists from a larger geographic area." It had also enlisted a New York–based firm that mounted trade shows, shareholder meetings, and "lollapalooza extravagances" for health-care companies.

Yet it fell to the reps to move ICRA (pronounced eye-ka-rah) from town to town, which McClellan did. He had to find a place big enough to park the beast near a hospital where busy doctors could walk in. Then he had to obtain permission to park his bus on the property. "Doctors like free publicity," so McClellan would often call the local newspapers and TV stations to cover the circus. Then he'd ingratiate himself with hospital maintenance crews so he could connect the motor home's power cable into a single-phase, 208-volt plug. After that, it was a matter of printing invitations, collecting RSVPs, calling reporters, and ordering a $350 buffet of cold cuts, sweet rolls, and hot coffee. On the day of the show, he'd arrive two hours early to meet the "producer" and run through the schedule of media interviews and guests. ICRA could handle eight doctors an hour, and McClellan tried to move fifty physicians through the circuit in one day.

Publicists in Raritan performed advance work marshaling wire services and medical journals to print news about the big blood rig. One visit was billed as "the first and only appearance of the simulator in the Bay Area and no additional stops are planned in the region this year." But there was always next year—and the year after that. ICRA turned up at hundreds of institutions, including Sloan-Kettering, Mayo Clinic, Duke, UCLA, Stanford, and Harvard. One wag called the parked theme ride "Chemo-World"; another dubbed it Epocot. It was Big Pharma's version of *Pirates of the Caribbean*. Ortho's thought leaders and advisors—Drs. Glaspy, Cella, and Vogelzang, among others—might as well have been singing "A Procrit's Life for Me" for all the world seemed to care. The Jolly J&J sailed on, plundering the treasure chests of community hospitals and snatching the purses of young and old, and no one seemed able to stop the ship. Procrit sales swelled.

—᙮—

MᴄCʟᴇʟʟᴀɴ was promoted to territory manager, given a raise, and began training other reps how to close deals. He taught them how to use minitrials, Phase IV marketing studies, and patient cards. "After a doc gets reimbursed for free drug the first time," he told his charges, "he'll become a loyal client."

McClellan's territory changed too. He no longer handled New Mexico but flew into Las Vegas every other week. He rented a full-size white Cadillac, drove slowly along the Strip, and stayed at all the big hotels, from the MGM Grand to Mandalay Bay. He rented a local storage facility in Vegas that he stuffed with Procrit mugs, eighteen-inch tote bags, medical textbooks, penlights, pads, chemo blankets, thermal glasses, and other tchotchkes. He missed the ornery enchantment of New Mexico, with its explosive lightning storms and miles of empty dirt roads, but he grew accustomed to the way reinforced concrete shadows fell on Nevada's gridlocked tourist basin. The sunsets all looked the same, but at least his clients were clustered in one convenient, eighty-four-square-mile area.

He'd turned maniacal in his job. To him, a doctor's no meant "Come back later." McClellan got thrown out of one office six times by a secretary who didn't like him. So the rep sat in the doctor's office for more than an hour one day until he saw the physician head for the men's room. McClellan abruptly got up, ran to the washroom, and sidled up to the man at the urinal. He struck up a conversation as the two men offloaded, and eventually, the rep made a sale. If he couldn't get any quality time with a prescriber in the daytime he'd wait until nightfall. Once he sat in his car in a dark parking lot until the doctor finally exited the building. McClellan jumped out of his car, met the man as he was unlocking the door to his Mercedes, and got an appointment. Another time, he tracked an important KOL by flying to a medical conference in Los Angeles, listening to his keynote address, and waylaying him at the reception. By the time their drinks were dry, McClellan had persuaded the doctor to speak at Ortho's next shindig. In time, hooking an oncologist was like shooting fish in a barrel.

As far as drugs went, Procrit was becoming the sine qua non for oncologists. They used the "buy-and-bill" model of business, purchasing epo (and other cancer drugs) in bulk at a nice discount. They marked it up for the patient, had their nurse administer the medicine, then billed insurers at high retail rates. The Big Five–managed health plans—the Cignas, Aetnas, and Prudentials—along with the commercial lines of Blue Cross and Blue Shield, were wise to this practice. So they paid providers at lower rates than the doctors billed. But many public plans paid full price. "The Railroad Retirement Fund pays real well," McClellan told one client. So, too, did many teachers', plumbers', and other labor unions and pension funds.

But Medicare paid the best, and for years it reimbursed doctors at 100 percent of AWP. In an effort to curb health-care spending, Congress had passed a Balanced Budget Act in 1997, which, among other things, reduced Medicare Part B payments to 95 percent of a drug's AWP—5 percent less than it had been paying. In January 1998 Ortho countered by increasing its drug sticker price 4 percent, again pushing up the AWP and insurers' reimbursements rates. It also offered even more in rebates, fees, and other goodies. McClellan believed his deals were good for patients, doctors, and nurses. "I feel like I'm really helping people," he often told his wife.

The rep grew close to Dr. Suresh Kattakar, an East Indian oncologist who owned his own practice. McClellan camped out at the doctor's Tucson office every week and bought him and his staff a meal almost every time. By 1996, he had finally converted Kattakar to Procrit, turning him into his single biggest account, amounting to $1 million worth of epo annually. At least once a year, McClellan paid Kattakar $500 for a daylong "clerkship." The salesman would don a white lab coat and follow the oncologist on his rounds examining breast cancer patients. It was a torturous experience, McClellan later told Duxbury. "I was so embarrassed. I spent the entire day looking at naked women."

"What did you do while the doctor was probing?" Duxbury wanted to know.

McClellan's voice turned peevish. "I didn't know what to do! I reviewed their charts, studied the ceiling, and commented on the weather. But mostly I just stood there looking stupid."

A few months later, when McClellan's boss said it was time to pay Kattakar for another clerkship, McClellan balked. "I've seen enough breasts to last me a lifetime." Instead, he handed Kattakar the $500 check and skipped the rounds. Meanwhile, Kattakar's practice grew and his staff expanded to forty-eight people. One day McClellan looked around and thought, "Every oncologist in Tucson is a millionaire because of Procrit. I know because I sell it to them."

He'd do anything for his clients, short of attending breast exams. He manned a huge booth at the American Society of Clinical Oncology (ASCO) convention, during which Ortho flew in the world-class tenor José Carreras to give a private concert for its friends. McClellan was boarding 117 flights a year, driving four thousand miles a week, and adding more trophies to his office shelf. He and his wife won a cruise to Baja California; a lavish trip to the Phoenician in Scottsdale; and a vacation in Santa Barbara, where they stayed at the elegant Biltmore, sailed on a catamaran, and visited a winery owned by Fess Parker, aka TV's Davy Crockett. The rep traveled to New Orleans, Manhattan, and Philadelphia, and became an oenophile, partial to Napa reds and $300 champagnes. Ortho treated him to private performances of the Eagles and Sheryl Crow, and he even met the cast of *Gilligan's Island*! For every company event, Beth bought a new gown and danced to the live music before collapsing at a table.

All those plates of roasted Colorado lamb and Tuscan-rubbed beef tenderloin left the salesman with a paunch. All those tee-offs with the newly installed vice chairman of Ortho, Carol Webb, Tom Amick, and new president Gary Reedy burned his cheeks a deep bronze. McClellan was making a base salary plus $15,000 in bonuses a quarter, totalling $120,000 a year, which bumped him into an upper-income tax bracket. He spent more time taking or arranging photographs than he'd admit. He asked someone to snap an especially nice one of him sitting next to a beaming Webb, his arm around the president. McClellan sent her a copy of the picture with a note: "The queen and prince of OBI." She replied like the former schoolteacher she was, saying, "If I were to give out gold stars for performance, this would have received five."

"I'm so proud of you," she wrote on another photo.

McClellan won three more President's Cups and three diamonds for his signet ring, along with other awards. Beth collected a gold bracelet, a Waterford crystal sailboat, and an expensive Lladró figurine, gifts that she brought home and placed carefully in her jewel box and curio cabinet.

15

Code Mistress

Duxbury scanned the entrance to the Puyallup Fair, looking for the ticket booth to one of the ten largest old-time fairs in the country. His pretty companion giggled as they passed under a flapping banner, and the woman's son ran ahead. The boy glimpsed the amusement park, then returned, his eyes as big as a wheel. "Can we go on some rides?" he said excitedly.

Duxbury assured him they could indeed, just as soon as he bought their tickets. He, too, was excited. This was his first date with Dr. Chinyelu "Bibi" Farris, a single mother, whom he already liked. Pleasingly plump, she moved with the unhurried majesty of a prizewinning float in a parade. Her skin was as dark and smooth as blackstrap molasses, her jet-black hair straight and sprayed, but her eyes had a tawny cast that in the right light looked green. Her overbite expanded her toothy smile into a communicable esprit. Duxbury caught the infectious grin and threw it back.

Bibi thought, "He's so cute." But she worried he'd find an excuse to cut short their date. Earlier that September 2000, she'd been trawling an Internet dating site when up popped a listing headlined "Ebony women only." It was Duxbury's and Bibi studied his photograph, swooning over his heart-shaped face and blue eyes. "Handsome," she thought. His bio said he liked hiking on the beach, cringed at plates of calves' brains, and loved playing music. He had a black daughter, which explained his racial choice in women. His nickname was Dux or El Marko. When asked what sort of body type Duxbury preferred, he'd written, "Doesn't matter." "Good," she thought. "He likes chubby women." But what really got her was his favorite saying: *Carpe diem. Seize the day.* Tiny fingers ran up her spine. Her motto had always been *Rapiamus, amici, occasionem de die,* or *Seize the opportunity from the moment, my friends.* Apparently, Bibi was more garrulous than El Marko, and she immediately answered his ad.

The next day, her heart stuck in her throat, she checked her e-mail. But there was no word from him. "He was such a good catch," she thought, "someone else probably nabbed him." She pushed herself away from the desk but stopped. She had turned thirty-seven three weeks before and was still single. Not one to beat around the bush, she leaned over the keyboard and tapped him a note: "Are you still interested?" A day later, Duxbury wrote back, explaining that he'd been out of town for the past few days. Delighted, she responded by sending her phone number. The next night, Friday, at 11:08 (she remembered it so clearly) her telephone trilled.

"Hi, this is Mark Duxbury," said the voice. "You responded to my ad, remember?"

She swallowed at the sound of his musky baritone. "Of course I do," she said, in a lilting, yet seductively breathy, tone.

The lonely hearts chatted away, and Bibi learned more about the eligible bachelor. For the past year, he'd been working for the French pharmaceutical firm Aventis Behring. "It's a leading promoter of plasma therapies," he explained. He sold blood-related products to hospitals, infectious disease clinics, and anyone else who treated HIV-infected patients, hemophiliacs, and other sick people. His territory encompassed Washington, Oregon, and Idaho, and he traveled more days than he'd like to admit. "It's a little rough on my social life," he explained. But he clearly loved his job.

"Thank God the blood business is more robust than oil, steel, or autos," he bragged. "Demand is up, supply is down, and the money's good."

"Very nice," she thought. She didn't date deadbeats or the jobless.

They talked about his work, and surprisingly, she spoke his language fluently. "I'm a retired physician," she said, laughing. "I had to close my family practice in Tacoma a few months ago, due to a disability."

"Oh, no," he thought, visions of wheelchairs and iron braces dancing in his head.

She heard the hesitation. Then she explained that her bipolar medicine, Seroquel, dulled her thinking and sometimes made her drowsy. (It also explained her weight gain.) She had struggled to put herself through the Philadelphia College of Osteopathic Medicine and hated to give up her practice. But at the same time she was loath to harm her patients by writing the wrong prescription. Fortunately, she'd bought a private disability insurance policy many years ago, so now she and her son lived comfortably on about $75,000 a year.

"Wow!" said Duxbury. *This is one smart woman.* "I always wanted to be a doctor," he confessed, hoping to impress. When he was seven, he used to catch dragonflies in a mayonnaise jar, stash them in the refrigerator, and wait until they were nearly dead. Then he'd unscrew the jar top, resuscitate them, and set them free. "I was a nerdy kid," he said. "One summer, when I was eleven, I read the entire *Encyclopaedia Britannica.*"

"My, my," she said, teasingly. "You must be a genius."

He laughed, feeling embarrassed. "My mom thinks I know everything." He told Bibi he was close to his mother, a retired nurse, and they often talked about medicine, and his late father had had a complicated medical history. "As you can tell, we've covered a few niches in the health-care field, even though no one's a doctor."

Then she regaled him with the story of *her* family. Born in Harlem in 1963, at the height of civil unrest, she was the middle of three children. Her father, John Farris, had been a fiery advocate for Black Power and a devoted bodyguard for Malcolm X. His was a full-time job, as millions of people detested Malcolm for harshly indicting white America. People repeatedly threatened the black Muslim leader and his family; they'd tried to bomb his car and may have burned down his house. In February 1965, when Bibi was just eighteen months old, her parents took her and her three-year-old brother to the Audubon Ballroom in Washington Heights to hear Malcolm speak. When the charismatic man finally came onstage, the crowd of four hundred stood up, but one man rushed forward, carrying something in his hand. Bibi's mother heard firecrackers pop and saw clouds of billowing smoke. Confused, she looked at a group screaming near the stage and, in a flash, understood what had happened. She threw her two babies on the floor, covered them with her pregnant body, and screamed as two other men opened fire on Malcolm, riddling his body with even more bullets.

"Jesus! You were at Malcolm X's assassination? What happened to your father?"

"He was devastated," she said. Her father had just been told to leave Brother Malik, as he affectionately called Malcolm X, and attend to his family in the audience. He rued the fact that he had not been able to protect his mentor. "He never got over that."

A long silence filled the telephone. Then the tête-à-tête resumed, first in a awkward murmur, then a rush, followed by a steady buzz. Somewhere a clock struck midnight. The two discovered they had more than medicine in common. Duxbury admitted that his six-year-old daughter, Sojie, was the apple of his eye. "She's black, her mother's black, and someday I'd like to be with a black woman who could be a role model for my daughter."

"How sweet," Bibi cooed. She chattered on about her six-year-old son, Richard, who rarely saw his white father. Soon the sky outside grew lighter; Duxbury noticed it was five A.M. They had been talking for six straight hours.

"When can I meet you?" he asked.

"How about tomorrow?" she said, feeling giddy. *Wait a minute! Tomorrow is today!* They laughed like kids horsing around. In a few hours Bibi and her son would attend Saturday service at a Messianic Jewish synagogue. Duxbury agreed to meet them there.

He showed up in pressed jeans and a brown leather World War II–style bomber jacket. She wore slacks and her most feminine top, and had piled blush on her cheeks in an obvious way. But instead of aging Bibi, the color made her look girlish, as if she'd been playing with her mother's makeup.

Years later, they'd both say it was love at first sight. That went for Richard too. He was a frightened six-year-old hiding behind his mother's leg, dressed in jeans and sneakers, with close-cropped hair and puffy eyes, as if sleep had just departed. Duxbury bent down to introduce himself, and they shook hands. The boy didn't smile, but when Duxbury asked if he could walk into synagogue with him and his mother, he nodded solemnly.

During the service, the two adults snuck sidelong glances at each other. "This is the weirdest date I've ever been on," thought Duxbury. Fortunately, the messianic Jews didn't believe in long services, and after the blessing, the congregation regrouped in the basement for refreshments. Duxbury milled about easily, but Bibi was quiet, and Richard looked sad. Duxbury turned to the boy and asked, "Would you like to go to the fair?"

"Would I?" his eyes opening wide. In reply, he ran outside to wait by the car.

And, now, here they were, thirty-five miles east of the city on the fairgrounds, swept up in a throng of a million other thrill seekers. It was early September, the sky was a brochure blue, and the hay underfoot green and sweet. A carnival organ pumped out sugary notes, and Duxbury squired his guests around to watch the milking of the cows, the hoof-dance of the pygmy goats, and the undisturbed sleep of piglets in pens. He bought cotton candy and watched as Richard tried to swallow the pink and blue swirls before they melted in his mouth. The three glided down the giant slide together, stacked like spoons, squealing in a carefree manner. "This is too good to be true," all of them thought. They rode the merry-go-round, the whirligig, the slingshot machine, and other rides. At dusk, they feasted on barbecued ribs and lemonade. For dessert, they watched bakers in red aprons rake flats of hot fudge. Finally, they gravitated toward the Ferris wheel, a giant circle magically lit by a string of stars. At the top, when the boy wasn't looking, Duxbury kissed his mother full on the mouth.

Two weeks later, he asked her to marry him.

—ᴍ—

HER eyes spitting flames, her nostrils flaring, an office assistant for a client slammed McClellan into the wall of the doctor's office, causing the hanging pictures to rattle. The henna-haired woman must have been six inches shorter than McClellan, but at 180 pounds she had the neck and shoulders to throw him to the ground. She was screaming, poking her stubby finger into his chest repeatedly, as horrified patients looked on. "Is this how you treat your big clients, hotshot?" she yelled. Several patients in the doctor's waiting room gasped loudly and a few stood up and slowly backed away from the scene. But the woman seemed oblivious to their fears, and hurled her words at her target. "If this is how you treat us, I'll just take my business to Amgen!"

McClellan winced. "Calm down a minute, will you? What are you talking about?"

"We are not"—*hard poke*—"getting our money"—*harder poke*—"like you said"—*stabbing pain*—"we would," she barked, jabbing her fork-finger at his bony sternum. "And," she added, her face inches from his, "We're not buying any more damn Procrit until we get reimbursed for what we've already bought."

Their eyes locked. He held his breath. "Okay. Let's talk."

She holstered her finger.

McClellan exhaled. He then stepped into the ring and executed a few swift, formal moves that helped him avoid yet another charging bull.

Ortho's nationwide off-label campaign was squeezing some of his clients, and he discovered that insurers such as Medicare weren't always reimbursing them for Procrit's new unapproved dosage. Angry clients from Yuma to Clifton were complaining about this, forcing McClellan to face down a potential stampede.

One prized client was Dr. Nafees Nagy, founder of the Nevada Cancer Center in Las Vegas, who had purchased about $800,000 worth of Ortho's drug. Based on McClellan's sales pitch, Nagy had expected to be paid at least $1 million from Medicare. But over a few years, and despite their repeated attempts, the office still hadn't gotten a cent.

"And the doctor is really pissed at you," one of Nagy's staffers confided.

That didn't sound right to McClellan. He knew that some of his doctors were getting paid by Medicare for their injectable drugs, even for the high doses. But Medicare didn't usually pay for off-label therapies that weren't considered "reasonable and necessary . . . according to accepted standards," and the 40,000-unit shots were not the accepted standard. The fact is that Medicare payments were decided on a regional not national basis, and some Medicare offices were more lenient than others. McClellan suspected that the reimbursement problem lay inside Nagy's office. He asked to take a look at the books.

The woman led him into her office. She pulled out the ledger and flipped it open. The salesman studied the pages for a few minutes, then discovered the problem. "You're using the wrong Medicare codes," he said jubilantly.

She looked over his shoulder. "Look," he said, pointing to the code she'd used. "This is wrong. You're supposed to use the code Q0136," he explained. McClellan knew this because Raritan had instructed its reps in the byzantine billing rules of insurers, ranging from profitable commercial firms to public nonprofits such as Medicare. He'd been taught how to fill out a HCFA 1500 form correctly, so the U.S. Health Care Financing Administration could dole out Medicare funds to Ortho's clients, including Nagy. An Ortho sheet explained that giving clients rebate payments in free product looks "more ethical and bring[s] less attention to the process." If the client asked if he could bill for this product, the reps were told to respond, "Yes, Doctor, you can. . . ." McClellan had dozens of other scripts and forms instructing him in the art of filing federal claims.

Now he looked up at Nagy's manager and said, "No wonder you're not getting paid!" Her face began to soften.

"Don't worry," he said rapidly. "Give me a few days, and we'll help you figure this out." He flew back to Tucson and reported the problem to his boss, Dwayne Marlowe. At the same time, the office manager related the incident to Dr. Nagy, who asked his attorney to set up a meeting with the Ortho guys.

McClellan and Marlowe flew to Las Vegas and met with the lawyer in Nagy's offices. He wasn't satisfied, so the salesmen agreed to pay $2,000 to fly a Medicare specialist—or "Code Mistress"—to Las Vegas to spend the day instructing Nagy's office manager in how to successfully bill the government for its Procrit. Marlowe reminded the attorney that Ortho helped clients avoid financial loss by assisting uninsured patients who are on Procrit, and providing doctors who didn't get reimbursed with complimentary drug. There were so many ways for supplier and client to make money (usually at taxpayers' expense) that all the angles didn't need to be sketched out.

But Nagy's attorney requested a list of every benefit, gift, and advantage that Ortho had extended to his client over the years. *Give us a reason to continue doing business with you, or we'll take our business elsewhere,* he implied. Since Nagy was a member of McClellan's Millionaires' Club, the Ortho men agreed. McClellan spent hours compiling his list; once he'd finished, he was amazed at Ortho's largesse. The company had paid Nagy $312,000 in grants, speaker's fees, Phase IV stipends, and other goodies. It had also given him access to ICRA, the blood mobile, with its attendant free publicity, estimated to be worth $150,000, and that didn't begin to include the dozens of staff lunches, CME nurses' programs, pens, pads, cups, chemo blankets, and other freebies McClellan had given him over the years.

However, Dr. Nagy still wasn't getting reimbursed for his high-dose Procrit. McClellan deduced that the office had ignored the advice of the Code Mistress, Bobbie Buell. It was a year later, and the problem had magnified; Nagy was on the verge of moving his account to Amgen, which had just unrolled the highly touted Aranesp for cancer patients. McClellan's stomach churned; he could not afford to lose this $1.6 million annual account.

He and his managers tried a different tactic. McClellan flew in the business manager from Dr. Kattakar's cancer office in Tucson, which for years had successfully billed Medicare for high-dose injections. McClellan booked the doctor's biller into the Mandalay Bay Hotel, treated her to steaks and drinks, and drove her to Nagy's office, where she spent two days reviewing more than a hundred rejected claims. To the relief of McClellan and Raritan, she found that most of the billing problems centered on other drugs, not Procrit. But she found serious flaws in Nagy's electronic billing system and learned that he had cut his billing staff in half while increasing the number of physicians at his center. And when Nagy's office *did* file a Procrit claim, it charged $48 per 1,000 units, versus Medicare's allotment of $12 (and Nagy's actual price of $8, factoring all the meals, rebates, and other fees he received).

McClellan gathered his information and made another appointment with Dr. Nagy. They met in the doctor's windowless, clockless conference room off Desert Inn Road and sat at a shiny wood table that smelled of money. The rep presented his findings, but halfway through, the oncologist interrupted rudely, his snarl sliding across the table. "You're a liar," he snapped.

McClellan's blood pressure jumped, his neck swelled, and a jolt of adrenaline shot through him. He'd had it up to here with these people and fought the impulse to tackle the doctor; instead he listened to the rant. "It's *Ortho's* responsibility to get this thing right and straighten out Medicare," Nagy insisted. "I'm not to blame for these rejections, and I want a line of credit *now*." He'd no longer pay for Ortho's drugs out of his own pocket, and demanded that Ortho start putting up its own money.

As generous as Raritan was with its big-volume clients, it couldn't give the doctor all of his drugs for free. *We don't do that for anybody.* "But," McClellan added, struggling to control his voice, "we'll make things right." He reported the quarrel to headquarters, and Nagy eventually straightened out his office problems. As for Ortho, it pledged to extend even more discounts if Nagy would amp up his orders. He did, and from then on, Nagy used so much high-dose epo, he bought nearly $2 million of the drug a year.

These false claims, subsidized by the hordes of primarily middle-class consumers, formed the heart of Ortho's business plan, as McClellan would later allege.

For years, Ortho's clients had been compensated well for injecting Procrit at the FDA-approved level, turning about a 25 percent profit. One of McClellan's most prized clients, Arizona Cancer Center in

Tucson, had received $80,000 worth of free commercial product over the years, and ACC had cashed in that drug for Medicare money, said McClellan. So why wouldn't that clinic join the crowd and amp up patient doses (and its own profits) by 33 percent?

But when ACC's oncology director, Dr. Daniel Von Hoff, complained that Medicare wasn't paying ACC for the 40,000-unit injections, Raritan had a huge problem. For one thing, Von Hoff's good friend, and Ortho's chief medical officer, Dr. Loretta Itri, had convinced him to escalate Procrit's dose in the first place. Plus, Von Hoff was no ordinary key opinion leader. He was a Big KOL-Kahuna, a "physician on steroids" who conducted more clinical trials for drug firms than nearly any other KOL. He collected advisory fees and perks from more than thirty pharmaceutical firms and sat on several companies' boards. "When I saw how many shares he owned in biotech and drug firms, my jaw dropped," McClellan told his boss, Marlowe. A good word from Von Hoff could catapult a drug's sales, and a bad word could . . . well, McClellan didn't want to imagine. He called his boss and explained, "We've got to solve this problem."

Raritan assigned a clinical affairs manager, Elizabeth Potente, to ghostwrite a letter to a Medicare official on behalf of Von Hoff. In it, she explained that off-label Procrit was "a treatment of choice at various institutions," and it had "significant clinical as well as financial impact" for doctors. Later McClellan would claim in a lawsuit that Von Hoff signed the October 2001 letter, and after a few more Ortho-instigated calls, *ipso presto!* The center began receiving more than $1 million for administering off-label Procrit.

In Von Hoff's letter, he and Ortho's manager had shrewdly cited an Ortho-funded trial that Ortho's point woman, Loretta Itri, had overseen. The Phase IV trial had looked at 3,012 patients with nonmyeloid tumors who were receiving chemo. The study claimed to have found that doses as high as 60,000 units a week were just as safe and effective as the lower, FDA-approved dose—and improved patients' quality of life. The study's lead researcher, Dr. Janice L. Gabrilove of Mount Sinai Medical Center in Manhattan, had taken money from Ortho, as had three other coauthors, and the fifth was Itri. Not the most unbiased report, yet the open-label, nonrandomized, multicenter study was published in a June 1, 2001, issue of the *Journal of Clinical Oncology* (*JCO*).

It was criticized for its many errors. A huge number of the study's patients—42 percent—had either dropped out of the study, or fallen through the cracks, or possibly even died. This glaring problem confounded two independent doctors who wrote a letter to the *JCO*'s editor. The study's rosy conclusion, they said, "wasn't supported by the data." Yet, shoddy as it was, the *JCO* study was a corporate coup. Ortho's sales crew carried stacks of reprints in their briefcases, and on tough sales calls, McClellan would whip one out, slap the copy on a physician's desk, and lean forward in his snakeskin boots. "Research shows that the high Procrit doses work, Doc," he'd say. "How much do you want to buy today?"

Headquarters made selling high doses even easier. It had just received FDA approval to manufacture a new 40,000-unit vial for surgery patients. That meant client-nurses didn't have to mess with mixing medicine from four 10,000 units, or add a 10,000-unit vial to a 30,000-unit dose. They could easily shoot up patients from one 40,000-unit vial. Ortho's president spread "the good news" in a memo. This was another ingenious way to market the high dose, and it became more difficult for nurses to find vials of the lower, FDA-approved 30,000-unit dose. Soon orders for the bigger glass vials boomed.

Throughout the client confrontations, McClellan managed to maintain the insistently sunny, all-American sales delusion that can poleax any Puritanical compunction. To help solve his *other* clients' billing problems, he flew the Code Mistress to offices in Arizona and Nevada. Bobbie Buell advised billers to be scrupulous and to never overbill; she warned that they couldn't bill for trial drugs that had been paid for by the trial's sponsor. But McClellan and his bosses winked at that caveat. Billing for free product was part of the magic of being a Procrit buyer.

The rep chartered a luxury bus and invited fifty nurses, billers, and coders to the four-star Ritz-Carlton in Phoenix, to hear Buell give an "Oncology Reimbursement Seminar" about Procrit. The event began

with a happy hour—pink cosmopolitans and bone-dry martinis—
accompanied by tinkling piano music in a setting reminiscent of a
mansion. At seven sharp, the group moved into a dining room taste-
fully decorated with sandy walls and hibiscus-colored carpets. Yawn-
ing windows faced a portico illuminated by lights from inside the
hotel, casting syrup-gold shadows across the lawn. McClellan stepped
to the front of the room, tapped his ring against his glass, and introduced Buell to a smattering of applause. The Code Mistress launched
into her presentation with MBA efficiency, while waiters balanced
trays of many courses and McClellan passed out material about how
to fill out HCFA forms. After forty-five minutes, Buell took questions
but left plenty of time for socializing. At nine, McClellan gaily herded
the nurses back to the bus, which trundled down Camelback Road
and deposited its riders at their destinations. So successful were these
events, headquarters began flying the speaker around the country to
address other Ortho clients. As McClellan told Duxbury, "We spend a
lot of money on Bobbie. But, boy, is she worth it! She helps us bring
in sales by teaching our clients about the HCFA 1500s."

—⟞⟝—

THE two men sat at a glass-topped table in Wang's Restaurant, a
Chinese eatery on a busy street in Bellevue, Washington. Duxbury
waited like an emperor, his arms out and his palms flat on the table in
anticipation. His favorite dish, kung pao chicken, had just arrived, and
he closed his eyes to savor the aroma of hot chili peppers and soy-
sesame. His companion, Paul Simmerly, bowed his head before the
sight of chopped chicken swimming in a plate of peanut sauce. From
that angle, Duxbury could see just how much bushier his friend's
broom mustache was compared to the brown hair that ringed his
monk's cap. Simmerly was a lawyer who considered himself a gour-
mand. He raised his head and lifted his chopsticks in the air. As if on
cue, the two men dove into their plates, each one deftly plying the
chopsticks as though wood had sprouted from their fingernails.

They'd known each other since 1995, when Duxbury and his

neighbors had hired the attorney to help settle a real estate matter. The developers of Cityscape, where Duxbury once lived, had sold its original units by touting the property's lakefront views. Yet once the last unit had been bought, the developer built another set of condos that blocked the owners' advertised views. Simmerly had dealt with irate homeowners and builders before, but one guy had stood out. "Mark was the most reasonable guy in the whole lot," he recalled. The blond salesman attended all of the meetings, was articulate, and tried to mediate among the bickering homeowners. In the end, the lawyer filed a class-action suit, and the thirty-two homeowners received a payout of about $80,000 after his fees. After that, the two men kept in sporadic touch; Simmerly knew about Duxbury's work troubles, and Duxbury had read in the newspaper about a few of Simmerly's cases.

"How's your rama?" Duxbury asked him.

"Fine, how's your mama?" the lawyer joked.

Duxbury rolled his eyes and the two chuckled. Both devoted dads, they shared the same middle name—Eugene—and the same brand of rascally humor. Paul's grandfather Zimmerly had left Germany to settle in Cleveland. When World War II broke out, he enlisted in the U.S. Army and became a drill sergeant. But the military refused to let a German-American fight against his fellow countrymen, and he soon changed the Z in his name to an S. Paul's dad was an electrical engineer who married the first female engineering graduate of Ohio State, a civil engineer named Edna. In the 1950s the couple moved to Seattle to take jobs at Boeing. Edna loved the Northwest, whose pure, Pine-Sol air and unpolluted, stain-free water came as a revelation to the Clevelander. Her son Paul, the middle of three kids, attended public schools and the University of Puget Sound Law School.

"Remind me again," Duxbury once asked him. "Why did you become a lawyer?"

"Because I wanted to help people," he said, simply.

Sometimes when Duxbury asked a question, Simmerly took so long to answer that his friend thought that perhaps he'd forgotten the query. But really the barrister was just examining the issue in his mind and forming his thoughts before allowing his words to roll out in stammer-free, grammatically sound sentences. He routinely weighed the diurnal issues of life: employment, real estate, and family. He hated divorce law—"sometimes you just want to shoot yourself"—but it was steady work, especially during the dot-com era, when Microsoft millionaires were falling out of trees. "You wouldn't believe the stories of unhappiness and betrayal I hear," he once told Duxbury.

"Spare me," groaned Duxbury. "I could tell a few of my own."

Indeed, that's one reason why they were there. They shared an unshakable, almost boyish belief in justice, and what Duxbury had told Simmerly about Ortho and J&J over the years sounded unjust in the extreme. Simmerly was now helping Duxbury with the subpoenas and declarations tied to the *Amgen v. Ortho* fight. He was disgusted at the level of secrecy between two publicly traded companies, believing in the words of U.S. Supreme Court Justice Louis Brandeis: "Sunlight is the best disinfectant." He thought shareholders, and especially patients, should know about the blood feud. Now he and his client considered mounting a shareholder fraud suit against the New Jersey conglomerate, claiming that J&J had made misleading statements and failed to disclose information, as was its fiduciary duty. Simmerly didn't have the artillery to take on such a case, so he and Duxbury batted about the names of some big-gun firms.

The salesman pined for justice and still bled from the memory of his Ortho days, when he had stooped over his lists, ground out the reports, and put his heart into pitching product in what turned out to be illegal ways, while Wood, Amick, and the others stood breathing down his neck, threatening him with their gaslights and traps. It didn't seem right that they had been rewarded for such behavior, while he was still trying to regain his foothold, renting a three-bedroom apartment in the tules.

On top of that, he had lost his well-paying job at Aventis Behring in early 2001, thanks to a recession that swept through Europe. Duxbury and several others were laid off. "But at least my manager was nice about it," Duxbury told Simmerly. After he turned in his company car, he was driven home in a limousine. He'd dusted off his résumé and, a month later, had landed an entry-level job selling a human growth hormone for Serono, a biopharmaceutical firm based in Switzerland. After striving for fifteen years in the drug business, he'd wound up back where he had started, motoring through the Pacific Northwest as a robo-rep.

He tried to avoid accidents. "But no matter how careful you are, if you spend enough time on the road, people will find a way to hit you," he said. The road warrior by now had driven more than a million miles on wet, snowy, dry, and mountainous roads. He'd been rear-ended, T-boned at an intersection, and struck by an airborne vehicle that had landed on his stationary car while he was inside, minding his own business. While he was selling his latest therapy, the passenger side of his automobile had been hit by another vehicle. Duxbury thought he was okay, but in early 2001 all the dents and fender benders of the traveler's life caught up to him. While driving to see a client one day, he experienced severe pain in his cervical spine. He noticed nerve problems in his left arm and a burning in his neck too. His doctor gave him local injections of corticosteroids, but he felt no relief. So, in May 2001, Duxbury underwent surgery to remove two discs in his back and to trim the bone in the inflamed area. The operation was a success, but his days on the medicine road were numbered.

Then there was his family. Mark had not married Bibi immediately as he had wanted, primarily because of Sojie. When Duxbury introduced his daughter to his fiancée, the eight-year-old girl had started to cry. "Daddy, I don't want you to get married," she said. That's not what he wanted to hear. He'd found love again with Bibi, who put the giddyap in his gitalong, the spigot in his fountain, the *joie* in his *vivre*. That autumn, he slowly introduced the idea of a new family, taking Sojie, Bibi, and Richard to the children's museum, the seashore, and the movies. That December Renee gave him two tickets to the Christmas train, so he and Sojie could ride it from Seattle to Tacoma. Bibi purchased two more tickets and surprised Duxbury by showing up at the station with Richard. The carriage pulled away from the station and, an hour later, pulled into Tacoma. The group then boarded a coach that whisked them to Point Defiance Zoo, which had been transformed into a snowy wonderland. The kids ran through the reindeer and owl exhibits together until it was time to board the train.

By January Sojie had given her blessing to the union. Overjoyed, the couple spent several weeks preparing the wedding and combining their households into Duxbury's apartment. On February 12, 2001, they borrowed the same old tropes and enactments that everyone else used and were married by a justice of the peace. The family that Duxbury had yearned for all these years celebrated. Duxbury had no Hamptons mansion, no driver, satellite phone, or even a 401(k). But he was as happy as a lord in his manor. As he told Simmerly that day over lunch, "My marriage to Renee seemed like a small crawl space, with the same fights and disagreements over and over again. But," he added, "life with Bibi is calmer. Every morning when we wake up, we kiss." His bride didn't drink, and Duxbury himself had given up drinking and smoking. Simmerly could see that the man was over the moon, even if his career was in limbo.

And now, as Chinese Muzak threaded the jasmine-scented air, the men's talk turned to action. Duxbury felt anything but secure in his present job, and now with a family to help support, he couldn't afford to lose it. But he resented the behind-the-closed-doors slurs of his previous employer. Ortho blamed its illegal dialysis sales on a "handful of Ortho Biotech salespeople acting in their own self-interest." The tens of millions of dollars of Procrit dialysis deals, J&J lawyers claimed, "were the creations of greedy, low-level sales representatives." *How dare they?*

"The bastards are ruining my good reputation," Duxbury told Simmerly. He couldn't help but think of how his dad, with his impossibly high standards, would have reacted, let alone his second cousin, Major Bruce "Snake" Crandall, whose code of honor and valorous deeds had helped inspire *We Were Soldiers Once . . . And Young,* written by retired Lieutenant General Harold J. Moore and UPI reporter Joseph Galloway. Crandall's Vietnam War heroism had deeply touched Duxbury. Moore had led Crandall and 450 other young men of the Seventh Cavalry into the remote Ia Drang Valley in November 1965. As a helicopter pilot, Crandall had transported the soldiers to a landing zone. After a few routine lifts, the men on the ground came under massive attack by two thousand North Vietnamese soldiers; three men on Crandall's Huey were killed and three more wounded, yet he kept his chopper on the ground so he could take on more wounded. After Crandall ferried them back to base, some said his mission was complete, but he returned, flying through smoke and bullets to deliver emergency supplies and carry out more wounded. He made twenty-two death-defying trips, and by the time Snake was through, he had evacuated more than seventy men in his dented, blood-drenched helicopter, many of whom tragically had to be wrapped in green rubber poncho-shrouds.

One element of Crandall's story especially sang out to Duxbury, and it was this: His cousin's tale focused on young soldiers who had nothing to do with the political machinations that put them in that deadly valley so far from home. Many didn't understand what the war was about; most had never chosen to be there. But once they landed together in the jungle, they fought ferociously and selflessly to help each other. As the book's coauthors wrote, "In battle, our world shrank to the man on our left, and the man on our right, and the enemy all around."

Duxbury claimed kinship with these men, and nothing would dissuade him from moving through his own valley of death to fight for what he believed was honorable. "J and J ruined my reputation and I want it back," he explained. There was Simmerly on his left, McClellan on his right, and J&J all around.

In July 2001 he sued Ortho for wrongful termination, breach of contract, and outrage. He claimed he'd suffered damages to be determined at trial, including lost income, back pay, lost benefits, humiliation, emotional distress, and mental suffering. He had more faith in the public legal system than in the kangaroo-like private courts. But there were tripwires in that system too.

—⚉—

THE wrong name for a global product can portend disaster. Ford Motors goofed when it unveiled its car Pinto—the name means "little penis" in Portuguese. Audi named its vehicle Etron, the French word for "feces." But Epogen seemed safe in translation. It was a distant cousin to the word *epigenetics,* the study of gene expression, and linguistically friendly to the name of the molecule that Amgen's scientist Fu-Kuen Lin had plucked from the human genome pool fifteen years before. As far as brand names go, "Ep-o-gen" had a sturdy ring to it.

But the word had other meanings, too, echoing "epigones," meaning "an imitative follower." Epogen did indeed imitate a human protein, but the private brand had followed decades of public subsidies.

While Goldwasser isolated the erythropoietin protein, it was the National Institutes of Health (NIH) that had funded his research for twenty years. Goldwasser had always believed that his discovery and its financial bonanza should be shared with the public; after all, taxpayers had funded his work. But after obtaining NIH's blessing, he had chosen to work only with Amgen. And that firm had managed to patent epo. The public never profited from the discovery, and ironically Americans continued to subsidize it in numerous ways: First, the Bayh-Dole Act in 1980 encouraged federally funded researchers to license their patented discoveries to industry, giving private firms public inventions. Second, when Epogen went to market, it was protected from competition by the Orphan Drug Law. The law was meant to encourage the creation of drugs for rare diseases in not-very-lucrative markets—Epogen was supposed to treat a universe of just three hundred thousand dialysis patients. But it and its sisters went on to rake in tens of billions of dollars, hardly the spoils of orphans and followers.

By the late 1990s, however, no act of Congress could rescue Epogen's slipping fortunes. Not only was Procrit outselling Epogen, but Wall Street worried that Ortho's archenemy had lost its edge: Amgen hadn't invented a blockbuster in over a decade. Now DuPont was sniffing around the Thousand Oaks campus, talking about buying the world's top independent biotech firm.

Epogen had indeed become an inferior imitator.

The real money was in the cancer market, where 1.2 million people a year were being diagnosed with the disease. The oncology drug class was the fastest-growing therapeutic category, with global sales set to double from the 2001 level of $7.6 billion, according to analysts. Amgen wanted a seat at that banquet table. Rather than continue re-searching an entirely new cancer drug, though, its scientists made a few minor changes to the epoetin alfa molecule, tweaking it just enough to get a new patent. The result was a longer-acting epo drug called Aranesp. Amgen planned to secure FDA approval to sell it as a new treatment for anemic dialysis and, eventually, for chemotherapy patients. When McClellan heard about this, he called Duxbury and howled. "Can you believe it? They're trying to elbow into our oncol-ogy market, where all the money is!"

"Clever," said Duxbury. "It sounds like a 'me too' drug, addressing symptoms that are already treatable with other drugs."

"I know! Why don't they use all of their money and brains to cre-ate a new drug that actually treats a disease that has no cure yet?" said McClellan.

J&J executives felt the same way. In 1999, the giant sued Amgen for breach of its PLA contract, dragging its partner back into Judge McGarr's chambers. J&J argued that it had exclusive rights to the cancer market and that Amgen was encroaching on its territory. But J&J lost. Aranesp would be launched at the more powerful dosage for cancer patients in the United States as well as in Europe, where J&J had long held a monopoly. New Brunswick swore that Ortho would "remain a market leader" and began promoting Procrit in even more aggressive ways, pushing on the clinical, regulatory, political, and mar-keting fronts.

—⁓—

Sitting on the couch next to Bibi, Duxbury flipped through the TV channels and found a rerun of the 2001 Tour de France. What a sight—the cyclists flew like parakeets, their multicolored jerseys of red, yellow, and green flashing by in a rainbow flock. The men kept their helmeted heads down, their mouths open, their legs pumping, and you just knew that their pulmonary valves were working double-time. The couple marveled at these super athletes, who probably used performance-enhancing drugs and were approaching the sort of genetically enhanced heroes of science-fiction novels. Duxbury felt certain many of these men were dopers. "They don't get that way on a diet of steak and lettuce," he told her. "Which one of these guys is high on epo?"

His was a reasonable question.

The world's top three cycling races had recently been rocked by scandals surrounding epo and other banned substances. In 1999, a race leader had been expelled on the next-to-last day of the three-week-long Giro d'Italia, after his blood test showed evidence of doping. Race organizers used new tests to detect epo, but it was generally known that cyclists continued to abuse the drug. Then, as Duxbury and Bibi watched the 2001 race, the station broke for a commercial—a Procrit commercial.

J&J's ad men had always had a long and lucrative connection with the cycling world. A century earlier, when the government tried to restrict drugmakers' popular self-medications, one of J&J's top sellers was Vino Kolafra, a mix of cheap sherry and cola nuts. J&J recommended the potion for "bicyclists, during long runs." Critics claimed the so-called lost vitality and blood disease cures were among the most depraved ads of them all. Eventually, the government agreed, and Vino Kolafra was pulled from the shelves.

Now, 105 years later, a new version of J&J's vitalizing blood drug was being peddled to the layman in just as cavalier a fashion. This drug ad looked similar to the one Duxbury had seen earlier. It featured an old, immobile man and a tired woman, both cured by a hit of Procrit. It was bad enough that J&J had run its misleading ads during prime time. But now, it was broadcasting the false spot during a sports event that had been rocked by epo scandals. "J and J might as well just sponsor the dopers' event," Duxbury said, snorting.

His sentiment was echoed by fans and critics on phone wires and in chat rooms. "I'm falling out of my chair, screaming with laughter," wrote a cyclist on an Internet bulletin board sponsored by the American Cycling Network. "You couldn't make this up." A former-cycling-champion-turned-sports-commentator agreed: "It's a stunner." How was it that the very drug that was staining the credibility of cycling was being touted during its most famous race?

Damage control teams in the East kicked into gear. The head of the network that had collected money for the ad said the entire incident was "pure coincidence." A J&J spokeswoman claimed to be unaware that the commercial had been running during the world-class cycling event. The network executive elaborated: "Obviously, we can't stop someone from getting a crooked doctor to write a prescription." But wasn't that what J&J was doing, crookedly promoting prescriptions for fatigue? In June 2002 J&J stopped placing its TV commercial on sports shows, saying it was "inappropriate."

But that was like closing the barn door after the cow had been sold. Dozens of Procrit ads had played on many other sporting events on other networks for years. J&J kept running its lush ads on other shows. By 2001, it had consolidated a $57 million ad campaign to go cheek by jowl against newcomer Aranesp and its mega-launch.

—⁂—

Behind the mirrored windows of an FDA building, Dr. Keegan navigated her way out of the paper minefield in her office and trudged to yet another meeting. The low drone from the six-lane thoroughfare outside didn't silence the static in her head. Regulators like Keegan were still getting squeezed by J&J to approve fatigue as a new Procrit indication. The company and its partner continued to submit the sponsored studies and data that it had presented in 1996, 1997, and the years leading up to 2000. Still, the regulators remained unimpressed. As Keegan repeated in the meetings, "Fatigue is not an indication." Later, an FDA official informed the J&J gang that "in the absence of a carefully monitored, adequate, and well-controlled clinical trial, conclusions about how patients would have responded in the absence of [epo] therapy cannot be drawn." Procrit could not be approved for fatigue. "There was a lot of back-and-forth on that," said Keegan.

Then, politics reared its head. George W. Bush named the first-ever political appointee to the Office of Chief Counsel. He chose a man who had spent much of his career suing the FDA on behalf of drug and tobacco companies that didn't like certain regulations, a man who was a self-styled activist for the free-speech rights of trusts and syndicates. As a partner in the Washington, D.C., firm Wiley Rein, he had billed more than $350,000 to Pfizer up until August 2001: That's when Bush appointed Daniel Troy as the FDA's top lawyer. The balding attorney looked older than his forty-one years, but he energetically took the agency in a radical new direction.

Even though the FDA was supposed to regulate drug safety, Troy sided with drug companies in lawsuits brought by patients who had been seriously harmed by drugs and devices made by Pfizer, Glaxo-SmithKline, and others. He argued that because these products had been approved by the FDA, patients' claims in state courts were therefore "preempted" by federal approval. Often the courts agreed and dismissed those cases. Troy actively undermined states' product liability laws that allowed consumers to sue drugmakers whose products were defective, pushing decades of consumer-friendly rulings back to the gilded days of quackery and Vino Kolafra. Troy became known as "the Prince of Preemption" and showed up at legal conferences urging white-collar defense attorneys to bring him their cases, so the FDA could file amicus briefs on behalf of pharmaceutical firms. Pick your cases carefully, he warned; make 'em "sound like a Hollywood pitch." And they did.

Before Troy's arrival, the FDA's Division of Drug Marketing, Advertising, and Communication had issued numerous warnings to J&J about its commercials. But Troy ordered that all such letters go through his office. On January 10, 2002, he met with Keegan and other staff members and told them to "readjust" their thinking on drug commercials. According to notes from that meeting, he reminded the regulator that conglomerates were "fully protected" by the First Amendment and that "context matters" in connection with commercial free-speech rights. After that, J&J grew bolder. It overtly resisted the FDA's requests. In April 2002 the company asked for more time to revise its advertising claims, asserting that that "the relationship between anemia and fatigue is universally accepted." Then its marketing experts started defending their misleading claims without providing any solid scientific evidence. In a May 29 meeting Troy ordered the FDA staff to surrender. "Try to find middle ground," he said. "Fix in content rather than yanking material."

For the first time in American history it seemed a corporation's so-called free-speech rights were deemed superior to the rights of trusting, injured, and even dead citizens. Before Troy signed on, the FDA's marketing supervision arm had issued about ninety letters a year warning drugmakers about their deceptive ads. After he started censoring the staff's reprimands, the number of warning letters dwindled to less than thirty. Time and again, he shot down their objections and scathingly overruled the drug safety staff. The staff's morale took a severe beating nearly every week. As Keegan said, "At the end of the day, the agency decided that the ads didn't really go too far." There'd be no more back-and-forth on the issue.

16

The Arbitrator

2001 to 2002

Prisoners, hermits, sinners, and rebels who say no to the normal constraints of society are often the ones who shape history. Sometimes rejection starts out with a small, insignificant act, like refusing to applaud a man onstage or declining to hug the office sycophant. Such decisions are almost never rational and often exact a personal cost. Sensible is going along with the crowd, adhering to the established order, doing exactly what your dad or boss tells you to do. But Duxbury had often said no, starting when he was thirteen, and his father had tried to control his musical tastes, and again at age sixteen when he ran away from home. Twenty years later he publicly repudiated Ortho's sales director, Tom Amick, and the overdose scheme. "We've all been trained to achieve and to never question orders," he realized. But Ortho had abused Duxbury's trust and had stepped over the line. It wasn't authority Duxbury disliked; it was the abuse of power. It was the one thing in the world that he could not abide.

McClellan had also been a middle child brought up by a strict, unforgiving father. But unlike Duxbury, McClellan followed the herd. He grew up with a grim, subservient mother. "I never saw my mother smile, probably because my dad was so gruesome," he told Duxbury. Abuse of power was a routine occurrence in his house, as regular as bedtime stories. When McClellan was four, he misbehaved, and his mother punished him by locking him in the basement. Alone in the dark, the toddler heard mice skittering in the rafters overhead. While trying to back away from the creepy sounds, he brushed against a spiderweb. Terrified, the boy screamed for his mother, who ignored him. Finally, he dove into a basket of dirty clothes and hid. Several hours later, his mother opened the door and let him out. But his father never gave him any quarter. A former street fighter who had grown up in the Depression, the senior McClellan had broken his nose so many times, it resembled a dumpling sliding down his face. The small-town policeman beat his son with belt buckles and electric cords. When Mc-Clellan was young, his mother sent the boy to live for the summer with first one aunt, then another. "That probably saved your life," Duxbury once told him. By the time McClellan was ten it was presumed that he could defend himself, but it didn't work out that way. His dad worked the night shift and slept during the day, and when the kids returned from school, he expected them to tiptoe around the house. But as soon as McClellan came through the door, his younger sister would purposely scream to wake up Dad, who'd come roaring out of his room to grab his son by the neck. "Time for a whipping," McClellan knew. The after-school routine didn't stop until McClellan grew taller than his sister and just as big as his father.

McClellan's older brother became a Golden Gloves boxer who often practiced on his little brother—as Mom watched. Seeking his own outlet, McClellan joined the track team. Even then, his father dictated the terms, making the scrawny kid run two miles in the snow every morning in heavy boots. "I'd take them off, and my feet would be bleeding." He joined the wrestling team, but somehow, all the log presses and kettlebells never turned McClellan into the bully that some of his male relatives became. He simply wasn't built physically or temperamentally to fight. "If I had stood up to my dad, I'd be dead right now," he said.

McClellan had been trained to respect, fear, and obey authority. He rarely said no. So perhaps it was inevitable that the two friends would bump against this basic difference in character, which they did, starting in late 2001. When Duxbury sued Ortho for wrongful termination, he didn't discuss it with McClellan. His friend believed that Duxbury had brought on his problems by speaking out so much. "You stir up trouble when you don't need to," he told Duxbury.

While Duxbury fielded subpoenas for the *Amgen v. Ortho* fight, McClellan criticized him for participating in the legal crossfire. "I don't understand why you're talking to Amgen," he told Duxbury. "The rivalry between these two companies is something I'd stay away from if I were you. It doesn't affect you."

"Oh, yes it does," Duxbury would say. "It affects you too," and Duxbury would start to explain what could happen to McClellan if Ortho were to be found guilty. But the Tucson rep didn't want to hear it.

"As far as I'm concerned, Amgen's the instigator of trouble," Mc-Clellan insisted. It paid rebates, incentives, and fees to McClellan's customers to encourage them to use Aransep. And he was right, according to later reports from *The New York Times* and others. "They're all over our territory, poaching our cancer patients and stealing our clients," he said, his voice rising as if he'd been cornered. "Every time Amgen gets mad, they run and file a suit against us."

Duxbury retorted that Ortho was guilty of the same wrongdoing. "Besides," he said, "Ortho is pushing the ethical envelope in a lot of other ways," like paying rebate kickers and requiring clients to give Ortho "first right of refusal" so it could match Amgen's sly deals. Duxbury explained that the U.S. district attorney was investigating TAP Pharmaceuticals for using similar sales ploys with its cancer drug Lupron. Owned partly by Abbott Laboratories, TAP had given away drugs, "grants," discounts, free trips, and other gifts to buy doctors' business—just as Ortho and McClellan were doing.

Duxbury said he'd been called to be deposed again on August 18, 2001, in the Amgen arbitration. Then he had to head to Chicago to testify in the hush-hush trial between the two. "You wouldn't believe what Ortho has done in its effort to gain market share, using the phony trials and such."

That's when McClellan exploded. "Look, it may sound corny, but I feel honored to be a part of the most admired company in the world.

I would never do anything to hurt this company," he said. He didn't want to listen to Duxbury's trash talk either. It could make him doubt everything he did at Ortho, and he couldn't function like that. "This is the best job I've ever had, and I'm not going to jeopardize it." After that, the two didn't talk about Duxbury's depositions, the arbitration, his wrongful termination suit, or any of the other cases that Duxbury couldn't help but tie to Ortho. He kept his low opinions of J&J to himself.

But then McClellan received a wake-up call. On October 3, 2001, TAP settled the criminal charges that Duxbury had told him about. The pharmaceutical paid an astounding fine of $875 million. It was the largest criminal award for Medicare fraud and sent shudders throughout the industry. McClellan probably wouldn't even have heard about the case, except that it was a big deal in Raritan, New Brunswick, and much of New Jersey. One morning after the announcement McClellan walked into his office and found a memo from headquarters. It recapped TAP's alleged crimes and assured reps that the J&J divisions complied with federal law. But just in case there was an issue, reps were ordered to suspend most sales efforts temporarily. *The legal department is reviewing our policies to make sure they comply with federal law,* McClellan was told. He raised an eyebrow and thought, "Guess Mark had a point." But instead of calling his friend in Olympia, the Tucson rep kept his appointments with clients. He didn't distribute any checks, however. A few days later J&J's lawyers gave Ortho reps a green light, and McClellan resumed doling out grants, discounts, free patient cards, and other gifts.

—⚶—

A LINE of thunderstorms pounded Chicago, unleashing shards of lightning that exploded old trees into thousands of dangerous wooden projectiles. Duxbury wasn't a superstitious man, but as he walked into a modern building in the city's Loop, he felt a bad omen. The turbulence didn't dissipate inside the lobby either. Men in blue overalls wheeled carts of boxes out of the elevator, making beelines for the curb. A dark-suited woman froze in the foyer, her mascara-streaked eyes dazed, her rouged face ashen. Haggard men in black moved zombielike across the lobby, carrying accordion files. Duxbury and Simmerly exchanged wide-eyed looks, wondering what sort of morality play they had just entered.

Riding the elevator up, they overheard snippets of conversation that explained the situation. Evidently, the two had just entered the headquarters of Arthur Andersen, and the previous week one of the firm's partners had been fired for destroying papers tied to a false audit of his top client, Enron Corporation, an energy firm built on elaborate financial deceptions. Now the accounting firm was under criminal investigation, and the Justice Department was seizing its documents. By the time Duxbury and Simmerly reached their floor, they'd grasped just how notorious this place was in the annals of white-collar crime.

Then they walked into an even stranger scene. Instead of entering a typical business lobby, with a chilly receptionist barricaded behind a counter, they faced a crude, cavernous arena with no walls, dividers, or even a potted plant. Amgen's attorneys at Holland & Knight had leased about twenty-four thousand square feet of space as part of the staging arena for the showdown, and standing in it were Amgen's Robert Brauer and attorney Hal Melton. The two greeted their guests, who looked around at a room big enough for grown men to play a game of regulation basketball; it was almost completely filled by racks of metal shelves, stacked to the ceiling with bankers' boxes.

Duxbury turned to the Amgen executive. "Are you guys getting ready to move?"

Brauer chuckled. "No. This is discovery for the arbitration."

Duxbury felt the hairs on his head stand up. He knew that the *Amgen v. Ortho* arbitration had been simmering for at least seven years, because he'd played a key role at critical junctures: first in 1995, when he had recounted his dialysis sales in a deposition in a related case; again in 1998, when he had contacted Amgen to expand his testimony, add his missing documents to the record, and pay back Ortho for blocking his employment benefits; then again in August

2001, when Ortho had forced him to repeat his earlier testimony. Now, on Monday, January 21, 2002, the biblical enmity of the two multinationals had boiled over again, threatening patients, shareholders, and the public welfare. Looking at the hundreds of boxes stacked high, Duxbury couldn't help but wonder, "What secrets do they hold?"

Amgen had not given up on trying to break its detested PLA and had again accused J&J and Ortho of a breach. In March 2000, a judge had decided that Amgen hadn't given its partner sufficient notice to begin a divorce, and the claim died. But on June 29, 2001, the California firm once again accused Ortho of marketing Procrit to dialysis centers. "We've been trying to get adjudication of [this] since 1995," Amgen cried. Meanwhile, the biotech firm claimed it had been forced to cut the price of Epogen just to remain competitive in its own market. But it *might* be persuaded to settle, it told the judge, *if* Ortho would admit to its breach, agree to stop hospital dialysis sales, pay $475 million in damages, and announce that Amgen had prevailed. What the accuser *didn't* say was that admitting a breach could cost Ortho its epo license.

The terms struck Ortho as excessive. It claimed that Amgen was reviving the same old market grievance they'd fixed in 1997 with their spillover formula. Losing its PLA would "have a material adverse effect" on Ortho, which had already spent hundreds of millions of dollars on clinical trials to obtain FDA approval for four nondialysis indications: nondialysis, HIV, cancer, and surgery. In the past ten years, those new markets had generated domestic sales of roughly $10 billion—some of which belonged to Amgen. All in all, J&J and Ortho had enhanced the value of epo tremendously, to their mutual benefit. Dissolving the union would annihilate Ortho, while giving Amgen a "wholly unwarranted" windfall of billions of dollars, a reward "vastly disproportionate to the elusive injuries it alleges."

All these briefs landed on Judge Frank McGarr's desk. An eighty-one-year-old retired federal judge, McGarr worked for Judicial Arbitration and Mediation Service (JAMS), a controversial firm that rents judges to wealthy litigants. A Chicago native, McGarr had been teethed on the ring of ambition, earning his degree from Loyola University's law school. Climbing the ladder at the U.S. attorney's office, he rose to first assistant Illinois attorney general. In 1970, President Richard Nixon nominated him to the U.S. District Court for the Northern District of Illinois. There, McGarr decided some colorful cases, including the sentencing of James Lewis, who had tried to extort money from J&J after seven people died from poisoned Tylenol capsules. In 1988, McGarr retired from the bench with a substantial public pension and immediately signed up for a more lucrative job with JAMS/Endispute, a California firm composed mostly of retired judges. Arbitration had originally been touted as a cheap and fast alternative to the public court system. But the number of litigators had increased, along with their convoluted suits, and by 2002, the second tier of justice had grown just as costly and time-consuming as the old courthouse. For proof, one need look no further than the Chicago staging room for *Amgen v. Ortho*.

After a decade of supervising the increasingly rancorous disputes, even McGarr was turning testy. When Amgen resurrected an old grievance, he chastised the firm. "It's no longer appropriate in this case to raise an issue . . . on the eve of trial." Now, in the third month of hearings, the two were locked inside a steel-reinforced room. Whether J&J won or lost depended on how well Duxbury and six other ex-employees performed. There was Oliver Medlock, who had secretly taped his superiors; Cynthia Kubas, who had sold to dialysis centers; Tom Fedorka, whom Tom Amick had ordered to help strike a deal with Charise Charles; and others. These people had either testified or were about to, and Duxbury was scheduled to appear on Tuesday. While he listened nervously to Melton outline the week's agenda, Simmerly counted the boxes on the shelves and figured there were between ten and twenty million pages of evidence.

The visitors were taken to a room and prepared for cross-examination. An Amgen attorney had already reviewed in minute detail all three of Duxbury's depositions and was ready to give him the third degree—just as J&J's attorney would shortly. The lawyer then went at Duxbury like a terrier on a squirrel. He sought to trap, rattle, and insult the witness, but Duxbury didn't rise to the bait. After a few hours, Duxbury, drenched in sweat, was given a break, along with a soda and sandwich. Then, the grilling resumed while, outside, thunder and lightning cracked across the swollen sky. It was as if Thor himself was having a seizure on the eve of Duxbury's ordeal. When the purple clouds turned to black, Duxbury raised his hand. "We've been at this for almost twelve hours, and it's becoming counterproductive. Can we stop?"

The Amgen crew took Duxbury and Simmerly to Morton's Steakhouse for dinner before dropping them off at the hotel they'd provided. Simmerly soaked in the tub as he watched television, while Duxbury reclined on the cushioned bed in his stocking feet, reading a mystery. Early the next morning, the two met for a breakfast of lobster eggs Benedict. A taxi took them back to the high-rise, where they ran into a TV crew lying in wait for Enron's number crunchers. The pair strode past the cameras, spun through a set of glass doors, and picked up snippets of gallows humor as they silently rode up to their own dreaded destination.

This time, they were led into a stadiumlike theater with tiered seats. "It's like a college lecture room," Duxbury whispered. Indeed, an aisle divided the room into prosecution and defense, and the plush seats were already filled with a hundred attorneys and paralegals. Everyone stared down at the stage where the distinguished-looking, white-haired Judge McGarr sat on a dais.

In one corner sat employees from Patterson Belknap Webb & Tyler, legal teams from Jenner & Block, Hedlund Hanley & John, and dozens of in-house lawyers, paralegals, and executives from J&J and Ortho. In the other corner were workers from Latham & Watkins; Holland & Knight; William J. Harte, Ltd.; and Richard J. Prendergast, Ltd., along with dozens of in-house counsel and representatives of Amgen. Standing in the aisle, Duxbury glanced at the men's indistinct faces; he figured that he shared with them the same average age, cholesterol level, and SAT scores but not their cash flow or net worth. "There's probably four hundred thousand dollars of billable hours sitting in this room here today," he figured. As if reading his mind, Simmerly leaned over and whispered, "I've never been exposed to a litigation that had such an unlimited war chest."

Melton glanced over at Duxbury. Earlier in the week, the witness had discovered that he'd forgotten to pack a tie, so the lawyer had lent him one. It was a drab, prosaic number, but when Duxbury's name was called, you would have thought he was wearing a jaunty green baize scarf with a joker grinning wild: All eyes followed the witness to the stand. He was led through the process of selling Procrit to dialysis clients, using rebates, discounts, and grants. Outside, thunder boomed once again, and Duxbury said to himself, "This is a massive déjà vu experience, only with more people watching." He was aware of thick-waisted men with hard jaws and soft coughs gauging his expression.

J&J's inquisitor asked him questions he'd answered a dozen times before, only now, they were delivered with a savage thrust. Conde-scension, innuendo, sarcasm, insult, outrage, disbelief—he felt sub-jected to them all. Duxbury was called a "disgruntled" employee and a "disaffected" rep, as if that implied he couldn't possibly be telling the truth. Someone repeated the lie that he'd been forced to resign due to "an incident involving an improper sexual comment to a customer." The witness turned red as he heard the slander against him, but man-aged to choke back his anger.

Simmerly watched this from the bleachers, waiting for an attorney to pounce on the elephant in the ring: Medicare. Epo had become the fastest-growing drug in the country, jumping 30 percent in 2001 from the prior year to over $5 billion in sales. The government reimbursed at least half of that at prices far beyond what the doctors so prized by Amgen and Ortho paid for it. Surely, in this room full of experts in health-care law, someone would pursue that line of questioning. Per-haps Judge McGarr himself would broach it, or some other member of the American Bar Association sworn to uphold the law. Simmerly felt certain that federal authorities would soon discover what was re-ally going on here. "This case is too big to keep secret," he thought. He was, however, mistaken, and that night, he returned to Seattle.

Duxbury, meanwhile, was asked to stay another day. He spent the morning on the stand and, at one point, grew distracted by the antics of a lawyer in the audience. First, the man stuck out his tongue; then he crossed his eyes. When he screwed his mouth into an exaggerated soundless scream, Duxbury realized the guy was trying to trip him up. The witness motioned for help, and Melton turned toward the rubber-facer wagging his eyebrows. "Your Honor," Melton said, clearing his throat. "Would you please direct the defendant's attorney to stop making faces at the witness?" *How pathetic.* If a $400-an-hour pantomime artist was the only arrow left in J&J's quiver, the witness must be doing all right. Two hours later, Judge McGarr excused Duxbury.

He unknotted the silk noose around his neck and returned it to Melton. Then Duxbury walked to the elevator and rode it down, rubbing elbows with grim-faced professionals who were hauling away yet more crooked accounting statements. When he stepped out of the car, he bumped into a man juggling files, who was smiling so broadly, he looked out of place.

"Well, you sure look happy," said Duxbury.

"I am!" he admitted. "I'm a lawyer!"

—⁓—

Over the next few weeks, Simmerly tried to make sense of the arbitration and what it seemed to epitomize. The lawyer wasn't naïve. He'd been involved in plenty of disputes. With his ruddy cheeks and pastry paunch, he could have been a *Bürgermeister* in one of those German towns his ancestors hailed from. He'd handled more than 150 trials and arbitrations and 1,000 hearings concerning fraud, employment, and other matters; he'd won several cases at the federal court of appeals. He'd testified before the Washington State Senate about fraud and nondisclosure in real estate sales and had successfully sued a few Fortune 500 companies himself. But he'd never seen anything like that Chicago production. Amgen and J&J were paying hundreds of millions of dollars to shroud their fight over a blockbuster drug.

"Why all the secrecy?" Simmerly wondered. Epo's formula was already part of the public record; trade secrets were not at issue; national security certainly wasn't at stake. "The only reason to hide the case is to save the companies from embarrassment." Some nights he'd lie awake, thinking about the injustice of the case and his client's situation. While searching for answers that summer, Simmerly came across a report by a Merrill Lynch analyst: "While we cannot dismiss the possibility [of] a few rogue J&J salespeople," he wrote, referring to Duxbury, "there is a fuzzy line" at issue. "Fuzzy my foot." To Simmerly, there was a clear boundary between right and wrong, and knowing when to draw the line required strength of character. But this wasn't just about Amgen and J&J. Corporate chicanery was breaking out all over the land. Tyco, Adelphia, Global Crossing, WorldCom, Dynergy, J.P. Morgan, Citigroup, AOL Time Warner, and others had become targets of valid shareholder suits. Dozens of other major entities had settled similar claims in the past few years, too, paying more than $100 million each. Investors big and small were furious at the growing legions of white-collar criminals who managed to deceive investors and skip town scot-free. What would shareholders think of the machinations of J&J, the "model of corporate citizenship and governance"?

Simmerly continued to advise his friend and client, but his outlook grew jaded by this case and the twists in Duxbury's wrongful termination suit. The crux of that claim, filed in King County's Superior Court, was that Duxbury had been fired for testifying truthfully in the *Charise Charles v. Amgen* case in 1995. But Judge Bruce Hilyer didn't see the connection. "Nothing in the 1995 testimony is obviously harmful to Ortho," he said. To prove otherwise, Duxbury requested pleadings from the *Amgen v. Ortho* arbitration that showed how extensively his testimony had been used. But Ortho's attorneys accused him of mounting a "fishing expedition" and claimed he wanted those papers only to "annoy," "embarrass," and "burden" the defendant.

Duxbury found himself in the impossible position of needing to obtain evidence for his case from a secret trial where all papers were sealed and under Ortho's control. Ortho did offer to show Duxbury some documents if he would agree to a protective order. But he refused, claiming his ex-employer wanted the gag simply to cover its tracks. It didn't help that Ortho's Seattle attorneys, Williams, Kastner & Gibbs, specialized in protecting white-collar clients from the new "heightened scrutiny" surrounding health-care fraud. Judge Hilyer refused to allow Duxbury to obtain his documents. Still, his suit gained ground. In late 2001, J&J flew an in-house attorney and a private mediator to Seattle to settle the case. Had Ortho made a respectable proffer of, say, $150,000, Duxbury would have settled. Instead, it offered $10,000, which didn't cover the five hundred hours that Simmerly had put into the case. "Don't be stubborn, Mark," his mother pleaded. "Take it!" Insulted, Duxbury spurned the pin money.

He continued selling human growth hormone for Serono but developed sleep apnea. His throat and tongue muscles obstructed his airways so much that during the night, he'd stop breathing and would awake, gasping for breath. He'd start breathing again, and would drift to sleep. But the frequent waking episodes left him exhausted. In the morning, he'd down a few cups of coffee and head out the door.

Meanwhile, Renee was growing uneasy with the time Sojie spent with her father's new family. She criticized Duxbury for discussing his lawsuits with their eight-year-old and objected to Sojie's sharing a room with her younger stepbrother, Richard. Even though each child had his or her own bunk bed, Renee wanted Sojie to have her own room inside Duxbury's three-bedroom apartment and requested "a written plan, at your earliest convenience, detailing how a new and more appropriate sleeping arrangement will be in place by September 30, 2001." Duxbury bought Sojie a cot, moved her into the third bedroom that functioned as his office, and started looking for a larger home. His unemployment spell had ruined his credit history to the point where he didn't qualify for an affordable mortgage. So Bibi took out the loan to buy a five-bedroom home in Gig Harbor. The night the family moved in, Duxbury joked, "It's nice to have a big roof over our head of instead of the Sword of Damocles."

Duxbury's sleep apnea worsened so that, one day, while driving a company car, he fell asleep at the wheel. "That's it!" he told himself. "It's no longer safe for me to be on the road." He sought treatment from a sleep clinic but was absent from work so much, he lost his Serono sales position in July 2002. He hunted for a new job but worried about the impact of his testimony in the Chicago arbitration, and the outcome of his Seattle lawsuit. Ortho obtained declarations of Duxbury's old tormentors, John Woodhouse and Melody Edgington, whose descriptions of him as a "failure" and a "leering" rep were refuted by others. Nevertheless, Duxbury felt the lynch mob coming his way, their words thrown up in his face like smoke from a burning stake.

For the first time, he wondered if his real opponent was neither J&J nor Ortho, but himself—defiantly cool and clenching his moral code in a white-knuckle grip. If so, he was perfectly matched against himself. He replayed every round in slow-mo until the fight became too close to call. Then the old familiar voices spoke up in his head. We all have voices, right? But have you ever heard people saying you were stupid and no good and that you should step in front of that bus? Duxbury did, and that's when he contacted his long-lost therapist, Vicki Boyd.

He walked into her Seattle office near the shores of Lake Union and brought her up to speed on what had transpired since their last visit in 1997. "My life is going better in so many ways," he said. "I've remarried and have an understanding wife. Things couldn't be better between Sojie and me. But my problems with Ortho have grown huge," he said. He explained that Ortho had fired him in 1998, had thwarted his efforts to land a new job for a year, and that he'd been subpoenaed three times to testify in Ortho's fight against Amgen. He'd sued Ortho for retaliating against him for his testimony but felt powerless against its legal maneuvers. "I expected this case to be a rough ride." But as the prospect of a trial loomed, his psychological symptoms had returned in spades. "I'm having a really hard time," he confessed.

Boyd recognized the signs as posttraumatic stress disorder. "Mark, you've always thought that someone behind the curtain at Ortho was doing bad things," she reminded him. "Now you're reliving those difficult experiences through your wrongful termination case." As they discussed his situation, Duxbury took a deep breath. But what his therapist didn't say was how shocked she was. "Maybe I'm naïve, but I didn't realize the lengths to which companies like his would go to threaten people," she said a few years later. "There were a lot of intimidation and threats against him. I worried about his physical safety."

The psychologist's fears were prescient if misplaced. Duxbury went on to see a neurologist for his involuntary spasms, an internist for a mysterious disorder, and a pharmacist for more prescriptions. Exacerbating his problems, Bibi stopped taking her bipolar medicine. As money grew tight in the Duxbury household and the pressures from Renee and Ortho rose, Bibi grew more agitated and Duxbury turned to drink. In December 2002, Bibi blew up and berated her husband for not getting a job. "I'm going to cut up all your fancy ties and suits because you're not using them," she yelled.

"Go ahead," he said, and tossed her his Swiss Army pocketknife with the blade closed. The tool grazed her face, and she screamed. Bibi picked up the telephone, dialed 911, and started to report a domestic violence incident. But before she could finish, Duxbury grabbed the telephone and cut her off. A black-and-white unit, however, was already shrieking toward Chez Duxbury. When officers arrived at the scene, they found the man of the house calmly waiting on the porch, the tip of his cigarette glowing in the dark. Later, Bibi admitted she had lied to the police, but by then her husband had been booked for assault in the second degree. He wound up pleading guilty for interfering with a 911 call—a misdemeanor.

Duxbury pursued his wrongful termination suit, seeking front pay, back pay, and the benefits he'd lost over the past four years. Amgen was willing to provide him with the arbitration documents he'd requested, but the judge fined him $2,600 for filing some materials without a protective seal. Duxbury was never even given a chance to prove his case at trial; the judge dismissed it. He appealed, but the State Appeals Court ruled that Duxbury had failed to link his 1995 testimony to his alleged retaliatory firing in 1998. As the court explained, "The record is remarkable mainly for what is missing."

—⁂—

AFTER several months, the latest battle of the drug titans ended, leaving Judge McGarr with a mess. "An enormous record, total disagreement by the parties as to what it means, and a varied assembly of contradictory calculations presents [me] with a difficult challenge," he wrote. Wall Street waited for the outcome, and one analyst speculated that J&J would have to pay a "modest" settlement. Another predicted a "multibillion-dollar figure." Both J&J and its accountant, Price Waterhouse, minimized that potential, however, on its financial statements and shareholder reports.

For its part, Amgen argued it had lost $1.24 billion in sales because of J&J's treachery and wanted to dissolve the PLA. Ortho claimed the loss was more like $102,148 and that Amgen was taking pretzel-logic positions. The star litigators at Patterson Belknap didn't just defend their client; they ridiculed Amgen's thesis, which was "that every senior member of Ortho's management has secretly conspired to breach the PLA and to lie about it when questioned under oath. This go-for-broke strategy collapses under the weight of its utter implausibility."

Yet it wasn't implausible to Judge McGarr, who rejected the testimony of every senior member of Ortho's management and, instead, believed Duxbury and the handful of "rogue" employees. On October 18, 2002, the jurist ruled that J&J's Ortho had intentionally breached its license rights by promoting Procrit to Amgen's clients in "egregious," "aggressive," "indefensible," and even "brazen" ways. But such actions weren't bad enough to break a corporate agreement, so the partners were stuck with one another. The judge ordered J&J to pay Amgen $150 million in damages, plus $150 million in attorney fees, in addition to its own legal bills of $150 million—or about $450 million. In press releases, each side claimed victory. But J&J was the real winner. By now, it had collected about $15 billion in global epo sales over the years and looked forward to reporting about that much again in the future. It had narrowly avoided losing the rights to the most lucrative drug ever created by biotechnology.

Duxbury felt vindicated by the ruling, but it wasn't enough. J&J had robbed him of his livelihood, his dreams, and a normal life with his daughter. The company was the architect of his downfall and the companion to his every waking thought. "J&J made me a criminal, and I want them to pay," he told Simmerly.

"But how?" his lawyer responded. Duxbury's own Washington State lawsuit against Ortho was dead; the arbitrator had spoken against J&J, but few outside that closed courtroom had heard. In fact, the arbitration trial had been so clandestine that shareholders and patients were in the dark about the spreading enmity behind the blood drug.

That autumn, Duxbury and Simmerly plotted a new course during a few weekend walks. As their feet scuffled through fallen leaves, they decided to bypass the state courts and secret panels. They'd mount a shareholder fraud suit against J&J and try to obtain some *real* justice in a U.S. district court.

17

For the King

2003 to 2004

DRESSED in their best suits, Simmerly and Duxbury walked toward
the Rainier Tower, a sensuous sheet of blue-gray textilelike steel that
at that moment was soaking up April's fickle sunlight. For an inani-
mate object, this building possessed a special type of mojo. It was
designed by one of Seattle's native sons, Minoru Yamasaki, the chief
architect of the twin towers of the World Trade Center in New York
City. As he did with many of his creations, he had tried to infuse this
one with a soaring spirit, building it atop an eleven-story concrete base
that, like an inverted pyramid, widened as it reached skyward. Locals
called it the "wineglass," visitors swore it had forty stories, but the
workers inside knew it supported only twenty-nine floors balanced on
an extremely narrow pedestal. Even so, it ranked as one of the safest
buildings in town.

Simmerly and Duxbury felt a little disoriented inside but finally
got their bearings. They headed to the law offices of Hagens Berman
Sobol Shapiro, a leader in complex litigation whose slogan was "Protecting the rights of investors, workers, consumers, and the environment." Simmerly had thought them perfect to press Duxbury's
shareholder fraud case against J&J and had made an appointment
to meet one of the firm's cofounders, Steve Berman. They entered the
firm's small lobby and waited until a secretary ushered them through

a corridor and into Berman's art-filled office, where they waited for him.

"Wow," said Duxbury, looking around. "This guy must be doing well." The office was long and narrow and bordered by windows that gave one the feeling of being in a crow's nest. Duxbury glanced down on Fifth Avenue and the tonier parts of downtown Seattle, then gazed straight ahead at the birds cartwheeling through the patch of clouds that stretched all the way to the violet-hued Olympic Mountains. He then scanned the office in his practiced way. There was a clean-topped desk, shelves behind it, and a framed story from *The Wall Street Journal* concerning a Big Tobacco case. Duxbury leaned forward to read the article. Berman had made his name serving as a special assistant attorney general for thirteen states in a landmark settlement in 1998. He'd been one of two private attorneys on the negotiating team and had devised the idea of using a huge tobacco company, Liggett Group, as a whistle-blower. That deed, among other factors, had added momentum to the case, which eventually led to a multistate $206 billion settlement. Duxbury spied three cigarette packs encased inside a Lucite block, a scalp from Berman's tobacco raid.

Just then, Berman burst into his own office and abruptly sat down. Clearly, the lawyer wasn't the grip-and-grin type, thought Duxbury. The five-foot-seven-inch man was known as a bare-knuckled litigator and had a lean cyclist's build and dark hair graying at the temples. His long face looked too big for his slight frame, and at the moment, he seemed harried and almost sad. Over the years, he had hatched clever legal strategies to use against Blue Cross, Microsoft, and Visa, making him a wealthy man. He sized up his guests, his small black eyes darting from one face to the other.

"What can I do for you?"

Berman listened as Duxbury outlined his case in clear, concise terms. He explained his background as an award-winning salesman, detailed the drug he had sold, and skimmed over the knock-down, drag-out fight between Amgen and Ortho. He spoke as if he were narrating the evening news, and gave examples of how both companies had committed fraud. Then Duxbury cut to the chase: *Help me mount a shareholder fraud suit against J&J.* Berman was impressed by Duxbury's warm voice and his smooth presentation. But he had ideas of his own.

His guests didn't know this yet, but Berman was ensnared in a price-fixing suit he'd filed against J&J and about forty-two other drugmakers and their subsidiaries. He was co–lead counsel in a class action suit called *In re Average Wholesale Price Pharmaceutical Litigation* MDL No. 1456, in Massachusetts. Maybe he had acted too hastily in filing the case in late 2001 without first learning to speak *la lingua pharma.* He and his partner Tom Sobol in Boston, along with dozens of other attorneys, claimed that since 1991, nearly all of the country's pharmaceutical firms had engaged in "a cartel and a conspiracy" to report fictitious AWPs for drugs. This inflated drug prices by as much as 1,000 percent at the expense of the self-insured laborers, retirees, and ordinary American consumers who made up his class of plaintiffs.

But Berman was going up against Pfizer, Abbott, Merck, and J&J without understanding the arcane terms they used or what they meant. He'd be loath to admit it, but he needed an insider to lead him through the hazy terrain. Berman asked Duxbury a few questions and listened hard, frowning as if the tumblers in his brain weren't clicking fast enough. Finally, he asked, "What do you know about the average wholesale price?"

"You mean AWP?" said Duxbury, smiling. "That means 'ain't what's paid.' It's supposed to be the real price that pharmaceuticals charge their customer. But it's a phony number. It's just another way for companies to rip off the government."

Bingo! Berman realized that the guide he so urgently needed was sitting right in front of him. The talk moved past shareholder fraud, and Berman explained his own multidistrict lawsuit against the drug firms. Then Berman made a most unusual suggestion.

"Would you to come and work for me for six months or so?" He needed someone who could decipher Big Pharma's practices to help him move his class action case forward. Terms were discussed, and before too long it was agreed: Duxbury would join Berman as a senior investigator on his AWP case. Eventually, Berman would represent Duxbury in what became a Procrit whistle-blowing case.

If ever a man got a lucky break, it was Mark Duxbury that day. He left Berman's penthouse office and descended to the airy lobby of the unorthodox, upside-down, mojo-heavy building. But he walked on clouds the entire way.

—⁓—

Duxbury could scarcely believe his good fortune. After working at several cruddy low-level jobs, he was now pulling down about $90,000 a year as "a glorified paralegal" in Berman's high-flying firm. Against all odds, he'd been able to turn his drug expertise and personal obsession into teaching skills, with a chance to show Berman, his associate Jeff Sprung, and the other lawyers how to spot the hidden ropes and pulleys that hoisted dodgy drugs into popular brands.

"I like to make the invisible visible," Duxbury told his new boss.

For the first time in who knows how long, Duxbury worked in an actual office with other people. For a man who had always loved company, he felt giddy to be among collaborators, smart people, and potentially friends. He'd been isolated at home for nine months, dealing with two difficult women and two pubescent kids and all the problems that entailed. Or he'd been plotting legal strategies against Ortho with his faithful friend Simmerly. But now he enjoyed things that company men took for granted. He had a capacious corner office that scraped the sky and gave him bird's-eye views of the clouds, the sea, and the busy lanes below of firemen, fishmongers, and financiers. There was a copy room, a receptionist, and a secretary whom he shared with others. The employees' lunchroom had a refrigerator filled not with clinking vials of Procrit, but brown lunch bags of sandwiches and yogurt, their owners' names scrawled in crayon on the front.

He began walking a little taller.

Berman's case hinged on proving how the nation's drug firms

"gamed" vulnerable patients and consumers by using AWP to inflate the cost of medicine. Duxbury taught the legal team which phrases to use and whom to contact when requesting information about grants, "continuing medical education" lunches, and whatnot. He wrote so many memos describing the perverse system that at one point Duxbury apologized "for the volume of information." Berman learned even more about the sleight-of-hand jiggery that engorged drug companies, and he had to acknowledge that his "expert" had the touch.

Duxbury traveled to obtain declarations and evidence for the suit. He wore his "God, I'm tired of traveling" tie, with its gaily colored toothbrush, hotel sink, and airlines baggage tag. During the city's jazz festivals, he wore his silk New Orleans tie painted with oysters, banjos, and signs for Bourbon Street. But this was a staid law firm, where solid-colored suspenders and bow ties were in vogue. So Duxbury bought himself a pair of suspenders and wore them just like the other guys. Some mornings he'd bring in a box of doughnuts to share with his office mates; other days he'd go to lunch to help celebrate a colleague's birthday. When he was stuck on an issue, he'd go shoot some pool with a lawyer at a billiards table across the hall from the office. Most co-workers liked Duxbury's "colorful personality and strong convictions," as one said, and he liked them back. As his work on Berman's AWP case began to pay off, Duxbury turned his attention to his own case and began researching the finer points of whistle-blower law.

—⁂—

THE False Claims Act stretches back to the thirteenth century, when English peasants who saw someone cheating the crown could sue on the king's behalf. That was the only way a commoner could gain access to the royal court, and if the accusations were deemed to be true, the peasant could be rewarded with a portion of the penalty the king levied against the cheater. Lawyers called such suits by the Latin term *qui tam*, which was an abbreviation of the phrase *qui tam pro domino rege quam pro se ipso in hac parte sequitur*. Loosely translated, that meant "he who pursues this action on our Lord King's behalf as well as his own." Egalitarian as it was, the principle was primarily a way for the king to enforce his own laws. Eventually, the deputized peasants grew a little too zealous in pursuing their bounties, and when the king's courts opened the gates to all legal disputes, *qui tam* actions withered away.

Yet the concept found a second life in America during the Civil War, when profiteers sold tainted pork and sawdust as gunpowder to the Union Army. President Abraham Lincoln condemned these merchants, saying, "Worse than traitors in arms are the men who pretend loyalty to the flag, feast and fatten on the misfortunes of the Nation while patriotic blood is crimsoning the plains of the South and their countrymen moldering the dust." In 1862 Congress held hearings on the unscrupulous contractors, which led to the court-martial of Major Justus McKinstry, an army quartermaster who ran a crooked procurement empire, complete with kickbacks. In 1863 Congress passed the False Claims Act, which became known as the Informer's Act, or Lincoln's Law. But at that time there was no Department of Justice to help enforce the law and, more importantly, no money to do so. *Qui tam* suits were considered legitimate, if uncommon, actions.

During the Reagan years, however, lucrative military government contracts exploded, and the law found new life. American taxpayers were shocked by claims that defense firms charged them and Uncle Sam $400 for a simple claw hammer. Once again the government lacked effective tools to combat such fraud until Senator Charles Grassley (R-Iowa), and Representative Howard Berman (D-California) championed amendments to the law that strengthened it. First of all, they made fraud onerous to defendants by tripling damages and penalties of up to $10,000 for each false claim. Then they made the whistle worth blowing by allowing citizens to share in a larger portion of whatever Uncle Sam recovered and, most importantly, by protecting them from retaliation. The law also required defendants to pay the legal fees of victorious whistle-blowers.

Duxbury learned all this late at night, after the cleaning crew had swept through his office with its vacuums and rags and after Bibi had fallen asleep at home. He read leather-bound law books about this arcane corner of law, which said that anyone with knowledge of federal fraud could file a claim on behalf of the government to recover funds. Duxbury could get between 15 and 30 percent of whatever the government recovered, depending on the extent to which he and Berman contributed to a successful government prosecution. If the government joined his case, it'd keep between 85 and 70 percent of its stolen funds, with Duxbury receiving the rest. Out of that, Duxbury would have to pay Berman's 40 percent commission, with something for Simmerly too. He figured that the Procrit case was worth a few billion dollars and that he personally could wind up with hundreds of millions.

Still, the road to riches was fraught with sheer drops, overhanging rocks, and the sort of windy isolation that induces hallucinations. First, an individual must be lucky enough to find an attorney willing to work for years on a contingency fee only. Then, the two must be brave (or foolish) enough to spend most of those years without pay, trying to get the Department of Justice to join their case. Without the full threat and might of the U.S. government behind Duxbury's claim, J&J would feel no need to take his case seriously. Duxbury and Berman would be up against armies of J&J's attorneys who were only too happy to run the clock, at a rate between $300 and $900 an hour. Duxbury's case could be swatted down before it even got to court. In his research, Duxbury had read of whistle-blowers who died before their case had even been heard. The *qui tam* journey was littered with more skeletons and iron carcasses than Russia's Trans-Siberian Highways, only with more red tape. You had to be the first to file, have direct knowledge of the scam, alert the U.S. attorney general before you filed, and follow dozens of other seemingly picayune rules.

But why wouldn't the government back Duxbury's case? Wasn't his the most deserving, most outstanding set of charges federal attorneys had ever seen?

—⚮—

Mᴇᴀɴᴡʜɪʟᴇ, Duxbury and McClellan continued to talk. One day, Duxbury asked what McClellan thought about J&J's $150 million fine from the latest Amgen arbitration. The Arizona rep was steamed. "I can't figure out what we've done to deserve that," he said. "We've been kept in the dark about this suit, but everyone I know thinks Amgen is the bad guy!"

The two had often disagreed on this point, which had strained their relationship. Duxbury had desperately needed help for his wrongful termination case against Ortho two years earlier, when McClellan was riding high as a territory manager. But the Tucson rep had refused to fax him documents. "I can't afford to risk my job by helping your legal case against my employer. Besides," McClellan had insisted, "I don't have any incriminating evidence." Duxbury had said he understood, but his friend's decision had really stung. He'd been blocked from getting a full copy of his personnel records, had been barred from using testimony in the *Amgen v. Ortho* arbitration, and his best friend and last hope wouldn't even mail him a copy of an old sales script. If McClellan had shared a few puny papers, Duxbury believed he would have won his case.

But now that Duxbury was an "expert" at a big-gun law firm, McClellan began to listen to his friend. "Dean, I'm seeing federal indictments of drug firms for the same types of fraud that we did at Ortho," Duxbury explained. Delving into these cases, he learned how the DOJ handled such claims. He even sent McClellan a few press releases about cases; one had involved reps who had given doctors free Lupron so they could bill Medicare and Medicaid at the full sticker price. McClellan remembered that deal—it had constricted his business for a few days. When Duxbury reminded him that TAP was the biggest Medicare fraud settlement, he grew quiet. "I'm not making this stuff up, Dean. The government is nailing companies for the same things Ortho's been doing."

After weeks of educating McClellan, Duxbury asked for help again, this time with his whistle-blowing effort. "You don't even have to put your name on the lawsuit," Duxbury promised his friend. That clinched the deal for McClellan, as he needed to remain anonymous so he could keep his job. One summer night in 2003, McClellan began to fax Duxbury patient trial cards, grant checks, and a few company memos. "Helping Mark seems like the right thing to do," McClellan thought. Yet he continued reporting to work every day.

With Berman's knowledge, Duxbury spent late nights collecting McClellan's faxes and drafting his brief. Much of the suit's boilerplate material came from Duxbury, who made a point of including the off-label promotion scheme in his suit. He'd send a draft to Berman and others, but every time it came back to Duxbury, the off-label clause had been erased. "Maybe it's a clerical mistake," he thought, but the paralegal who prepared the papers denied it. Finally, a few nights before the suit was filed, Duxbury realized that Berman was the one who was erasing his pet phrase. The former rep walked into his boss's office and began to argue.

Berman didn't want to include the phrase. "It's too jargony," he said. "We're going to concentrate only on the AWP aspect."

"But you can't drop off-label," Duxbury insisted. "The high-dose campaign was absolutely illegal. We have to keep it in." He tried explaining the deed in financial terms. The fraud tied to inflating Procrit's AWP figure was at most 40 percent of the drug's cost and therefore would amount to a 40 percent payday. Duxbury explained that off-label promotions were 100 percent wrong and therefore potentially more lucrative.

Berman replied that the term *off-label* hadn't been used much before. *The judge won't understand it.*

"I don't care if it's *never* been done before," said Duxbury. "I'm the pharmaceutical expert here, and my case revolves around this illegal promotion." Finally, Berman stuck in a simple clause that described off-label promotions without actually using those words. Specifically, the *qui tam* suit said that Ortho paid doctors "to use the drug in a way which is inconsistent with its FDA approved indications. . . ." As it turned out, that awkward, fifteen-word phrase would become absolutely critical.

That night, Duxbury stayed even later to make sure the brief was complete. He crossed out McClellan's name at least once, but when he saw that Berman had kept in his pet clause, Duxbury was so tired, he didn't proofread the entire final document. Apparently, neither did Berman.

The day before Halloween, Berman and Duxbury sent their allegations to the U.S. attorney general, John Ashcroft, as required by the rules of *qui tam* law. On November 3, 2003, they filed Duxbury's suit in U.S. District Court in Boston, home to some of the nation's most consumer-friendly laws. It remained under seal so that the government could investigate the allegations without revealing them to the defendant or to the public. When Duxbury finally completed his task, a slow leak of breath escaped his clenched jaw. "Yes," he thought, and silently raised his fist in the air.

—⟶∭⟵—

A WEEK or so later, Duxbury reread his case and saw a mistake. "Oh, shit!" he cried. In all of the brouhaha with Berman over the off-label clause, Duxbury and his lawyer had forgotten to redact McClellan's name out of the final version. Duxbury felt awful about this and spent days worrying about it. But he didn't call McClellan to explain or even apologize. "I had a brain fart," he rationalized. "It was completely by accident and it's all my fault." Duxbury figured he could make it up to his friend later. That, too, was a mistake.

—⟶∭⟵—

THE Rainier Tower had been designed to include sun panels, a shopping mall, music concerts, and a courtyard big enough for a thirty-yard dash. But the modern amenities couldn't change some of the outdated, biased views of some of the building's tenants. As helpful as Duxbury was to Berman's team, some office mates viewed him with skepticism and even disdain. "You need a rogue to catch a rogue," judges used to say about whistle-blowers, and a few people at Hagens

Berman seemed to adopt that attitude. One such man was Berman's partner Jeff Sprung, who considered Duxbury a scoundrel who had committed the crimes he was now getting paid to uncover. Or that's what Duxbury suspected after working with him. Short and balding, Sprung was married to a doctor and often objected to Duxbury's proposals. One day, after a particularly tough meeting, Duxbury had to face it: "This guy just doesn't like me."

Duxbury had continued to wear his Ortho signet ring proudly. It was a constant reminder of his former sale stardom and also of what Ortho had put him through. Whenever someone asked him about it, he'd explain all that and include the significance of the symbol. But invariably the well-meaning professional would stare at him with incomprehension and draw back. "How can you wear that thing after all that company has done?" *Inflating drug prices, cheating orphans and old ladies, robbing state capitals.* They didn't understand that Duxbury had been tricked too. "I was shocked to learn that nearly everything I did at Ortho was illegal," he'd explain. "They cheated not just the government but their own people too!" Yet, somehow, his words didn't come through, and the conversation would peter out with a weak promise to do lunch.

One or two people actually avoided the so-called Brainiac. At the time, Duxbury was reading *The Human Stain,* a novel by Philip Roth in which a man is falsely accused of a politically incorrect crime—with tragic, ironic results. Duxbury so identified with that character that he replaced the nameplate on his door with one that read, THE STAIN. On his toughest, most discouraging days, he'd pass THE STAIN, look at his ring, and redouble his efforts to keep pushing. He so wanted to regain his once-sterling reputation, and to be able to say that he was "doing well by doing good" and really mean it.

An unexpected bit of fallout from the job was the strain it put on Duxbury's marriage. He now had to drive ninety minutes from his home in Gig Harbor to downtown Seattle, usually in rush-hour traffic. He'd leave his home at seven A.M. and return twelve hours later—or more. The couple had reconciled from their volatile arrest incident. But they were still circling each other uneasily, trying to find a way back to the heart-galloping spot from which they'd started. Bibi would call him frequently at the office to say she missed him, but some days she was particularly needy. Renee, too, was still nervous about Sojie staying in Duxbury's new home, the one purchased to give Sojie her own room. Bibi thought Sojie was spoiled; Renee disapproved of Bibi, accusing the woman of being too tough on her nine-year-old. Nor did Renee want Sojie playing with her eight-year-old stepbrother Richard because, sometimes, they squabbled and fought. "That's what kids do sometimes," an exasperated Duxbury tried to explain.

But it was no use, and he did not want to fight Renee in court. Caught between two women pulling at him from opposite ends, by the needs of his daughter and his stepson, and strained by the drive between work and home, he decided to shell out $900 a month to rent a separate apartment. In July 2003, he moved some of his things to a two-bedroom place in Surprise Lake, a planned community in Milton. That cut his commute in half, gave him time away from his wife, and accommodated Renee by allowing him to spend quality time with Sojie without other family members. Bibi resumed her medication and grew more emotionally stable, which improved her relationship with her husband too. By 2004, Duxbury was seeing Sojie on Wednesday evenings and every other weekend in his own apartment. That place would soon rip his world apart.

—⚂—

Back in the office, Duxbury realized he had an affinity for law. All that logic and debate, the parsing of intent and meaning, the sparring with scholars and fools ... he liked the to-and-fro of fighting with words and ideas. After seven years of being deposed for other battles, he'd gotten a hard-knock education in law *for free,* he told Simmerly, and it showed. "Every time I order takeout, I swear to tell the truth, the whole truth, and nothing but the truth, so help me God!" Duxbury knew how to take declarations, whom to subpoena, and which exhibits to hunt down. And every once in a while, he got the feeling that maybe, just maybe, justice was being served. Once, after Berman won a particularly difficult round in the AWP case, Duxbury felt a surge of pride. "What a thrill!" Maybe his efforts were actually lifting the cause. "This is why I love the law."

He had helped accomplish a lot in Berman's drug-price-fixing case. On February 26, 2004, U.S. District Court Judge Patti Saris, in Boston, had ruled that finally, after two years in limbo, Berman's AWP case could lurch forward. With the additional information that Duxbury had supplied, the lawyer amended his original complaint to include some new, meatier details. "I don't know if I'm going to settle these cases or go to trial, but the judge is pretty outraged at the facts," Berman told his star consultant. Sure enough, that summer, U.S. District Court Judge Patti Saris rejected nearly every argument made by the defendants in their efforts to kill the AWP case.

With Duxbury's help, Berman began looking at other government pools, or "honeypots," that doled out health-care money to grandfathers, the disabled, and babies and their mothers. Medicaid plans in most states insured large numbers of the poor and elderly, paying what Duxbury suspected were illegally steep prices for Procrit doses. Duxbury helped Berman file two suits on behalf of California and Illinois.

———

SOMETHING thrashed in a burlap bag. Harsh laughter, a flame moving closer, and a howl as the thing in the bag flailed harder. Stuck in that wild borderland between sleep and nightmare, Duxbury awoke, gasping for air. Alone, he didn't know where he was until he remembered— Boston. It was early February. The sun wouldn't rise for a few more hours and his meeting with federal prosecutors wouldn't start until hours after that. Blurry-eyed, Duxbury rose and made himself a cup of coffee. He flung open the drapes and stared at the harbor outside his window. A bitter wind whined through the hotel's ducts and rippled the water's surface. In the distance, he could see runway torches and pier signs flickering bravely in the dark.

When the sun finally rose, as pale as topaz, Duxbury snapped a picture of the dawn. He had flown in yesterday with the purpose of meeting Berman's well-known partner Tom Sobol. A veteran of the tobacco settlement, the attorney and his client were scheduled to present their *qui tam* case to prosecutors in the federal courthouse at two P.M. today. It was critical to convince authorities that Duxbury's case was solid. If the DOJ lawyers decided to join him, they'd need to be certain they could prove his charges in court. Duxbury had been told that Sobol had all the supporting evidence and would help prepare him for his two P.M. session.

Confident, Duxbury took his time with his morning ablutions. He ordered breakfast and read *The Boston Globe* while surfing the news channels. He showered, shaved, and donned a designer suit along with one of his lucky ties. At midmorning, he squared his shoulders and walked outside to the blistering wind of Rowes Wharf. He strolled a few blocks until he found the right address. Upstairs, in the lobby of Sobol's firm, he introduced himself to the receptionist. "Mr. Sobol will be right with you," she said, and Duxbury took a seat.

Twenty minutes went by and a secretary appeared to offer Duxbury some coffee. Thirty more minutes passed and Duxbury grew antsy. "It's getting late," he thought. After a while, the secretary returned and said, "I'm sorry, but Mr. Sobol has an urgent deadline and can't meet with you." Instead, he'd send Ed Notargiacomo, who had joined the firm eighteen months earlier. The younger man seemed nice enough, but Duxbury blanched. An associate joining the DOJ meeting wasn't as impressive as a partner. "Oh, well," Duxbury thought. "Maybe this guy knows his stuff."

There was no time for lunch, so the two grabbed a taxi. In the cab, Duxbury learned that Notargiacomo was working on the firm's AWP litigation but knew little about Duxbury's *qui tam* case. Duxbury tried to summarize his sixteen-page complaint, but when the taxi halted in front of the new brick courthouse, he gave up. The men climbed the stairs to a room where they met the federal lawyers assigned to

Duxbury's case: an assistant U.S. attorney and DOJ attorney Jamie Ann Yavelberg.

Yavelberg didn't look very happy. Berman had insisted that the trial attorney fly from her home in Washington, D.C., to Boston to meet his lawyers at their convenience. Now, Duxbury realized, Berman had insulted her again by sending Ed. The short, normally chatty woman turned to Notargiacomo and essentially asked why the government should intervene in this case. The associate floundered, so Duxbury seized control and gave Yavelberg an overview. The legal concept of "off-label" was relatively new, so Duxbury, in his best FM-radio voice, outlined how it worked at Ortho.

"And what documents do you have to prove your claims?" she asked.

Notargiacomo remained silent, so Duxbury answered. "I don't have any in hand, but we can send them to you."

If Yavelberg had a hard time understanding Duxbury's fraud claims against J&J and Ortho, it was understandable. Life inside her under-staffed division was so chaotic, there was a backlog of 200 *qui tam* cases collecting dust. The overwhelming number of these suits accused health-care and pharmaceutical companies of illegal practices, seeding a cottage industry for white-collar defense lawyers. Yavelberg and Connolly asked a few more questions, but after an uninspiring hour the meeting broke up.

Duxbury flew back to Seattle and waited for word from Washington. February passed, then March. In April, Yavelberg replied. Berman considered her letter "high-handed," but Duxbury was happy to hear she was investigating his case. Her two-page epistle asked for more information, and she summarized his suit with its kickbacks and grants. Strangely, she didn't mention the most important element of all, Ortho's marketing trials and illegal promotions.

Duxbury wrote a draft amplifying his claims. This time, he used the term *off-label dosing* and threw in some numbers. In 2002 alone, the government paid $1 billion for Procrit injections, making this a multi-billion-dollar case, he wrote. Berman added his thoughts, too, with a chaser of disdain: We "are not sure you have grasped [our case] based on your letter and the interview of Mr. Duxbury. In this submission, we again explain the key aspects." he wrote. Berman signed the seventeen-page letter, and Duxbury's hopes rose on the thin expression of Yavelberg's interest and the inflamed response of his boss. Then, a more urgent matter forced Duxbury to push the matter aside. McClellan needed help.

18

Black Ops

2004

GRIPPING a black leather overnight bag and briefcase, Duxbury stepped off the airplane at the Tucson International Airport and onto the tarmac. It was Friday, the last day of April 2004, yet a blast of furnace-hot air smacked him in the face. He'd boarded the plane that morning in temperate Seattle, dressed in a powder-blue button-down shirt, khaki slacks, and cordovan-colored loafers. But at noon in this godforsaken region near Fort Apache, Duxbury might as well have been wearing a parka and snow boots. He tried to walk briskly out of the oppressive heat and toward shade, but energy seeped out of him like air from a punctured tire. As the concourse shimmered a few hundred feet ahead, he reminded himself why he was here.

Earlier that week, on Monday, April 26, Duxbury had gotten a late-night telephone call from his friend, who was clearly upset. "They fired me," wailed McClellan, his voice panic-stricken. The shorthand version of McClellan's crisis was that his managers had just asked him to resign his job or be fired. They'd surprised him by corralling him into a conference room and asking him to sign a severance agreement. They also wanted all of his Ortho records. Duxbury commiserated with his friend on the phone for nearly an hour. "I don't understand this," McClellan kept saying. "I've won all these sales contests and prizes." Duxbury agreed that McClellan's firing was low-down. But he thought it was also disastrous for his whistle-blowing case. Whatever dribs and drabs of evidence that McClellan had been secretly faxing to Duxbury over the past few months would stop once McClellan left Ortho. And that would weaken Duxbury's suit and dissuade the government from joining his case.

The morning after McClellan's call, Duxbury had marched into Berman's office. "We need to see what records Dean has—and pronto," he had urged. "Otherwise, Ortho is going to destroy his papers, and we'll lose some critical evidence." Duxbury suggested that Berman send him to Tucson over the weekend to investigate.

Three days later, here he was, on a reconnaissance mission in the baking Sonoran Desert, sweating pellets. "I can't wait to see what Dean has," he thought. He reached the air-conditioned airport terminal and exhaled loudly. He walked past a barista stand with its aroma of strong coffee and resisted the pull of the smoke-filled bar and its sports-TV chatter. He kept an eye peeled for McClellan and was just about to step out to the curb, when he spied his buddy, dressed in gray flannel slacks, a starched white shirt, and a striped tie held in place with an old-fashioned tie chain. Duxbury hadn't seen him since that ill-fated national sales meeting in Seattle six years before. Duxbury put down his bags to better study his friend. The Tucson man was still a trim 185-pound manager with a full head of hair and a thick, tidy mustache. But now his face looked more beaten than weathered. At that moment, McClellan was pressing his cell phone against his one good ear, a frown creasing his brow as he listened to a voice on the other end of the line. Duxbury waited for him to finish. Then he stepped into McClellan's line of sight.

"Hey there, stranger," he said.

"Mark!" cried McClellan, throwing open his arms.

The two embraced in a bear hug, then, at arm's length, sized up one another.

Duxbury was no longer the scrawny, hunted-looking guy with unkempt hair and a rumpled suit, which is how he had looked when Ortho had launched its Phase IV promotions. The man standing before McClellan was clear-eyed and well rested, wearing casual new clothes and the cool assurance that McClellan recognized in young climbers—the same confidence that McClellan himself had possessed only a few months ago. McClellan bent down to pick up Duxbury's overnight bag and led him to the parking lot. There he fumbled for his keys and stopped in front of a new luxury Saab sedan.

Duxbury whistled as he slid into the car's passenger's seat. "Nice wheels!"

McClellan started the engine. "Headquarters just sent it two months ago, because of my 2003 sales. I hit a record $10.5 million."

"So why are they asking you to resign?"

As he drove out of the lot, McClellan rattled off a few possible reasons: He was too old, and a younger rep would be less expensive; his bosses were jealous of him. Or, he said, throwing out his pet theory, "Someone at corporate knows I'm talking to you, and they don't like it."

The two discussed that possibility as McClellan drove out of the south end of town, passing the boneyard of decommissioned bombers lined up at Davis-Monthan Air Force Base. Beginning in 1999, the year after Duxbury left Ortho, some of McClellan's bosses would ask about Duxbury out of the blue. "What's new with Mark?" they'd say, or "Have you heard from Duxbury?" This was odd, since none of McClellan's bosses had liked Duxbury. "One guy who asked about you hadn't even met you!" Their questions were disingenuous at best.

"That *is* strange," Duxbury agreed. "Maybe they were trying to learn details about my suit." *The one you didn't help me with*, Duxbury wanted to add.

McClellan's silver Saab headed north under the piercing blue sky. "I never told them anything about you," McClellan insisted. "But they kept quizzing me over the years. '*What's Mark doing?*' It really bugged me." McClellan shopped short of saying he resented being tarred by his friend's brush.

Duxbury himself had a grievance or two. McClellan's firing had brought up memories of his own ignoble sacking half a dozen years earlier. He thought of those days when he'd needed help from his friend and had been batted away. Duxbury had said that he understood, but those words had stung. The two drove in silence over the lunar landscape, each man weighing feelings of abandonment and betrayal against the pure joy of seeing an old friend.

The two-lane highway started to climb toward the red-rock Santa Catalina Mountains. Here was a strangely beautiful landscape, full of prickly pear cactus, mesquite trees, and creosote shrubs. The plants were bursting with so many white, pink, and yellow blossoms that a visitor might forget that those flowers concealed two-inch-long thorns and sharp needles. Danger was everywhere, even under Arizona's state flower, the bloom of the tall saguaro cactus. McClellan had loved these plants ever since he first saw a saguaro as a kid, watching a Roy Rogers western on a black-and-white TV. It was only later, after he brushed against the cactus, that he learned just how hurtful the spines could be. Funny how he'd once thought that only good could come from collaborating with Duxbury too. But now, as McClellan's car sped over the deceptively hostile terrain, he was wiser than that.

McClellan debated whether he should bring up his complaint. A few weeks ago, he'd finally gotten around to reading a copy of Duxbury's *qui tam* suit when, there, in the middle of page 10, he saw his name. "One Ortho Biotech sales representative Mr. Dean McClellan had over 400 patient trial cards in his possession. . . ." McClellan had been furious. "Mark had promised he'd keep my name out of the suit, but he hadn't." As soon as McClellan had seen himself mentioned in the whistle-blowing suit, he knew he was a dead duck. "The biggest reason I'm getting fired is because of Mark."

McClellan believed that his friend had betrayed him. Had he broached the topic that day, he would have gotten an apology. "I screwed up," Duxbury would have told him. But Duxbury was too embarrassed to apologize, and McClellan hated confrontation. As he steered the car through the prickly terrain, he decided not to bring up the sore topic. "Besides," he told himself, "there's nothing anyone can do about it now."

The car continued its climb as McClellan and Duxbury brooded about the past and the rather treacherous present. Each man stood to lose a lot of time and energy in this *qui tam* thing; their efforts could boomerang into a breach-of-contract action against them for violating J&J's secrecy agreements. But sometimes friendship exacts a price. These two had shared sales expeditions and late-night goofball missions and had been commemorated in commercial cathedrals. They'd collected medals, cups, and rings, only to reach the pinnacle of their careers then get absolutely thrashed. It dawned on them that perhaps their entire journey had been a ruse, a hoax, or worse, a perversion, and that somewhere along the way, they had lost their best, most noble intentions.

They had traveled many roads together, and as the Saab sped toward town on this new venture, each man silently let go of his accusations. They both relaxed inside the well-insulated luxury sedan and made room for the easygoing bonhomie and brotherly trust that cemented their remarkable, stubbornly durable bond.

—Ⅲ—

McCLELLAN finally pulled his car into an upscale neighborhood and parked in the flagstone driveway he had built himself. He led Duxbury into the low-slung ranch house, past the large kitchen, and through a side door to a breezeway. He unlocked the mother-in-law unit that he had also built and, with a sweep of the arm, said, "This is where you'll be sleeping." It looked like it had been built in the 1970s with its wood siding, brown shag carpet, and avocado-green bedspread. Nailed to the wall were a mail-order plaque of the McClellan coat of arms (two spears crossed behind a shield), a framed shot of McClellan paragliding over a beach in Puerto Vallarta, and a personalized autographed photo of model Cindy Crawford. Remnants of his drug stewardship were strewn about the room: a mug emblazoned with the name Procrit; a solar-powered calculator stamped with an insulin drug logo; and a two-inch-long flashlight-pen from Amgen. The bookcase held a set of Time-Life history books—*The Scouts, The Indians,* and *The Frontiersmen*—along with several photo albums marked by year.

Later, the two sat in the white-tiled kitchen and gossiped over beers.

McClellan, however, wasn't in the mood for chitchat. He perched on the bar stool, lost in blue thoughts, the fan whirring overhead. Duxbury offered to make dinner, and while he rolled out pizza dough, chopped garlic, and grated cheese, McClellan disgorged the humiliating details of his dismissal.

The previous Monday, his boss, Scott Hudson, had shown up to shadow McClellan on his weekly sales calls. "I should have suspected something right away," he said. McClellan didn't think much of it and had started the day by bringing his boss along on a visit to Dr. Suresh Katakkar, who was set to buy $900,000 worth of Procrit that year. The doctor warmly greeted McClellan. A few weeks earlier, on April 12, McClellan had given him an Ortho check for $19,278.73—the physician's bonus for exceeding his first-quarter purchase agreement. "Katakkar is happy with us as usual," McClellan had told Hudson. McClellan was about to drop in on Dr. Von Hoff next, when Hudson deviated from the schedule. He ordered McClellan to head to the Kinko's store on Broadway. There, in a conference room and on the speakerphone was a woman from human resources. "I've been ambushed," McClellan thought.

But he could not for the life of him recall what CLiM (Career Limiting Move) he had committed.

It wasn't as if the fifty-four-year-old McClellan was an extravagant line item on J&J's ledger. In 2003, he earned about $165,000 (not including benefits and perks), making him one of the top-paid sales reps. But that was a fraction of the $6.6 million total compensation of CEO William Weldon. More to the point was that, come June 15, McClellan would turn fifty-five and be eligible for a pension that would pay him 70 percent of his salary. If, for some reason, McClellan were to resign before that date, then Ortho wouldn't have to pay him so much. Plus, it could replace the salesman with a less expensive rep. The trick was to push McClellan off the moving train without making a mess.

An employer can legally fire someone for any cause except for race, sex, or age; Ortho needed a good reason to terminate its agent. So, in January, McClellan's bosses had started to strip away the rep's hospital clients, which accounted for half of his sales. By April, the die was cast: McClellan's sales were down 53 percent.

As a result, Hudson gave him an ultimatum that day in the Kinko's conference room: Retire or be fired. McClellan's stomach had churned. The HR woman would mail his separation papers shortly, she had said. "Make sure you seek the advice of an attorney before you sign them."

Now the forlorn rep looked at Duxbury. "I don't even know an attorney," he wailed. Duxbury suggested he talk to Berman. Then he sketched out their weekend mission.

After a dinner of pepperoni-and-cheese pizza, McClellan mixed some gin-and-tonics and led his guest out into the warm spring night. They had only forty-eight hours to comb through McClellan's files. He had collected so much material over the years that Ortho bins and boxes filled his garage, two sheds, and a company-paid storage unit. McClellan had grown attached to those files. "I can't remember a deal or contract unless I have the piece of paper in front of me," he confessed. When his job had begun to sour a few months earlier, he had moved many of his papers out of his garage and sheds and into an even bigger rental unit a few miles away. "I figured the company might send someone to steal my papers, and I didn't want them around my family," he explained. After all, Duxbury's papers had been seized by an ex-FBI-agent-turned-Ortho-security-guard, and the same thing could happen to McClellan.

"I'm not being paranoid," he insisted defensively. In fact, a stranger in a red pickup had been cruising past his home every morning for a few weeks. "I live on a cul-de-sac and know all my neighbors," McClellan said. "But no one recognizes this guy in the red truck, and believe me, I've asked."

"I believe you, Dean," said Duxbury.

The moon rose and cast its pale light on the outcroppings of the Santa Catalina Mountains. In the foreground, just beyond McClellan's fence, loomed a thirty-foot-tall saguaro. Its trunk stood silhouetted against the dusk, its thick, handless arms reaching for the sky like a cardboard villain from a Tom Mix western. The men talked and laughed as the moon arched over the patio.

The next morning, coffee cups in hand, they walked outside to begin the day's work. Just then, the mysterious red pickup truck slowly drove by. "Good morning!" McClellan yelled, waving to the startled driver. The man sped off, and McClellan turned to his friend. "What'd I tell you?" he said, triumphantly. They climbed into the sedan and zipped toward Bear Canyon Self-Storage. McClellan sped seventy miles an hour in a fifty-five-mile-per-hour zone, and Duxbury nervously glanced at the black box perched on the dashboard. "I hope your radar jammer is working," he said.

"Oh, yeah," McClellan assured him. "I got me a laser jammer too." Since both devices thwarted lawmen who tried to enforce speed limits, they were illegal in many states, but not in Arizona. "Haven't had a ticket in nearly twelve years, even though my average speed is ninety-four miles per hour," McClellan added.

A few minutes later they pulled into a gated lot across the street from the sheriff's station. Near a clump of horse tongue and a security panel, McClellan stopped the car long enough to punch in a code, and the gate swung open. They parked near the end of a maze of industrial-looking sheds. McClellan unlocked his storage unit and stepped inside. Duxbury heard the sound of tiny nails skittering across the cement floor; McClellan spotted a rodent the size of a squirrel. "It's just a pack rat," he said. "They make their homes out of anything, paper, cans, cacti . . ."

"How convenient for them," said Duxbury, goose bumps prickling his arm. He gingerly took the top off a box, which in turn startled a black spider inside. At the opposite end of the room, McClellan nearly stepped on a poisonous scorpion; he stomped it dead with his boot heel. When the critters had finally retreated, the men reviewed the dust-covered files. Duxbury found the list of top oncologists who had been paid as Ortho advisors. He ran across sales materials, scripts about how to pitch off-label uses, and other incriminating evidence. Some documents were stained with rat urine; others held dead ants. But nearly all were legible, and Duxbury became engrossed in their content.

Of particular interest were Ortho's guidelines for "Free Goods and

Patient Assistance." All samples were supposed to be marked "Sample Drug—Not for Resale, Insurance Billing, or Reimbursement." But neither McClellan nor Duxbury had ever seen such a Procrit label. Free drug was supposed to be limited to introducing a customer to a product, but it was widely used to entice and appease clients. Reps were supposed to advise doctors that they "may not bill third party programs" for free drug, but the opposite occurred time and again. Grant money should be given to "educational centers," read the guidebook, but the rule that made Duxbury choke was this one: "Patient confidentiality must be maintained."

"Jesus! We were taught to violate nearly every one of Ortho's rules," he said.

McClellan grunted. He was immersed in a box containing his old expense reports. He saw one that stopped him cold—a 2003 telephone bill had several numbers blacked out. McClellan remembered that a New Jersey manager had asked him why he'd redacted the numbers, and he had explained, "They're personal contacts, not business." In fact, they had been telephone calls he'd made to Duxbury. McClellan had wanted to hide the fact that he was not simply talking to his friend but faxing him Ortho memos for Duxbury's whistle-blowing lawsuit. McClellan had always suspected that management knew he still talked to Duxbury, but as he stared at the marked-up telephone bill, he realized that he himself had tipped them off.

When he had copied the bill, he had redacted Duxbury's 206-area-code number. But when he had copied that page, the "light" button on the copier had turned the black mark into a light gray line that had highlighted, rather than concealed, Duxbury's number. McClellan felt a chill climb up his spine.

"Mark, look at this," he said, raising the sheaf of papers in the air. "I was sacked for cooperating with you and your suit."

Duxbury flipped through the report, then looked into his friend's hurt blue eyes. "I'm sorry, Dean. I didn't mean for this to happen."

"It's my own fault," he admitted. Besides, he knew there were other forces at work. The two returned to the business of pawing through manila folders, vellum sheets, and WAR reports until evening and returned the next morning to find even more astonishing evidence. On their last night together, they dined on red meat and drank Mexican beer. Then they poured themselves after-dinner drinks and stepped out to the patio, where the intricate rocks that formed Thimble Peak reached for the stars. Duxbury explained the status of his case and added that, if all went well, he could win $1 billion or so, and that Berman would take 40 percent of that. "Whatever is left, I'll split with you evenly," he said.

"Really?"

Duxbury wasn't kidding. He had already laid out Ortho's illegal schemes with his own documents, though he wasn't sure that'd be sufficient. But if McClellan agreed to serve up his cache of papers and if his case triumphed in court, then it was only right that McClellan share in the spoils.

The friends clinked their glasses under the indigo blanket of Arizona's sky.

The next morning, McClellan drove Duxbury to the airport. Before they parted, McClellan told him one last thing:

"I don't want to get sued by Ortho for helping your case, Mark."

"Hey, it's your case now, too, remember?"

On Tuesday, May 4, McClellan received a six-page letter signed by the director of human resources. It confirmed his separation and stirred up his anxieties with this standard clause: "You agree that you will not cause or permit to be filed any lawsuit against the Company." "Too late," he thought grimly.

McClellan tried to sleep that night, but sirens, coyotes, and other sounds of lunacy filled the air. He rose from his bed and padded outside, where the full moon was in the midst of an eclipse. The Indians who had once lived in this basin believed that eclipses brought cataclysm. McClellan didn't like change, least of all the kind followed by misfortune. He reviewed his position and wondered, how bad would things get?

—‍⟋⟍‍—

Jim Lenox was back in the hospital, only this time it wasn't cancer. It was double pneumonia and both lungs were so infected that the bacteria had spread to his blood system. Doctors realized that their patient had septic shock, a life-threatening condition that few people survive. The fifty-one-year-old man was moved into intensive care and placed on a ventilator. His prognosis was so bad that family members were allowed to gather around his bed, dressed in sterile gowns and masks, to say good-bye. Ten-year-old Christopher was especially upset at the sight of his dying grandfather. But a week later, Jim miraculously walked out of the hospital. He had beaten the odds for the second time in his life, and the prospect of growing old and toothless never looked so good.

—∿—

A few miles away, Dr. Patricia Keegan sat nervously at the head of a meeting room inside a chain hotel in Gaithersburg, Maryland. This upwardly mobile city, with its family eateries and street fairs, didn't look like a suburb of the Maryland-D.C.-Virginia business corridor. But it was only thirty miles from Capitol Hill and the site of many regulatory meetings. Keegan craned her neck to study the room of oncologists, analysts, lawyers, and reporters. Enormous bowl-shaped lights cast some of the faces in shadow, making them unrecognizable. But Keegan knew many people at this gathering of the Oncologic Drugs Advisory Committee—an FDA advisory panel known as ODAC.

This May 4 session had been convened to help the FDA figure out how to address some disturbing news about epo. An independent study published in the October 2003 issue of the British medical journal *Lancet* had tested European patients in a well-defined scientific trial. The *ENHANCE Study* had all the right components and was a randomized, double-blind, placebo-controlled trial of 351 head and neck cancer patients receiving radiation therapy. The researchers had expected that patients who had received the drug before their radiation treatments would fare better than the control group who skipped injections. Some oncologists hoped epo might even help study patients live longer, which would have been a boon for patients and drugmakers alike.

But to everyone's shock, the epo group fared much worse; they were 69 percent more likely to experience disease progression and 39 percent more likely to die. It was such a horror that when its German author, Dr. Michael Henke, reviewed it on Christmas day, he broke down and cried. The trials had focused on boosting hemoglobin levels to 14.5 for women and 15 for men—higher than was ordinarily prescribed to treat anemia.

At the same time, Keegan and her peers learned of the *BEST Study*. This even bigger European study enrolled 939 patients who received Procrit/Eprex in high doses for twelve months to maintain hemoglobin levels of 12–14, as much as 40 percent above prudent levels. Again, survival was poorer for the sick people on epo than for those on placebos. J&J itself had been forced to halt four of its own high-dose trials after too many patients suffered blood clots. The health-care giant had been hoping to expand its drug's market by showing that it helped treat cancer—the golden goose of the pharmaceutical industry. In a way, the trial had been a good idea, since epo oxygenates the blood and radiation tends to work better in the presence of oxygen. Some in the ODAC audience wondered how many study patients had died in J&J's high-dose trials; perhaps the loved ones of the 4 million or so global patients who'd taken the drug might like to know too. But J&J declined to reveal those numbers and, at the time, the FDA had no authority to obtain them.

Most alarming of all was that these studies indicated that epo could grow tumor cells, along with red blood cells. The evidence wasn't conclusive, and attendees of that daylong meeting listened to the polished executives from Amgen and J&J defend their products. They unfurled their charts, waved their pointers, and explained that, as most doctors know, patients tend to develop blood clots when you give them epo at higher-than-approved dosages. The *BEST* and *ENHANCE* studies, they concluded, were flawed.

Even so, the ODAC panel asked the firms for more trials. Regulators needed to know if the widely prescribed drugs worsened outcomes for cancer patients. The committee even recommended a set of protocols to create rigorous, science-based studies, and Amgen and J&J executives told regulators that they had already begun signing up patients for new trials. But what the FDA didn't know was that there were already problems with those studies. Neither Amgen nor J&J had designed them to meet the high standards ODAC had just recommended. It seemed as if the aim of these trials was not so much to determine if epo was safe but to evaluate its effect on anemia and thereby to expand the product's already huge market.

News of the ODAC advice and the sponsors' pending studies trickled out to the medical community. But not many epo patients heard the word. Reports of the trials' fatalities got lost somewhere in the Maryland-D.C.-Virginia triangle, and J&J did not create a new Procrit commercial, nor did Amgen sit down with an NPR correspondent. Procrit specialist McClellan talked to doctors all day long, but he didn't learn about the shocking trials until Ortho circulated a memo. If asked about the trials, he should say that Procrit was "safe and effective" when used according to the label. "Reflect confidence," the script said. "Do not deviate from approved core messages."

In some other time, scientific indications that a class of drugs might actually grow malignant tumors would have been enough to yank those drugs off the market. But this was 2004, when the regulated were mightier than the regulators. All the FDA did was revise the drugs' labels a bit by including a description of the trials and warning of risks such as tumor growth and death. Although Keegan and staff requested that J&J and Amgen perform more clinical trials, they didn't give them a deadline. But they did mention the long-promised safety studies, and once again, the two companies pledged to provide them with their new batch of trials. "We relied on what they said they were going to do," Keegan later recalled.

J&J, meanwhile, had a pending request. Ortho's staff over the past five years had managed to spread the unapproved, 40,000-unit Procrit dosage throughout the American oncology community. The off-label therapy was now considered to be "community standard." So a month after ODAC heard the tragic effects of high-dose epo, J&J asked the FDA to approve the new dosage. Incredibly, it did, and Medicare began paying for the more expensive shots, endangering hundreds of thousands more sick people.

19

The Eleventh Hour

2004 to 2005

WHEN Duxbury returned from Tucson, dehydrated but elated, he marched into Berman's office and presented him with some of McClellan's documents. Berman couldn't believe his eyes. He grilled Duxbury. "Where'd Dean get these?" And "Why did he save these documents?" Berman badly needed evidence to persuade the DOJ to join their whistle-blowing suit, but he was suspicious of easy pickings. "This is outrageous stuff, if it's real," he said. Before the attorney staked his reputation on these gems, he needed to ensure that the source was credible. "Get him in here," he told Duxbury.

On Tuesday, May 11, McClellan appeared in the penthouse lobby of Hagens Berman Sobol Shapiro. Duxbury led his friend into the main conference room, with its thirty-foot-long windowed wall. "What a view!" McClellan cried. He pressed his face to the glass and looked down from a height of forty stories. He saw tiny fishmongers at Pike Place Market, pedestrian-ants on Waterfront Park, and white-and-green toy ferries chugging across Puget Sound. Sunlight danced around the whitecaps in the distance, and looming over it all was the westernmost mountain range in the continental United States.

The two sat at one end of the long, polished cherrywood table. Finally, Berman walked in and greeted McClellan brusquely. The lawyer sat as far away from his guest as possible, in his usual power seat at the head of the table. McClellan thought the man lacked charm, if not manners. As Berman talked twenty-five feet away, McClellan had a hard time hearing him, but the drug rep was too vain to tell his host about his deaf ear so, instead, he asked him, "Would you like me to move closer to you?"

"No," Berman replied. Clearly, he needed to demonstrate his power, even if it made his guest squirm. Duxbury winced as the tension in the room mounted.

Trying to mediate, Duxbury positioned himself between the two. He explained that McClellan possessed valuable documents that could move their *qui tam* case forward. To prove it, Duxbury held up the list of elite doctors who had participated in Procrit's promotion.

"Is this from your files?" Duxbury asked McClellan.

"Of course it is," McClellan said, surprised at his friend's short memory. He realized that Berman was scrutinizing him, and he fidgeted. Then Berman interrupted Duxbury and questioned McClellan himself. "How do you bribe doctors?"

McClellan told him about speaking fees and preceptorships. Duxbury noted the puzzled look on Berman's face and quickly translated. "Preceptorships occur when reps pay doctors money for the privilege of following them on their rounds," he explained. Berman asked about bonuses tied to high-dose Procrit sales, and McClellan described the Maximum Value Programs and others. Eventually, the lawyer and the stranger connected, and after an hour, Berman seemed satisfied. McClellan left the meeting for the four-star hotel room that Berman had paid for.

Then, Berman huddled with Duxbury and said, "I get it now."

"Good," said Duxbury. "Dean's not a nut, or at least he's not a nut in the way you thought he was."

Berman's eyes bored into Duxbury's. "Well, he's enough of a nut that I can understand why he'd keep company memos for years on end."

"With his help, we can deliver truckloads of evidence to the DOJ."

Berman then reviewed McClellan's separation papers from Ortho and, the next day, advised the rep to sign them. "I'll take care of you," he promised. McClellan returned to Tucson and reviewed his severance agreement. It said he'd receive his usual $6,500 monthly salary, bonuses, health-care coverage, and his other benefits until year's end. In return, McClellan must agree to "turn over to the Company, all documents, records and property in [his] possession" related to Ortho business. On May 21 McClellan signed the papers and mailed them to New Jersey. That evening, he called Duxbury to announce his formal retirement.

"If you want to make copies of my files, Mark, you'd better hurry," he warned.

Early Monday morning Duxbury marched into Berman's office. "We *have* to move on this. Dean's leaving the company. On Thursday morning his bosses are going to cart away all of his papers, so we have to copy them first."

With Berman's permission, Duxbury hired a legal copy service in Phoenix, a hundred miles away from McClellan's home. That night, Duxbury called his friend to alert him to the plan, a plan they had only forty-eight hours to execute. McClellan agreed to it all.

On Tuesday, May 25, a U-Haul truck pulled out of Phoenix, headed south, and three hours later pulled up to McClellan's storage facility in Tucson. The driver, wearing a tight T-shirt, hopped out of the cab and introduced himself. His burly helper wore earrings and tattoos. A suspicious McClellan showed them his jam-packed locker, whose metal shelves groaned under the weight of binders, reports, and brochures. The driver opened the aluminum tailgate of his truck with a clatter, pulled out a stack of cardboard, and tossed a few sheets to McClellan. The three worked rapidly, assembling stiff, flat pieces into a fleet of bankers' boxes. Each man grabbed an armful of binders off the shelf, dumped them into a box, and loaded the box onto the truck. As the afternoon sun beat down on the ovenlike vault, sweat poured down the movers' faces. McClellan kept an eye on them. As Duxbury had warned the movers a few days ago, "My friend has a fit whenever anyone handles his papers." But McClellan had cause to be anxious. "I don't know who these guys are, or whether I'll ever see my boxes again," he thought. If his boxes weren't returned by the following day, he could be sued by J&J for aiding a "lawsuit against the Company." He didn't want to lose his salary or hurt his chances of landing a new job, so his entire future lay in the hands of these brawny strangers.

After three hours or so, they had packed and loaded fifty-five storage boxes into the ten-foot truck bed. By four P.M. the U-Haul had pulled away. They had only twenty-four hours to drive to Phoenix, unload the truck, disassemble the binders, make the copies, reassemble the binders, and drive back to Tucson in time to return the cache in perfect order—before McClellan's bosses arrived on Thursday. "I have no idea what will happen to me if these guys screw up," McClellan told Duxbury that night.

"I just hope they get back by morning," Duxbury agreed.

That night, McClellan sat in his backyard and contemplated the rocky minarets that rose beyond his cowboy cactus. He didn't know how long he'd be unemployed, what sort of job he'd find, or whether his role in Duxbury's suit would be worth the trouble. While he fretted, a crew of people in a nondescript building a hundred miles away stood over photocopy machines and handled fifteen thousand pages that catalogued McClellan's career. Under sickly green fluorescent lights, they unsnapped binders, unstapled reports, stacked papers in chutes, and slapped brochures on glass. Squat, tall, multifunction copiers whirred and buzzed as workers restapled, reclipped, and replaced the stacks of papers in their original files and boxes. They repeated the dull, methodical motions for hours. It was labor-intensive, monotonous work that required one's full attention, which is why the service charged as much as $1.50 per page, or roughly $10,000 for the job. All night the crew worked, moving robotically in the low-humming, drum-droning, light-flashing room.

Early the next morning, the files were loaded back into the U-Haul, and the orange-and-white truck swung onto Highway 10 and headed south. At noon, the tattooed driver pulled up to the storage unit where McClellan paced. "Boy, you got here in the nick of time," McClellan said with a grin. The two began moving his original files from the truck into the vault, and by midafternoon all fifty-five boxes were again stacked inside. McClellan thanked the driver profusely. "I'm amazed that you guys copied so much so quickly." The muscle-shirted driver nodded, then slowly backed the truck, gears grinding, out of the lot and turned the corner.

For the next few hours, McClellan emptied boxes and stacked his binders on their rightful shelves. He arranged the sales contracts, brochures, and memos in chronological order. Then he broke down the empty boxes and placed them in trash barrels scattered around the grounds. It was after six o'clock.

The next morning, McClellan slumped in his beloved company car outside the storage vault. Sadness, grief, and anger bubbled up inside him, but he pushed his emotions down. "I'm losing a big part of myself," he had to admit, and that included his silver Saab, a computer, printer, laptop, and other property he'd grown accustomed to using over the years. Nearby was an older car he had rented so he could drive himself home. Then Hudson pulled up in a gray luxury sedan. Sitting shotgun was a handsome young hire who was obviously McClellan's replacement. McClellan climbed out of his car, but no one offered to shake hands.

Hudson and his aide picked over the files, while McClellan watched from the doorway. The young man grabbed a binder full of contracts from doctors who belonged to U.S. Oncology, until yesterday a huge McClellan client. The Houston-based cancer treatment network had purchased some $350 million worth of Procrit in 2004, allegedly lured by about $70 million in kickbacks and profit. As the young man stuffed the binder into a box, McClellan, just to be ornery, told him, "I don't know what you want with that old binder." The two ignored the older man. When they had crammed Hudson's car full of McClellan's books, they filled the Saab too.

At last, the vault was empty, except for the naked metal shelf units and a pile of trash on the floor. Satisfied that he had seized every trace of McClellan's success, Hudson stepped into his crowded car, while the younger man slid behind the wheel of McClellan's former sedan. They drove away, and the erstwhile territory manager of oncology in the Western Region crumpled over the wheel of his cheap rental.

Meanwhile, twelve hundred miles away, copies of those very same documents were being unloaded from an airplane at Sea-Tac International Airport and onto a truck. The vehicle headed north then lumbered into the underground garage of the Rainier Tower, where workmen stacked the boxes onto dollies and wheeled them to the top floor. Duxbury directed the shipment to a windowless room. He sat at a long table and began to sort through twelve years of Ortho correspondence and 1,375 pounds of paper, searching for any explosive communiqué he could load into his *qui tam* case.

—⚌—

Duxbury and Berman continued to wait for the government to intervene in their suit, certain they had a good case. Yet as head of the Department of Justice, U.S. Attorney General John Ashcroft discouraged whistle-blowing. This was strange, since the whole idea of *qui tam* law was to crack down on government fraud, waste, and abuse—the mantra of many a politician. But Ashcroft and others grew so lax about pursuing those whom Lincoln had despised as "worse than traitors in arms" that Senator Grassley cosponsored a bill to protect whistle-blowers. In the dead of night, however, that bill was shot down, contributing to a decade of hostile rulings, and eventually, a 3–210 track record, *against* those who blew whistles. President Bush was hardly a fan of deputized citizens either. After Enron's implosion, he may have signed the 2002 Sarbanes-Oxley Act (SOX), which purported to protect whistle-blowers from retaliation, but his administration interpreted it very narrowly. If you reported fraud at a parent company, you were safe from reprisal. But if you worked for one of its many subsidiaries, good luck. Duxbury was long past retaliation, but others like him were now persona non grata.

Still, Duxbury continued nursing high hopes. That summer, he and Sojie spent their days around Surprise Lake, where squadrons of damselflies and green darners flitted around like toy copters. The *buzz-buzz-buzz* of their breeding and speeding filled the warm afternoon air with lullabies. The father and his ten-year-old daughter usually ended their days at sundown, tired but content. One evening, after Duxbury had put Sojie to bed, he took out his gun. He hadn't cleaned it for quite some time, and that chore tended to relax him.

While Sojie slept on that hot evening, he opened her bedroom window to let in the cool air. He then spread his tools on the coffee table. It was late on July 29, 2004, and a burst of untimely fireworks filled the air along with a man's loud voice. He was clomping up from the dock near the man-made lake, intoxicated and yelling. As he walked closer to Sojie's opened window, Duxbury got up. He opened the sliding glass door that faced the lake and tried to hush the carouser. "Hey, kids are sleeping, okay? Please hold it down." A neighbor overheard the exchange through his open window and appreciated the intercession; he was working at his computer. But then the drunken reveler saw a weapon in Duxbury's hand and took umbrage. "Are you trying to scare me? Why are you flashing a gun?" he asked, adding a few profanities. "What if I come over and shove that gun up your ass?" He charged toward Duxbury.

The father held out his palm. The oily black weapon glinted in the glaring porch light. The drunk backed away. But he continued taunting Duxbury so that the neighbor grew worried. It was clear "that the man was being very belligerent" and that Duxbury was "speaking very quietly," the neighbor later reported. Duxbury continued asking the intruder to please leave, but the boor continued shouting until another neighbor across the way finally hollered, "What are you to trying to do? Bother *everyone* in the neighborhood?"

Finally, the drunkard stumbled off. Duxbury retreated into his apartment and, exhaling nervously, put his gun down and poured himself a drink. He fell asleep. An hour later, neighbors saw police cars and a van pull up. A SWAT team in black masks and full helmets spilled out of the van and, ninjalike, ran silently and rapidly up to Duxbury's apartment, splitting off into two streams. One approached from the front of his place and the other from the rear. At a prearranged signal, the first group burst into his apartment, and the next thing Duxbury knew he was on the floor, facedown, his hands wrenched behind his neck as masked men yelled and danced around him. Unarmed and prone, Duxbury was hit four times with a Taser gun. Each time, he yelled out in excruciating pain, two prongs and sixty-five thousand volts' worth.

As neighbors watched, Duxbury was handcuffed and placed into a car. Officers waited until Renee arrived on the scene to take Sojie home. Duxbury, meanwhile, was driven to a precinct and booked on several counts of assault with a deadly weapon.

He was absolutely livid. "This is wrong, flat-out wrong," he kept thinking. But the final indignity was being strip-searched. An officer inspected each orifice until he finally reached the man's most intimate one. Buck-naked and bent over, Duxbury could no longer hold his tongue. "You know," he said to the officer, "I've had a lot of shit jobs in my life, but yours definitely takes the cake." The lawman didn't reply, but the cords on his neck bulged like a gargoyle's. He let Duxbury dress, then threw him into solitary confinement for twenty-four hours. "Enjoy yourself, wise guy." Duxbury turned to face the wall and wound up counting all 167 of the cinder blocks in his claustrophobic cell. For the rest of the night, he struggled to keep from choking on his bile or crying out in rage.

When he got out of solitary, he composed a letter to his daughter, explaining what had happened. Renee intercepted that missive, though, and responded a few days later, while her ex-husband was still in jail. "Surprise, it's me writing," she wrote. Renee had expected that Duxbury's "first priority" in jail would have been to write her and "agree on a communication plan that is emotionally best for Sojie." But actually Duxbury's top goal had been to get out of jail, deal with the charges, and somehow return to work.

He was allowed to call Berman, who gallantly tried to rescue him. The lawyer wrote a letter "to whom it may concern" and explained that it was critical that Duxbury return to work as the firm's health-care expert, and pronto. "We are in the midst of a critical deadline looming [*sic*] and we need his assistance." Berman needed Duxbury's help in a filing for his AWP case, due in a few weeks, and on a similar case on behalf of several states. Berman also threw in the *qui tam* suit, since "the prosecutors have asked for [Duxbury] to gather information."

Other people wrote to the court on Duxbury's behalf, too, and before long, he was back at work in the Rainier Tower. However, the entire episode had upset Sojie and Renee, who filed a suit against her ex-husband to keep him away from their daughter. On September 3, 2004, she filed for a modified custody agreement and got restraining orders as well. Duxbury was now prohibited "from going onto the grounds of or entering the home, working place, or school of the other party or the day care" of Sojie. He had to keep a hundred yards away from her, give up his gun, and agree that from now on, his daughter would reside with her mother only. Duxbury tried to fight the case in court and even sold a saxophone or two to pay for legal expenses. But he lost. There'd be no more birthdays, Easters, summer picnics, or Christmas train rides with Sojie. He had no input into her education, health, or safety. Before he could see her again, he had to submit to drug and alcohol evaluation, psychology evaluation, and cooperate with a guardian. He was absolutely inconsolable, crying in the car on the way to work and trying to collect himself before walking into work on time.

Court dates were set, and events turned ugly, as these things do. For Sojie, the court appointed a guardian ad litem, who conducted cursory criminal history investigations of the parents, including Bibi. Lots of dirty laundry got aired. In fact, all three adults had been investigated regarding allegations of domestic violence—Renee and Duxbury had actually been prosecuted. All three grown-ups were also on medication of some sort.

The guardian recommended that Duxbury and Renee take parenting classes, and that Sojie and her father have professionally supervised visits that he pay for. The court-appointed guardian wanted the court's permission to delve even deeper into the adults' personal lives by performing a more thorough criminal investigation and contacting their health insurers to review their medical and psychological records. She wanted Duxbury to undergo drug and alcohol evaluation and for Renee to continue her counseling.

Oddly enough, the guardian never did get around to interviewing Sojie, the only person she was supposed to represent. Months later, the drunken man who had triggered these horrible events returned to the fray. He had repeatedly contacted the police to try and recant his statements, and in 2005, he finally got through. Once his new truthful statement was filed, it was clear that no assault with a deadly weapon had actually occurred that night at Surprise Lake. Duxbury pleaded no-contest to one charge of unlawfully handling a weapon, a misdemeanor. By then, however, it was too late. "I've been made to look like an unstable, violent, suicidal nut," he thought. But worse than that, he'd lost his child.

—⁓—

In September 2004, Ortho Biotech was served with a subpoena from the Office of the Inspector General of the Department of Health and Human Services, probing the marketing practices of Procrit. Investigators wanted to look at the period from 1997, when Duxbury was first told to sell the high-dose drug, to the present. They also demanded documents tied to Ortho's dealings with U.S. Oncology. New York's attorney general issued a subpoena to Ortho for the same marketing documents, though Duxbury didn't hear about these developments until later. When he did, he felt as if he was finally getting a break. Could justice be far behind?

—⁓—

Back at work, Duxbury kept telling himself that his *qui tam* case was gathering steam. At least he still had that going for him. If Berman won the case, Duxbury could receive enough money to regain custody of his daughter and live a decent life. Berman had also promised to give him a big bonus for all of his work on the successful AWP suit. They hadn't signed a contract or even written a letter of agreement, but Duxbury trusted the man, especially after the lawyer had bailed him out of jail. But then the winds changed. In May 2005, Berman was well on his way to winning his multimillion-dollar case against the pharmaceuticals and Duxbury sensed that he had essentially worked himself out of a job. Still, he wasn't worried—Berman had promised to pay him a huge bonus when it was all over. And Duxbury believed him.

The last week of May, Duxbury walked into work ready to discuss his case with Berman, but stopped to chat with some coworkers. Duxbury began describing all the reasons why he was optimistic about his case when one of them poured cold water over him. "I'm sorry, Mark. But the DOJ isn't going to intervene," he let slip.

"What do you mean?"

I just heard that it doesn't look good.

His associates walked away, but Duxbury didn't move. Without the imprimatur of the federal government, his *qui tam* case was all but dead. "I feel like I've been kicked in the teeth," he realized. Duxbury went to the men's room and tried to decipher the code that was tap-tapping out on a frequency that was just a little out of his range. Berman obviously didn't want to tell him yet, and there could be only one reason why, he concluded. The lawyer had decided to drop Duxbury's *qui tam* case too.

That realization felt like sixty-five thousand volts burning through his body. Duxbury left the office in a daze and tried to get his moorings. Around him, office workers poured out of the towers and buildings along Seattle's Fifth Avenue as if school had just let out. Record-breaking heat had ushered in Memorial Day weekend, and people were strolling toward the waterfront and congregating in open-air cafés, giddily celebrating the unofficial arrival of summer. Packs of young professionals passed by Duxbury, and a few revelers even bumped his shoulder. Yet he didn't take offense or even notice; his eyes might as well have had X's over them, like a dead man's in an old-fashioned comic strip.

Rewinding the film of his life over the past decade, he couldn't figure out where he had gone wrong. J&J was raking in nearly $4 billion a year selling a drug that harmed people, yet he couldn't stop it. He was the spontaneous type and had never orchestrated a long-range plan or figured all the angles of a particular course in life. He'd always led from the heart, taking life as it had come, even if it that meant getting licked. But, now, he kicked himself. He should have seen this one coming even if he was a shade off his best.

He had always imagined someday telling his daughter, Sojie, that he might have failed at many things (like fatherhood) but he'd always stood up for what he believed was right. "The thought of Sojie was the one thing that kept me fighting," he rationalized. "I wanted to show her that I'd done something with my life. I wanted her to see that there was a big reason why I'd been kept out of her life all these years." He had needed to prove to his daughter—and maybe to himself too—that he had *not* spent a good part of his life chasing windmills, as Renee so often claimed.

Now he'd been stripped of even that shred of dignity.

Duxbury had failed Sojie. On top of that, he was about to lose his job, again, his fourth one in seven years. Who would take on a broken, forty-five-year-old has-been? Without his livelihood, his child, or even his burning mission, he saw no reason to live.

While pacing the streets, he spied Sojie in a fabric store, giggling with her girlfriend. He had gone through hell over the years to keep her in his life but had been prohibited from seeing his own flesh and blood for nearly a year. Now the sight of his beautiful eleven-year-old shocked him. She was no longer the little girl who had watched *Blues Clues* cartoons with him, or had chased damselflies down by the lake. She had sprouted into a petite young woman, with dark ropes of curly hair, skin the color of tea, and the profile of a Mayflower descendent. God, it was painful to be so close yet so far out of reach! He yearned to hug her but recalled the restraining order that Renee had obtained against him. He tried to stay a hundred feet away but managed to catch Sojie's eye. He smiled. Sojie looked away, embarrassed at the sight of her father. Duxbury beckoned to her friend, who walked over to where he stood. It took everything he had, but he mustered a smile for her, too, and greeted the girl by name. "Do me a favor, will you? Tell Sojie that I love her." She nodded and ran back to deliver his message. Without a further sign to him, the two girls bent their heads together and, in quick, arpeggio steps, walked away.

He felt as if he'd been walloped in the gut with a baseball bat.

Standing in the aisle, he tried to catch his breath. Then he made his way home and hatched a plan.

—⚍—

As was his custom, Duxbury made dinner that night. Since Richard was spending the night at a friend's house, he and Bibi dined alone. He didn't divulge much about his day, but instead listened as Bibi chattered away. Then the two settled on the couch to watch a movie. She drank a soda, while he poured himself a Long Island iced tea in a tall plastic cup. He could hear the sounds of partiers outside, laughter floating over the harbor's surface and bouncing around his gated neighborhood. Everyone, it seemed, was celebrating tonight. After an hour or so, he heard Bibi's steady, snuffling snore; she'd fallen asleep next to him. It was near midnight and time. Heavy-limbed, Duxbury moved to the kitchen sink and set down his tall glass. He glanced out the kitchen window. Fog had already cloaked his property, obscuring the tops of the blue spruce and conifers that encircled his backyard. Long spears of moonlight filtered through the green arches. Swaths of ivy tumbled over his fence and joined the piles of dead pine needles and acorn caps. A damp darkness enveloped him, and involuntarily Duxbury shivered.

He picked up the vial of barbiturates on his right. Dumping a bunch into his hand, he threw them into his mouth and tried to swallow them. Some pills got stuck in his throat, so he washed them down with a drink on his left, the vodka cocktail he'd been sipping all night. He repeated the motions—dump pills, swallow, follow them with alcohol—until no drugs remained. The liquor had already made him wobbly, so he didn't have much time. He left the kitchen, headed to the stairs, and began to climb, placing one flat foot above the other. At the top of the landing, he bumped against the rail but steadied himself. He proceeded down the hall, his path lit by the moonlight stealing through the blinds. Instinctively, he paused at the doorway of his den and, for a second, wavered. Here was the graveyard of his quixotic quest for justice, spread on the floor: his moldering depositions from the *Amgen v. Ortho* case, his fruitless wrongful termination suit, the short-lived shareholder fraud suit, his custody battles, arrest records, visitation schedules, and rotten restraining order. On the floor near the door was his latest, and last, resort—the *qui tam* suit. The bones of himself stared back from what looked like a madman's bunker but was actually his home. There was nothing left of his work but shame, rage, and depression, and he could no longer stomach such gruel.

He moved on down the hall and finally made it to his bedroom. The shades were drawn but he could see his bed. He sat on the edge, and then it started: A warm wave rose slowly in his chest like syrup laced with lead. It spread to his heart and washed over his long-aching pain. Great drifts of bliss flowed into his belly, then shot out to his arms, legs, and face. The benzodiazepines began to shut down his cardiovascular and respiratory systems, and slowed down the thrumming air around him. His mind sideslipped, then spun, as the molten river hit his central nervous system. "God, this feels good," thought Duxbury, and he fell back onto his comforter and let the pharmaceutical torch blaze through his body. He lay spread-eagled on the bed and placed his right arm on his chest. The last thing he saw before he passed out was his gold champion ring, glinting like a lump of fool's gold. Then Duxbury slipped into unconsciousness.

PART IV

20

Twice Saved

2005 to 2006

THE sleeping man thrashed in his hospital bed. "Sojie?" he moaned.
"Is that you?" Yellow threads of light pulled him to semiconscious-
ness. Duxbury opened his eyes, which felt like pinpricks in a tarp. His
throat burned as if a frayed rope had been wrenched down his gullet.
For a minute, he wondered, "Am I in that hellhole Tombstone?" He
looked around, and objects clicked into place: Small plastic sacks held
clear liquid dispensed through tubes that ended in his arm; black cords
ran across white sheets; a shadow moved outside a window even as
sunlight slid in, glancing off a glass-fronted TV set. The room had a
streaky luminescence like an old black-and-white movie, the kind
where the walls close in. Duxbury turned his head and saw Bibi sitting
next to him. She tilted her face, so her liquid eyes were even with his
gritty slits.

"How are you doing, hon?" she asked tenderly.

Cruelly, he didn't answer. Instead, he turned his face to the wall.

Over the next few days, the groggy man pieced together events
with the help of his wife and doctors. While he had surrendered to the
lethal warm undertow that had flooded his system, his wife had been
downstairs, dressed in an African-patterned muumuu. She had awak-
ened on the couch, clicked off the TV, and taken her glass to the
kitchen. Woozily, she noticed the cups and plate that her man had left

on the counter and made a mental note to scold them in the morning. As she walked upstairs, her slippers scuffling the carpet, her way was lit by little parallelograms of moonlight slipping through the drapes. Bibi turned the corner into her room and saw her husband splayed across the king-size bed, fully dressed, with one arm flung over the side and both feet touching the floor. The picture didn't register; his breathing didn't sound right. She drew closer. "Mark!" she whispered and nudged his shoulder. No response. "Mark," she said louder. Then, she grabbed his shoulders and shook him roughly. "*Wake up, Mark!*" In that instant, her mind's eye flickered on the kitchen counter: the vodka bottle, the giant plastic cup, the *empty prescription bottle*. In a flash, she knew that her husband had swallowed the entire bottle of clonazepam.

They say that when a person is in the midst of a life-or-death crisis, he or she can perform unimaginable acts of strength and courage. In those crystalline seconds, one's senses are also magnified to a superhuman degree, as Bibi herself discovered. The 170-pound woman bent over Duxbury, grabbed him by the trunk, and hoisted him over her shoulder as if he were a sack of potatoes. A smell of alcohol slapped her face; the sound of shallow breathing hummed in her ears; yet the weight of this lumpy, 210-pound body felt like a laundry load of fluffy cottons. Something came over Bibi, and the physician in her took over. She found herself cakewalking through zero-gravity space, as though someone had given her a shot of 100,000 units of recombinant erythropoietin. She carried the deadweight down the hall and carefully maneuvered the stairs to the bottom; she leaned against the corner to steady herself. Then, she took another step and managed to fling open the door that led to the garage. With one more stride, she opened the door of her SUV and slid her husband's body into the backseat.

Pressing buttons, turning keys, and shifting gears, she backed her Nissan Xterra out of the garage and sped to the hospital ten miles away. It was past midnight, and the two-lane road twisted under black pillars of trees and boughs. The highway was empty as she raced up the hill at Hollycroft Street, moving faster than she'd ever driven before. "C'mon, Mark, please don't leave me." She rolled down the windows, turned up the music as loud as she could stand it, and continued her soliloquy of prayer and babble. After crossing the Tacoma Narrows Bridge, she passed strip malls and ghostly stores. Finally, she saw the honeycombed tower of St. Joseph Hospital. She screeched to a halt in front of the emergency room, ran inside, and explained her mission. White-coated attendants rushed out to the car with a gurney and returned with Duxbury on it. They disappeared into a room to try to resuscitate the patient while his wife tried to fill out the paperwork. Over the next few hours, Bibi imagined half a dozen scenarios and braced herself for the possibility that her husband might emerge brain-damaged, doomed to live out the rest of his years in a vegetative state.

Finally, a doctor came out. "Dr. Duxbury," he said, poker-faced. "Your husband is going to be fine." She slumped on the couch. Then, she remembered her son sleeping at home. Richard had just turned eleven two days earlier, and in a few hours, ten of his friends would join him for a birthday bash at the house. Anxiety about her husband's condition turned into anger over his selfish deed. "How could Mark try and kill himself on the eve of his stepson's birthday party?" she thought. It was past three A.M., and she needed to be home for her son. Too distraught to drive, Bibi called a friend to pick her up.

That afternoon, Richard's party went off without a hitch. Bibi didn't explain why his stepfather was absent—nor did the boy ask. She kept the suicide attempt a secret. Several hours later, she returned to the hospital and her husband's bedside just as Duxbury had started to surface in that strange luminescent space. Doctors and nurses glided in and out of his room, quietly pleased that their measures had helped save his life. At last, Duxbury faced his wife and spoke for the first time.

"I wanted to end it," he explained. "Why didn't you let me die at home?"

—⁂—

AROUND the first day of June, Duxbury left his bed at St. Joseph Hospital. A nurse helped him into a wheelchair and rolled him across the floor he knew so well. He used to walk these corridors on his own, upright and poised, his fancy shoes clickety-clacking down the halls. Here's where Duxbury had made his first Procrit sale, his first big conversion, and one of the country's largest Procrit conversions of its day. Now those accomplishments seemed to mock him. He was delivered to the curb, where Bibi waited with the silver SUV, ready to ferry him across the Tacoma Narrows. A bitter grief climbed up his throat.

Those first few weeks back in the office were strange, disjointed ones, full of bits and pieces that at the time seemed insignificant and disconnected. He tried to sort through the jumble of faces, names, and phrases, but they ran together under the blur that passed for comprehension. It was only later in hindsight that all those little things rearranged themselves neatly into the high-stakes board game that he should have seen all along. For example, he noticed how Berman had intermingled the documents of Duxbury's *qui tam* case with those from the firm's more successful AWP case. That struck Duxbury as questionable at best. Was his own attorney using papers from a client's *qui tam* cache to further the firm's other drug case? A clammy paranoia settled upon Duxbury's shoulders like an old bathrobe.

On the surface, however, life continued normally. His office mates burst in most mornings refreshed and unsuspecting of Duxbury's botched ritual of despair. He resumed his cigarette breaks, calling himself a "born-again smoker," and joined the thin herd that walked out mid-morning to pass around the Bic lighter and strike up. He listened to the litany of ailments—the aching backs, the neurotic tics, and the "mother of all hangovers." After ten minutes of office palaver, he'd grind out his butt and return to work. Did anyone notice? The man who cherished human connections had always been the cynic of this lighthearted tribe. But now his jokes had a cur's bite. "A friend is just a stranger who hasn't given you the brush-off yet," he cracked one day. No one laughed.

Duxbury fixated on Berman. A big part of sales is knowing that people will lie to you at their convenience, and during those first few weeks back at work, Duxbury's BS detector was turned up high. Whereas his boss had once greeted his employee in the hallway with a quick glance and nod, Berman now refused to meet the man's gaze. *Beep, beep.* His boss begged off discussing Duxbury's *qui tam* case and seemed uncomfortable in meetings. *Beep, beep.* Berman was not even sharing what others were talking about—the DOJ's cold shoulder. At one point, Duxbury reviewed his options: He could either ride this thing out to the last bitter moment, and keep sipping the office Kool-Aid. Or he could find himself a new project.

One day, he walked into Berman's office and suggested that they look into publicly funded clinics that treat poor, uninsured children and their parents. "Clinics are supposed to get special pricing on drugs, which should be a huge discount." But Duxbury felt certain that the drug companies didn't extend the full legal discounts to the clinics, instead charging them illegally high prices. Since these costs were borne by the government and the average taxpayer, this constituted Medicare and Medicaid fraud, said Duxbury. "These deals are always rigged in the drug companies' favor," he explained. When Berman asked Jeff Sprung what he thought of the idea, Duxbury felt a pang. "Jeff doesn't think that drug companies would actually rip off old ladies and orphans," he thought. But escalating drug costs in 2005 were starting to force some states to slash services to precisely these types of vulnerable patients. Duxbury wanted to work on this case in the worst way, largely because it'd give him another year or so of income. In his meeting with the partners, the glorified paralegal defended his idea with a stentorian delivery: "Give me six months, and I'll make friends with some of the billers at these clinics." Reluctantly, Berman agreed.

Then tiny shards of information began to appear. On July 12, 2005, the DOJ formally declined to intervene in Duxbury's *qui tam* complaint, for the time being anyway. The district court judge in Boston would soon unseal his suit for all the world to see. That was the one glittering note in the DOJ's rejection slip, and Duxbury hoped that some intrepid reporter would soon pick up on his allegations against J&J.

Down the hall, meanwhile, Sprung had begun to study how the DOJ's rebuff impacted the firm's whistle-blowing case. The lawyer looked at all the angles of the arcane law: Was Duxbury the first guy to blow the whistle on this particular alleged fraud? How did the public disclosure rule relate to its chances of success? In December, Berman paid a consultant $500 an hour to analyze Procrit's recent dosage studies, and the FDA's revised label. It was almost as if the firm needed to rationalize its decision to drop Duxbury's *qui tam*. Sprung would later claim that he'd given Duxbury a copy of his resulting twenty-six-page memo, but Duxbury would counterswear that he'd never seen it.

As the year drew to a close, Duxbury put on his best face and designer duds. In the last days of October, he congregated with his peers around bowls of candy corn, wearing a spooky-looking tie. At Thanksgiving, he sported a harvest-toned number and shared a favorite stuffing recipe with a coworker. During Yuletide, he wore festive suspenders that featured toy soldiers dressed in red-and-gold-trimmed jackets, their drums and swords at the ready. Yet if you looked closely at his braces, you'd see that the toy soldiers weren't smiling, starry-eyed boys but gray-haired old men with scraggly beards and dismal eyes. The prankster inside Duxbury was still alive, although his humor had blackened.

No amount of goodwill among men could change his course. In December, Berman pulled the plug on Duxbury's investigation of indigent clinics and officially terminated his expert. Then on January 18, 2006, Hagens Berman Sobol Shapiro officially ceased representing Duxbury because it "could find no evidence corroborating his theory" that Ortho's dose-ups were illegal. Yet, oddly, the partners continued filing papers in his case, even after Duxbury asked them to stop. One of these filings would soon be used against him.

—ᴍ—

Duxbury retraced the song-and-dance routine that qualified as a job search. He called recruiters, but if his name had been mud several years ago, it was now fresh manure. Wherever his résumé landed, he could almost hear the bellowing: "Duxbury?" *Hell, no!* The ex-rep was now notorious among the polypharmaceuticals: If they hadn't heard about his work on Berman's AWP case against dozens of drug companies, they'd gotten wind of his role in the multimillion-dollar arbitration—or maybe his unlawful dismissal case against Ortho. The job seeker had three strikes against him, and that didn't include his whistle-blowing suit, which had just been unsealed for public consumption.

He applied for a job stocking shelves at Home Depot but was turned away for being overqualified. He tried to see his now-thirteen-year-old daughter but was rebuffed. He wasn't even sure his messages were getting passed on to her. When he learned that the FDA in October 2005 had approved Procrit for anemic children receiving chemotherapy, he nearly lost it. "That's incredible," he shouted, slapping his forehead. Procrit's label had just been modified to warn of its growing risks, yet it was good enough to treat weak ten-year-olds. That one match relit his fire.

He called Simmerly, and, after a spell, they decided to search for new cocounsel to pick up their *qui tam* action. Graciously, Berman had referred them to the firm Phillips & Cohen, which had successfully brought the action against TAP Pharmaceutical years ago, nabbing a huge settlement. The firm spent weeks investigating the pros and cons of Duxbury's claims, but recognized that unlike the TAP case, the DOJ had refused to intervene. Whoever took on Duxbury's suit would have to push it uphill, like Sisyphus, without the aid of Uncle Sam and against the tribal ire and legal artillery of a $180-billion leviathan.

On the March morning of his forty-sixth birthday, Duxbury was weighing his long shot when he read a newspaper article about Hagens Berman Sobol Shapiro. A jury had just ordered the firm to pay $10.8 million for dumping one set of clients in order to pursue a more lucrative class action against the same defendant. The firm had been hired to help three small water bottlers go up against the giant Nestlé Corporation over a misleading label on its Poland Spring water. The lawyers were close to completing a $20 million mediated deal with Nestlé that would correct the situation, when, at the last minute, Hagens Berman pulled out and filed a class-action claim against Nestlé in five states. That went against the wishes of their original clients and caused Nestlé to withdraw its offer and stop negotiating.

But the attorneys had underestimated their own clients. One of their aggrieved plaintiffs was the small bottler Tear of the Clouds, co-owned by Robert J. Kennedy Jr., who used proceeds from that venture to fund his water-protection efforts. In the news article, which Dux-bury devoured, Kennedy blasted Berman and Sobol, saying, "This was a case of the attorneys grabbing everything they could for themselves." It turned out that the lawyer who had represented Kennedy from the start and who had brought in Berman and Sobol was none other than Jan Schlichtmann, the attorney made famous in the bestselling book and Oscar-nominated movie *A Civil Action*.

A chill ran up Duxbury's spine. He sat back at the kitchen table and digested the news. He had enjoyed reading Jonathan Harr's 1995 non-fiction book and even liked the 1999 movie version in which Schlicht-mann was portrayed by John Travolta. He figured that this article was a good omen and birthday gift. He called Simmerly, who not only liked the idea of hiring Schlichtmann but offered to contact him. "Why not?" he asked. "At this point, we've nothing to lose." But first, the two men had to make sure that no other law firm was interested in their case and—lucky break! They were on their own. In July, Simmerly composed a letter to Schlichtmann, enclosed the *qui tam* complaint, and invited him to chat. There wasn't much time, Simmerly added. The court had twice extended their deadline so that Duxbury could find new counsel. In five weeks the last bell would ring and, without a new lawyer, their case would die.

—◊—

THREE thousand miles away, Jan Richard Schlichtmann was working in his office in Prides Crossing, Massachusetts, and spied the message. Ever since the attorney had been portrayed on the big screen by a Hol-lywood dreamboat, he'd been inundated with requests, including sev-eral related to his law practice. The fifty-four-year-old Schlichtmann was no Travolta. Rather, he looked like an embattled raptor, with a large wingspan, a hawklike visage, and a crest of white, wavy hair. A lean six feet five inches, he swam almost daily in a lap pool built inside his seaside home and lunched on small crustaceans and filtered water. The Boston lawyer had turned down many requests to take on cases in the past decade. But something about Simmerly's package grabbed him. He read the pleading of a case that set off his internal Geiger counter: Here was a rare David fighting one of many Goliaths over a radioactive charge that a product might be harming a large class of people. The lawyer reread the pleading, looked out his office window toward the Misery Islands, and realized with excitement, "I've always wanted to try a whistle-blower case."

Schlichtmann had made his name with a liability lawsuit filed by eight Woburn families who had lost children to cancer. The 1982 case accused W. R. Grace, Beatrice Foods, and another firm of dumping chemicals, including a probable human carcinogen, near Woburn's water supply. His partners didn't want the case, but Schlichtmann believed they could win big. Instead, Woburn snowballed into a Manichean battle between two blue-blood law firms on one side and the then-cocky, self-styled Atticus Finch on the other. Adjudicating it all was Judge Walter J. Skinner, who openly disliked Schlichtmann. After a four-month trial, twelve jurors found Beatrice "not guilty." But then Schlichtmann discovered that Beatrice had withheld a damning report showing that the toxic chemicals on its property were "the probable source" of water contamination. Outraged, he asked for a new trial, but Skinner declined. Schlichtman went to the U.S. Court of Appeals, where Judge Juan Torruella and two others heard his case. On December 7, 1988, the bench found that Beatrice had committed an "outright breach" of rules and deprived plaintiffs of a "fair chance" to develop their case. It sent the case back to Skinner for "an aggressive inquiry." When Skinner again found no reason to retry the case, Schlichtmann appealed *that* decision, too, and by the time *A Civil Action* was flying out of bookstores, the Environmental Protection Agency and DOJ had sued Beatrice and Grace for a $70-million Superfund cleanup of Woburn, and Boston's judges and lawyers—including Schlichtmann—looked inept, at best.

Schlichtmann eventually settled Woburn for $8 million, giving each family about $350,000 after expenses and leaving their attorneys $2.5 million in debt. Woburn was a painful experience for Schlichtmann. "It bankrupted me, not just financially but spiritually too," he said to anyone who would listen. But what really ate at him was the fact that he'd let down his clients. They had wanted an apology from the corporations whose toxins had killed their children, and all Schlictmann had been able to extract was a mixed verdict and relatively modest payout. Disgusted with himself and the law, he had borrowed just enough money to buy a plane ticket to the island of Kauai. There, he slept on the beach, cooked over a campfire, and contemplated his "wasted" life. "Everything I've done has been nothing but failure," he believed. One day, the long-limbed man swam into the open sea and considered swimming until he couldn't see land. But as the sun set, so did his suicidal ideation. He turned back to shore.

In Hawaii, he built an energy-efficient lighting business and retrofitted two high-rises. Yet Boston kept calling. During Woburn's appeal in 1988, he had met a petite blonde named Claudia Barragan at a charity auction of bachelors. She had had no intention of bidding on Schlichtmann until she saw him across the room. "There's something about him," she told her girlfriend. They watched him entertain a klatch of glamorous, well-dressed women whose laughter bubbled over. The plain-looking Barragan elbowed her way to the circle, introduced herself to the man, and made a pretty witty comment herself, only it was about Woburn. "That piqued his interest more than any of the women he was with," she thought. That evening, she bid a measly $25 for a date with him and lost to a wealthy woman. But Schlichtmann was so taken by Barragan and her bravado, he drove her home that night.

So began their on-again, off-again courtship. At first Schlichtmann's passion for his work was contagious, and she got swept up in his cause du jour. "Boy, when you believe in something, you give one thousand percent," she once told him. But after a while she recognized the habits of a workaholic, and his obsessions dampened their romance. Over the following seven years, the couple broke up several times, but in 1993, Schlichtmann gave in and returned to Boston. He moved in with Barragan, and the couple soon purchased a run-down property on Beverly Beach, built by a Russian scientist who had worked on the secret Manhattan Project. Choked by brambles, the 1940s-era place had metal doors and gloomy interiors. The couple began to renovate it as their funds allowed. One day, Barragan came home from work to find Schlichtmann clearing the weeds with a sickle. He looked up, sweat dripping from his brow, and nonchalantly suggested that they marry. Barragan immediately accepted, took his hand, and dragged him inside their gutted home. She slipped a Patsy Cline CD into the stereo, selected the song "Crazy," and led him in a slow dance. "Life with you is going to be one wild ride," she whispered, and he laughed. In November 1994, they were wed in a small Jewish ceremony in the 1889 office/shed next to their home-in-progress.

Schlichtmann had finally found peace. Standing on his cleared property one day and looking out to sea, he had an epiphany. "In that instant," he later said, "I integrated the whole experience of Woburn. I accepted it and realized that the whole experience had taught me a lot." America's adversarial system of law is deeply flawed, he believed. Instead of solving problems, it creates more problems. "Court fights are a bloodletting process that wastes time and money," he said. "The system is screwed up, and we're not being honest about it."

Suddenly, he saw his role in a new light. Rather than continue working *inside* the system, he wanted to find creative ways to solve disputes *out* of court. When the Oscar-nominated movie based on Woburn elevated his profile, he lectured about this with a convert's zeal. In 1998, when a group of parents from Toms River, New Jersey, with cancer-stricken children approached him, he urged them to mediate. They agreed to an eighteen-month legal moratorium, while government officials analyzed the town's toxic water supply. Schlichtmann convinced the families to sit at the table with Union Carbide and Ciba Specialty Chemicals. It took three years, and the companies never admitted guilt, but damn if they didn't settle with some parents for $13.2 million. "You should measure success by how satisfied your clients are with the result," Schlichtmann told himself. "Or that's how *I'm* going to measure it from now on."

Yet, the Duxbury lawsuit touched him on several levels. For one, Schlichtmann's grandfather in the early 1900s had owned a drugstore and soda fountain in the Jewish part of South Philadelphia. The pharmacist probably stocked items like John Wyeth's Cocaine Tablets and Johnson & Johnson's belladonna plasters, yet he himself abstained from drugs. A folk doctor, he preferred herbal cures, exercise, and the natural manipulation of the body. He taught his son to avoid chemicals and to learn how to let his body heal itself. As a result, Schlichtmann's father learned how to read food and drug labels decades before that was common; when he finally had children, he insisted on doing the family grocery shopping.

That must have been difficult since Schlichtmann's dad was also a traveling salesman for the S&H Green Stamps company. Every Monday, he'd leave his home on Lake Cochituate, near Framingham, Massachusetts, and hit the road to call on grocery stores throughout New England. He'd sell dinner plates and baby buggies that store customers could buy with redeemable stamps. "It's a way for the grocers to reward customer loyalty," he'd tell his son. Schlichtmann grew up waiting for Fridays, when his peripatetic father would return home. Later, he took a stab at the sales trade himself, peddling life insurance to college kids. The twenty-three-year-old was so good, he sold nearly $1 million in policies in six months. But he hated the job.

So, in a very visceral way, Schlichtmann "knew" about drugs and salesmen. But what really got him was how Duxbury's case stirred up the old juices. The former medical malpractice attorney couldn't help but be drawn to this big noble cause: a harmful drug, a big corporation, a few underdogs, and a class of innocents. The more Schlichtmann explored this crusade, the deeper the hook sank into him. After a few days, he asked Simmerly if he could talk to his client.

Over the following weeks, in a series of transcontinental calls, Schlichtmann got to know Duxbury. The personable ex–drug rep led the gung-ho salesman's son through the business model of the industry. He explained its hierarchy, it practices, its promotional "kickapoo

trials," and its own customer kickback and rewards system. Schlichtmann came to see not just the heart of Duxbury's claims, but also the
gristle of Big Pharma itself. At one point, he recognized his good fortune: "This guy has an encyclopedic knowledge of the industry." It
wasn't often that a lawyer met a client who could also be a partner.
That's when Schlichtmann knew he simply had to take this case.

Yet he was no longer a swinging bachelor with a black Porsche 928
and a rack of Piero Dimitri suits. He had gone up against two giants
twenty-five years ago and had lost nearly everything. Now, at fifty-
four, he had a wife, three kids, and an ocean-front home that he and
his wife had painstakingly renovated, appraised at nearly $2 million.
He wasn't about to slip off the edge again, at least not without a safety
net. So he contacted a friend, class-action attorney Bob Foote, and
asked if he'd like to finance a big health-care case.

—⚬—

A SNOWY-HAIRED, tall man lay supine on the floor of a staid conference room, like a big bird in pain. "Oh my gawd, I'm dying!" he pro-
claimed, adding a profanity. He moved one knee to his shoulder,
knocking one of the expensive leather chairs into the polished table.
Duxbury, McClellan, Simmerly, and the others in the room politely
turned away, giving the moaning exerciser a little privacy. One of their
hosts stood up and pointed outside through the spectacular stainless-
steel-framed windows that faced north onto the Chamber of Commerce panorama. Each law firm's conference room was just slightly
different from the next, and up here, forty-plus stories high, Duxbury
could admire the limestone walkways, Art Deco streetlamps, and
jewel-like dome of a former speakeasy run by Al Capone. McClellan
looked down on the murky Chicago River. A lawyer noticed his gaze
and said: "On St. Patrick's Day, we throw dye in the river to make it
look green."

McClellan scratched his head. "You don't need to do that. It's already green."

The man on the floor writhed in pain: "Ouwooo."

As the others sat down to discuss Duxbury's case, Schlichtmann tried to relax the muscles in his back. Earlier in the day, he had boarded a commercial plane to Chicago and had squeezed his body like an accordian to fit into the snug space. Now he was paying the price of contortion. High above the river in the urban sanctuary of the 153-year-old firm Winston & Strawn, Schlichtmann rolled around on the carpet. He performed a few more therapeutic moves in hopes he could stand up and complete his presentation.

Word had rippled through the halls of the venerable firm that the noted lawyer was planted right here in the conference room. At first, just a few associates nonchalantly walked by, their heads swiveling ever so slightly to peek through the glass-paned window at the great man. But as soon as a few passersby spotted Schlichtmann rolling on the floor like a wounded heron, they'd disappear and return snickering, this time with a few more disbelieving friends in tow. McClellan watched as the line of rubbernecked lawyers thickened, their eyes bugging out, their Adam's apples bobbing, looking like a flock of hyperthyroid turkeys jockeying for a clear view.

McClellan chicken-winged Duxbury, who took in the scene and stifled his own cackle. "Jan," he said. "Are you still with us?"

The man on the floor moaned.

Schlichtmann had called this September 15 meeting partly to meet McClellan and to introduce his new clients to their co-counsel, Robert M. Foote. Schlichtmann had met Foote a few years earlier at a legal conference. In 2003, after Berman and Sobol bailed on the Nestlé/ Poland Springs case, a furious Schlichtmann had enlisted Foote to help him resuscitate some sort of settlement for his clients. Foote had filed a class-action suit against the water giant in Illinois state court and, three weeks later, shook hands with the Nestlé camp on a deal similar to the $27 million one that Schlichtmann had parlayed. For that, Schlichtmann and Foote had divided an $8 million fee.

When the Boston lawyer asked his Chicago friend to partner on the Duxbury case, Foote contacted Duxbury's original lawyers and floated the idea of linking forces with them. Berman presented the idea to his firm's partners and come back with their response: "You remember . . .

Hannibal [Lecter] in *Silence of the Lambs*?" he wrote, naming a movie's serial killer. "Folks here view Jan as worse and just as tricky." Berman added that a Seattle professor had penned an article detailing how Schlichtmann had "sold out" his Woburn clients. When Duxbury saw the response, he just shook his head.

So, Foote agreed to fund expenses in this case if Schlichtmann would do the heavy lifting. Duxbury needed to give the court a status report by September 5, and Berman and Sobol had already notified the judge that Duxbury intended to pursue his case "independent of the government." Schlichtmann then filed his papers with the court indicating he was Duxbury's new counsel along with Simmerly, Foote, and Kathleen Chavez.

Now the entire crew was holed up on Wacker Drive in the offices where Edward Foote, Bob's father, had once been a partner. This meeting spot was more convenient than Bob's smaller bureau thirty-six miles away in Geneva, Illinois, and once Schlichtmann got off the floor, the team spread out their documents. In just ten days, they'd try again to lure the DOJ onto the good side of Duxbury's case. Everything in their PowerPoint presentation to the government had to be clear, accurate, and powerful.

The group identified specific examples of how Duxbury had used a form letter to give free commercial drugs to doctors at Rainier Oncology for a "minitrial"; how McClellan had encouraged Dr. Kattakar to bill the government; and how an Ortho manager had ghostwritten a Medicare letter on behalf of Dr. Von Hoff. The lawyers also discussed how to amend the complaint, and everyone understood the importance of the AWP claim. "Let's go with it," Foote said.

"It's not enough," Duxbury explained. It had always bothered him that Berman had resisted developing the off-label claim in his suit, and he wasn't about to repeat that mistake. As it was, Pfizer, Eli Lilly, and others were settling off-label claims for fines ranging from $36 million to $430 million. Duxbury had learned that epo ranked at the top of Medicare's reimbursement list to the tune of several billion dollars. "From 1992 through 2004, every Procrit claim submitted to Medicare was false," Duxbury asserted. Ortho inflated the real price of its product with its discounts, rebates, and other off-invoice, under-the-table fees. "But more importantly," he said, "it increased the dosage using sham trials." It took all of Duxbury's skills to sell them on his idea, and he'd have to repeat himself several times over the next few months. But that day, they finally agreed on the documents they'd use to bolster their two-pronged claim.

When the meeting broke up, the whistle-blowers and lawyers walked outside toward Chicago's sluggish river, whose surface reflected the steel towers and arching bridges overhead. It was an Indian summer day, with temperatures in the mid-seventies, and when Duxbury pointed to the House of Blues across the water, his best friend made a crack about his "horn." Duxbury laughed; he hadn't felt this good in a long time. McClellan, too, looked as proud as pie, with a paperback copy of *A Civil Action* under his arm. Earlier that day, he'd asked Schlichtmann to autograph his book, which the lawyer had done by scratching out a few large hoops crossed by a heavy bar. The attorney had also scrawled a note that memorialized the day "as we begin another journey to justice!" As an afterthought, McClellan had asked Schlichtmann to pose for a photograph, and in that moment, the pale-faced Bostonian looked bewildered standing next to the tanned desert rat.

Later, when Duxbury and McClellan returned to the hotel, Duxbury loosened his knotted tie and asked his friend: "What do you think of Jan?"

"I didn't recognize him at all," said McClellan. "He doesn't look a thing like John Travolta."

21

Miracle-Gro

2006 to 2007

IT'S safe to say that the relationship between a whistle-blower and government attorneys is not a laugh a minute. The rules of the game place him in the most vulnerable spot. The whistle-blower files his case under seal so the DOJ can investigate and save the accused company from any false charges and undue embarrassment. Next, the whistle-blower must tell the government everything he knows about the alleged fraud, which usually happens in a meeting. Then, the government sits down with the accused and reveals all to the company, recording its side of the story. However, the feds don't usually report back to the whistle-blower, not even regarding the progress of its investigation. The probe can take years, with the suit under seal and the company free to go about its business. But most whistle-blowers lose their careers, suffer physical deterioration, and battle depression, according to a May 13, 2010, study in *The New England Journal of Medicine*. Another study found about 20 percent of them lose their wives and homes, and 10 percent attempt suicide. The hapless citizen who started the entire legal process is usually the last one to know the fate of his initiative—whether he'll live in poverty or win the lottery. It's like a three-member downhill race team where only one guy has to ski down a black diamond run. Naked and blindfolded.

Duxbury and crew weren't considered experts at this type of law.

In September 2006, Duxbury and Simmerly flew to Washington, D.C., to meet McClellan, Schlichtmann, Foote, and Chavez. The whistle-blowers stayed at the DoubleTree Hotel downtown with its nubby bedspreads, faux maple desks, and busman's rates. On Monday, September 25, they met at the chalky federal building on Pennsylvania Avenue to present their case to the DOJ. Passing through the security system, they were escorted to a room in the commercial litigation branch, where Jamie Ann Yavelberg greeted them pleasantly. Short and pear-shaped, the thirty-nine-year-old tended to dress like the harried mother of two and schoolteacher's wife she was: casual skirt, mismatched blouse, long hair pulled back, and impossibly high heels. Duxbury thrust out his hand in greeting but got a limp apathetic clasp in return. His psychic radar went off: Berman had admitted he'd "pissed off" the feds in 2004, supposedly by not naming McClellan as a source in the suit. That never made sense since McClellan's name could be found on page 10 of the original complaint. Duxbury realized a more likely reason for the DOJ's chilliness was that Berman had treated Yavelberg rudely. He watched as Schlichtmann now tried to make up for that.

The attorney fired up his portable computer. Solicitous yet brief, he click-clacked through his thirty-three PowerPoint slides, beginning with the AWP claim. As each framed flashed on, Schlichtmann's face was bathed in light while the rest of the room seemed cloaked in conjecture. Duxbury couldn't read Yavelberg's expression. But when Schlichtmann unfurled the second part of his *qui tam*, the off-label promotion, the government attorney turned downright inscrutable. After the presentation, Yavelberg asked a few questions and Duxbury and his attorneys answered as best they could. An hour or so later, the crew left the marbled corridors of the run-down justice building. "I thought it went well, didn't you?" Schlichtmann asked perkily. Everyone nodded, but Duxbury wasn't convinced.

Later, Yavelberg reviewed the Boston attorney's case with her bosses, and contacted Schlichtmann. "Procrit has a 'halo effect,'" she let slip. Oncologists all across the country prescribed this wonder drug to millions of cancer patients. Even if Ortho had illegally promoted the high doses, so what? The conventional wisdom said the doses worked.

Schlichtmann called his client and relayed the conversation.

"Procrit has a *halo* effect?" Duxbury repeated, incredulous.

"Mark, maybe we should drop the off-label claim and stick with AWP."

"No," he insisted. "Off-label is the only thing that makes this case worthwhile." AWP was inflated by 25 percent or so. But illegal promotions "are one hundred percent wrong. Don't you see?" he pressed. "It's a much bigger crime."

Duxbury, meanwhile, asked Berman to return his *qui tam* files, which included many of his and McClellan's original notes. Berman e-mailed him back later that day. "Right now no one is free to separate out awp [*sic*]... work product from file but we will perhaps next week." Duxbury made a mental note to follow up. But events would overtake him.

A few weeks later, in late October, Schlichtmann filed Duxbury's amended complaint and served it to J&J in New Brunswick. This time, McClellan was listed prominently in the head as a co-relator; crucially, the off-label claim was strengthened and developed over several pages. The suit laid out the fraud perpetuated by inflated AWP prices, kickbacks, "phony drug studies," and "the inflated dosing scheme." Once it was filed, the seventy-two-page lawsuit pulled J&J and its indomitable legal team into U.S. District Court in Boston.

—⚬—

W HILE the cylinders on his *qui tam* fired up again, Duxbury returned to his life. He kept applying for jobs. But over the past two years, the pool of applicants had expanded into a lake, making him just another fish shivering on the line. He didn't see Sojie often, and when he did, it wasn't for long. They spoke in halting, chest-constricting, haiku-like verses, and before he knew it, he'd be waving good-bye, his intestines twisting inside him as the car disappeared from sight. Renee ridiculed his windmill-tilting joust with Ortho and warned him not to burden

Sojie with such nonsense. Some days, Duxbury wondered if he really was some man from La Mancha and Simmerly his loyal, donkey-riding companion.

One place that Duxbury felt appreciated was in Richard's life. The boy seemed to thrive on his stepdad's attention. One day, Duxbury gave Richard a songbook and clarinet and taught him a few ditties. To Duxbury's delight, the boy had the touch and set loose his sarabandes in the air like they were so many doves. Some nights when Richard practiced, Duxbury thought he heard the sound of another lonely soul. For the boy's twelfth birthday, Duxbury gave him a saxophone and they practiced for months for a school talent show. Performance night found the two onstage dressed in identical shirts and skinny ties, swaying through a duet of G. F. Handel's "Adagio et Allegro." Richard won a "superior" rating, the first he'd ever received. "You're one of the few dads who actually performs with his kid," the boy told his stepdad, and Richard began earning better marks in school.

But as far as the "real" world was concerned, Duxbury was at the bottom of the power helix: He had no job, no title, and no visible means of support. This fact drove a wedge between him and Bibi. She spent her monthly life insurance check on the mortgage, the kid, the cars, and clothes; he tried to reassure her that he was working too. "Someday, honey, this *qui tam* suit will pay off for us," he promised. But Bibi would just put her hands on her hips and scold him: "Someday doesn't cut it, Mark." Then, they'd verbally fight until their lips turned blue.

He began feeling poorly. He already had spinal problems due to compression, but then a doctor diagnosed him with low testosterone levels. He was given one prescription, then another—an off-label treatment of human growth hormone. That only increased his blood pressure and worsened his sleep apnea. To help pay for the mounting medical expenses, the couple took out an equity loan on their home. Duxbury made up for it by shopping for groceries, cooking the meals, picking up Richard from school, and taking care of the cars. One minute he'd be buzzing around the house like a bumblebee on a pollen jag, and the next minute he'd crash and feel like dying.

He missed his daughter so badly, he started seeing a therapist. After a few sessions, that doctor diagnosed Duxbury with a bipolar disorder and chronic severe depression, again. "It's unreasonable to expect you to show up for work, and I'll write a letter saying that." The psychiatrist gave the patient some *more* medicine and suggested he apply for disability. Duxbury began the long, drawn-out process, hoping he'd get a monthly stipend, but Bibi grew frightened they'd lose their house. "Don't worry, honey," he told her. "We'll be okay." *We're survivors.*

The Duxbury medicine chest that once held mostly palliatives for sore gums and rinses for trench mouth grew crowded with bottles of anti-inflammatories and mood stabilizers. Duxbury didn't want these drugs and one day he looked in the mirror and asked himself, "Is this self-destructive?" His reflection couldn't say. But Duxbury just wanted to feel like a normal guy.

Then, things turned ominous. Duxbury's home was middle-class and low-security, tucked behind a community gate and packed next to other units. He bolted his doors, locked his garage, and displayed a sign that warned prowlers about nonexistent guard dogs. But he also had his own security measures. While most people let a padlock dangle down from a gate's latch, Duxbury laid his combination lock sideways on a ledge with its numbers facing out. "That way, I can tell whenever it's been moved," he told Bibi.

One night, while Duxbury's father-in-law slept in the downstairs bedroom, the guest awoke to see a man peering in his window. The former bodyguard of the late Malcolm X crept upstairs to alert Duxbury, who quickly dressed and slipped out the back. He scanned the trees that stood like sentries over his sloping yard and held back the invading gloom. He walked the yard's perimeter. But he didn't see a soul.

The next morning, he circled the property again. This time, he found that the knee-high grass on the side of his house had been trampled down. And the gate padlock that Duxbury had placed on its side? It was swinging down from the ledge; someone had moved it. Duxbury called the police, who took a report about a prowler. "If you see him again, call us," an officer suggested. They'd send a unit to patrol the area that night, but there was nothing more they could do. When the police left, Duxbury told his family, "Let's not make a big deal out of this." The jobless man was already stressed; no need to become paranoid too.

That summer, he took his family to Cannon Beach on Oregon's isolated coast. The night they returned, they heard noises in the yard, only this time unmistakably close. Duxbury crept out to investigate but found nothing. So he devised a plan. The following evening, Richard was sent to sleep at a friend's house, while his parents prepared to keep an all-night watch. Duxbury retrieved a large-scope air rifle and handed his wife an air pistol. She shuddered, but he explained, "We only want to *frighten* the prowler, not hurt him. All you have to do is wave the pistol and call 911 when I tell you to." They opened the windows so they could hear every muffler backfire and owl screech, and turned on all the house lights so they could see and be seen.

Then they settled in with sodas and snacks; Duxbury stretched out on the couch facing the kitchen window and Bibi reclined in the easy chair. Around midnight, they had dozed off, when Duxbury awoke to the noise of something—or someone—scraping against his house. He looked out the kitchen window and saw a man about six feet tall peering in the window. Duxbury ran outside, brandishing his air rifle and yelling, but the spooklike figure had disappeared. The next day, Duxbury went out to investigate, and this time, he found a live bullet shell about sixteen inches from his home and directly in front of the kitchen. He picked up the bullet, and Bibi gasped, her eyes as big as platters: "Is someone trying to kill us?"

"I don't know," he answered. But for the first time since he'd filed his *qui tam*, he felt the sharp, metal taste of danger.

—⁂—

IN November 2006, *The New England Journal of Medicine* published a controversial study. It showed that patients given epo doses to achieve a hemoglobin level above the level recommended by the FDA had a 34 percent greater incidence of deaths and heart attacks. Researchers had divided 1,432 anemic patients with kidney disease into two groups: 715 were injected to target an average hemoglobin level of 13.5 g/dl, and 717 took a lower dose to reach an average of 11.3 grams. These patients were not yet on dialysis, but the study's death rate was so shockingly high, it had to be terminated. This so-called *CHOIR* study reinforced concerns that kidney patients were being given too much epo.

The study's lead author, Dr. Ajay Singh, said that his trial didn't necessarily *prove* that epo was dangerous—just that high doses were. But by 2006, every doctor was using high doses. Ortho had spent years making sure that the off-label regime prevailed, as had Amgen, it turns out. It had helped develop guidelines for the National Kidney Foundation, so that Amgen's client/nephrologists considered doses targeting levels of 13 g/dl appropriate.

The idea that more was better had spread far and wide, at least among the Yanks. The amount of epo given to the typical U.S. dialysis patient had tripled since 1997, along with the expense and number of fatalities. The death rate for epo-injected dialysis patients in the United States was nearly fifty times higher than it was in Europe, where there was no financial incentive to "blood dope them up," as one buyer had said.

Duxbury thought the *NEJM* article a damning one and sent it to Schlichtmann. But the lawyer wanted to know, "How does this apply to our case?" Ortho's business centered on cancer, not dialysis.

"Yeah, but it confirms our theory," said Duxbury.

Not really. Schlichtmann wanted a triangle of evidence connecting Procrit, cancer, and death. The feds needed to see that Procrit did not wear a "goddamn" halo, but horns and hooves.

That autumn, the lawyer hunkered down in his wood-framed office. The structure had been built in 1889 as a workshop/boathouse for a Boston Brahmin who summered there on Kings Point, close to the Cabot Lodge Estate, steel baron Henry Frick's manor, and the home of Teddy Roosevelt's daughter Alice. The workshop was by no means palatial: It was a snug eighteen feet by eighteen feet and contained two desks, three computers, a copier, a fax machine, and the latest video and audio equipment, on which Schlichtmann podcasted legal commentary. Cocooned in his Waspish digs on the New England shore, surrounded by the latest Scandanavian technology, the Jewish attorney searched for a foothold in a lawsuit based on a medieval Anglo-Saxon concept.

Then, the rains started and the rat-tat-tat symphony on his roof swelled. In December 2006, epo took another blow. An independent trial called the *Danish Head and Neck Cancer (DAHANCA) Study Group 10* looked at 516 patients who received high doses of Aranesp. Researchers had set out to see if the anemia drug could be used to treat head and neck cancer. Patients receiving radiation for this painful form of cancer were treated to raise hemoglobin levels to between 14 and 15.5 g/dl. But tragically, those on Aranesp were 10 percent more likely to suffer tumor growth. This was huge!

Amgen notified the FDA about the negative results. But despite the company's boast about its "pharmaco-vigilance" program, it failed to share the news with investors, clients, or patients—and regulators didn't either. The mainstream press wouldn't get wind of the devastating trial for several months, leaving Schlichtmann in the dark about a critical cancer study that could fortify his case.

As storms threatened New England, Schlichtmann kept racking his brain. He ached for *something* to keep his *qui tam* afloat and talked with Duxbury several times a week about it. But it was no use. Lost in a flurry of papers, his eyeballs seared from reading the few mind-bending studies, he felt as if someone had stuffed his brain with wet socks.

In January 2007, J&J leaders faced an onslaught of quietly damning trials about its blockbuster drug. The numbers were so fatal that J&J and Amgen had to send out "dear doctor" letters. They highlighted some of the recent trial results and warned doctors about using their drugs in an off-label, high-dose manner. There were a few tepid reports, buried mostly in the back pages of newspapers, near the stock tables and, again, Schlichtmann and Duxbury missed them.

J&J's attorneys, meanwhile, filed its argument against Duxbury's complaint. The well-written thirty-six-page motion didn't address the serious criminal claims directly, yet called them "parasitic." Other whistle-blowers had already accused J&J's division of similar crimes, they argued; therefore, Duxbury's suit should be dismissed. Under *qui tam* rules, only the first to file can take a shot at collecting a bounty, and this rule, among other technical aspects of the law, formed the basis for Ortho's defense. Its outside counsel was skilled in defending pharmaceutical fraud claims and Schlichtmann studied their response like it was a chart of oriental waters.

Days passed; the stakes on both sides mounted; Schlichtmann kept looking for his break. In mid-February, the *JCO* published a paper online describing a small Canadian trial in 70 lung cancer patients. The study had been stopped because patients taking Eprex at higher levels were dying sooner. Yet news of the mounting body count slipped under the glassy surface. J&J reported record earnings growth, Schlichtmann grew despondent, and Duxbury urged his attorney forward. He spun the tale of how his ancestors had been kicked out of England in the 1640s and had sailed to Plymouth Rock to seek refuge. It was all hooey, of course. But Duxbury asked Schlichtmann if he'd ever heard the bells of the Duxbury Pier lighthouse, located eighty miles south of Prides Crossing. It used to warn fogbound seafarers of dangerous shoals. "You're doing that, too, Jan," the client told his lawyer. *Now, bring us safely in to shore.*

In February, the FDA began composing a safety update to epo's label, based on the terrifying trial results. J&J now sold $3.5 billion annually of Procrit and Eprex, its European brand, while Amgen collected even more, $5.6 billion, in Aranesp and Epogen sales. By now, there were other companies selling epo, but J&J and Amgen owned 70 percent of the market. Any official warning about these products could drag down their stock prices.

Then, along came Daniel Troy, the corporate attorney who had been the de facto chief of the FDA just a few years earlier. During his government tenure, he'd held 129 meetings with lobbyists and executives who had issues before the FDA, versus his predecessor's single meeting. He had blocked the FDA staff from protecting children from dangerous antidepressants and their parents from false advertising. He had resigned in December 2004—just as a congressional committee seemed ready to call him to testify under oath. Representative Maurice Hinchey (D-NY) called Troy's departure "a rare bright spot in what has been a dark period for the FDA," but the lawyer had never really left. In 2007, Troy was ensconced at Sidley Austin, a large law and lobbying firm located two blocks from the Bush White House, in a beautifully renovated Beaux-Arts building. The firm was known for its platinum clients such as J&J and Amgen. As Keegan and staff reviewed changes to epo's label, Troy contacted his former colleagues at the Office of Chief Counsel on February 27 and asked a favor: *Will you set up a meeting with FDA staff and my clients, the makers of epo?* "It would be great if you could make sure that someone at OCC makes sure that people understand the limits of their authority," he reminded them. The next day, Amgen's and Ortho's managers were negotiating with the FDA over the precise wording of "a safety update" that would affect Aransep, Epogen, and Procrit.

Schlichtmann had no clue about any of this, and like Jonah in the belly of the whale, he wrestled with his predicament. The lawyer now had eight days to finish his brief. He checked in with Yavelberg to see how her investigation was coming along, but her response was morbid. As he later reported to his client, "Not only is the off-label claim dead, it's being transferred out of the morgue and into the graveyard for burial!"

Duxbury continued to insist adamantly that his claim had merit. During long, rainy-night telephone calls, he patiently repeated what he'd been saying for months, and Schlichtmann listened until his ears rang. He needed to respond to Ortho's motion to dismiss by February 22 but wanted confirmation that Procrit's high doses had been both illegal *and perilous.* The spark he needed lay inside those four unpublished or unpublicized studies, just beyond reach. As his deadline approached, he asked for another extension, and the judge gave it to him. But the future looked bleak; Schlichtmann had only three more weeks to deliver.

By now, he wasn't sleeping well. He'd rise at four A.M., dress in jeans and a flannel shirt, and pad downstairs. He'd slip out the door, walk a few steps to his "boathouse," where he'd light the propane-fueled fireplace. While warming his hands, he'd admire his rare mantel carved by the Salem craftsman Samuel McIntyre. Schlichtmann had salvaged that piece, too, he remembered, and he'd turn back to try and save the Duxbury case too. February turned to March, and Schlichtmann was still chained to his albatross, rubbing his tuft of white hair as if the answer was hooked in his scalp. "What can I say to move this case farther along?" he'd cry. Four days before his brief was due, he wondered if he had made a mistake: "Is this case a loser?" *Is this another Woburn?*

Then the telephone rang. It was Jamie Yavelberg, who sounded excited. "Did you see the *New York Times* story today?" she asked.

"Oh, yeah," he said, in a breezy tone he didn't feel. "How about that story?" He had no clue what she was talking about, but as he listened, it grew clear. The damning little-known epo studies that had been piling up over the last five months had finally forced regulators to take action. As the DOJ attorney went on, Schlichtmann searched online for the story, and there it was, headlined: "FDA Warning Is Issued on Anemia Drugs' Overuse."

Regulators had just issued their sternest alert for Procrit and her sisters, and the so-called black box warning was one step short of yanking the drug off the market. The FDA had already alerted healthcare professionals about the newly discovered dangers, and Schlichtmann's spine straigthened as he read: "Avoid serious venous thromboembolic events by using the lowest dose. . . . Additional warnings about increased mortality, cardiovascular events, tumor progression and uncontrolled hypertension . . ." The red flags described all the study results that Schlichtmann had missed that fall and winter. Now researchers believed that Procrit triggered blood clots, strokes, heart attacks, and deaths in patients with chronic renal failure, on chemotherapy, and even *surgical candidates*. "Jesus," thought Schlichtmann: "This drug couldn't be worse."

Yavelberg pointed out that Procrit was in trouble. Then, she added, "We want you to know that we'll file an amicus brief with the court."

Schlichtmann couldn't believe his ears. The government intended to file a motion, presumably in support of his case. He thanked her profusely and hung up.

"Eureka!" he shouted.

Schlichtmann's breakthrough was as much logical as it was emotional. He'd been waiting to *feel* the whole *ganze megillah* of this case so he could defend it passionately. Now, as news of epo crashed over the wires like waves off Misery Island, Schlichtmann realized he had little more than seventy-two hours to file his brief. He locked himself in his boathouse that weekend, writing feverishly and trancelike, stopping only to eat, drink, and rest. On March 13, he filed his papers with the court, on time.

Later, he realized that his client had been right all along: The high doses had not only been illegal but deadly. "Mark has been a goddamned voice in the wilderness all these months," he thought. From then on, he treated his client more like a valued a friend.

—ᴧᴥ—

SIMMERLY, meanwhile, worked another part of the case. For months, he'd been writing letters to attorneys general in states such as Illinois, California, and New York, and to legislators in Washington, Oregon, and New Jersey. He wrote to the Office of the Inspector General and to members of the House Committee on Energy and Commerce, the Senate Committee on Finance, and others. As Duxbury's case shuddered to life again, he contacted reporters at *The New York Times*, *The Washington Post*, *The Seattle Times*, and others, hoping to bring attention to the claims. Here was Sancho Panza, an ever faithful squire in service to his friend. In Simmerly's mind, a brilliantly vivid cavalcade of horses would soon glide into view and he felt sure that once the couriers grasped his message, the red-hot poker of consequences would strike. That spring, Simmerly got through to two reporters at *The Wall Street Journal*. But Procrit's tale was so complicated, it took weeks for the *qui tam* plaintiffs to tell it clearly. At one point, Duxbury helped McClellan compile a collection of their evidence to help the journalists. McClellan entitled his booklet "Justice Shall Prevail" and printed a gavel on its cover. When the reporters needed even more information, McClellan produced a second "Justice" booklet and, later, gave every member of the "team" a copy.

On May 10, 2007, the story finally appeared in *The Wall Street Journal*, along with the newspaper's signature mark: a dot-ink portrait of one of the article's subjects, Dean McClellan, dressed in a tuxedo and bow tie. "Suit Details How J&J Pushed Sales of Procrit," the headline trumpeted, and the piece laid out the scheme. "The documents provide a rare window into the complex case that is adding to the legal problems piling up on the health giant (J&J)." The day before, *The New York Times* had published a related exposé about how epo's two partners were paying hundreds of millions of doctors every year to pump anemic patients with unsafe doses. In fact, a cancer clinic near Seattle had received $2.7 million from Amgen just for prescribing $9 million worth of its drug in 2006 alone. "Damn!" Duxbury told McClellan. "I know those oncologists—and the reps who paid them." Now that *two* national newspapers had broken the crime story, the two believed that someone would surely have to pay.

—⚏—

EXCUSE me. Pardon me. A woman dressed in high heels stepped on the wing-tip toes of a man already seated in the huge conference room. A dark-suited man bumped the knees of an older woman, jostling her papers as he strained to reach an empty seat. *Pardon me. So sorry.* It wasn't even eight A.M., yet four hundred people had packed the tight rows of a ballroom at the Hilton Hotel in Silver Springs, Maryland. Those who couldn't find a chair had to park themselves against the bone-colored walls, being careful not to brain themselves on the wrought-iron fixtures. The mood was suspenseful, the air thick. Competing aftershaves and colognes assaulted the senses like Coco Chanel on Pepé Le Pew.

Dozens of grim-faced people sat at the front of the room, their tables forming a horseshoe. On one side was Dr. Patricia Keegan and her colleagues from the FDA; in the middle sat members of the advisory committee, mostly oncologists; and the other leg was for the managers of Amgen and J&J. These players faced a sea of consumer advocates, stock analysts, hedge fund reps, lawyers, corporate spies, and about fifty reporters. Keegan was braced for what was sure to be a long day.

The FDA had called this May 10 meeting to discuss epo in the wake of its black-box warning. After so many studies had demonstrated the risks of aggressive doses, regulators wanted the seventeen-member panel to reevaluate the safety of the top-selling drugs and advise them on what to do. For Procrit, Epogen, and Aranesp the implications of this meeting were enormous, if unthinkable. Could it be that for nearly fifteen years, oncologists had been giving cancer patients a biologic that was essentially killing them?

The crowd settled, and the show opened with Amgen's executive vice president Roger M. Perlmutter. At one time, the internist had chaired the immunology department at the University of Washington. Now, after six years at Amgen the fifty-six-year-old pulled down about $5 million a year and his hairline had receded to the point where it looked as if his curly, gray corona might slip off any minute. He assured the crowd that "patient safety is our highest priority," then went on to review the thirty-six oncology studies that had been performed since the last ODAC meeting, in 2004.

Perlmutter then introduced a series of six experts who stressed the benefits of epo. One of them, Dr. Jeffrey Crawford, urged the committee to reaffirm the value of Aranesp and "preserve the role of the physician in clinical decision making." Other experts from Stanford, Duke, and USC unsheathed their pointers and described in bloodless terms hazard ratios, cerebral "accidents," and overlapping patterns. A listener could be forgiven for thinking she had wandered into a Montgomery County traffic planning session rather than a national drug alert. But after an hour or so, a hint of trouble bubbled up. It came during the presentation from Alex Zukiwski, the head of a division at J&J Pharmaceutical Research and Development (J&JPRD). Dressed in a blue oxford shirt and navy suit, he spoke in a clipped British accent about J&J's "Phase IV" trials and "noninferiority" studies. Perhaps it was the effect of standing in the harsh spotlight; or maybe it was the room's warm, stultifying air. But as slides of incomplete Pro-crit studies flashed across the screen, Zukiwski started to perspire pro-fusely. At one point, he stopped reading his prepared remarks, pulled out a white handkerchief, and mopped his brow. Then he plunged ahead with the script. It was hard not to feel sorry for Zukiwski, who, consciously or not, seemed to be signaling that no one at the horseshoe table had the foggiest idea if epo was safe.

Excuse me. So sorry.

After nearly two decades of peddling their medicine with minitrials and marketing studies, both drug promoters were having difficulties conducting a scientifically sound clinical experiment. By 2001, they could not find enough patients in the United States or Western Europe willing to participate in a science-based trial. They needed to enroll enough of the right sort of patients with the same disease that were at the same stage of progression and follow them through the duration of double-blind, placebo-controlled research—ideally to measure epo's safety at the *approved* dosage. Zukiwski admitted the "challenges" of this project and explained that, at this very moment, senior members of his staff were flying around the globe visiting fifty trial sites trying to enroll enough patients. Despite these problems, he insisted that "our data continue to support the safe use of (epo) as labeled and show no discernible effect on tumor growth and overall survival."

Someone in the audience coughed loudly.

Then, Keegan and her peers took the floor to run through the fatal data from the recent studies. Staff member Dr. Vinni Juneja criticized the two companies for not providing the data they had promised at the last ODAC meeting in 2004. In fact, the regulator announced that both Amgen and J&J had designed their current studies to *not* answer critical questions, and at this gasps and yelps ran through the crowd as if a surfeit of skunks had been set loose. As one analyst said to his neighbor: "It's worse than we expected," although it wasn't clear if he was referring to the companies' disingenuous behavior or their public outing. The FDA's Dr. Juneja then added that "no completed or ongo-ing trial has addressed [epo] safety issues in cancer patients." Report-ers peck-pecked on their portable devices.

Usually, panel meetings like this one featured eloquent pleas from patients to keep a drug on the market. But not this time. During the public comment period, a stream of consumer advocates and cancer survivors lined up at the microphone. Bob Erwin, head of the Marti Nelson Cancer Foundation, noticed that the elephant in the room—money—had not been discussed. After the black-box warning, insurers such as WellPoint and UnitedHealthcare had restricted their payouts for epo. Erwin wondered if the drug prescriptions had been "reimbursement-driven rather than guided by professional judgment about what may be best . . . for the patient."

The next speaker went a step further. "The story of these anemia drugs and how they were oversold to the public . . . is truly outrageous," said Maryann Napoli of the Center for Medical Consumers. The ubiquitous Procrit commercials showed actors after they'd gotten their happy shots. The ads ran for about nine years and were so persuasive, "what cancer patient *wouldn't* ask their doctor for this drug?" So imagine Napoli's surprise when the FDA announced its black-box warning *two months ago.*

"Why did the FDA allow J&J to run those Procrit ads?"

Bravo to regulators for sending warning letters to doctors, Napoli added. "But what about patients?" *How are they going to get the word?* Just then, the public address system squealed slightly and her words skidded around the narrow room. (Some months later, Napoli's question would echo back and haunt those at the horseshoe table.)

But she reserved most of her ire for the cancer doctors. "Oncologists are in effect running their own pharmacies," Napoli explained. We're suspicious of healers who treat patients with herbs—then sell those herbs as a cure. "Why not treat oncologists in the same way?"

Other patients had more to say. "We trust you to look after our best interests as you evaluate the benefits and harms of (our) drugs," said Carolina Hinestrosa of the National Breast Cancer Coalition. Instead, the doctors sold out their patients and took advantage of "perverse financial incentives" to enrich themselves. "How come we have no answers?" Hinestrosa asked. *Can't you guys at the Fortune 500 companies come up with one well-defined study?*

So sorry. Pardon me. Excuse me.

At the lunch break, several reporters and analysts sprinted out of the room to telephone their editors and chiefs. The hotel's small café was mobbed with about a hundred patrons and indignation jostled indigestion. Sixty minutes later, spectators returned to their seats and wall spaces. The meeting resumed, and the blunt talk from the morning's speakers spread now to the ODAC panelists. At one point, committee member Dr. Otis Brawley, blurted out: "I'm concerned that this compound is a stimulant [and] fertilizer for epidermal tumors."

"What data do you have to assure me that this is not Miracle-Gro for cancer?"

The crowd was so shocked, it laughed. Brawley had spent weeks coming up with that quip, and now, as his colleagues stared at him in disbelief, he just grinned.

The companies' representatives and federal regulators scrambled to answer his question. When they couldn't, Dr. John Glaspy took a stab. He had written the *JCO* fatigue study for Ortho and had taken many dollars from both sponsors over the years. Now he addressed the issue of whether "perverse financial incentives" drove the boom in epo prescriptions.

"If there is inappropriate use going on that is driven by reimbursement, that is a bad thing. I am not here to defend that," Glaspy said. He went on to say that if these drugs were to be banned, nearly half a million people a year would need blood transfusions. Generally, people aren't given transfusions unless their hemoglobin levels fall to 8. But the idea of returning to transfusions evoked images of the Dark Ages, circa 1980, when people died from infected blood banks during the AIDS plague. The nation's supply was in much better shape in 2007. But could the country handle the loss of the blood drugs? Glaspy wondered.

The real problem? Brawley countered, "A hell of a lot of people get growth factors because doctors make twelve hundred bucks a shot off it, not because [patients] need it."

"The burning question," added ODAC panelist Dr. Silvana Martino, is this: "Does this thing [epo] actually kill people?"

The most horrifying aspect of the recent studies was that cancer cells seemed to have epo receptors that might allow the drug to oxygenate—and breed—malignant tumor cells. In other words, epo could possibly grow cancer cells and thereby hasten a patient's death.

Amgen's vice president tried to stop this train wreck. Perlmutter stood up and explained that it was mere "speculation" that cancer cells had epo receptors. But an FDA staffer, Dr. Barry Cherney, jumped in to correct the executive. "There is an extensive body of literature that counteracts what you say."

Perlmutter turned pugnacious. Shall we "go into it and talk about exactly how confounded that literature is?" he asked.

"No," ODAC's chairman interjected.

Then came the cliff-hanger, the moment when ODAC voted on what the FDA should do with its black-box blockbuster. There was $12 billion in annual global sales at stake. What ODAC recommended, the FDA often put in stone, followed by Medicaid, WellPoint, and the others. Medicare Part B had supported this drug for years and spent more on epo than any other drug, or $4 billion in 2006. If the FDA banned these agents, the fortunes of Amgen and, to a lesser degree, J&J would plummet along with their vaunted reputations.

The votes were tallied: The group agreed (15–2) that regulators should restrict the use of drugs (and their marketing) until safety studies were completed. It agreed (12–5) that epo should *not* be given to people with some tumors, but ODAC didn't say which kinds of tumors. The hemoglobin baseline should be lowered (15–2) but the level wasn't specified. And, despite all the danger signs about high hemoglobin targets, the panel of oncologists concluded (11–6) that the dose should *not* be aimed at a lower level, like 9 or 10, but kept at the label's current measure of 12. *So sorry. Pardon me.*

Certainly, the FDA needed to reeducate people about the drugs' risks, but ODAC didn't say how. Importantly, ODAC repeated that epo shots be discontinued as soon as a patient stopped his chemotherapy.

But would patients get that message?

—m—

W HEN Duxbury heard about the patient deaths, he felt the worm crawl down his ribs, inch by inch. It had been hard enough for him to accept that, for most of his career, he'd been a trained thief. He thought he had come to terms with that contradiction, winking back at him from mirrors and windowpanes. But now he realized he'd been an assassin too. Ten percent of the cancer patients for whom he'd sold Procrit had died! The glass panes were now crowded with ghostly faces—and he didn't recognize the shell-shocked man staring back at him.

—⚊⚊—

J IM Lenox felt as fit as a horse. The handsome fifty-three-year-old had been cancer free for nearly nine years now. He had welcomed a few other grandchildren in the last decade and had remained close to Christopher, who was now fifteen. Jim's health concerns focused only on a worsening shoulder pain. So, in March 2007, Jim went in for a checkup. An X-ray found tumor nodules, this time in his upper right lung. They were small, he told his wife. "It's nothing to worry about." They'd been down this road before.

On April 10, he got his first round of chemotherapy, Carboplatin, along with some other drugs: Taxotere supposedly stopped the growth of red blood cells and Avastin, at $8,000 a month, allegedly starved his tumors. Jim also received Amgen's drug Neulasta after every chemo treatment to help him fight infection, and Aranesp injections, at $2,500 per shot. Sharon's health insurance through the post office was pretty good, but it didn't completely cover the cost of these expensive drugs, adding possible bankruptcy to the list of risky side effects. Despite the high-end treatments, Jim lost weight, developed sores in his mouth, and sometimes felt as if vats of oil were burning in his veins. In May, after four weeks of treatment, a CT scan showed improvement. Though he was enervated and bald, Jim and his wife were heartened. At the doctor's suggestions, he agreed to undergo a few more sessions of chemo and drug therapy.

Sharon and her daughters accompanied Jim to the hospital, and while he sat in a room getting poked with needles, they waited in the lobby. Sometimes drug reps and their caterers would pass by, wheeling carts of piping hot plates of veal piccata and chicken salads earmarked for the doctors and nurses. The aromas wafted through the oncology ward, irking the Lenoxes. "Why does this happen every time we're here?" said daughter Joanne.

"I don't know," Sharon replied. "But I'm so hungry, I'm drooling."

Even a whiff of melted cheese made Jim want to gag, however. Nurses took his blood every week to measure his hemoglobin levels, and every third week, he received Carboplatin through an IV. His arms turned into the limbs of a junkie, with purple bruises and collapsed veins, and he suffered from constipation or diarrhea, depending on the day. Sharon herself would grow sick at the sight of their medical bills. But they soldiered on.

Jim actually wanted to receive blood transfusions instead of epo shots, and though his request was initially denied, his blood count fell so low, he had to be transfused with two pints of blood. That made him happy, but it worried Sharon. She took the nurse aside and said, "I thought the Aranesp was supposed to eliminate the need for blood transfusions."

Jim's last chemotherapy session occurred on July 25, and later, he and his wife heard the prognosis: Tests "showed significant improvement and tumor shrinkage," the doctor said. Jim no longer needed chemotherapy. The family celebrated by throwing a barbecue.

But for some unknown reason, Jim continued receiving high doses of epo even though he was off chemotherapy. The FDA had never approved epo for any other cancer patient but those on chemo. Yet Jim was injected with several shots of the risky, expensive drug in September, in October, and throughout November. As a result, his prognosis did not look good.

22

Brothers

2007

"THEY say, right here, that McClellan has no connection to Duxbury," said a voice along the table.

"That's nuts!" McClellan caterwauled.

"We can show a connection," Duxbury said, fishing through a pile
of papers.

"Damn it," said Schlichtmann, pacing the floor. "Where's that roster from the early 1990s that listed both of your names?"

"Hang on, Jan. I'm looking for it."

The nine people in this meeting room at the Seaport Hotel along
Boston's waterfront kept rifling through the folders and briefcases that
lay everywhere. Duxbury, McClellan, Simmerly, and Bibi sat on one
side of a long table, and Foote, Chavez, a law clerk, and a paralegal
had spread out on the other side. Now some of them moved to their
laptops and tap-tapped frantically through the labyrinth of files. Duxbury was rooting around in a paper mound, trying not to spill the cups
of coffee and soda on the table, and pushing aside plates of half-eaten
bacon-lettuce-and-tomato sandwiches. Though it was only mid-
morning, most of them had been up half the night. Schlichtmann had
worked until dawn, taken a power nap, then come marching in with
his satchel and binders.

"Call your wife, Dean, and ask her to look for it."

McClellan mumbled something inaudible.

But Schlichtmann wasn't listening. He continued pacing, hovering over the shoulder of first one person, then another, flitting down the table in his cobalt-blue shirt and dark slacks, looking like a raven hopping along a fence.

"I found it!" shouted Bob Foote, and the room exhaled.

Duxbury made a quip that seemed funny at the time, followed by a howl from McClellan. Foote managed to get the image onto the large white screen at the head of the room. "Look at that, will you?" Schlichtmann shouted, his head turning from the screen to the table, then back again. The document listed the names of the Ortho hires—including Duxbury and McClellan—who had attended the training session in the wooded New Jersey compound so many years ago.

"Well," the attorney intoned in mock solemnity, "so much for the defendant's claim that our co-relators didn't know each other." He unleashed a few choice profanities, then shouted, "They've been @#% best friends for fifteen years!"

His colleagues whistled and shouted as if they were at a ball game. Then there was a knock on the door. They were so engrossed in their work they didn't even hear it, but the rap sounded again, only louder. Someone rushed to open the door abruptly and a man in shirtsleeves stepped back. "We're next door, in a meeting, but we can't hear each other talk. Could you keep it down?"

"Certainly, no problem," said everyone at once.

The door closed. Sheepish glances flicked across the table.

Then, the tittering resumed, but Schlichtmann seized control. In a few hours, at 2:30 P.M., to be exact, *United States of America ex rel Mark Duxbury and Dean McClellan vs. Ortho Biotech* would be considered by a federal judge, and their presentation had to be thorough. Heads bent over yellow highlighters and black-and-white briefs.

Duxbury, dressed in one of his old sales suits, was nervous but elated. His case wasn't actually in trial yet. But this was the closest it had gotten to a judge since he had filed his *qui tam* four years earlier. Preparing for this presentation was like water rising behind a cardboard dam. Everything that Duxbury had been collecting over the years had been funneled into this room. Now it was all reaching critical mass. Each drop of energy that Duxbury had poured into his mission was about to be unleashed in a new form, but what would it be? The torrent was gaining momentum and sweeping everyone along; in this moment, McClellan forgot that he had never wanted to be a part of this, Simmerly didn't mind that he was on the sidelines, and Duxbury almost believed that he had never given up, not only on his case but on life itself. Of course, he had, and that only made this day sweeter. He and his "team" were lost in the driving pulse of creativity, surrendering to something big and melding into a perfectly calibrated machine.

The group had been here for a day or so, lodged in a part of Boston undergoing gentrification. The Federalist Revival style of the ten-year-old Seaport Hotel blended in with the city's historic warehouses, as did the new federal courthouse and public archways. But this was not a tour group. They ordered in food and bottled water. The PowerPoint they would deliver to Judge Rya Zobel this afternoon, on May 23, 2007, was more critical than the one they'd presented to Yavelberg. Schlichtmann wanted the courts to recognize Duxbury as the guy who'd been "first to file" the off-label and AWP claims; he also needed the judge to recognize McClellan as a co-relator who'd been involved in this suit since the beginning.

This time, it was Simmerly who wore the novelty tie, a navy blue sash with the words *Illegitimi Non Carborundum*; that was pseudo-Latin for "Don't let the bastards grind you down." He promenaded around the room, glancing occasionally at his wrist, keeping track of the time. "An hour and a half, people," he said, his hands patting his belly. There was a spate of discussion. "Fifty-six more minutes," he said later as another slide fell into place. "Okay," he yelled finally. "Let's pack up." Simmerly had also been waiting for years for this moment and he wasn't about to be late.

Duxbury straightened his tie, a hand-painted number that looked like a giant blood clot, McClellan tugged at his Hopi-patterned sweater, and Schlichtmann put on his coat: The dam spilled out to the street. One group hailed a taxi, loading in briefcases and video equipment. But since it was a gorgeous, windswept day, the plaintiffs and their attorney strolled a few blocks to the federal courthouse. Duxbury hung back a bit so he could smoke a cigarette without disturbing anyone, McClellan leaned into the wind, while Schlichtmann's long camel coat whipped around his matchstick legs. He tried to keep a positive attitude about the courts without inflating hopes, but he had already warned Duxbury, "I've been in this situation so many times before where I think we have a great airtight case and it turns out we don't. So remember it's a crapshoot." But this case had already worked its way inside Schlichtmann: His blood pressure had jumped recently, his shoulders looked a little bonier, and his pupils had turned a redder shade of brown. If his usually coifed hair was the only thing that got roughed up today, he'd be happy.

Schlichtmann led this ragtag crew into the new John Joseph Moakley Federal Courthouse on Fan Pier. Erected on the site of a dilapidated port, the complex was a glass and brick building overlooking the Inner Harbor. From the street, the $250 million complex didn't look like much. But once Duxbury and McClellan got past the armed guards and metal detectors, they looked around in awe. There were no dark corners here or the stench of twenty-to-life, only light pouring through a nine-story shaft that reached skyward. When Duxbury turned a corner, he walked a passageway that was rimmed by an enormous glass wall, rippling seven stories high. From here he could look down upon the whitecapped harbor as if he were riding the crow's nest of a ship. He wasn't sure whether it was the vertiginous view or the majestic venue, but his knees turned rubbery. "Jees," he told McClellan. "I feel like I'm in an opera house."

"Stop it," said McClellan. "We've got enough drama as it is."

And the hearing hadn't even started.

Duxbury and McClellan walked into Room 12, with its perfect acoustics and wood panels, and took seats in the spectators' well. The room was empty except for their four attorneys, who were already behind the bar, unpacking their evidence at a table. Ortho's three attorneys had already settled themselves and were chatting like old friends. Susan Burke wore her blond hair straight and her navy blue silk jacket extra long over her ample hips. The forty-three-year-old had started her career working for the DOJ, then, for a time, was at Covington & Burling. She'd been a lawyer for a regional division of Tenet Healthcare, which, in 2006, had paid the government $900 million in penalties for Medicare fraud. Now Burke had her own practice, and she sometimes defended clients accused of health-care fraud. Lately, she'd taken on civil cases on behalf of Iraqi detainees who had been tortured at Abu Ghraib prison and against American contractors.

Next to Burke was her cocounsel, Patrick Davies, a partner at Covington & Burling, who had helped manage the Latin American branch of the notorious Whitecoat Project. Led by client Philip Morris, that global effort had tried to roll back smoking bans and refute the idea that secondhand smoke was harmful. Davies defended Chiquita Brands in suits brought by Colombian nationals who claimed, under the Alien Tort Statute, that Chiquita had paid paramilitary groups to kill their family members. Davies was also a member of the pharmaceutical defense team.

Then there was Covington partner Ethan Posner, who earlier in the year had been named one of the top 50 rising stars by the *American Lawyer*. The forty-four-year-old had the broad shoulders and wide stance of a college baseball batter, but too many client dinners had thickened his figure. He had fleshy lips, and a bull neck that supported a broad, open face. He had joined Covington & Burling in 1990, left for two years to work in the Justice Department, made a few connections, and returned to Covington in 2001. The partner now cochaired its pharmaceutical litigation group, defended clients in Berman's AWP suit, and had just helped GlaxoSmithKline reach a $70 million settlement in that case. He billed $750 an hour and was said to be worth every dollar.

Ortho had a formidable defense team.

Suddenly, the clerk ordered, "All rise," and Judge Rya Zobel stepped to the dais, all five feet five inches of her. The handsome jurist wore her thick black hair in a stylish short cut. She had been one of the first women appointed to the federal bench by President Carter and looked to be in her early sixties but was actually seventy-six. At the throat of her dark magisterial robe was a splash of red silk, and a hint of gold flashed on her ears.

Zobel acknowledged the "very good" amicus brief written by Patricia Connolly, assistant U.S. attorney for the district of Massachusetts. Below Connolly's name was that of Jamie Yavelberg, and both women were in the courtroom. Schlichtmann had hoped that the DOJ would actually support his case, but no such luck. Its brief indicated that it simply wanted to protect its right to pursue Duxbury's claims against Procrit's promoter at some later time, even if Duxbury's case died.

Zobel now wanted to know if Schlichtmann agreed with Posner about the issues regarding public disclosure. "No," he replied. And so the fencing began.

Posner's job was to zealously defend J&J and Ortho. His strategy apparently was to conflate other suits with Duxbury's, cite some case law, and stir up confusion and doubts. His brief said that Ortho denied the allegations: "In fact Procrit was approved as safe and effective by the FDA for once weekly dosing at 40,000 units for chemotherapy patients, the alleged 'off-label' use in this case." What he didn't say was that Duxbury claimed the off-label crime ran from 1997 until the FDA approved the high dose in 2004. As for "violations"? Never mind. "The court need not wade into the merits" here because the whistleblower didn't follow *qui tam* rules.

Posner dragged in Duxbury's first attorney, Berman, and some of the filings that Berman had made in this *qui tam* case after he'd dropped it—and after his ex-client Duxbury had asked him to stop filing briefs. Now Ortho's lawyer quoted from those papers, telling the judge that Duxbury's old counsel "had consulted with medical experts" and "researched the public bar and first to file" rules. Since Berman and Sobol had dropped Duxbury's case, the implication was that they hadn't found merit in it.

Duxbury felt he had already been shafted six ways to Sunday, and now Ortho's lawyer was parading his trussed up body in front of the court. Duxbury felt betrayed by his ex-lawyers and believed there'd been no good reason for them to file their self-serving papers at his expense. "Whatever happened to attorney-client privilege?" he wondered.

Posner then claimed that Duxbury's AWP claims were suspiciously similar to Berman's claims in a multidistrict litigation that was unspooling in a room down the hall. The two claims share "the same headers [and] the same text [which] is not surprising," Posner explained. Berman had written both cases, and Posner's voice struck just the right tone between disgust and gloat.

"The Average Wholesale Price case," Posner said, had been pending for a year and a half before Duxbury brought his Ortho/Procrit claim. Berman's AWP case had also alleged that Ortho had falsely inflated Procrit's price; therefore, Duxbury's "copy cat" claim didn't qualify him as the "first to file" that allegation. Posner interpreted the *qui tam* rules to say that Duxbury couldn't allege an AWP crime since Berman had beat him to it.

Rubbing his beefy hands, Posner then set about dismantling Duxbury's remaining claim of off-label promotion. Your Honor, he said, "they don't even use the phrase 'off-label'" in their original complaint. He accused Duxbury and Schlichtmann of lifting verbiage from a similar Procrit suit and pasting it into their amended complaint, a no-no in these types of cases. The suit Posner referred to had been filed by an Ortho manager based near Denver and it was breathtaking in its detail.

Kurt Blair had claimed that Ortho had "engaged in a widespread scheme to market and promote" Procrit at high, unapproved levels, causing doctors and pharmacists to file "hundreds of thousands of false claims" to Medicare and Medicaid over the years. His suit described Tom Amick's illegal high-dose promotions and detailed Ortho's "purportedly independent clinical studies," including one influenced by Loretta Itri, vice president of Ortho's clinical affairs. Blair described the "promotional junkets" for Procrit-praising doctors on its Speakers Bureau, and how they were "carefully selected and trained" and "given slide kits created by Ortho Biotech which contained the message, including off-label information, that Ortho" wanted them to convey.

The Denver whistle-blower also detailed Ortho's national "slush funds," including the $4 million per year "educational" grant budget and a $1 million-a-year fund earmarked for $300 clerkships. Furthermore, Blair claimed, Ortho had paid $1 million a year to U.S. Oncology so its reps could get in the door and pitch the company's 1,300 physicians. In thirty-four pages, Blair and his attorneys had arguably written a juicier and more impressive complaint than Berman and Sobol had in their sixteen-page brief. And, as Posner told the court, Blair focused "almost exclusively on the alleged off-label promotion of the 40,000 once weekly dose [scheme]."

Posner neglected to state clearly that Duxbury had filed his suit seven weeks before Blair, making Duxbury the first to file. The Colorado whistle-blower had spent months trying to get the DOJ to intervene in his case too. After two years, when his suit was about to be unsealed, Blair and his attorney, Michael Berger, pleaded with a judge to give them more time to persuade the DOJ to join. The judge refused and broke the suit's seal, which prompted Blair and his lawyer to drop their case; they had weighed the odds and didn't want to fight J&J alone.

Now Posner informed the room that the DOJ was still investigating it.

"And seeking lots of extensions," said Zobel, shooting Yavelberg a withering glance. The judge was clearly displeased with the DOJ's foot-dragging in not just the Blair case, but in Duxbury's too.

Posner stepped back to his notes. He claimed that Duxbury had copied Blair's dead case, making him "the classic parasitic relator."

Duxbury felt as if he were being slowly mauled, the delicate layers of his skin peeling away so that Ortho could eat him later at its gluttonous leisure.

Posner wasn't done. He'd been raised in a lower-income block of Manhattan and schooled in a rough neighborhood of the South Bronx. He knew that con men tell a complicated story to get away with a simple crime. Since he'd joined the white-collar crime beat, he had learned to defend his clients in a silky, sophisticated way no matter what they had *allegedly* done. So he didn't belabor any points. Instead, he just pulled out a new blade to rip another hole in some schmoe's suit. Take Duxbury and McClellan: They "don't have any direct and independent knowledge of any false claims because they" didn't specify the date and amount of each fraudulent Medicare bill. *Rule 9B, Your Honor.*

Posner then punched Duxbury below the belt by ridiculing his "misguided campaign to exact revenge for a firing caused by his own wrongdoing," i.e., for "making racially and sexually harassing remarks and for failing to complete his expense reports timely and accurately." Duxbury had brought his wrongful termination lawsuit against Ortho but had lost, said Posner. Then, he and Berman had filed a *qui tam* which "went nowhere." So Duxbury had amended his complaint in 2006 and dragged in McClellan. "But McClellan is out. . . ."

"Because there is no relation between the two?" asked the judge, fully engaged.

"That's correct," Posner said quickly.

McClellan poked Duxbury's ribs. "We got him there," he whispered.

Posner then summed up his case: Duxbury doesn't actually allege a single fraudulent bill paid by Medicare, and even if he had, he doesn't show how Ortho caused it. "We ask Your Honor to dismiss the case."

At last, it was Schlichtmann's turn. He'd already set up a white screen for his PowerPoint show. Now he softened his tone into one of a mediator seeking common ground. He greeted his opponent, Posner, as "my brother." The judge looked amused.

Schlichtmann then took Zobel through the history of *qui tam* law and how even the U.S. Supreme Court had said, "Look at the plain words of the statute." Public disclosure of a fraud doesn't kill a *qui tam* case *if* a relator has independent and direct knowledge of the fraud.

The judge leaned forward. "What that means . . . is that you could have ten relators coming in after the public disclosure, each of whom has independent information and [they] file a complaint and they're all okay?"

"No," said Schlichtmann. *Only the first one to file is okay.*

Zobel nodded.

The lawyer added that when a relator amends a complaint, he can do so as long as the new allegations aren't fundamentally different from the original scheme. *So we're in!*

Now he bore into the crux of his case, which was that Duxbury included the off-label claim in his original November 2003 lawsuit. He may not have used the term, but he had certainly explained it in his fifteen-word phrase. Duxbury had claimed that Ortho "use[d] the drug in a way which is inconsistent with its FDA approved indications." He had elaborated on the fraud by calling it "the 40,000 unit dosage scheme" and citing "phony drug studies." Some judges might accept this as the English definition of "off-label," but courts were split on this and other exacting rules of *qui tam*. Zobel now had the duty to clarify this point.

"Assume for the moment," Zobel told Schlichtmann, "that I disagree with you and find that the off-label claim is not in the original complaint. Are you dead on that claim?"

No, Your Honor. "I'm severely wounded but not dead."

Perspiring under his royal blue shirt, the lawyer explained that the original off-label charge was one count in a "very simple complaint." Then, he flicked on another slide and moved into how Duxbury's amended complaint that Schlichtman himself had written had separated the allegations into an AWP count and an off-label count.

"And kickbacks too," said the judge eagerly.

"Well, kickbacks actually were used to promote both [schemes]." That's how Ortho got doctors to bill Medicare for inflated AWP, he explained. Meanwhile, "phony studies" succeeded in providing kickbacks like "cash payments to a physician . . . to influence [him] to use more of the drug" and "to spread the once-a-week unapproved dosing," he said, quoting from Duxbury's original complaint.

So, Your Honor, "our complaint is pregnant with the claim [and] although my brother says it's just a little bit pregnant. . . . That is sufficient." Schlichtmann then addressed Posner's assertion that there was no connection between Duxbury and McClellan. "They're flat wrong," he said, and flashed the slide of the 1992 Procrit training school that listed Duxbury and McClellan.

"So we've got the goods," said Schlichtmann excitedly. McClellan and Duxbury sat grinning from the bleachers.

"My brother has [said] that we haven't identified even one false claim. Judge, that's just not true." Schlichtmann showed a slide related to Dr. Kattakar and how Ortho had showed the doctor how he could profit from Procrit's spread, and how McClellan had showed his office how to file for Medicare, and how the Ortho rep had actually seen the submitted form. Schlichtmann went on to say that McClellan "obtained firsthand knowledge" that the doctor had received reimbursement, which over the years amounted to more than $3 million of false claims.

Schlichtmann had warmed up, and he clicked through slides the way Dillinger must have gone through bullets. Here was Rainier Oncology and its $20,000 of free drug; here's Dr. Von Hoff and Ortho's letter on his behalf; here's our claim that his center received $1 million in government payouts for years of off-label dosing.

At the sound of $1 million, Posner 's face went white.

Schlichtmann continued. "How can one say that we have not identified a specific amount of money [and] a specific provider?" He let those words hang in the air. "Those three alone are the evidence, Your Honor." With that, he sat down.

The judge asked the government if they'd like to be heard. Yavelberg, wearing a short skirt and patent leather heels, walked up to face the judge and clear up a "small nuance" in both men's presentations.

Ortho's attorney was given one more chance to gut Duxbury's claims. Posner had been raised as an only child and had been truly touched by Schlichtmann's nod to him as "my brother." He had always wanted a brother. But that didn't stop the defense lawyer from moving in for the kill. He scattergunned subjunctives all over the courtroom without so much as a by-your-leave. He argued that Duxbury's off-label claim wasn't in his original complaint. "It doesn't even say 'off.'"

The judge pushed him on this point. "Well, what it describes is exactly what off-label in this context means, doesn't it?"

"No," said Posner, a little too loudly. "There should not have been one count, as AWP and off-label are two completely different legal theor[ies]."

In the end, that is what the case boiled down to. It didn't matter that a multibillion-dollar fraud might have been perpetrated against the citizens of the United States. What counted was that you follow a complex arrangement of man-made rules and frame them in legal theories.

Even so, by the time Judge Zobel cracked her gavel, it looked as if Posner and Ortho were severely wounded, and Duxbury was very much alive.

—⁓—

THEY wound up back at the hotel, in the crowded downstairs bar. It was past three-thirty and the sounds of Thursday's happy hour rang around them like Friday's school bell. A bossa nova tune glided beneath the other patrons' laughter; singles were shooting back doubles, and the sun streamed through the transom windows, glancing off the potted plants. Simmerly lined up a few upholstered chairs as the old party hands, Duxbury and McClellan, slid together two low coffee tables for the food and drinks that Schlichtmann had started to order.

Foote and Chavez took the couch against the wall, forming the base of a U, while the others arranged themselves in chairs on either side. A waitress took orders and returned to plop down plates of cheese, crackers, vegetables, and shrimp as big as your finger. Glasses of martinis, chardonnay, vodka tonics, beers, and sodas were passed around and people took their first sips, then leaned back. You could almost hear the collective sigh of relief, but after a few chord changes, the group began chattering. This was Schlichtmann's favorite part of a case, the dissection of a court hearing. He could spend hours with friends evaluating his courtroom arguments and those of his opponent, parsing every pause and clause. "I think we did well in front of the judge, don't you?" he asked the table.

"Oh yeah," everyone responded. "You did great, Jan."

"Posner, by the way, did not do his homework," said Duxbury.

"The guy looked stricken when he heard the $1 million figure regarding Von Hoff."

Hoots erupted, followed by a few cocktail slurps.

"The judge is not prejudiced," said Foote. "She's one of the best. Plus, she's done a lot of litigation with big companies."

"Well, this is the biggest case she'll ever see," said Simmerly, leaning into the ring. "Procrit and the others are Medicare's most-reimbursed drug."

"And almost all of the sales involved high doses," said Schlichtmann.

"We figured it out once, and it came to sixty billion dollars in potential damages," said Simmerly.

"*What*?" Bibi asked, astounded.

"In fraud cases, the government can fine a company as much as triple the damages," Simmerly explained, then waited for a reaction.

He got some googly eyes and slow whistles.

"So how much could you get?" a voice asked.

"Maybe six billion dollars," Simmerly said. When the government recovered money from a whistle-blower's case, they could share anywhere between 10 percent and 30 percent. "But I don't think the government would ever levy such a steep fine." In fact, Simmerly's estimates were high.

"That's okay," said McClellan. "I'll take a few million."

Duxbury started recounting his war stories, and Berman's name came up. "You know where his AWP case is now?" Duxbury asked. So far, Berman had won or settled about $120 million in AWP claims and had obtained a "groundbreaking settlement" of a 4 percent rollback of prices on hundreds of drugs. Berman had announced that this could save consumer health plans $4 billion. "Except it probably won't," Duxbury explained. "AWP may be gone as a benchmark, but it's already been replaced by a whole bunch of other alphabet soup names": WAC (Warehouse Acquistion Cost), ASP (Average Sales Price), AMP (Average Manufacturer Price), and others.

Schlichtmann snorted. He didn't like the way Berman had used Duxbury in his huge case. Berman would eventually collect about $40 million in fees on the AWP case, but forget to pay Duxbury his long-promised bonus.

By now, the glasses had been drained, and another round had been ordered, along with more hors d'oeuvres. A few people left, and the circle grew tighter.

"Paul," laughed Schlichtmann, "you're a real goddamn lawyer. You've stuck by Mark through thick and thin over the years." He looked around the table and added, "This guy actually believes the oath he took to 'zealously' defend a client."

Simmerly looked pleased.

Schlichtmann recounted the dark days of last year, when he kept seeking extensions to respond to Ortho's motion to dismiss. Duxbury threw in his own two cents, and McClellan chimed in with a story about scorpions nesting under Ortho memos in his storage facility. Pretty soon everyone was shouting and laughing. None of them had had a good night's sleep, all of them had worked hard throughout the morning, and the afternoon legal match had jangled their nerves. Now they were huddled on a sheer cliff overhanging *Qui Tam* Road hallucinating about the riches they could collect. Their eyes sparkled.

Around six, the sun slanted low in the windows, and Schlichtmann raised his glass. The group fell quiet. "I want us all to get along," he said apropos of nothing. What he didn't want was a repeat of Woburn, with clients feeling abandoned or the nasty infighting that big-stakes lawsuits can engender. That was worse than losing, he believed. Basking in the dusky glow of the tight circle, he looked into every face. "You know the feeling in this room right now?" he asked. The remaining fellows nodded. "I just want this feeling to always be alive.

"I want us to *always* be like this with one another." *Brothers.*

Duxbury would try to hang on to that feeling over the next seven, rocky months.

23

As the World Spins

2008

Dressed in her mourning clothes, her heart beating fast, Sharon Lenox stood at the local gas station and wiped the residue of fuel from her hands. She had just scrounged through her car console to find enough change to buy some gas and had put ten dollars' worth into her old Acura Integra. That would be enough for her to drive to a place she abhorred, to do something she'd never, ever done. It was early Thursday morning, March 13, 2008, and a quick glance at her windup watch said time was running short. She climbed back in the car and pulled onto a back road near her home in Crofton, Maryland. This route would be faster than crawling along the interstate at rush hour, and she glanced in the rearview mirror to check the traffic. For a moment, she didn't recognize the face staring back—that of a tired, sad, fifty-four-year-old woman. She still had her dimples, turned-up nose, and a sorrel-colored mane. But the crow's-feet had really dug in over the winter, and if Sharon had gotten a decent night's sleep lately, she couldn't say when. She moved her eyes back to the road and concentrated on the fifty-minute drive to Gaithersburg. In about an hour, the FDA's advisors would begin another ODAC meeting to discuss epo, and Sharon was determined to get the drug yanked from the shelves.

As she drove, Sharon took in the chilly rural scene. The bare trees waved their branches at the wind, their black quills scratching calligraphic notes across a vellum sky. She tried to erase the disturbing images that kept jumping through her head. Just seven months ago, Jim's doctor had proudly announced that her husband's tumors were shrinking and that Jim had shown "significant improvement." He could stop the ghastly chemo treatments. Jim had turned to her with a big, toothy grin and said: "See, honey? I *told* you we'd beat this thing!" Incredulous, she had laughed, then fought back tears of joy. How many people beat cancer twice in their life?

That fall and winter, the couple returned to the doctor every three weeks, just to test Jim's blood. If his hemoglobin dropped, the oncologist would reach for a syringe. *Hold still now for a shot of Aranesp.* During that time, he had received at least five shots though the label clearly dictated that only patients undergoing chemo should get them. No one told Jim that the FDA had slapped a black-box warning on the drugs in March 2007, nor did anyone mentioned May's urgent bulletins of new risks, increased death rates, and tumor growth. In response to epo's mounting deaths, the FDA in November had issued a stronger "dear doctor" letter, incorporating some of ODAC's recommendations from its May 2007 panel: Oncologists should use the lowest drug dose possible, it said, and understand that the lower 30,000-unit doses aren't necessarily safe, either.

In December, Jim called Sharon at the post office but didn't know why he had or even who she was. In an uncharacteristic move, Sharon burst out crying and left work. She found Jim at home, confused and slurring his words. She brought him back to the doctor, who said, "I don't think his cancer has spread." But Sharon insisted that her husband get a CT scan, and, sure enough, the cancer had now metastasized to his brain. He slumped; she choked.

Radiation was ordered, but first a mesh mask had to be made for Jim's face. It wasn't iron, but it might as well have been, given its torturous effect. Part medieval device and part science fiction prop, the mask was placed over Jim's head every week. A white-coated technician would bolt the mask to a table. As Jim lay there, nailed down so he couldn't move, the table would slide into a claustrophobic cone where his head was zapped with gamma rays. "Take a deep breath and hold it," the lab coat would tell the man in his horror chamber. Jim tried not to freak out. "It's just for five minutes," he'd tell himself. "I can endure anything for five minutes." Then, that ear-shattering sound: *screech, zap-boom!* When it was over, he'd go home, only to return the next day.

Sharon turned off Old Washington Road, closer to her destination, but still mired in the past. Last year, she had researched Jim's therapy carefully, yet she had missed epo's dangers. As she steered onto a sinuous two-lane road that twisted past fallow farms and the listless Patuxent River, her mind drifted to happier times. Two months ago, Jim had completed his radiation treatment, and the doctor had said that his tumors had shrunk too. Sharon wanted to know, *How much longer does he have?* He "could live for three to six months, or longer," the oncologist said. That was January 7, 2008, five days after his fifty-fourth birthday, and he was to return again in two weeks.

That afternoon, the couple drove home as the sun slipped down. It rays bled into the horizon, staining the steel-blue sky with swabs of rust and kohl. "My God!" Jim whispered. "What a beautiful sunset!"

A few days later, he became dehydrated, and Sharon took him to the hospital. His hemoglobin was fine. "All he needs is fluids," a doctor reassured them. After two days on an IV drip, he was released. But as Jim was putting on his jacket, a nurse ran up with a loaded syringe.

"What are you doing?" Sharon asked. "He needs some Procrit," the nurse explained. But he'd always had Aranesp, Sharon objected. "Honey," the nurse explained, "we can't afford that expensive stuff." And with that, she injected Jim with 40,000 units of Procrit.

Sharon felt an itchy intuition. But she kept silent and took him home. That Friday evening, fifty friends and relatives came over to toast Jim with gifts and cupcakes. They left two hours later, and that's when Sharon witnessed something straight out of a zombie film: her husband's mouth oozing thick, dark blood. He coughed and struggled to breathe. His eyes grew wide with fear. She struggled to comprehend what was happening. Then, she snapped to her senses and dialed 911, begging for help as blood spurted out of Jim's nose and mouth and down his chest, a huge, muddy, scarlet river. Worse, he started coughing up pieces of tumor and lung—then passed out. Sharon fell to her knees and gave her husband CPR until her nose, hair, and mouth were covered in his un-anemic blood. After twenty minutes or so, she looked down at Jim, his eyes frozen in fear, his mouth gaping, his head a Procrit halo of sputum and bloody chunks.

Now, two months later, she pulled into the Holiday Inn in Gaithersburg and parked. Walking into the lobby, she found a woman at the registration desk. "I'd like to speak to this committee," she said. Fortunately, there was one spot left, and Sharon took it. But she would have only three minutes to comment, and if she went over, they'd cut off the microphone. She nodded and walked into the grand ballroom, where 350 people were crammed into a low-ceilinged, mustard-colored room.

The panel members sat at tables in the front, cordoned off as if they were royalty. Today's agenda had many items, but the underlying question was simple: Should epo be withdrawn as a therapy for cancer patients?

One oncologist, Dr. Bruce Redman, stomped his foot at some of the plain English flying around. "Just because these are public meetings, the term 'tumor progression' should not be used," he said. He had an aversion to the term and preferred the medical jargon "decreased risk of local control."

However, some colleagues preferred the plain talk. "I'm really struck at the very protracted timeline for an assessment of safety," said Dr. Judith Kramer of Duke. Beginning in 2001, the drug companies had been enrolling patients in twelve safety studies. "Yet those trials were either just being submitted" or were still unfinished. Why the delay?

An Ortho executive thanked her for the question and proceeded to glissade through some PowerPoint slides. But he didn't answer her query.

Kramer then asked if "physician incentives" were tied to prescriptions, and this time, Joshua Ofman, an Amgen vice president, stood up. "Slide on," he ordered, and launched into an explanation of the "buy and bill model" unique to this country. But he stepped mambo-smooth over Dr. Kramer's question without answering it. She frowned.

One of her colleagues tried to pitch in: "I didn't hear the word 'bundling,'" said Dr. Michael Perry. "It's my impression that discount prices are given when you buy several of the sponsors' products at [once]," he said, describing J&J's and Amgen's sales practices. Doesn't that "influence the rate at which you might prescribe these drugs?"

Ofman sprang up, jig quick. He said that if incentives were used, one would see doctors targeting hemoglobin numbers above 12, or high weekly doses of epo, or some other imaginary thing. He tap-tapped around the issue until Dr. Perry interrupted:

"You ought to be on *Dancing with the Stars*," he said, naming a hit TV show.

"Well, in the current system," Ofman began, but his audience burst out laughing.

"Can you say the word *yes?*" Perry prompted.

"Yes," said Ofman, blushing, and then sat down.

All of this shocked Sharon, who was appalled at the deferential treatment accorded the panelists and corporate men, even when they were dissembling. "Why are they allowed to dominate the daylong meeting with their incomplete trials, while patients and others who *know* these drugs are only given three minutes? Something's wrong here," she thought.

One panelist, oncologist Joanne Mortimer, veered into a serious area. The "elephant in the room is [this]," she said. "Would this committee opt to approve this drug based on what we have heard today?" *Raise your hand if you'd approve epo.*

Not one went up.

After that jaw-dropping moment, the chair called for public comment, and Dr. Charles Bennett stood up. He was widely respected for his independent assessments, which often clashed with the drug sponsors' studies. He was beginning a new meta-analysis of some fifty-two studies that would soon show a more deadly 17 percent chance of dying from these drugs. *Seventeen percent of patient deaths!* But that day, he said: "There is no basic science at all to show" much of anything regarding epo's safety. Bennett then rattled off the hazards ratios from his published epo studies—14 percent deaths among one epo group, 18 percent among another, and 29 percent mortality in a third. He had more to say, but his three minutes were up. Oncologists, a nephrologist, and a few others spoke warmly about the drug and were applauded.

Then it was Sharon's turn. She'd never spoken publicly before and her stomach felt like an aviary with hundreds of wings beating to get out. Wearing the same dark outfit she'd worn to Jim's funeral, she said, "I'm not a scientist or a doctor. I'm a mail carrier," and she skimmed Jim's story.

"My husband of thirty-seven years took well to his treatment and could have lived six months or longer," she said. Instead, he bled to death four hours after he got 40,000 units of Procrit. *We were never told of warnings.* "We have to sign a HIPAA law [form]. We sign for prescriptions at the pharmacy. Even McDonald's tells you their coffee is hot." *Why don't you require patients to sign informed consent papers before giving us this drug?*

She wondered if her husband would still be alive if he had not been injected with epo. "We don't know," she said. "But that should have been his choice, not the doctor's."

As the widow walked back to her seat, the room was hushed; some panelists squirmed in their seats. Sharon sat down and said aloud, "Dang, no one applauded *me* for my speech."

Her words were still hanging in the air as the panelists started to vote. By 8–5, ODAC recommended requiring informed consent procedures for every patient placed on the drugs. It voted 9–5 to exclude breast and head and neck cancer from epo therapy. It had the chance to take the drugs off the market, but voted 13–1 to keep selling them. Should the label warn against using this iffy drug on patients who might be cured? Yes, they voted 11–2. In other words, epo should be given only to those with no hope of living. Hardly a ringing endorsement, and at one point, Dr. Kramer wailed, "How long do patients have to continue to be exposed to a drug that we're not sure is safe?"

When the meeting broke up, Dr. Keegan gathered her papers and looked up. She could see Sharon Lenox walking out the door. She thought back to that day in 1993 when the FDA had first approved epo for cancer patients, despite the clinical trial that had indicated that the drug could fertilize tumors.

Just then, a reporter Keegan knew approached her. Their eyes met and Keegan's face crumpled. All the regulator could say was: "I wish we had known about this fifteen years ago."

—⁊⁊—

Wᴴɪʟᴇ the nation was growing more aware of Procrit's dangers and "J&J's sharp practices," as Rep. John Dingell called them, the courts were not. On January 28, 2008, Judge Zobel made a devastating ruling in the Duxbury case. He had not been the first to file an off-label claim; Blair had been. And Duxbury had failed to prove a single claim of fraud. "It was a horrible decision," said Jeb White, head of Taxpayers Against Fraud, a nonprofit dedicated to supporting whistle-blowers. To begin with, Duxbury had beaten Blair to the courthouse by six weeks; plus Blair's case had died, making it irrelevant to Duxbury's claim, according to the byzantine rules of *qui tam* law. Also, Duxbury had been specific in his claims, listing precisely how Ortho had induced Drs. Naggy, Von Hoff, and others to commit fraud. But Judge Zobel threw Schlichtmann's *qui tam* case out of her court, handing Posner and Ortho a win.

A few months later, Ortho offered to settle the embarrassing suit for $100,000 but Duxbury wouldn't even consider it. Schlichtmann was crushed by the entire affair and wobbled between enthusiastic despair and profane disgust. By June, he had rallied himself, driven by his stubborn client and his own crusading tendencies. "We're going down fighting, Mark," he told his client and fell to work on writing an appeal.

While the team conferred over the details, the former sales reps scrambled to keep their families together. McClellan was now earning "peanuts" working as a drug "marketer," the lowest rung on pharma's totem pole. He made cold calls, talked up promotions, and basically smoothed the way for a better-paid drug rep to waltz in and seal a deal. His computer signaled every twenty minutes or so, reminding him it was time to make the next overture, and, by five P.M., he had to send a report to a much younger man, confirming that he'd met his quota. The sixty-year-old was weary of earning a quarter of what he'd made ten years before. He yearned for the day when he could draw his Ortho pension and get on Medicare's roll.

He talked to Duxbury almost every week, and they groused about their conditions. "Why don't you come down for the weekend," Mc-Clellan suggested. "We'll take the top off my blue Corvette and race around town together." *Won't we look cool in the custom 1975 classic, with her Edelbrock headers, Cragar wheels, and four-barrel Edelbrock carburetor? Can't you hear the rumble of the engine's race cam beneath us and see the flirty cutout fender skirts?*

"Come on, Mark. We'll have some fun!"

"I can't do that right now," Duxbury said. "My house is about to fall into foreclosure." In 2007 Countrywide Mortgage had started to foreclose on them, and he and Bibi were desperately trying to keep their house. A financial advisor had told them to "walk away" from their mortgage, but then where would they be? Duxbury couldn't see them living on the streets. Instead, he contacted the lender and wrote Countrywide a heartfelt letter explaining why they'd missed so many payments. Part of the reason stemmed from Duxbury's mounting health problems; he also found it hard to pay $700 a month for private health insurance. If only his disability request would come through, then he'd be good. But who knew when that would be?

Both men, meanwhile, had become notorious in the small world of drug reps. *The Wall Street Journal* article had raised their profiles, and now some of their old friends and enemies were watching their legal battle with zest. Their attention wasn't all welcome, however. In online chat rooms, some Ortho reps ridiculed the pair and their *qui tam*. "Like a prison inmate who reads law manuals, Mr. D. believed that 'learning the law' made him able to challenge it. McClellan was just a bitter & stoic [*sic*] old man who wasn't able to change," wrote one poster. "That's what happens to old smelly fish."

"McDux, the latest superhero tag team," another poster called them. "What [will] he do, use a saxophone to stop corruption? Give us a break!"

Within days, a chat-room brawl broke out, replete with figurative headlocks and sucker punches. One clever poster stood to the side, reciting "The J&J Reality Credo: We must strive to reduce costs in order to maintain a high stock price. . . . Customer orders must be serviced [with] bundled products, rebates and performance kickers. . . . In private, we can screw [our employees] when they least expect it. . . ." and so on. "Wow," thought Duxbury, "this guy is even more cynical than me."

Both relators began to suffer bouts of clammy paranoia; Duxbury fielded strange, cryptic e-mails from unknown senders and, one day, found fresh footprints at the side of his house. McClellan began to suspect that someone was trying to hack into his computer and bought a new one, along with a high-tech security system. Schlichtmann was no help. The attorney wouldn't return their calls or e-mails for days or even weeks. Perhaps he'd lost interest and was on to the next exciting case; maybe he was suffering a bout of rudeness or was lost in one of his periodic funks, during which he'd "hide under his rock," as Duxbury would say.

Then, a small miracle occurred: Renee and Sojie were fighting so much that the older woman finally threw up her hands. Sojie had nowhere else to go but to her father. The fifteen-year-old moved back in with Duxbury, Bibi, and her stepbrother, Richard. Duxbury was overjoyed. "I never fought for full custody of you because I had such a hard time enforcing my visitation rights," he told his daughter. "But this is great!" Looking into her melancholy eyes, Duxbury could see his child had been through a difficult time. He told her how wonderful she was and how great it was to have her back. In time, Sojie started to think better of herself, and incidentally, so did he. "I feel reborn," he told McClellan.

Most evenings, he and Sojie would put their heads together over her textbooks, and tenderness would well up inside him. He loved his child in that dumb, helpless, oxlike way that fathers do. When she began studying anatomy, she asked about the sciatic pain he suffered, and they talked about his medicine. When she read about the brain, he shared how his synapses misfired and brought on his caveman depression. Sojie came to understand and even adore her dad, which was no small thing for a teenager. After dinner, when the kids had cleared the dishes and scattered to different corners of the house, Duxbury would sit alone in the dark and listen to the house breathe. He'd hear Sojie chatter to friends on the telephone; he'd keep time as his fifteen-year-old stepson tried to master the strains of some new song; he'd listen to the sounds of his ordinary life curling around the banisters and through the halls, consecrating him and this suburban moment. At those times, Duxbury felt like crying, not necessarily because he was unhappy but because he felt so full. His family was finally home.

Other nights, Duxbury would contemplate the way the modern world was spun into whatever pleasing images the weavers decreed—everything from the institutional Ponzi schemes concocted by mortgage bankers to the racketeering drug operations defended by Washington's high-priced lawyers. Reality no longer consisted of what the average guy could see, touch, or hear. Oh no, it was honed and polished to precise specifications by market researchers, brand experts, and invisible committees. The most defining characteristic of our era, Duxbury decided, was spin.

—◊—

J&J, it seemed, had always been a wizard of spin.

The company had been founded in early 1886 by two brothers, Edward and James Johnson, who had worked as medicinal "travelers" in antebellum days. They'd tried their hands at other jobs, but as the two approached middle age, they had little to show for their efforts. Their older brother, Robert, however, had grown rich as a drug and chemical importer during the heyday of patented medicines, whose secret ingredients often included morphine, opium, and 40-proof alcohol. The Johnson boys saw there was money to be made. So they took over the top floor of an abandoned wallpaper factory in New Brunswick, on the banks of New Jersey's Raritan River, borrowed $1,000, and began manufacturing medicinal plasters and cotton dressings.

The mild-mannered men were no match for their snake-oil competitors, however, and Johnson & Johnson floundered for several months until late 1886, when Robert stepped in. A brash businessman and Wall Street investor, he seized control, infused the company with $100,000, and hired a hundred immigrant laborers. He also added a twist. For years, he'd been taken by the radical ideas of a famous British surgeon, Joseph Lister, who believed that airborne germs were "invisible assassins" and who advocated sterilizing surgical tools. Robert borrowed the doctor's theories and began manufacturing not just mustard packs and corn plasters but also antiseptic dressings "according to Lister's formula." There's no sign that Johnson ever signed a PLA with the British physician, but Lister's name was promiscuously displayed on J&J fumigators, toothpaste, and even Lister's Dog Soap. It also helped that Robert fiercely slashed his price lists to beat his rivals. As he told one traveler, "We have concluded to stick the knife right into the bowels of the plaster business."

Ministering to Americans' pains and illnesses, J&J grew. Over the years, the brothers competed fiercely against the Wyeth brothers' Sun Opium Tablets, Bayer's Heroin Cough Suppressant, and the Parke Davis Cocaine Injection Kit. J&J responded with its own products, and soon dockworkers on the busy Raritan River were unloading shipments of Indian rubber, Tasmanian poppies, and 100,000 pounds of belladonna *a year*. Indeed, J&J was importing so much of the deadly nightshade that Robert decided to grow the exotic plant himself. He even advertised an "extra high grade" of the narcotic to sell only to J&J "friends" at "the highest prices in the world," two dollars a pound, with a limit of three jars per person. Carts and buggies lined up at Johnson's Bellevue Farm across the river from where his factory hummed. Dangerous and addictive ingredients were mixed into J&J's liver poultices, headache compresses, and "female" remedies. Robert no doubt considered J&J a reputable firm, but there was a trace of *Doc Johnson's Travelling Miracle Medicine Show* rolling through his factory floor.

More than most, Robert knew the value of a good ad man. In 1889, he hired a clever pharmacist and copy writer named Fred Kilmer. The son of an Episcopalian preacher, Kilmer made effusive claims in J&J's ads, affixed "Doctor" to his name, and coined catchy names for J&J products, like Mosquitoons for an insect fumigator. He, too, borrowed liberally from others, such as Clara Barton, the nurse and founder of the American Red Cross. Kilmer used her nonprofit group's name for J&J's commercial needs, mailing out his own "Red Cross Messenger" pamphlet that interspersed practical business tips with advertising features about J&J soaps, creams, and ointments. Kilmer encouraged parents to send in photographs of their diapered darlings playing with tins of Baby Powder, a product that he invented.

In 1894, J&J introduced the first of its "kola" preparations that increased stamina and suppressed the appetite. By then, the brothers' self-adhesive belladonna plasters dominated druggists' shelves, with their promises, written in several languages, to cure mothers' headaches and baby's whooping cough. The poisonous treatments often resulted in slurred speech, urinary problems, constipation, convulsions, delirium, hallucinations, and even death. Yet who could prove it?

Robert also capitalized on calamity to enhance profits. Through friends in high places, J&J was able to move medical supplies to the U.S. military during the Spanish-American War of 1898, including a new cloth stretcher to carry the wounded. When the Galveston hurricane of 1900 blew out that town's pharmacies, J&J replaced its company's goods at no charge. After the 1906 San Francisco earthquake and fire, J&J forgave most of the city's druggists' debts and then became the largest donor of supplies. Good deeds translated into smart business and after eight years of chasing fire, war, and rain, J&J's revenues had tripled to an astounding $3 million.

Yet all this was threatened by a growing progressive movement to force "public druggers" to print the ingredients of their "medicines" on the label. The industry fought off the threat. Only tiny North Dakota required that compounds containing morphine, opium, cocaine, hashish, bromine, iodine, or 5 percent of alcohol say so clearly on their tags. Unlucky consumers in all the other states had to guess what was inside those pretty green bottles, and babies continued dying from opium syrups, more children grew addicted to spiked sarsaparilla, and young mothers kept hiding their flasks.

In 1905, *Collier's Weekly* magazine published a muckraking piece that exposed the drug industry's chicanery. "Legislation is the most obvious remedy," it famously wrote. The series so outraged the public that Congress was shamed into passing the first federal drug law, the Pure Food and Drug Act of 1906. That law banned the manufacture and sale of poisonous patent medicines, but it had no teeth. J&J's "Doc" Kilmer claimed to have "devoted time to the passage" of that law, but regulation seemed contrary to the interests of commerce. Kilmer's altruistic devotion may have been smart PR or it may have been all spin. But what's clear is that, law or no law, many harmful drugs remained on the shelves because their peddlers faced no dire consequences.

Still, the muckrackers and rabble-rousers had put all "druggers" on notice. That same year, 1906, Robert Wood Johnson began providing company housing, medical care, and some progressive benefits to the immigrants—mostly Hungarians—who worked in his factories. This engendered enormous loyalty from his employees, and thanks to Kilmer, word spread about the company's benevolence. J&J's kola potions and narcotic cures continued flying out of stores until 1912, when laws finally required all drugmakers to list the contents of their patented products on their labels. Sales of J&J's belladonna poultices and other untested products slowed but didn't quite stop. Only in 1938, when the Food, Drug, and Cosmetic Act passed, did Congress finally put some teeth into its consumer protection laws. And this time, there really were some J&J representatives in the wings helping craft this seminal act: the firm's lawyers at Covington & Burling, which had been formed in 1919 with J&J as one of its first clients, and a charismatic lobbyist, Tommy "the Cork" Corcoran, one of FDR's brain trust.

"Community standards" sagged and old beliefs that arsenic, for one, effectively treated psoriasis or that laudanum safely cured the ladies' "hysteria" fell by the wayside—along with product revenues. The new legislation said that the government no longer needed proof of fraud to stop the sale of a drug; it could seize any drug it suspected of being dangerous, from Mosquitoons to Vino Kolfra. For the first time in U.S. history, the burden of proof shifted to the manufacturers, who had to submit data based on scientific experiments to demonstrate that their drug was safe before it could be sold. Evidence-based science became the rule. In fact, that's how the U.S. pharmaceutical business operated for many years. Mass production of insulin in the 1920s; tests with lifesaving penicillin in the 1930s; the discovery of the antibiotic for tuberculosis in the 1940s; the distribution of miraculous vaccines against polio, measles, mumps, and rubella in the 1950s and 1960s; the wildly popular contraceptive pill in the 1970s; the advent of genetically engineered drugs in the 1980s—all of these innovations boosted America's drug business.

In 1992, when Congress passed the Prescription Drug User Fee Act, it helped grease the skids for faster approval of drugs. Pharmaceuticals began paying the regulator annual fees so the FDA could review their applications quickly. The PDUFA was renewed in 1997, in 2002, and again in 2007, and each time Congress allocated less money to the safety side of drug review and more to the expedited approval section. By 2008, when ODAC was left without any evidence for epo's safety, one scientist said it was time to return to the tenets of 1938 law and to basic science itself.

J&J's campus still lay forty miles southwest of New York City, in New Brunswick. No armed guard appeared as you drove through its gate, and no pretentious driveway swept up to a grand entrance. Two flags—the stars and stripes and New Jersey's gold banner, which depicted the goddess Liberty—waved in front of the sixteen-story white tower that vaguely resembled a giant tin of Band-Aids. The twenty-acre campus was bordered on one side by the mighty Raritan River, on another by Rutgers University, and was skirted by the rolling green lawns. Inside its buildings friendly, smiling people bustled about and a corridor of photographs testified to J&J's philanthropy in such far-flung places as Malaysia and Mumbai. Visitors to J&J's headquarters got "just the impression that Johnson [& Johnson] wanted to create," as a reporter noted in 1924, and it all seemed benevolent, pristine, and humble.

There was still the redbrick power house said to be the last remaining structure from Robert Johnson's era. Up a rise and across a lawn was another brick office, whose quaint porch conjured visions of an "adobe of some alchemist of olden times," as the 1920s scribe said, with its "red peculiar cross, the symbol of the firm's cabalistic (ways), suggestive of the arts and lore of the Rosicrucian. . . . Not an unsuitable first impression."

Only now, not quite a century later, J&J was a health-care goliath that oversaw more than 230 divisions sprawled across 57 countries and sold more than 100 drugs and even more consumer products. Its products affected the lives of a billion people around the world, and its market capitalization was bigger than the gross domestic product of Hungary and Tasmania, combined. It had friends all over the world, including Michael Mukasey, a former partner with J&J's law firm, Patterson, Belknap & Webb.

In 2008, Mukasey vacated his office as U.S. attorney general and as chief of the DOJ, and bid his staff good-bye. How would J&J fare in the new administration? Duxbury, McClellan, and Schlichtmann had high hopes that the new attorney general would put things right.

24

The Burden

2009 to 2010

SCHLICHTMANN'S eyes scanned the horizon for an omen. Crossing the snow-covered street outside the federal courthouse in Boston, he glimpsed the blue patch poking through the gray sky and thought, "A break in the storm, good sign." Boston was in the midst of one of its coldest winters ever and parts of the area had been buried in eight-foot snowdrifts for the last few days. Schlichtmann had been anticipating his day at the First Circuit Court of Appeals for months, and his team had arrived yesterday to watch him argue Judge Zobel's disastrous opinion. Friday morning, January 9, 2009, had dawned hopefully with sun streaming through spools of heavenly lamb's wool. But it was 26 degrees outside, and he was a superstitious lawyer who needed a stronger sign than a respite from stormy weather.

Schlichtmann hurried up the stairs to plead what he believed would be the most important case in his career, *U.S. ex rel. Duxbury and McClellan vs. Ortho Biotech.* His retinue lagged behind, struggling to keep up without slipping in the slush. They reached the courthouse rotunda and passed the guards and vestibules. While waiting for the elevator, Duxbury noticed for the first time the absence of the traditional judicial icons: Why no statue of blindfolded Justitia or painting of King Solomon with his sword? Was that a good sign or a bad one? Duxbury kept his mouth shut and waited next to his attorney.

The room on the fifth floor was so hot and crowded, it felt like a Dutch oven, roasting the supplicants: old men in hats; well-heeled developers; and at least one street-corner junkie. For many, this circuit was the last resort, and some appealers conferred nervously with one another or stared ahead at the arches at the front of the room, puzzling over stenciled swirls. (Good signs or bad?) Probity and restraint reigned here, but at that moment the room crackled with impatience. Schlichtmann slipped off his dark wool coat and took a seat, his long back bent like a bow over his binder. Behind him sat his clients, one dressed in a hemoglobin-colored tie and the other in "lucky" cuff links made of Indian-head copper pennies.

The room waited for the three-judge panel to appear. Schlichtmann had no idea who'd be hearing his case today. Judges take these cases according to a lottery system, and no litigant knew which three judges would adjudicate his case until the robed ones walked through the chamber door. All the fifty-seven-year-old attorney wanted was a fair hearing, even though this court had twice denied him that very thing on other cases.

The first, of course, had been Woburn in 1988.

Then, an unlucky thirteen years later, in 2001, Schlichtmann had squared off a *second* time with the First Circuit. He had begged for relief in his personal bankruptcy, a case wreaked by the Woburn havoc. His court-approved bankruptcy had allowed him to wipe his debts clean, but a collection agency had hounded him for years. Its tactics were so onerous that Massachusetts and Texas had chased the company out of their states. But a First Circuit panel had rejected Schlichtmann's argument in a bizarre ruling that was ridiculed in a respected legal publication and was subsequently reversed.

Now eight more years had elapsed, and today, Schlichtmann had to argue before the circuit for a third time. He watched the judge's chute like a grouse on the first day of open season. Within minutes, that door finally opened, and three wizened men in long ebony robes swept onto the high bench. Schlichtmann all but gasped. "Oh my God," he thought. "Is this a sign from the universe that I'm about to get screwed?"

Sitting in the middle of the bench was his nemesis, seventy-six-year-old Judge Juan R. Torruella. The man with the walrus mustache was the same judge who had ruled against Schlichtmann in his two other appeals cases. The attorney's heart sank as he braced himself for arguments.

When his case was called, Schlichtmann stepped up to the podium and nodded to Judge Torruella. "Hello, Mr. Schlichtmann," the judge replied, smiling pleasantly.

The attorney froze. He could do this one of two ways. Duxbury had been urging him to change his strategy and drop the conciliatory approach. Stop calling Posner, Ortho's attorney and the opponent, "my brother," his client had urged. "You're too damn nice." The lawyer had held back partly because of criticism he'd received for his youthful arrogant behavior. He had once thought nothing of arguing with a judge and openly disrespecting his opponent when he believed they were wrong or, worse, lying. He'd gotten a reputation for that over the years, though not all of it was fair. All the notoriety surrounding Woburn had made Schlichtmann a boldface name, but it had turned him into a lightning rod too.

As he stood in front of the judge, wavering, Duxbury tried to beam him a message: *Go for the jugular, Jan.*

The attorney took a deep breath and prepared to draw blood. "The district court was wrong," he began. "These two gentlemen were, in fact, the first to blow the whistle on one of the largest Medicare frauds in history." The forty-eight-year-old Duxbury felt a low-level electrical current run up the back of his neck, just as sixty-year-old McClellan threw an elbow into his ribs. "This dosing scheme threatened the lives of hundred of thousands of patients and may have led to the unnecessary deaths of tens of thousands [of people]," he told the judges, "and resulted in U.S. taxpayers paying billions of dollars in fraudulently obtained Medicare . . . claims." As his voice rose, his mind raced: "Will Judge Torruella rule against me this time too?"

By then, his wife, Claudia, had snuck into the courtroom, dressed in slacks and a red embroidered jacket. The last time she'd seen her husband in front of a judge was twenty-one years before, when her then boyfriend had appealed the Woburn case. She had attended that hearing to give him moral support, but now the petite mother guided the couple's two sons into a row. Twelve-year-old Zack and thirteen-year-old Max listened as their father argued a case he'd been talking about for months. It was a way to teach a larger life lesson, said Claudia, and later, Schlichtmann added, "I wanted the kids to see how their father tried to stand up for something he believed was right, no matter what a court might say." It was the first time the boys had seen Dad in action.

Schlichtmann spoke passionately, his long arms flapping, and his body rocking back and forth. Here was a man with nothing to lose, making a last-ditch effort to save what he called his biggest case ever. He had to argue the public disclosure rule and the off-label claim, and dismiss any doubt that the Duxbury case had been first to file. He had to focus on all the technicalities, when it was the broad outlines of this case that electrified him: how Ortho bribed oncologists, rigged phony medical trials, pushed higher, illegal doses, and abetted billions of dollars in false Medicare claims. Then there were the deaths. He thought, "A lot of people haven't even heard of these problems, so they're still getting Procrit." But he didn't actually say that to the court.

Posner, dressed in a dapper pinstripe suit, got up to respond. He essentially repeated the argument he'd made in Zobel's courtroom eight months earlier, only in clearer sentences. He began citing rules such as (e)(3) and 9(b). The off-label claim, he said, was related to the Food, Drug, and Cosmetic Act, while the AWP claim was Medicare fraud, and this complaint didn't distinguish between the two. He talked with the lulling precision of one practiced in delivering eviscerating blows, claiming that the dearly deceased Blair suit alleged the same thing as this not-quite-dead *qui tam*. "Duxbury literally copies lots of sentences from the Blair complaints," Posner said with a flourish.

"Great," Duxbury thought. "Here we are being called plagiarists by a bunch of murderers."

Not to be left out, the DOJ had filed its brief too. But again, it simply wanted to hold its place in line if it ever decided to pursue this case. Dressed in a business suit, Yavelberg answered questions, but in a slip of the lip, she called the whistle-blowers "tipsters," as if they had done little more than alert the schoolteacher's wife that someone had made off with the rolling chalkboard. That choice of word, more than anything else she said, suddenly explained a lot, thought Duxbury. "The reason the DOJ hasn't joined our case is because they don't take us seriously." *Tipsters indeed!*

—⁓—

AFTER the hearing, the Duxbury contingent made their way to a hotel bar, only this time it was an empty, dimly lit pub with no celebratory happy hour. It was a little before noon, and the smaller group teetered between a steady patter and a worried silence. Duxbury, McClellan, and Simmerly ordered sandwiches while their attorney lunched on fish. "Did you think I was clear?" Schlichtmann asked his clients. "Did I do okay?" He had asked his wife the same questions, but she had studied his exhausted-looking face without really answering. She'd lived with him long enough to know that courts could be maddening, and she didn't want to give her husband any false hope since the crash of disappointment would wallop the entire family.

But here in the hotel bar, Schlichtmann listed all the reasons why Torruella and his peers should rule in his favor, his long fingers and spatula-shaped hands stirring the air. His listeners chuckled, but the undercurrent of uncertainty dragged them down.

Then, Schlichtmann drove the hour up the coast to have dinner at home. Duxbury and his doppelgänger reminisced about their rep days and how they had once taken over entire hotel floors, racing each other down gilded staircases. *Thumpeta thumpeta thumpeta.* Now the two men poked their heads into an old watering hole and asked the bartender if he'd ever heard of Jan Schlichtmann. "Oh, yeah," said the man. "Last I heard, he was somewhere in Hawaii, being a bum."

"Well, let me bring you up to speed," Duxbury said, and laid out his attorney's current whereabouts and his latest case. Impressed, the bartender bought the two men another round, and Doppel and Gänger toasted to Schlichtmann and his latest ill-fated lawsuit.

At dinner, Simmerly joined the two co-relators, and the three weighed their chances for success. McClellan didn't think they'd win this round, Simmerly didn't see how they could lose, and Duxbury was of two minds. "Well, Deano, if you're right and we lose, we can park ourselves on your patio and turn up your stereo really, really loud and play 'Don't Fear the Reaper,'" he said, naming a Blue Oyster Cult song. Duxbury then gripped the table and grimaced, as if stereo woofers were about to blow him away. Simmerly laughed. McClellan, a Johnny Cash fan, was unfamiliar with that particular tune. But he nodded affably and said "Okeydoke." It was agreed.

Later that night, Schlichtmann slipped away from his family dining table and surreptitiously called his client for what Duxbury dubbed "Jan's therapy session." The anxious attorney wanted to talk about the case again and endlessly refigure the odds against them—and their chances for success. At one point, Duxbury needed to get something off his chest. "I'm like a rock climber, Jan. As long as I can see my next move, I can keep going, one step at a time. That way," he said, "I don't get depressed."

But he needed to know how far Schlichtmann was willing to go. "What happens if we lose the appeal?"

"If that happens, we'll ask for a hearing from the full First Circuit court," the lawyer replied immediately. "And if that fails, we'll take it to the Supreme Court." Duxbury felt relief, but now Schlichtmann was all fired up. "Mark, I'm so proud to be involved with you and this case." *Sure, I want to win, who doesn't?* "But if we lose, it won't be because we didn't give it our all." Win, lose, or draw, Schlichtmann was determined to pursue this thing until there was nothing left to do. "This is without a doubt the best moment in my legal career.

"I love this case."

That was all Duxbury needed to hear.

—〰—

WHILE waiting to hear from the court, the four men coped with their rising stress in varying ways. In Prides Crossing, Schlichtmann rose at four A.M. to work in his office by the sea. In Tucson, McClellan drank a little more than usual, and in Gig Harbor, Duxbury went on the wagon and tried to keep the blues at bay. But something had shifted in Boston. Suddenly, it wasn't so much about winning this case anymore as it was about telling this story—again and again if necessary. "Somebody needs to be held accountable," said Duxbury.

—⁂—

IN May, Duxbury finally received notice that he qualified for disability under Social Security. "Hallelujah!" he shouted. He reaped more money than he had since his golden days at Ortho fourteen years ago: a $20,000 lump sum; the promise of a steady $2,000 check every month; some funds for his dependent, which he intended to save for Sojie; and a place on the rolls of government health insurance. He felt like Neptune, lord of the soggy realms, and grabbed a conch shell he had found years ago during a sales junket to a tropical isle. He blew the beach wind instrument like a trumpet, but it sounded low and muffled. "Just as well," he thought. He didn't need the neighbors calling the cops over some domestic disturbance.

Bibi was relieved by the extra income. But the tension at home didn't dissipate. The couple fought about money, the kids, and the Ortho case. After one nasty row, Duxbury showed up on Simmerly's porch tossing out a pun. "It's love among the ruined at my place," he said. The two passed a few companionable hours together; then Duxbury drove home. Later, he decided to spend his windfall fixing up the homestead and painted the kitchen a bright coral, the living room a marine blue, and the foyer an oyster shade. To Bibi, it looked like a day-care center. But when her husband's back gave out, she relented. He chose the carpet, trashed the old couch, and bought some Ikea furniture. He also bought himself an electric guitar with as many custom features as a rock star's.

In August, Duxbury sent the two kids to a relative's house for a few days and took his wife to the end of the earth. It was Bibi's birthday and they needed time alone together. They tossed their bags and CDs into the car and motored south to one of the more spectacular spots in the country. The 400-mile-long Oregon coast is protected by rocky headlands and, in some places, pillowed by sand dunes. They passed Astoria, once a camp for the Lewis and Clark expedition and later a fur trading post of New York baron John Jacob Astor. Victorian houses, operating canneries, and other remnants of the nineteenth century poked up. But Duxbury kept driving until he reached the shores of Cannon Beach. He pulled into a lodge, unpacked their bags, and set out to explore.

When Mark was a boy, his mom and dad would load the family into their aluminum Airstream and steer the silver torpedo down the highway. One summer, they set down their trailer here on Cannon Beach and popped up the awnings. While the rest of the family made camp, the tow-haired Mark changed into his bathing suit and ran out to Haystack Rock. At 235 feet tall, it was the third largest intertidal rock in the world, and it teemed with marine and bird life. At its feet were orange starfish, green sea anemones, and purple barnacles, and its crown was festooned with nests of baby falcons and puffin chicks. It was irresistible to the bucktoothed boy, and depending on the ocean's mood, he'd find a foothold on the monolith and start scampering up. Seagulls would scream and drop guano on his slippery climb, cormorants would circle his head without a peck, while tufted puffins would cry as if daring him to continue. He'd climb that craggy ladder until he couldn't go any farther. Turning out to sea, he'd holler at the wheeling birds then stand shivering on a ledge. He'd study the waves below. The tide had to be just right, the wind calm, and his timing absolutely perfect. When he felt the forces align, he'd fling out his arms and dive. The wind would whip his face, the birds would trace his arc, and he'd hit the cold surface and plummet down. For a second, his world would go silent, his vision clouded by churning sand and seaweed. He'd get his bearings and, just before his lungs burst, would kick off the bottom and resurface, jubilantly sucking air.

At forty-nine, however, he was saddled with a bad back and weak bones. He didn't dare attempt such a foolhardy feat, at least not on Haystack Rock. But he recounted the story for Bibi, and she marveled that he never cracked his skull. That morning they held hands and walked the beach. They slipped into a nearby forest, venturing a few yards in until they found a restroom. Bibi went inside, while Duxbury rested near a boulder. When his telephone rang, he almost didn't answer it. But it was Schlichtmann, and it had been eight months since they'd last seen each other, after the Appeals Court argument. Duxbury answered, bracing himself for bad news.

"We fucking won!" yelled Schlichtmann. His next few words were so garbled, Duxbury had to ask him to repeat.

"We broke through the barrier." Schlichtmann could hardly contain himself. "The Appeals Court ruled in our favor. I can't believe it myself, but Judge Torruella actually did the right thing this time!"

Duxbury sat on the boulder. As he listened to the ecstatic voice on the other coast, Duxbury learned that he *had* pled with "sufficient particularity under Rule 9(b)." The court said he could now try to prove that J&J and Ortho had paid doctors with drugs, discounts, honoraria, and other kickbacks for their Procrit business. Duxbury didn't have to show every fraudulent invoice before going to trial either. "The government has evidence of Medicare fraud right there in its file cabinets," said Schlichtman. The court said that the whistle-blower simply has to *tell* the government about alleged fraud.

It wasn't a total victory: McClellan was still not a co-relator, even though the Appeals Court had hinted that it would have considered a plea to reinstate him. Nor could Duxbury try his off-label promotion claim since his fifteen-word phrase hadn't developed the facts as had Blair's. But Duxbury's case could move to trial with all his kickback claims, making Schlichtmann deliriously happy.

"Hell, everything in this case is a kickback, no matter what you call it," he shouted. "This is huge!"

The case had risen from the dead. The Appeals Court even rejected the DOJ's own arguments against Duxbury. The government had said that pubic disclosure preempted a whistle-blower from bringing *qui tam* charges, but the court said no. *Read the statute.* Anyone with firsthand knowledge can bring a claim even if the fraud has already been publicly disclosed. All in all, the ruling lifted not just Duxbury's case but hundreds of other *qui tam* suits too. Schlichtmann told his client they'd set a precedent. Then he hung up. By the time Bibi emerged from the ladies' room, tears were running down Duxbury's face. He couldn't even speak. She took him in her arms, and he broke down. Finally, he choked out some words: "We won!"

Then, his heart went into atrial fibrillation. That night, against Bibi's wishes, he bought himself a bottle of vodka and mixed a drink to calm himself down.

———※———

LAWYERS are a cliquish group, and among the stalwart few who press *qui tam* cases, the circle is even tighter. So when the decision was posted, word of Duxbury's victory spread like kelp on an artificial reef. From the desert floor of Tucson to the high-rise of Covington & Burling, the decision rocked the participants in the suit. The case would now return to Zobel's court, but Schlichtmann needed to obtain a court schedule, begin discovery, take depositions, and file motions. Why, there might even be a mediated settlement and a decent offering. It looked as if Duxbury had finally gotten what he wanted and the story was about to bust wide open. As it was, the House Committee on Energy and Commerce had already started investigating the off-label promotions of J&J and Amgen and had asked the companies to stop their advertisements, halt payments to doctors, and turn over marketing materials.

The whistle-blower, meanwhile, spent hours working with a freelance reporter on a story for *Vanity Fair*. One day, in the midst of an interview, he asked her: "Is Annie Leibovitz going to take my picture?"

"I don't know," she responded. The glossy magazine usually commissioned color photographic spreads that accompanied its stories. But most of its articles featured the rich and famous, and Duxbury was neither—yet. "I always thought my life story would sound like

Death of a Salesman, but it's turned out to be *Birth of a Whistle-blower.*" But what Duxbury really wanted was his good name restored along with some semblance of fair play. "I guarantee you, once news of this scheme is published, someone will be held accountable," he said. That summer, he prepared himself for trial and a photo shoot. His self-improvement regime consisted of buying new walking shoes to shed some pounds, having his teeth professionally whitened, and switching from Menthols to Lights.

—⁓—

AN October wind kicked up dry mounds of leaves. Stands of ever-greens blurred into the far edge of an inky backyard. Inside the house, shafts of moonlight stole through the blinds. Deeper, in Duxbury's bedroom, a night-light glowed near a baseboard.

Duxbury's sleep apnea was so bad, he needed a breathing mecha-nism to get a decent night's sleep. He wore a mask over his nose and mouth that had a tube connected to a continuous positive airway pres-sure. The whir of the CPAP machine sounded like a ghostly compan-ion whispering near his ear: *Wheeze pant, wheeze pant.* Sometimes those chords gave him nightmares of Ortho pursuing him; other times he dreamed of tackling the beast and the steady respirating rhythm lulled him to sleep. No one knows where his nocturnal flight took him on October 12. Bibi had fallen asleep in front of the TV. Around mid-night, she climbed the stairs and rolled into bed next to her husband. She noticed that his mask was askew or maybe it had slipped off. She thought of waking him up but fell asleep instead.

The next morning she arose before Duxbury, as usual. Richard went off to class, but Sojie didn't feel well and stayed home from school. At eleven A.M., Bibi went upstairs to check on her husband. "Mark," she said, and gently nudged him. "Mark," she said louder, and pushed him hard. This time, his body felt stiff. She saw that his left arm was purpled. She cried to Sojie for help, and the girl came running up the stairs. When she saw her father lying there lifeless, she screamed. Bibi dialed 911 and tried to administer CPR. But Duxbury's jaw was shut tight. By the time the paramedics arrived, one thing was clear. Duxbury was dead.

—◈—

QUESTIONS of malfeasance surrounding Procrit began piling up. An elderly woman who had terminal lung cancer didn't want to endure any more treatments and moved into a nursing home's hospice program, ready to die. Yet her oncologist ordered twenty Procrit doses and sent them to her at the nursing home. The cache must have been worth $10,000, yet she was never given a single shot. Her grown children and friends wondered: How much profit did the oncologist reap from that Medicare prescription?

A middle-aged woman, diagnosed with lung cancer in her prime, received a Procrit shot one morning and ran chores that afternoon. But later that night, she apparently suffered a heart attack. The nurses were shocked at how quickly she had passed. "That doesn't make sense," one of them told the patient's mother. The patient had paid for each epo dose three times: once with an out-of-pocket payment, again through her private insurer, and once more through her federal taxes that went to Medicare. Even so, the nurse asked the grieving mother to send back the daughter's unused Procrit vials, which she did.

Had the daughter died naturally? Or had she been killed by the effects of Ortho's aggressive marketing studies? This and other anecdotes never made it into the pages of a medical journal. No detective ever showed up; no photographs were ever taken or else they were lost; and potential witnesses were allowed to slip away before they could be questioned. The deputies who arrived to remove the corpses pronounced death without ever suspecting foul play; therefore, county coroners never performed the autopsies. These were sick people with failed kidneys and malignant tumors, and what ordinary person would consider an FDA-approved drug as the prime suspect in 17 percent of these deaths? Those tinkling glass Procrit vials were either tossed or shipped.

At Christmastime in 2009, the FDA finally released epo guidelines to the public. Dialysis patients could still receive low doses of the drug. But only terminally ill cancer patients with no hope of living six months could be injected. Even then they had to sign a consent form. For a former miracle drug, it was quite an indictment.

Posner, meanwhile, appealed Duxbury's Appeals Court victory and asked the U.S. Supreme Court to hear him. It was a long shot, but both sides tried to drum up support for their separate causes.

Schlichtmann and McClellan returned to Washington, D.C., haunting the marble corridors of the DOJ and trying to see someone at the attorney general's office. "I feel more earnest about the case now that Mark is gone," McClellan told his lawyer. "Mark spent the last ten years of his life doing this, and we owe it to him." Schlichtmann agreed and unleashed his manic brand of energy. Posner had become a skilled adversary in pharmaceutical *qui tams,* billing J&J about $1 million a year on the Duxbury case. He moved comfortably through the federal halls, where he had more friends in the U.S. Attorney General's Office than Schlichtmann did. One of them was the AG himself.

In 1999, during the Clinton administration, Posner had worked at the DOJ under Eric Holder, then the deputy attorney general. During Holder's tenure, the DOJ issued its guidelines on the criminal prosecution of corporations, and on the use of the False Claims Act in health care. Two years later, both men returned to Covington & Burling, where they parlayed their experience and contacts into new business. In November 2001, the two cowrote a report warning Merck, Pfizer, and their other clients about "The Feds' Increasing Focus on the Pharmaceutical Industry." They and other lawyers advised J&J about how to manage their mounting number of *qui tam* suits (over drugs such as Risperdal and Ortho Evra), accusations of executive criminal behavior (as in the cases of Michael Dormer and Robert John Dougall), and problems with tainted or defective products (including Children's Motrin and DePuy hip replacements).

In 2009, Eric Holder left Covington & Burling to become U.S. attorney general and head of the DOJ. Holder no doubt signed an ethics pledge and promised to recuse himself from certain pharmaceutical cases. But, in late 2010, Sen. Charles Grassley grew worried about the

DOJ's stagnant number of criminal prosecutions under Holder. Health-care fraud was pegged at $100 billion to $400 billion a year, yet in fiscal year 2009 the DOJ had filed twenty-one *fewer* fraud cases than the prior year, when George Bush had been in office. And many of Holder's legal colleagues saw nothing wrong with him shuttling between the private and public spheres of justice. In a December 17, 2010, letter, Grassley told Holder and the secretary of the Department of Health and Human Services, Kathleen Sebelius, that he had serious questions about how they were spending taxpayer money "to combat criminal health care fraud." It looked as if Holder had a conflict of interest bigger than Jan Schlichtmann's beaked nose.

That's what McClellan saw on his trip to the nation's capital. He couldn't help but notice how thin the walls were between government authority and corporate power. "I thought this kind of stuff was unethical. But here, it seems so blatant!" The revolving door between the highest levels of public office and private corporations was spinning so rapidly, it was hard to tell who was representing whom. McClellan's head hurt just thinking about it.

Neither the AG nor the DOJ made a stand for Duxbury against J&J that year. But then again, neither did the Supreme Court. The high bench declined to hear J&J's case against the relator, which kicked Duxbury's case back to district court. Months passed and the eighty-year-old Judge Rya Zobel seemed to have forgotten all about it.

Then, in September 2010, Zobel made one of the more bizarre rulings in *qui tam* law. The statute of limitations had already shrunk Duxury's claims incidents within a small nine-month period from November 1997 to July 1998; Schlichtmann had to prove Ortho's criminal acts in that small window. Then, Zobel cut the suit alleging a national, long-running $6 billion fraud scheme down to about seven counts in the Seattle area.

The decision stunned the close-knit world of *qui tam* lawyers. "It's the narrowest ruling on the books," said Jeb White of Taxpayers Against Fraud. The courts had already ruled that Duxbury was the original source of the nationwide allegations, and that he'd been specific in his claims. Yet Zobel had arbitrarily shrunk his national case to a tiny section of the Pacific Northwest. "You can't limit a whistle-blower to that extent," said White. "It undercuts the government's fraud-fighting efforts."

Zobel had created a nightmare for the DOJ too. Her parochial ruling opened the door for Procrit whistle-blowers from Sacramento, Dallas, Des Moines, and hundreds of other cities around the nation. Following her lead, it would take decades for orphans and widows to recoup the medical funds they'd lost to J&J's alleged scheme.

Schlichtmann had already lost his star witness and crusader client. "Now I've been handed an absurdity for a case." He spewed forth an impressive string of blasphemies that ended on a note of surrender. "The judge has taken every opportunity to kill this case, and by God, I think she's finally done it!" He despaired of ever getting a fair hearing.

—⚌—

On J&J's campus sits a large sculpture of a mother cradling her baby. It is located near J&J's gleaming white tower and the brick pump house left over from the early days. Created by the British sculptor Henry Moore, the artwork was installed in 1986—the year the federal whistle-blower law was revamped. The bronze statue nestles under some elms, and when the afternoon breeze blows through the leaves, light and shadow dance upon the primordial shape. Back when Duxbury was selling $3.6 million worth of Procrit and flying to New Brunswick for meetings, he'd stroll out to the corporate gardens and admire the piece. Moore once said that the secret of life was "to have a task, something you devote your entire life to . . . something you bring everything to every minute of the day. . . . And the most important thing is, it must be something you cannot possibly do."

Perhaps Duxbury already knew this secret of life. He had devoted most of his adult life to chasing an elusive goal. But he had been stopped in the middle of his third act. He never got to finish his story. By early 2010, his autopsy had come back, and it showed that the night he died, he had Big Pharma coursing through his veins. He had Lipitor and Tricor for high cholesterol; albuterol for asthma; diltiazem, digoxin, and warfarin for his atrial fibrillation and heart ailment; and Topiramate and Trileptal to help soften the edges of his bipolar disorder. He'd been prescribed methadone and Oxycontin for pain, and on his last night, he had mixed himself a vodka tonic. His cause of death was "acute intoxication by the combined effects of ethanol, oxycodon, oxcarbazepine, methadone"—in short, drugs and alcohol, a lethal but common nightcap not just for whistle-blowers but for many Americans.

When Duxbury died, nearly half of the country was taking at least one prescription drug—150 million people—including one out of every five children. The licensed drug business was an $800-billion-a-year global industry that routinely peddled insufficiently tested medicine in unsafe ways. Incredible as it seems, the FDA was still waiting for safety studies, epo was still a blockbuster with more companies selling $11 billion a year, and Amgen and J&J were still feuding in arbitration. Yet Duxbury's case had still to get a trial. Maybe his *qui tam* was flawed from the very beginning; maybe he had pleaded with more idealism than expertise; maybe his attorneys had dropped the ball. On those days when the invading gloom enveloped him in brutal honesty, Duxbury wondered if he himself was his own worst enemy.

Five months before Duxbury died, he finally took off his Ortho ring. His journey had started with a quest for that shiny piece of jewelry, beginning in the early days at Ortho, when Duxbury had bounded through the linoleum-floored hospitals spreading Procrit's tidings. He had believed in the drug. He had striven to earn the respect of his clients, peers, and superiors. That inch-thick gold band had spurred him on to achieve many big, seemingly impossible feats and had led him to a seat at the champions' table.

For the longest time, he assumed the signet ring symbolized a balanced moral order, in which a basic set of ethics ran alongside his pack's social values. Duxbury had felt the heft of the ring and had worn it throughout his depositions and testimony in the *Amgen vs. Ortho* arbitration, his misadventures on the AWP case, his wrongful-termination suit, and his own inglorious *qui tam*. He'd always known the ring wasn't 24-karat gold. But by 2009, he was coming to see the

10-karat trinket for what it was—the last unexamined clue in a long trail of scattered but invisibly connected stones.

"That ring used to mean something to me," he confessed. "But it's odious to me now."

In a prescient note of May 5, 2009, Duxbury wrote, "Looks like I'm entering the ranks of the former crusaders sometime next week." He was tired of his quest. "I've done everything I could to make up for what I did at Ortho," he said. He figured epo had killed half a million people over the years, yet he couldn't comprehend why the drug was still on the market, approaching $100 billion in global sales. Whatever debt he felt he owed to society, he had repaid in spades, and if he couldn't get a full pardon, then he'd take a get-out-of-jail card.

Duxbury no longer wanted the stain of Procrit gold on his hand. Yet he dared not throw away his old talisman. He decided to pass on the burden of the black-edged ring to someone else. "Maybe you can play a role in shedding light on this real-life crime," he told the next one in line. Duxbury had devoted himself to something he could not possibly do, and it was time for someone else to shoulder the load. He wasn't giving up entirely; he'd be around to help. "You, on the other hand, have agreed to perform the hardest job of all." He handed off the ring, along with the papers, photos, and records from his extraordinary, twenty-year-long odyssey, so that his story could be told. Before Duxbury left, he said: "You're on the inside of it now. Maybe you can do something I couldn't to ensure that justice really will prevail."

Notes

Much of the book's material comes from hundreds of interviews conducted from 2007 to 2011 with Duxbury, McClellan, Simmerly, and Schlichtmann. The author tried to verify each source's recollection with photos, another interviewed source, or supporting documents. Some additional sources from each chapter are listed below but not all.

Prologue

Interviews with Sharon Lenox, daughter Joanne Groseclose, and son-in law Dan Groseclose, including those of November 13, 2008, and December 2, 2008; incident report from Anne Arundel County Police Department, January 12, 2008, medical report of January 8, 2008, and records from radiation oncologists at the Tate Cancer Center and Baltimore Washington Medical Center.

PART I
Chapter 1: Meet and Greet

J&J reception: picture of Nicole Miller ties; brochure of Wyndham Princeton Forrestal Hotel and Conference Center, formerly called the Merrill Lynch Conference and Training Center; Longstreet's online biography sheet; his speech recalled by McClellan, Duxbury, and sales rep Henry Lovett; January 26, 1996, deposition of Dennis Longstreet from *Charise Charles Ltd. v. Amgen Inc.*; McClellan résumé; Duxbury résumé; March 10, 2003, declaration of Duxbury in *Mark E. Duxbury v. Ortho Biotech*, Superior Court of Washington, King County; event roster of March 1, 1992.

History of epo: *The $800 Million Pill: The Truth Behind the Cost of New Drugs*, by Merrill Goozner (Berkeley: University of California Press, 2004); Michel Rosen, "The Birth of Biotech," The Wisconsin Technology Network LLC, August 25, 2004; *Science Lessons: What the Business of Biotech Taught Me about Management*, by Gordon Binder and Philip Bashe (Boston: Harvard Business Press, 2008).

Oil shale: http://ostseis.anl.gov/guide/oilshale/index.cfm; Robert Langreth, "Biotech Behemoth," *Forbes* magazine, January 10, 2005; Amgen Factsheet, http://amgen.com/media/fact sheet/; "Amgen: Up from Biotech," *BusinessWeek* magazine, March 18, 2002; interview with Richard Erwin, November 7, 2008.

J&J history: *Robert Wood Johnson, Gentleman Rebel*, by Lawrence G. Foster (State College, Pa.: Lillian Press, 1999). Winnie-the-Pooh tie: *Ortho Pharmaceutical v. Amgen* arbitration, deposition of Thomas Amick, July 28, 1995.

"Amgen, J&J, and division of market," described in Judge Frank McGarr opinions in *Ortho v. Amgen*. Duxbury's December 2, 1998, deposition. Details about Providence St. Peter Hospital: Hospital-data.com/hospitals/Providence St. Peters; also interview with Loretta Green at St. Peter, February 19, 2010, and Providence Web site.

Tom Amick letter to sales force and "Physician Supply & Surgical Supply," winter 1992.

Duxbury family background and photos from Faye Duxbury, October 15, 2009, among other interview dates; declaration in *Duxbury v. Ortho Biotech*, Superior Court of the State of Washington for the County of King, March 10, 2003 ("wrongful termination case").

Chapter 2: The Deal

Dialogue of Longstreet and Dawson taken from dozens of their letters contained in Vols. I and II of exhibits cited by Amgen in opposition to Ortho's motion for Summary Judgment in *Ortho v. Amgen;* maps and pictures of Ortho's and Amgen's site.

Bicyclists: *From Lance to Landis: Inside the American Doping Controversy at the Tour de France*, by David Walsh (New York: Ballantine Books, 2007). "The Physiological Effects of Two Cycling Drugs," by Mark Cannon; "The EPO Dossier," report issued by Sandro Donati, 1994; interview with FDA's Patricia Keegan, November 12, 2008; Amgen and J&J history from McGarr opinion, April 4, 1990.

"Stamina-Building Drug Linked to Athlete's Deaths," by Lawrence M. Fisher, *New York Times,* May 19, 1991; McGarr's opinion, April 1990.

SF trip: photographs; sales material and Charise Charles flyer of 1992 and deposition of Bennie Thompson, September 14, 1995; Oliver Medlock depositions from July 17, 18, 20, 1995. McGarr about Rathmann opposing cross-license agreements: "Business People," by Lawrence M. Fisher, *New York Times,* October 27, 1988. Binder plays tennis: "Amgen's Ace," *BusinessWeek*, January 10, 2000. List of diseases from April 19, 1989, letter to Amgen's attorney Lloyd Day from Ortho's attorney John Sipos at Patterson Belknap.

"Follow the Pill": Understanding the U.S. Commercial Pharmaceutical Supply Chain," by the Health Strategies Consultancy LLC, March 2005. Drug Distribution Chain: "U.S. Prescription Drug System under Attack," by Gilbert M. Gaul and Mary Pat Flaherty, *Washington Post,* October 18, 2003.

Duxbury's deposition, August 24, 1995, and December 2, 1998; Binder and Longstreet meeting in Miami, March 21, 1991; $164 million payment from Amgen to Ortho and $90 million payment from Ortho to Amgen issued in September 1992, arbitration papers; declaration of Paul Fedoka, March 10, 2003.

National sales and Southwest outperforming Northwest: Duxbury deposition, December 2, 1998; struggling to keep the lights on from Memorandum of Law in Opposition to Amgen's Cross Motion for Summary Judgment, November 1, 1999.

Chapter 3: Medicine Road

CIA history of plausible deniability: "CIA and Assassinations: The Guatemala 1954 Documents," *National Security Archive,* http://www.gwu.edu/~nsarchiv/NSAEBB/NSAEBB4/index.html.

Information on the towns: Wikipedia, and *Oregon & Washington Tour Book* (AAA Publishing, 2009), pp. 173, 198, 199, 205, 281; Energy Northwest (http://www.energy-northwest.com/who/); Longstreet and plausible deniability, deposition of April 27, 1994; Bob Nelson affidavit October 27, 1999; Bill Ball deposition, May 18, 1995; interview with Dr. Charles

Bennett, September 10, 2009; McGarr's April 1990 history of epo; Boykin's bio; Duxbury's declaration of November 12, 1998; Boykin invoice from Charise Charles dated January 27, 1993; Duxbury's deposition of 1995 and 1998; also Carleen Brown's request for Ortho rebate submitted November 19, 1993.

Charise Charles flyer, "Reimbursement Assurance Program," circa September 1992.

Description of conversation between Boykin, Duxbury, and Brown from Duxbury depositions and declarations in *Amgen v. Ortho*; Dr. Balthasar and his Medicine Show devised by an education interpreter from the Ohio Historical Society in Cincinnati, http://www.blm.gov/or/oregon-trail/files/NRDRBalthasar.pdf.

Early reps and elixirs containing alcohol from *The Gentleman Rebel*, and Hofmann description and stories from the same book, pp. 239, 457, 460–2.

Boykin's fourth-floor shipping address: from Charise Charles invoices of November 19, 1992, and February 18, 1993. Also *Tri-City Herald*, March 30, 1988, p. 9, "Dialysis Center Likely New Tenant for Kadlec." Nassif set up account: Duxbury 1998 deposition; Amick letter to Duxbury, January 6, 1993; Duxbury's bonus checks listed in his 1992 compensation sheet.

DDD books for Duxbury from February in *Charise Charles v. Amgen*; also from July 1997 to March 1998; Animal Tests: "Veterinary Spotlight: Abuse with Unknown Perils, *Thoroughbred Times*, January 17, 2004: "CU Vet Researchers Start Clinical Trials of Drug to Combat Feline Anemia," by Roger Segelken, *Cornell Chronicle*, July 21, 2001.

Conversation between Duxbury and hospital people from Al Linggi deposition of September 12, 1995. Memos: Dimino notes; memos between Duxbury, Nelson, and Ball; copies of checks given to St. Joseph.

Chapter 4: Raise the Stakes

Meeting Renee Matson: from Matson's declaration in wrongful termination suit, March 10, 2003; Amick's congratulations memo to groom, May 20, 1993; Duxbury's awards and memos from Amick. "Procrit They Wrote" contest: January 4, 1993, memo to Duxbury from Melanie Baglioni. His $20,000 sales a month from Duxbury 1998 deposition.

John Hess, manager of Minneapolis District, to Bill Ball, memo of February 25, 1993; St. Joe had been among the first dialysis units in the U.S. to buy epo and was a big customer of Amgen: Linggi deposition, September 12, 1995; Putnam Report—Mark Duxbury Territory, June 23, 1993; memo to William Ball from Robert Nelson, with copy to Duxbury.

Description of Linggi conversation from interviews with Duxbury, and September 12, 1995, deposition of Al Linggi *(Ortho v. Amgen);* memos, gifts, and thank-you notes from and to Duxbury and Nelson to Dimino and Linggi, dated December 10, 1992, and December 15, 1992, and check to St. Joseph's Pharmacy from Ortho dated January 20, 1993; St. Joe's called it a "charitable gift," letter from 1994; memos from Duxbury to regional manager Bill Ball and supervisor Robert Nelson, April 16, 1993.

DDD efforts between Duxbury, Bill Ball, and Nelson, from Duxbury deposition, December 2, 1998; February 25, 1993, memo to Ball from John Hess of Minneapolis Division; destroying DDD books, Duxbury deposition, December 2, 1998.

Amgen rep threatened to subpoena Linggi's deal: from Duxbury deposition, 1995. On St. Joseph's Hospital appearance: photographs and *Healthcare Architecture in an Era of Radical Transformation,* by Stephen Verderber and David J. Fine (New Haven: Yale University Press, 2000), pp. 73–77. Duxbury talked to Amick in La Jolla about the forecasts: Duxbury deposition, December 2, 1998.

Chapter 5: The Cancer Indication

FDA cancer approval from Keegan interview and records; St. Peter's, http://www2.providence.org/phs/archives/history-online/Pages/Memorials.aspx.

$25,000 for another fund: DOJ's February 4, 2004, interview with Duxbury. Also Procrit label from 1993. Bicyclists: *From Lance to Landis;* McGarr's history of epo, April 1990.

St. Peter's history with Duxbury: Duxbury deposition, August 25, 1995—the portion of it referring to the Early Purchasing Incentive Program; and memo about the region's business to Nelson from Duxbury, December 4, 1993.

Memorial Clinic: Duxbury deposition, August 25, 1995. Story of Memorial

Clinic and nephrologists sending patients across the street, Duxbury deposition; also Memorial Clinic: "Mid-Twentieth Century Olympia: A Contest Statement on Local History and Modern Architecture, 1945–1975," http:// www.ci.olympia.wa.us/~/media/Files/CPD/Hist-Preservation/MAContext-StatementAPRIL2008reformatted.ashx.

"Defunct Clinic Home to New Doctor Roster," by Lorrine Thompson, *The Olympian,* January 7, 2002. Discussion between Duxbury and Nelson re: patient trial cards: Duxbury statement, April 1999, U.S. ex rel. *Duxbury v. Ortho Biotech,* first amended complaint.

Details of Northwest territory and sales issues from Ball's May 18, 1995, deposition; Ortho's dialysis sales descriptions from McGarr's October 2002 opinion. Explanation of Medicare filings use HCFA Medicare claim form.

Money to St. Joseph outlined in October 26, 1993, memo from Ball to Nelson; Linggi's second check of $20,000, Duxbury deposition of August 18, 2001; letter of thanks from James A. Plourde, director of St. Joe's foundation, written March 3, 1994; memos from Duxbury to Nelson re: St. Joe's, December 4, 1993.

Matson declaration, March 10, 2003. Also, Interim Report of The Guardian Ad Litem in the custody case between Renee Matson and Mark Duxbury, April 19, 2005. Details of Duxbury's sales: January 22, 1994, memo from Nelson, Ball, and Amick; stock contract agreement; Montana trips detailed in 1998 Duxbury deposition.

Chapter 6: Chosen One

Photos of Duxbury's condo; "History of St. Peter's" from Web site, and spwmw.org; http://www.energystar.gov/index.cfm?fuseaction=labeled_buildings.showProfile&profile_id=1001284; architectural details of St. Pete's from "Mid-Twentieth Century Olympia: A Context Statement on Local History and Modern Architecture 1945–1975."

Duxbury's depositions of 1995, 1998; St. Peter payment from memos of 1995; Longstreet deposition, April 27, 1994; March 26, 1993, deposition of Phil Vacchiano of Huntington Artificial Kidney, New York, in *Charise Charles v. Amgen;* Amick, July 28, 1995, deposition in *Ortho v. Amgen;* also February 8, 1996, deposition in *Charlise Charles v. Amgen;* deposition of Mark Johnson, CEO of third-party supplier Chapin Medical, on

August 18, 1994. Dr. Joseph Letteri, CEO of Huntington, deposition, August 4, 1993.

JJHCS info from Scott Bartz; bios of Nelson, Thompson, Longstreet, and Webb.

Barton bio and letter November 2, 1994, March 10, 1995, July 7, 1995.

Interviews with Beth McClellan, December 17, 2008, and April 27, 28, 2010; McClellan photos, event schedule, menus, and other materials; congratulatory letters from Amick to Duxbury March 28, 1994; from Webb and from Longstreet April 5, 1994; Webb kissed him on the cheek: Duxbury deposition, August 18, 2001, p. 105; Rancho Mirage Web site.

Ortho memento book and photographs from McClellan. Duxbury's ring: eyewitness account and description by Thomas Johovic, gemologist, Goleta Jewelers. Nelson says everyone's forecast increased: Duxbury deposition, 1998. Amgen fighting with Ortho over dialysis sales: from McGarr's opinion of October 18, 2002.

Duxbury genealogy history from interview with Alyn Duxbury, January 11, 2010. Amgen documents: monthly summary, April 1993, "Amgen's profit margins are exorbitant. . . ." Memo re: Territorial Update 81804 Hackensack, September 18, 1992.

PART II
Chapter 7: The Deposition

Duxbury landing new business: CMMA account from April 1999 chronology; Duxbury deposition, August 25, 1995. The study of patients by oncologists: "Phase IV timeline study . . . A Two-Year Process." Giving money to St. Joe's to ease financial pain: Barton memo to Duxbury, February 21, 1995. Duxbury's performance: Planning and Review Form for Barton, 1994 to 1995.

Duxbury's deposition in *Charise Charles v. Amgen* of August 1995; history of Patterson Belknap Webb & Tyler; "The Boss," *ABA Journal,* June 1, 2010.

Duxbury chronology of April 1999; bios of Paul Pizzo, Thomas DeRosa, Jerry Linscott; Patricia Buchsel declaration, March 2003, verified in interview March 31, 2011.

Dorie Good's deposition, April 18, 1995, and April 25, 1995, in *Ortho v. Amgen.*

Chapter 8: On the Border

The Most Beautiful Villages & Towns of the Southwest by Joan Tapper (New York: Thames & Hudson). McClellan's and Duxbury's WAR memos from February 14 to 28, 1996; altercation between Duxbury and Renee in Seattle Police Report, July 19, 1994, and court files; Duxbury's personal files disappearing, 1998 deposition; McClellan photos of himself and Duxbury in Tombstone and Tucson.

Duxbury receiving "most improved retail market share" in 1996, 1995 from Duxbury deposition and Barton's letter of April 6, 1996: letter to Duxbury of October 29, 2002; Mooney's letter to Bill Pearson of April 25, 1996, and Mooney's letter to Barton of May 30, 1996; Barton deposition, March 4, 2003, in *Duxbury v. Ortho;* Pearson deposition, September 12, 1995; *Amgen v. Ortho* suit and McGarr's October 2002 opinion.

No study has demonstrated that Procrit improves symptoms of anemia: Procrit Rx List, Internet Drug List. Massive turnover: Duxbury deposition, August 18, 2001. Washing dialysis out of sales figures: Duxbury 1998 deposition.

Wood from April 1999 chronology; El Conquistador pictures and materials; 1996 POA sales rep handouts and booklet; Procrit and Epogen label; Keegan interview, November 2008; Webb's deposition, March 15, 1996, and June 1, 1998, in *Charise Charles v. Amgen* and *Ortho v. Amgen.*

Chapter 9: Blues

"Performance Update and DD analysis" letter, February 24, 1997, from Keith Wood to Duxbury; "Current Performance Rating," March 10, 1997, from Duxbury to Wood; Amick deposition of 1995; J&J employee Mark Sutton interview, October 1, 2008, and November 12, 2009; St. Joe's and Julie Peerboom, from Duxbury deposition 2001; interview with Bibi Duxbury and Richard about music.

Webb's memo, July 24, 1996; FDA site about approval of 40,000 units. Charlotte, North Carolina, meeting: photos and materials; Peter Tattle bio and writings; news reports of Ortho Dematologic.

Chapter 10: Quality of Life

Keith Wood's letter to Duxbury, March 24, 1997; Duxbury's response, April 15, 1997; affidavits from Madigan receptionist Rosie Choiniere, April 7, 1997; a copy of the receptionist's sheet with time and dates of Duxbury and Wood's visit; letter from Duxbury, March 14, 1997, to Lieutenant Ken Bertram; Julie Peerboom's written statement or affidavit of April 8, 1997, used in Duxbury's employment case; Duxbury's response to Wood on visitation rights, April 15, 1997. Swedish grant in Duxbury amended complaint.

"Procrit Epoetin Alfa, Clinical Outcomes: Effectiveness and Safety in the Community Setting, Backgrounder"; in-service training order from Wood to Duxbury, March 24, 1997.

JCO March 1997 article: "Impact of Therapy with Epoetin Alfa on Clinical Outcomes in Patients with Nonmyeloid Malignancies during Cancer Chemotherapy in Community Oncology Practice."

Ortho had no compliance officer or ethics auditor: Duxbury interview with DOJ, February 4, 2004; lack of paperwork on grants, etc., Duxbury's interview, February 4, 2004, at DOJ; Buschel letter; Hilton Dempsey memo of April 22, 1996; "Memorandum of Law in Support of Ortho Biotech's Motion for Summary Judgment," July 30, 1999.

Duxbury deposition, August 25, 1995, and December 2, 1998.

Note to Gelbman (draft), April 8, 1997; e-mail to Gelbman, April 9, 1997; Gelbman's response, April 11, 1997; complaint to personnel from Duxbury; state of Washington unemployment office.

Chapter 11: Gaslighting

Vicki Boyd interview, March 10, 2009, and Duxbury notes and records; Boyd deposition in termination suit, November 25, 2002; billing slips, Metra Health Benefits bills for 1996 and 1997; Kemper National Services, June 17, 23, August 6, 1997, with medication payments and notes from Donna Poole, M.S.N., A.R.N.P. Letter to Duxbury from George Mooney, September 8, 1997, and to John Woodhouse, and to Marilyn Drake; October 2, 1997, letter to J&J Appeals Committee and Boyd's letter to same party (used with Duxbury's permission).

Duxbury's April 1999 chronology, filings at Washington State unemployment department, Duxbury 1998 and 2001 depositions.

Chapter 12 : The Overdose Plan

McGarr's October 2002 opinion; McGarr's rulings and fines traced in November 1, 1999, motions from Amgen and Ortho. Also, "Amgen to Pay $96 Million in Drug Dispute," *New York Times,* September 16, 1997; Ortho Memo to Oncology Business Franchise from Bob Ashe, "Hospital Cleaning Process," September 9, 1997; DDD figures from 1997; Webb deposition, March 15, 1996; and "Rivalry between the Drug Companies." From Procritlawsuit.com.

Photos, materials, and memos from Seattle Ortho meeting January 1998; recap of POA Meeting, February 2, 1998, memo to San Diego District from Dwayne Marlowe; Dorren McCullough letter, April 14, 1998, to Nutan Parikh re: Phase IV studies; June 4, 1998, letter to Amick, et al., from Doreen McCullough, M.B.A., R.N., re: "Phase IV Weekly Dosing Study Status Update." Sales figures from Ortho and Amgen releases.

Western Washington Cancer Treatment claim in *Duxbury,* second amended complaint filed October 27, 2006; Melody Edgington declaration and Pat Buchsel declaration and Relay for Life material.

Numerous memos between John Woodhouse and Duxbury, as well as June 30, 1998, letters to Ortho managers from Kellee Bergstrom, Connie Thomassen, Dr. Sujata Rao; July 1, 1998, letter to Duxbury from Thom Murray; and March 14, 2003, declarations from Bergstrom and Murray, along with photos. Also Duxbury's April 1999 chronology and claims from termination lawsuit.

PART III
Chapter 13: The Millionaires' Club

Duxbury secrecy agreement signed February 21, 1992; Duxbury's resignation letter to John Woodhouse, July 20, 1998; Duxbury's letter to the State of Washington Employment Security Department, August 10, 1998; Eligibility Profile, State of Washington ESD, August 14, 1998; Reemployment Worker Profile, North Seattle Job Service Center, August 14, 1998; Duxbury's declaration of November 12, 1998.

McClellan and the Millionaires' Club in Laguna Niguel: interviews and photographs of Dr. and Mrs. Katakkar, Bill Pearson, and McClellan from November 1997. Reps' pitches to multiple myeloma: October 28, 1993, memo from Ortho manager Jennifer Hopwood to San Diego district.

Study passed around to reps: "Recombinant Human Erythropoietin and the Anemia of Multiple Myeloma," by Bart Barlogie and Thad Beck, *Stem Cells* 11 (1993), 88–94; Ortho product insert package warnings on 1990 label and on 2000 label.

McClellan and Advisory Board members or KOLs: McClellan interviews, Ortho memo for February 26, 1997, and accompanying ten-page list of doctors; presentation by Dr. David Cella, May 23, 2001, Arizona Cancer Center, five-page document; Dr. Gaylor treating "mildly anemic patients," from McClellan's WAR report of May 20, 1997; free Procrit Trial Cards, supplied by McClellan, including sequenced numbers and data; McClellan's homemade sheets: Procrit QW 40 K Study Master Sheet; Procrit Phase IV study, 1996, by Dean McClellan, Ortho Biotech, Tucson #1 MD-A; Tucson #1 MD-B; AZ #1, MD-E, et al.; Vogelzang quoted in "Personal Health" by Jane E. Brody, *New York Times*, April 2, 1997; Fatigue Coalition funded by a grant from Ortho—from "Strength for Caring," according to J&J Web site; standing orders for Davis-Monthan AFB.

Jim Lenox: Johns Hopkins doctors on Ortho's advisory board included Arleen A. Forastiere, associate professor of oncology and cochair of the head and neck advisory group; Mario Eisenberger, associate professor and specialist in genitourinary cancer; and Nancy E. Davidson, cochair of the Procrit breast cancer group. There were other Ortho thought leaders, adherents of Procrit, at Johns Hopkins in 1998.

McClellan's background and résumé. Also Jerome Groopman, quoted in "New Drug Approved to Treat AIDS Anemia," by Gina Kolata, *New York Times*, January 3, 1991.

By the spring of 1999, the FDA had received complaints regarding Ortho's promotion of its high-dose campaign: detailed in two letters by William Purvis, director of Advertising and Promotional Labeling Staff at CBER, to Ralph Smalling at Amgen; one dated March 30, 1999, regarding marketing "east of the Mississippi river," and another letter dated May 11, 1999, regarding "west of the Mississippi" marketing.

McClellan's homemade Phase IV study reports about patients: McClellan and his millionaire desires from interviews; ticket stub from "Success 1998," February 17, 1998, along with flyer and online material from various speakers cited, including Zig Ziglar.

Amgen approached Duxbury with a job: from his 1998 deposition.

One critic of the Washington Mutual Tower that opened in 1988 was the

New York Times' Paul Goldberger, "Proud of Its Height, a New Tower Rules over Seattle," November 27, 1988.

Duxbury's letter to the state ESD, October 15, 1998; weather reports for Seattle, December 2, 1998; State of Washington Office of Administrative Hearings for the Employment Security Department, Doc. No. 01-1998-80403.

Chapter 14: "Strength for Living"

Pizza boy scene from Duxbury: Procrit commercials include the 1999 "Grandfather and Camera"; but this refers to the "Anthem" 2000 ad, which is similar to the "Dressmaker" 2001, "Veteran" 2001, "Big Boy Bed" 2001 (both thirty-second and sixty-second commercials), all of which have similar story lines. Script is from the 2001 "Anthem" commercial.

Cancers diagnosed in 2000 amounted to 1.2 million, according to the American Cancer Society.

FDA and advertisements: interview with Keegan, November 2008; Keegan résumé; visit to FDA in November 2008; reviewed letters, meeting notes, and attachments from September 17, 1996, to July 3, 2002, between drugmakers Amgen, J&J, and FDA regulators, including letter from FDA to Amgen/J&J. J&J's "tardy submission of materials [was] not acceptable," said Mary A. Malarkey, director of the compliance office at the CBER unit; letter from William V. Purvis, director of Advertising and Promotional Labeling Staff at FDA, to Ralph J. Smalling, November 6, 1998, about the October 25, 1998, *Parade* advertisement.

Procrit advertisements: USF Spotlight, October 29, 2001, said $14 billion a year on all drug promotions, 15 percent of which was direct-to-consumer. Regarding $1.4 billion on TV ads: *Pharmaceutical Marketing:* "The Facts Speak for Themselves," Part I in a Two-Part Series by W. Richard Bukata, M.D.; *Emergency Medicine News* 24: 8 (August 2002), 3, 43–44; assertion that the cost of drug ads in 1995 was $313 million, from "FDA Loosens Restrictions on Drug Ads," by Kasper Zeuthen, *Los Angeles Times,* August 9, 1997.

24-7 call center, with ten thousand pieces of patient education mailed, from American Advertising Federation "Mosaic Award Case Studies" for Procrit ads.

History of DTC (direct-to-consumer advertising): http://www.kevinmd.com/ blog/2010/09/dtc-advertising-history-fda.html.

McClellan and Las Vegas segment: details of gifts and money given to Dr. Nagy, totaling about $460,000, from a March 30, 1998, letter from McClellan to Nagy's attorney Fred Waid. Also detailed in Duxbury's amended complaint, p. 50. Biller from Kattakar's office was Nanette van der Sander.

In 1999, high-dose Procrit was approved in 40,000-unit vials, from a January 7, 1999, memo from Ortho president Gary Reedy to a string of Ortho executives and managers.

McClellan's notes regarding ICRA include directions, Ortho "ICRA" invitation, Ortho-faxed information to McClellan's boss Dwayne Marlowe; advertisement in Las Vegas for Party Rental Place, along with eight receipts for party itself, advertising, and other costs from February 1999. The New York–based firm was RJO Group, cited in Ortho's instructions to rep. Quote from young guide taken from "Chemo Disney: Ortho Biotech Markets Procrit Using Virtual Reality," by Lauren John of *Breast Cancer Action* newsletter, October 24, 2007. Raritan publicists contacted advance press: from "Advisory/Virtual Reality Helps Doctors Empathize with Cancer Patients," BW HealthWire, November 11, 1998; online press release about ICRA.

"I'm manager of all the trials," Dean McClellan, March 30, 2009; Medicare Balanced Budget law; Ortho raised its Procrit price, said William C. Pearson in November 17, 2006, deposition for Pharmaceutical Industry Average Wholesale Price litigation against J&J: MDL No 1456, Civil Action 01-12257-PBS. Pearson's declaration was withdrawn six weeks later, on January 5, 2007; master list of minitrial doctors from McClellan's files of 1998; McClellan's 1999 QW business goals and bonus objectives; Arizona Inn, where Ortho housed some of its speakers.

Children's study: *JCO*, August 2006, "Double-blind, placebo controlled study of QOL . . ." by B. I. Razzouk, J. D. Hord, M. Hockenberry, P. S. Hinds, J. Feusner, et al. Keegan's old office: description from FDA spokesperson Karen Riley and Paul Goldberg, editor of *The Cancer Letter*.

Examples of Ortho's teachings regarding HCFA 1500: Procrit Appropriate Use Guarantee Program Fact Sheet (January 2001) and slide presentation; Preferred Purchasing Program; Loyalty Multipliers; script of Anticipated Objections and Responses; photo of McClellan giving $40,000 to UAZ; State Medicare Guidelines CMS 1500 from Ortho. Kattakar details in Duxbury amended complaint, October 27, 2006.

Chapter 15: Code Mistress

Interviews with Bibi; her résumé; Duxbury and his résumé.

Rapidamus, amici: http://www.personal.kent.edu/~bkharvey/latin/morph/verb ssub.htm.

Warning letters to GlaxoSmith Kline and Schering, etc., from "Misleading Drug Ads Persist," by Jennifer Warner, Medscape Medical News, December 4, 2002.

Daniel Von Hoff and reimbursement issues: from amended original complaint, pp. 48–49. Also, letter to Medicare official John Clarke, written on Ortho stationery by Elizabeth Potente, pharmacy director at Ortho who reported to Loretta Itri, and, according to McClellan, signed by Dr. Von Hoff, dated October 5, 2011; also Von Hoff's résumé; also memo regarding May 11, 2004, meeting with McClellan, relayed in Jeff Sprung declaration of May 14, 2004.

Code Mistress details: from Roberta Lee Buell, M.B.A., and her Web site; also, December 4, 2001, flyer of seminar hosted by Ortho and McClellan at Ritz-Carlton; McClellan interviews; Procrit "Billing and Reimbursement" guidelines show how to fill out Medicare HCFA form. Ortho's four-page directions regarding codes for surgery and QW dosing, dated April 19, 2004, before approval of QW dosing.

Endispute Arbitration, Chicago, Illinois: *Ortho Pharmaceutical Corp. v. Amgen,* Amgen's reply to Ortho's Memorandum of Law Opposition to Amgen's Motion for Partial Summary Judgment, December 17, 1999.

Simmerly and Duxbury section: interviews with both and reenactments of luncheon with both at a Chinese restaurant; Duxbury's medical records provided by Dr. Bibi Duxbury; Ortho blamed its actions on low-level reps: from its December 17, 1999, brief and Amgen's reply, same date; also "Alex and Joel Newsletter," 1993, regarding Simmerly's family.

Harold G. Moore and Joseph L. Galloway, *We Were Soldiers Once . . . and Young: La Drang, the Battle That Changed the War in Vietnam* (New York: Random House, 1992), describing Crandall, as well as interviews with Faye, Alyn, and Mark Duxbury. Section on Aranesp and brand names: famous goof-ups in corporate branding, ESPN Radio, November

12, 2007. The importance of sound in names: "If the Candidates Were Pharmaceuticals," by Bill Radke and Michael Raphael, American Public Media, March 1, 2008.

Amgen's advertising: *The $800 Million Pill: The Truth Behind the Cost of New Drugs,* by Merrill Gozner (Berkeley: University of California Press, 2004); also December 30, 2010, obituary for Gene Goldwasser, ACP Internist blog by John H. Schumann; cancer diagnosis figures and market from an independent science study, "Cancer: Facts and Thoughts," by Dave Kristula, May 31, 2000; Amgen and Ortho fight from McGarr's rulings, October 2002.

Procrit commercials during reruns of 2001 Tour de France: "Fell out of my chair laughing," from velonews.competitor.com, and from american-cycling.org bulletin board; "Cycling: As Seen on Television, Prohibited EPO on Sale," by Edward Wyatt, *New York Times,* June 2, 2002.

Vino Kolafra: Kilmerhouse.com: The drink was made by a J&J subsidiary, the Brunswick Pharmacal Company, from 1894 to 1896. A J&J Web site called it one of J&J's more unusual products. Other information about Vino Kolafra comes from a November 1896 ad in *Popular Science.* Regarding the new ad campaign for Procrit: "DDB Shop Gets J&J's Procrit," by David Goetzl, *Advertising Age,* October 2001. About J&J a hundred years earlier and its Vino Kolafra: The quoted line is from "The Great American Fraud" by Samuel Hopkins Adams, *Collier's* magazine, October 1905.

Daniel Troy at FDA: Keegan interviews; "FDA's Counsel's Rise Embodies U.S. Shift," by Michael Kranish, *Boston Globe,* December 22, 2002; "Daniel Troy: Godfather of Big Pharma Protection Racket," by Evelyn Pringle, LawyersandSettlements.com, September 27, 2006; "FDA Career Staff Objected to Agency Preemption Policies," prepared for Chairman Henry A. Waxman, U.S. House Committee on Oversight and Government Reform, Majority Staff Report, October 2008; Web site of Representative Maurice Hinchey (D-NY), "FDA Is Placing Corporations above People"; and many other links. "Hollywood pitch" aspect of Troy's appearing at the 8th Annual Conference for In-House Counsel and Trial Attorneys in Drug and Medical Device Litigation in New York City: affidavit from attendee Jessica Dart, March 1, 2004.

Chapter 16: The Arbitrator

McClellan résumé; Duxbury's August 18, 2001, testimony; Keegan interviews and FDA letters, including letters, meeting notes, and attachments from September 17, 1996, to July 3, 2002, between Amgen, J&J, and FDA regulators (see Chapter 14 notes).

McClellan and Duxbury continue to talk and disagree over DOJ announcements: TAP Pharmaceutical press release, October 3, 2001, from DOJ; Pharmwatch, "Criminal Prosecution of TAP Pharmaceutical," December 25, 2005.

The scene in which Mark testifies in the Amgen case in Chicago, January 22, 2002: weather, http://www.crh.noaa.gov/ilx/trivia/jantriv.php; Duxbury and Simmerly interviews; flight records, hotel receipts, Duxbury and Simmerly interviews of March 13, 2009; also map of downtown Chicago; "Holland & Knight Comes to Dearborn," by Brian Burden, in CoStar Realty Information, August 9, 2000; "Arthur Andersen's Fall from Grace," by Ken Brown and Ianthe Jeanne Dugan, *Wall Street Journal*, June 7, 2002; "Arthur Andersen to Stay Put," *Chicago Tribune*, March 17, 1992, listing address as 33 West Monroe; and interview with Kristen at The Grillroom, March 20, 2008.

About Judge McGarr: his ruling on the state being founded under the Christian religion, which should not be denied: http://www.missiontoisrael .org/gods-covenant-people/chapter8.php; "Frank McGarr. . . . did nothing to move the case": from "In the 1980s, a Chicago Newspaper Investigated Cardinal Cody," by Roy Larsen, Nieman Reports, spring 2003 (retrieved June 26, 2009); biographical information from Judgepedia, Wikipedia, and Loyola University.

McGarr's ruling "on the eve of trial," August 13, 2001; also his October 18, 2002, ruling.

Press releases from Amgen, one premature, March 13, 2002; one from Ortho on October 18, 2002; a belated one from Amgen on January 24, 2003. The "most lucrative drug ever produced by the biotechnology industry," taken from story "Johnson & Johnson to Pay $150 Million in Amgen Suit," by Andre Pollack, *New York Times*, October 19, 2002; Figure of $9 billion came from addition of Procrit sales from 1992 to 2000.

July 30, 1999, "Memorandum of Law in Support of Ortho Biotech's Motion for Summary Judgment"; list of attorneys from the documents from Endispute Arbitration, December 17, 1999: Amgen's Reply to Ortho's Memorandum of Law in Opposition to Amgen's Motion for Partial Summary Judgment and Reply Memorandum of Law in Further Support of Ortho Biotech's Motion for Summary Judgment; names of the other reps deposed in the *Amgen v. Ortho* papers, pp. 26, 238–241.

Epo fastest-growing drug, from "IMS Reports 16.9 Percent Growth in 2001 U.S. Prescription Sales," in IMS Press Release, April 2, 2001. July 16, 2002, Goldman Sachs report and a Merrill Lynch report of July 12, 2002, that quoted "corporate governance issues"; UBS Warburg report estimate of "multibillion-dollar" settlement from J&J.

Wrongful termination suit file, including July 2001 complaint case 01-2-19764-9 filed in Superior Court of King County; defendants' response and motions; judge's rulings; various witnesses' declarations and statements; *Duxbury v. Ortho Biotech*, No. 52348-1-1, in Court of Appeals for the State of Washington, Division I, May 24, 2004; Appeals Court Opinion.

"Corporate Accountability and Compliance in Health Care: Will Health Care Be the Next Enron?"—a February 27, 2004, presentation by Kimberly Baker and Arissa Peterson of Williams Kastner & Gibbs; domestic violence case explained by Mark and Bibi Duxbury; medical reports from Boyd and oral examination notes, November 25, 2002; letters from Matson filed with court, including one regarding the father's parenting skills, April 29, 2001; Pierce County property records of Duxbury's five-bedroom home; McGarr's opinion, October 18, 2002, and associated records.

Chapter 17: For the King

Visit to Steve Berman's office and interview with Berman, November 6, 2007 (on behalf of *Mother Jones* magazine); Rainier Tower details from visit, Emporis Web site; biography of architect Minoru Yamasaki from www.historylink.org; Berman letter and materials to author, November 6, 2007; *In re Average Wholesale Price Pharmaceutical Litigation*, MDL No. 1456 Memorandum and Order, November 12, 2007; Findings of Fact and Conclusions of Law, June 21, 2007.

Whistle-blower law explained thanks to: John T. Boese, *Civil False Claims and Qui Tam Actions*, Third Edition, Volume 1 (New York: Aspen Publishers, 2006), pp. 1, 3, 23; Also to Joel Hesch, former DOJ attorney, interview, January 23, 2009; also *Whistleblowing: A Guide to Government Rewards Programs,* by Joel Hesch (Lynchburg, Va.: Goshen Press, 2008).

Medicaid suits filed by Berman with Duxbury for California and Illinois; also letter for Hon. John Ashcroft, October 30, 2003, from Berman re: *Ex rel. Mark Duxbury v. Ortho Biotech Products;* Duxbury's original *qui tam* suit filed November 3, 2003.

February 4, 2004, meeting with DOJ's Jamie Yavelberg in Boston: Yavelberg résumé and letter April 6, 2004; Berman's response, June 18, 2004, and related memos. Ashcroft unfriendly to *qui tam* law: "Who Killed the Whistleblower Bill?" by Tom Devine, *Los Angeles Times,* January 10, 2011; also *Wall Street Journal* report, September 4, 2008; September 9, 2008, letter to Secretary of Labor Elaine Chao from senators Charles Grassley and Patrick Leahy, of the Committee on the Judiciary.

Chapter 18: Black Ops

Interviews with Duxbury and McClellan; visit to McClellan and scene of events on December 17, 2009, and again on April 27, 2010. Telephone bills; Kattakar records and others from Duxbury amended complaint of 2006; Weldon's salary from J&J annual report, 2003; McClellan's salary and benefits from him; May 4, 2004, letter to McClellan from JoAnne Stehr, director of human resources, signed May 21, 2004; McClellan's calendar and flight receipts; eclipses during 2004, by Fred Espenak, *Observer's Handbook 2004,* Royal Astronomical Society of Canada (May 4); and weather report and full moon eclipse.

May 4, 2004, ODAC meeting description from Keegan interview and FDA transcripts; October 2003 *Lancet* study by Dr. Henke, and *ENHANCE Study* and *BEST Study* cited in ODAC; also, "The Dark Side of Epotein," by Chaya Venkat, *Lancet,* November 22, 2003; Oncologic Drugs Advisory Committee, "Safety Concerns Associated with Aranesp, Amgen Inc., and Procrit, Ortho Biotech, for Treatment of Anemia Associated with Cancer Chemotherapy," FDA Briefing Document, May 4, 2004; map of Gaithersburg and triangle. Also Lenox interviews.

"Drug Company Halts Trials of Procrit," by Andrew Pollack, *New York Times,* November 27, 2003; Dr. Robert DeLap bio, http://www

.acceleratingworkshop.org/modules/faculty1/index.php; DeLap's quote from *New York Times* story.

Chapter 19: The Eleventh Hour

McClellan and Duxbury interviews regarding Berman visit; McClellan date-book for dates and times; U-Haul contact from McClellan; Duxbury bills; U.S. oncology records.

July 29, 2004: events for incident at Surprise Lake: maps of area and records from King County Sheriff's Office; declaration of neighbor Thomas Houha, August 19, 2004; letter on behalf of Duxbury from Robert Taylor-Manning, September 20, 2004; letter to Duxbury from Renee, August 19, 2004, among others; *Matson v. Duxbury;* Interim Report of the Guardian ad Litem; note from Dr. Michael Pearson re: Bibi and how she is "not a danger to herself or anyone else."

Berman sends letter to Mr. Dennis Burns, August 18, 2004, listing need to have Duxbury back; September 20, 2004, letter from Robert Taylor Manning.

Renee Matson v. Mark Duxbury, September 3, 2004, modification of custody decree and ex parte restraining order to show cause; also parenting plan; September 23, 2004, hearing at which judge signed restraining order.

Interim Report of the Guardian ad Litem Kelly Theriot LeBlanc, filed April 19, 2005; and sixteen-page rebuttal to that report detailing errors; motion to quash subpoenas, November 5, 2004, granted.

Subpoena: "U.S. Seeks Johnson & Johnson Procrit Documents," by Scott Hensley, *Wall Street Journal,* October 4, 2004.

Night of suicide from interviews with Bibi, Duxbury, and reenactment at their house; weather report; medical records.

PART IV
Chapter 20: Twice Saved

Schlichtmann: This chapter relied on Jonathan Harr's fine book *A Civil Action* (New York: Random House, 1995), especially pp. 464–491; "Toxic Legacy" by Dan Kennedy, *Boston Phoenix,* December 17–24, 1998; numerous interviews with Schlichtmann, especially on November 20, 2008, and with Barragan, January 9 and 16, 2009; and visit to house, November 20, 2008. Also, *Ann Anderson et al. v. Beatrice Foods,* U.S. Court of Appeals, First

Circuit (862, F. 2nd, 910), decided December 7, 1988; SJC-09790 *The Cadel Co. v Jan. R. Schlichtmann,* January 17, 2007; *Commonwealth of Mass. vs. The Cadle Co.,* December 7, 2007; Adam Cohen, "Next Case," *Time* magazine, January 18, 1999; Mary Kugler, R.N., "Toms River Cancer Cluster Settlement," Rarediseases.about.com, December 9, 2003, post; Jean Milke, "Toms River N.J. Cluster Update," *Asbury Park Press,* October 5, 2004.

Associated Press story "Jury awards more than $10 million in water bottlers' lawsuit," March 23, 2006; also Commonwealth of Massachusetts, Superior Court Civil Action No. 03-4462-BLSi, *Garve Ivey et al. vs. W Henry Shaw et al.* consolidated with others.

Hagens Berman Sobol filings in *U.S. of America ex. Rel. Mark E. Duxbury,* "Status Report," September 5, 2006; Schlichtmann's filing of "Notice of Appearance," September 7, 2006; among others; also relied on numerous e-mails between Duxbury, Berman, and Sprung.

Chapter 21: Miracle Gro

Civil False Claims and Qui Tam Actions, Third Edition, Vol. I, by John T. Boese (Aspen Publishers, 2006) law; travel receipts and notes from Duxbury, McClellan, and Simmerly.

New England Journal of Medicine, November 2006; *Danish Head and Neck Cancer Study,* December 2006; FDA briefing document for ODAC meeting of May 10, 2007; "Heart Risk Seen in Drug for Anemia," by Alex Berenson, November 16, 2006, *New York Times;* "Some See Profiteering in Clinics Use of Drug," by Christopher Rowland, October 24, 2006, *Boston Globe.*

J&J 2007 year-end results; e-mails regarding Daniel Troy, Sidley Austin associates, from congressional investigations mounted by Committee on Energy and Commerce and Reps. John D. Dingell (D-MI), chairman of the Committee on Energy and Commerce, and Bart Stupak (D-MI), chairman of the Oversight and Investigations Subcommittee, specifically hearings of House Committee on Energy and Commerce Subcommittee on Oversight and Investigation, on May 8, 2008.

Ortho Biotech press release, February 28, 2007; *FDA News,* March 9, 2007.

Eyewitness account of May 10, 2007, meeting of FDA Oncologic Drugs Advisory Committee at Hilton Washington DC/Silver Spring; ODAC 2007 transcript and final vote.

Lenox medical records (referred to in other chapters).

Chapter 22: Brothers

Eyewitness account of May 22, 23, 24 court preparations, meetings, and court appearances in Duxbury case and its various parties. Biographies of Susan Burke, Patrick Davies, Jamie Yavelberg, Ethan Posner, Judge Rya Zobel; May 2007 interviews with Foote and Schlichtmann.

Amended Duxbury *qui tam* complaint October 27, 2006; Ortho's Motion to Dismiss *qui tam*, January 17, 2007; Duxbury's Response to Ortho's Motion to Dismiss, filed March 13, 2007; U.S. Amicus Brief, March 16, 2007, Ortho's Reply Brief, April 24, 2007; Duxbury's Sur-Reply, April 30, 2007. Also court transcripts of May 23, 2007.

Chapter 23: As the World Spins

J&J campus: visit to New Brunswick campus and tour, November 17, 2008.

History: Robert Wood Johnson: *The Gentleman Rebel,* by Lawrence G. Foster (State College, Pa.: Lillian Press, 1999).

J&J history: *The Gentleman Rebel,* pp. 36–90; concerning Johnson's experiments with belladonna, ibid., pp. 86–89; http://en.wikipedia.org/wiki/Parke-Davis; Belladonna Plasters, 1912, see Kilmerhouse.com; "Great American Fraud," by Samuel Hopkins Adams, in *Collier's, The National Weekly,* October 7, 1905. About opium and drugs: http://www.opioids.com/timeline/index.html.

Opium, cannabis, and drugs: http://www.opioids.com/timeline/index.html; http://antiquecannabisbook.com/Appendix/MfgIndex.htm; Index of Pre-1937 Medical Cannabis Manufacturers, *420 Magazine; The Scientist,* March 2008, "Poppy Power Almost a Century Old," Bayer Aspirin Heroin advertisement; Worthopedia, Premier Price Guide for J&J Vintage Belladona Plaster Full Tin; eBay, Wyeth "Sun" Cholera Mixture Bottle with Opium.

Chapter 24: The Burden

Eyewitness account of January 9, 2009, court scene in First Circuit Court of Appeals, with accompanying briefs and transcript of the session's arguments. Also copy of Duxbury grievance against Steve Berman filed February 2009 with the Washington State Bar Association, including supporting documents.

Biographies of Judges Juan Torruella, Eugene Siler Jr., and Jeffrey Howard. Also Duxbury interviews of Daniel Dee Miles and Charles Barnhill and review of their Medicaid cases.

Notes about Mark's health from Bibi's notes; Washington State Medical Quality Assurance Commission, File #200801-00070P; statement of Chinyelu A. Duxbury, M.D.; autopsy report from Pierce County Coroner; police report, Duxbury's notes and conversation, May 5 and 6, 2009.

Acknowledgments

Not every story finds a home, and this journey started with Paul Simmerly, who spent three years pitching it before the author finally understood its significance. My deep gratitude to the four main characters and their families, who graciously opened their homes and lives to me. This story couldn't have been told without their patience and the generosity of the Lenox family. I appreciate the time Dr. Patricia Keegan, Karen Riley, JoAnn Minor and the late Patty Delaney, Charles Miller of the Department of Justice, Joel D. Hesche formerly of the DOJ, Paul Goldberg of the *Cancer Letter*, the librarians at the U.S. Courthouse in Boston, and legislative aides for Senator Charles Grassley and Representative John D. Dingell spent with me. I regret that representatives of Johnson & Johnson declined my numerous requests to participate in this project.

I'm especially grateful to the gifted Lisa Erbach Vance of the Aaron M. Priest Literary Agency for her unerring instincts, to John Richmond, and to Aaron himself.

Several friends acted as devil's advocates and guardian angels, including Gayle Lynds, who introduced me to the world of thrillers, and Melodie Johnson Howe, who guided me through the realm of mysteries. Mary A. Fischer gave invaluable expert advice; the talented Joan Tapper helped shape this project; and Eileen Welsome read chunks of the manuscript. Margery Nelson, Bill Link, Cheryl Ebner, Steve Chawkins, Jane Hulse, Pat Robertson, Doug Preston, Jon Land, Jutta Haase, Sharon and Mike Davis, Carrie and Ann Yusko, Fritz and Barb Mondau, and the late, great Shirley Lampasona gave constant encouragement.

I'm much obliged to Harry Moses, Robert Sam Anson, and Dana Brown for their early encouragement. Rita Beamish helped me focus on the heart of the story, while Martha Shirk, Michelle Levendar, and the California Endowment Health Journalism Fellowship at USC's Annenberg School for Communication provided ballast. I also thank Monika Bauerlein at *Mother Jones* for her initial support and Katie Orenstein, Katharine Mieszkowski, and the inspiring voices at The Op-Ed Project.

I salute the wonderful team at Dutton, beginning with my excellent editor Stephen Morrow. I so appreciate the talents of Brian Tart, Alex Gigante, Andy Celli, Christine Ball, Amanda Walker, Rich Hasselberger, Julia Gilroy, Susan Schwartz, Leonard Telesca, and Stephanie Hitchcock. It was my great fortune to wind up with you all.

Particular gratitude goes to Scott Bartz and Robert Erwin, who read portions of this story for accuracy. If there are mistakes herein, they are all mine.

And finally to my expanded family and the ones at home: Timothy, Emily, James, and Oliver have been very understanding throughout it all, and none of this would have happened without magnanimous Ray.